Unidentified

The National Intelligence Problem of UFOs

Also by Larry Hancock

Shadow Warfare: The History of America's Undeclared Wars (Hardcover/Softcover) by Larry Hancock and Stuart Wexler

Surprise Attack: From Pearl Harbor to 9/11 to Benghazi (Hardcover/Softcover)

Nexus: The CIA and Political Assassination (Softcover)

Unidentified

The National Intelligence Problem of UFOs

by

Larry Hancock

TREATISE PUBLISHING

Trea-tise, noun, a written work dealing formally and systematically with a subject.

Unidentified, The National Intelligence Problem of UFOs

Copyright © 2017 Larry Hancock

All rights reserved. No part of this publication may be reproduced, distributed, or transmitted in any form or by any means, including photocopying, recording, or other electronic or mechanical methods, without the prior written permission of the publisher, except in the case of brief quotations embodied in critical reviews and certain other noncommercial uses permitted by copyright law. For permission requests, write to the publisher, addressed "Attention: Permissions Coordinator," at the address below.

ISBN: 978-0-692-89229-9
Printed in the United States

Treatise Publications
P.O. Box 92874
Southlake, TX 76092

Treatise publishing contact for Group, Club or Wholesale orders: http://www.treatisepublishing.com

Images for this book are copyrighted by their respective copyright holders and may not be reproduced for any reason or in any format without express permission from the owner or copyright holder.

About the Author

Larry Hancock brings his formal training in history and cultural anthropology to his research and writing on military history and national security subjects. Following service in the United States Air Force, his career in computer/communications and technology marketing allowed him the opportunity to become involved in and consult on strategic analysis and planning studies related to capital investment and long range business planning. With six books in print, Hancock's writings focus on topics of Cold War history; his most recent books have explored long term patterns in covert action and deniable warfare ("Shadow Warfare") as well as national command authority and command and control practices ("Surprise Attack").

INTRO

"In view of the... persistent reports of unusual flying objects over parts of the United States, particularly the east and west coast and the vicinity of the atomic energy testing and production facilities, it is apparent that positive action must be taken to determine the nature of these objects and their origin."

Brigadier W. M. Garland, Directorate of Intelligence, U.S. Air Force, January 3, 1952

There is simply no doubt that unidentified aerial objects were a serious problem for the military. In the beginning they represented a challenge for the Army Air Force, then for the newly independent United States Air Force, its Directorate of Air Intelligence, and its Air Technical Intelligence Center. As time passed that fundamental military problem was largely buried in the massive number of newspaper headlines, magazine articles and movie titles. UFOs became part of the popular American culture in the 20th culture and continue in a lead role in the 21st.

The much more serious challenge to the national intelligence community – including not just the Air Force but the CIA, the FBI and even the Atomic Energy Commission – remained hidden behind the movie titles and the deluge of colorful aliens from outer space. The Air Force was never entertained by that but in a way it was better that the public was going to the movies rather than asking much more serious and embarrassing questions about what was going on in the nation's air space at the height of the Cold War.

The public would not have been reassured by a number of the actual statements contained within assessments being circulated within certain security agencies. That certainly would have included comments in an internal CIA memo prepared within the agencies Office of Scientific Intelligence:

"Sightings of unidentified flying objects at great altitudes and traveling in the vicinity of major U.S. defense installations are of such a nature that they are not attributable to natural phenomena or known types

of aerial vehicles." Marshall Chadwell, Assistant Director, Office of Scientific Intelligence, Central Intelligence Agency, December, 1952

As time passed, the continued observation of unidentified aerial objects became more than just a question of identification, at some levels of the military it became a matter of whether or not an actual threat existed. Such concerns increasingly pitted field commands against senior decision makers in Washington D.C.

> *"In view of the fact that this sighting suggests a possibility of a different type of threat to the Continental United States, request this Headquarters, ATTN: ADODI, be advised of your final analysis regarding this sighting."* Strategic Air Command, UFO incident investigation, Northern Montana / 1959

> *"This sighting was a positive observation, under ideal circumstances, of a definite object of an unconventional nature – possibly of foreign origin, which could be a threat to national security.*" Strategic Air Command, UFO incident investigation, Carswell AFB, Texas / 1965

> *"Malmstrom, AFB Montana received seven cuts on the height finder radar at altitudes between 9,500 and 15,500 feet...objects could not be intercepted...Four Strategic Air Command sites observed intercepting F-106's arrive in the area; sighted objects turned their lights off on arrival of interceptors and back on upon their departure."* National Military Command Center, Unidentified Sightings, November 8. 1975

In the real world of military operations, screened by Air Force public relations statements, UFO incidents were taken quite seriously. At higher levels they became a serious challenge to the overall national intelligence system.

How that system dealt with the challenge of UFOs, what it did, what it failed to do and might it have done are all the explored in the following pages.

Acknowledgements

The author would like to express his admiration and thanks to the UFO historical researchers who spent years doing Freedom of Information requests as well as all the other tasks necessary to build the body of information cited in this work. Every effort has been made to name and include credit for all for individual efforts. Undoubtedly some will have been missed or left out and for that, sincere apologies.

In memory of Sherry Fiester for her lifelong quest for truths.

Table of Contents

Chapter 1: Bogies and Bandits 11

Chapter 2: Nightmare Devices 29

Chapter 3: Fear Factors 49

Chapter 4: Weight of Evidence 64

Chapter 5: Something Real 78

Chapter 6: Foreign Origins? 111

Chapter 7: Failure to Identify 141

Chapter 8: Security Concerns 159

Chapter 9: Reduction and Reassurance 189

Chapter 10: I Want Answers 209

Chapter 11: Defense of the Capital 278

Chapter 12: Identified or Unknown 255

Chapter 13: Ownership 278

Chapter 14: Ownership and Tasking 305

Chapter 15: Beyond BLUE BOOK 331

Chapter 16: Indications of Reconnissance 356

Chapter 17: Not the Russians 381

Chapter 18: Parties Unknown 395

Chapter 19: Threat? 423

Chapter 20: The Challenge 443

Chapter 1

Bogies and Bandits

In this chapter

- An in depth examination of the response by Allied field and staff intelligence groups to widespread reports of unidentified and unconventional aerial objects in both the European and Pacific theaters of war.

- Proof that military personnel were able to accurately describe and characterize very real, although unexpected and unconventional aerial objects – even under the stress of combat conditions.

- A detailing of the military security and media control practices used to deal with actual, well defined threats posed by wartime unconventional aerial objects.

The Hurricane fighter was on night patrol beyond the French coast; it was December, 1943 and British fliers had been in combat for some four years. As he neared the mouth of the Somme River, pilot B.C. Lumsden saw two orange/amber lights climbing upwards towards his airplane. His first thought was that he was taking antiaircraft fire, with incoming "flak". Instead, he quickly realized that the lights were moving far too slowly to be tracer rounds. The lights brightened, reached his altitude and moved into level flight, maintaining course with his aircraft.[1]

Lumsden responded as any combat pilot would – if you can't identify it, you treat it as a threat. During the war years, enemy aircraft were referred to by pilots and aircrews as "bandits". If they could not positively be identified as a threat, unknown craft were described as "bogies" – in Scotland a term associated with phantoms and ghosts. Lumsden responded to his "bogie" in what was a standard reaction for fighter pilots – he jettisoned his external fuel tanks, began evasive action and dived several thousand feet to reach an air speed of some 260 miles per hour. The lights dived with him, passed him, pulled up and took position over his fighter.

There was no sign of an aircraft associated with the lights, they clearly were not flak nor were they any type of flare or searchlights shining on clouds. What they were was a mystery, but they were clearly focused on him and his plane. Lumsden pushed his Hurricane to its maximum speed and left the scene, leaving the bogies behind. In the years following his bogie encounter would be repeated dozens of times on night missions, both in the European and Pacific theaters. Nighttime bogie sightings became a serious concern for aircrews, a potential threat to morale and a real headache for the Allied intelligence groups – as well as the bane of both field units and headquarters staff.

During World War II, Allied intelligence in Europe, and to a lesser extent, American intelligence in the Pacific, became very involved and proactive in dealing with a variety of reports relating to unidentified aerial objects. That war time experience gives us an invaluable introduction into how military intelligence responds to reports of unidentified and unconventional objects. It also establishes the context for how those same intelligence groups would initially respond to similar reports immediately following the war, during both 1946 and 1947. Finally, the wartime experience provides a vital test of observer reliability, with combat sightings being made under some of the most challenging conditions imaginable.

By 1943, the world was fully engaged in the second major global conflict in two decades – the only real question about the bogies being reported in the European and Pacific theaters was whether or not they actually represented active threats. The vast majority of the sightings involved anomalous nighttime lights, a great many types of lights – all of which behaved mysteriously, often quite unlike known enemy aircraft. However there were a few such encounters where solid objects could be clearly seen and their shapes defined.

One of those incidents occurred in May of 1943, during a large scale British night bombing mission against Essen, Germany. The crew of an RAF Halifax bomber observed a long cylindrical object, silver gold in color. The object was sharply defined and apparently motionless, sitting at an altitude of around 18,000 feet and tilted at a 45 degree angle to the ground.[2] The bomber's crew noted a number of individual lights which they took to be windows or portholes in the side facing them, evenly spaced down the object's length. The cylinder itself was estimated to be larger than their own bomber.

As the crew continued to watch the cylinder it suddenly began to move away from them, accelerating at a very high speed and becoming blurred, with its appearance foreshortened. Upon their return to base following their mission, the crew members described the encounter during their debriefing, but were apparently not questioned further about it.³ At the time, given that the object showed no sign of hostility the report was simply filed. Military intelligence was already busy with studies of a stream of reports which suggested much more obvious threats to ongoing combat missions.

British and later U.S. Army Air Force air crews frequently observed a wide variety of unidentified aerial objects and light phenomena. Debriefing and intelligence reports routinely mentioned them because such reports could provide warning of new enemy weapons as well as other potential threats to combat missions. As early as September, 1942, after collecting data from some three years of debriefing reports, British Bomber Command issued "A Note on Pyrotechnic Activity over Germany". The report described three categories of phenomena being reported by air crews – including balls of fire coming up from the ground, lights which appeared to be multiple parachute flares dropped by enemy aircraft and small colored balls seen at altitudes up to seven thousand feet – thought to be bomber raid tracking flares deployed by the German air defenses.⁴

None of those mystery lights were seen to involve a direct threat to Allied aircraft, although it was noted that some might be a new psychological ploy. For example the balls of fire which dramatically exploded might be mistaken by air crew as friendly aircraft being destroyed around them. By October, 1943 that category of sighting was being reported in British memoranda as "Enemy Defenses Phenomena" and through December reports continued to describe "Chandelier flares", "Scarecrow flares", "Track Indicating flares" and a new category of "Meteor projectiles, possibly being related to enemy aircraft carried rockets or in some cases anti-aircraft type rockets".⁵

German forces also observed similar light phenomena. During 1944, a German staff officer prepared a very detailed report on British pathfinder aircraft operations.⁶ Pathfinder aircraft operated in advance of the larger bomber groups and provided navigational and operations support for large scale (800-900 aircraft) bombing raids into occupied Europe and Germany. The German report gives an insight into the variety of indicator bombs and flares used by Allied aircraft over the period of 1942-1944. Those devices may well have generated aircrew reports of mystery lights, especially under certain weather and combat conditions.

The German report included red, green and yellow "cascade bombs", dropped from heights of 5,000 to 8,000 meters, which fell burning and remained burning on the ground. Lights/flares were observed dropping not only into the target areas but also along the bomber flight paths; they were presumed to be route markers for the bomber stream. Average burning time for the markers was reported as three to four minutes. In addition to air dropped ground markers, "skymarkers" (parachute flares) were in common use, often placed singly and at regular intervals. These were reported to be red, in combination with quick burning green flares ("dripping green stars). Less frequently seen were green markers with red stars and green markers with yellow stars. White and yellowish flares were used for target illumination. During the fall of 1943, the Germans had observed Allied efforts to mark approach corridors with numerous flares – but that practice seems to have ceased over time, possibly because of the heavy bomber losses inflicted by German night fighters defending the target areas.

The report also discussed new types of light markers, not yet clearly identified at that time. These included quick falling flares with columns of sparks – these were reported descending in many colors. A large reddish-yellow "fireball" was reported, apparently used to designate the beginning and end of attacks. The fireballs were seen to produce red flares and were reported as unusually bright. Red "multi flash" flares were also described, apparently being used as bombing guides, but of very short – two to three second – duration.

The German study also noted that with the very large night air raids, repeat flare drops would be used to re-center targeting so that bombers to the rear of the stream would not drop their bombs short as the attack progressed. Different colored sky markers were used in the setting of the repeat markers. For the large scale raids, new route markers would also have to be deployed as the bomber stream progressed. Markers dropped at prominent navigation points or turning points could be red, green, yellow or white and were noted to be set to the side of the designated flight path (a defense against German night-fighters).

Other sources also reported that as part of the German night-fighter effort, selected anti-aircraft batteries – located near German airfields – fired colored flare patterns at regular intervals to aid Luftwaffe night fighters with navigation. In some instances, the Germans also launched flares for area illumination in an effort to help define Allied bombers to night fighters which attacked them from above. As early as 1942, the Luftwaffe had established an extensive series of night fighter belts complete with extensive support from their Mammut and Wasserman ground based radars; the ground radar was complemented by radar equipped Bf-110 night fighters. The night fighter/radar defense lines extended for several hundred miles across Germany and into German occupied territories from France northward into Denmark.[7]

In reviewing aerial phenomena military reports for 1942 – 1944, we find night mission observations of bright white lights, a reddish orange object giving off a green star, an airborne red light, glowing orange balls and globes, small colored balls, a light blue ball of fire, red lights disappearing in streaks, yellow streaks of flame, orange lights singly and in pairs and moving slowly before disappearing, white flares, a cluster of colored flares and balls of orange fire. However in no instance were actual attacks on allied aircraft reported in conjunction with the mystery lights. As a result, Bomber Command's intelligence assessment – "A Note on Pyrotechnic Activity over Germany" – was that aircrews were observing German defensive light devices, including some specifically designed for psychological warfare.[8]

Yet even if the majority of the nighttime "bogies" were pyrotechnic devices (either Allied or German), new types of potential "bandits" began to be appear in late 1943 and early 1944. That period saw the first reports of: "silver discs", "streak like vapor trails", rockets with "blazing sterns which altered course in flight", projectiles resembling "glider bombs", a "glowing red object shooting straight up, doing a wing over then going into a dive and disappearing" – with the appearance of a "flying wing".[9] The many types of nighttime light reports had proved time consuming and frustrating for intelligence groups, however this new series of observations began to reveal what eventually proved to be very real threats, associated with several new types of German weapons.

In two instances (in the Stuttgart area of Germany, during September and October, 1943) Allied air crews began to submit reports which were interpreted as possible aerial anti-aircraft bombs. In September of 1943, a 1st Bombardment Wing mission against Stuttgart reported "objects resembling silver discs about the size of half dollars" floating down into the formation. One cluster of falling discs was estimated to be approximately eight feet wide and four feet in height. The mass of material fell into the path of the formation and one group of discs was seen to fall onto the wing of a B-17. The aircraft's wing immediately caught fire and the aircraft did not return from the mission.[10] In an October report, a plane from the American 546th Heavy Bomb Group described a cluster of small silver discs dropping into their formation's path. Unable to avoid the discs, the crew could hear them striking the plane's tail section, but with no apparent effect or damage. A mass of black debris was observed about twenty feet from the discs. The crew observed two other instances of a black debris field and associated cluster of discs. Another B-17 flying behind the crew later reported that they thought that German fighters were dropping "pie plates" on them.[11]

There is confirmation that the Germans were indeed experimenting with various types of aerial bombs, in fact the Peenemunde technology center had developed and tested advanced parachute bombs which were to be dropped in masses in front of bomber formations. They had also developed canisters which could be filled with large quantities of small explosive or incendiary bombs.[12] Similar aerial bombs and advanced dispensers were developed for use by the new German jet fighter bombers – the Me 262s. Actual air bombing tests were conducted with a formation of four of the jet fighters in December, 1944; the aircraft were equipped with special optical sights for the air to air bombing.

At the same time the silver discs were being reported, Allied intelligence began to receive observations which led to the identification of new German weapons ranging from rocket powered glide bombs to advanced missiles and aircraft. Sightings of smoke trails and lights led to the confirmation of glide bombs launched from aircraft and directed by operators visually targeting the devices – either by smoke trails (daylight) or green/blue lights in the tails of the weapons (night use). The early observations were validated by the positive identification of the German Henschel Hs 293, the first "standoff", guided aerial weapon to enter service in large numbers. The Hs 293 had an airplane-like configuration, an under-slung rocket engine and was carried and dropped from German bombers.

Radio control of the device was standard and a flare was burned in the tail to help operator tracking. There were also glide bombs with wire guidance and even a later version using crude television assisted control. The first operational use of the Henschel guided weapon was in the summer of 1943 and over 2,300 Hs 293s were eventually deployed in combat, sinking a variety of Allied vessels including five destroyers. The November 1943 issue of *Impact*, a confidential USAAF intelligence newsletter, carried an article entitled "New Buck Rogers Development"; the article provided construction details and actual photos of the Hs 293 in flight; the photos had been taken by a British ship.[13]

The Germans also deployed the Fritz X (FX 1400), an armor piercing bomb fitted with four cruciform wings and steered by radio command. Two Fritz X hits sunk the Italian battleship Roma and others seriously damaged Allied ships, including cruisers. Approximately 1,400 were used during the war. The Germans even tested anti-radar missiles such as the BV 246 (Hagelkorn). That device was a very streamlined but un-powered, long-range glide bomb with a range of up to 200 kilometers. Over 1,100 were produced before the project was canceled.

On December 11, 1943 an American bomber crew reported encountering an "unidentified" object over Edman, Germany. It was described as being about the size of a Thunderbolt aircraft and passed around 75 yards beneath the bomber formation. The object was flying straight and at a "terrific speed"; it left a white streak like a vapor trail, which remained visible for some time. In retrospect this sighting was an almost perfect description of the prototype German rocket fighters then in development. On April 25, 1944 the crew of an American B-17 flying over France watched a "small black airplane" fly past at a distance of only three or four miles. It had a thick, teardrop shaped body, sharply swept back wings and lacked any horizontal control surfaces; the description was a perfect match for the newly deployed German Komet rocket fighter.[14] The typical Komet rocket fighter attack leveraged its awesome speed of almost 600 miles per hour to burst up and through bomber formations faster than any Allied fighter could intercept it. That maneuver offered the Komet the ability to fire both going up and down in passes against bomber formations.

A somewhat similar observation, but one occurring at night, was reported by a bomber crew in December, 1944. The object was first seen as a glowing red light but upon closer approach it appeared to be a winged craft which, after shooting past, performed a wingover and went into a steep dive. Although impossible to confirm, this observation is another good description of both the appearance and tactics of the Me 163 Komet rocket fighter –which began actual combat operations in May, 1944. The issue with the December sighting is that, as far as is known, the Komets were never used for night operations due to the immense risk of landing a powerless craft in the dark. Whether or not the December sighting might have been an experiment is impossible to say. Overall, the Komet rocket fighter proved to be an operational failure, especially as compared to the German Me 262 jet fighter. The Komets shot down sixteen Allied aircraft and required truly exceptional pilots. Komet operations were actually shut down in the spring of 1945 and many of their pilots were sent to the more successful jets.

German jet aircraft were quickly described and accurately reported by Allied aircrews when they began to enter combat several months after the advent of the rocket fighters.[15] The Me 262 was the only German jet fighter to become fully operational during the war. It had been approved for production in June of 1943 and the first special unit of jet pilots went into training in December, 1943. Preproduction aircraft were accepted by the Luftwaffe in April, 1944 and the first operational sorties began that month. A reconnaissance unit of the jets was formed in December of 1944 and a special night fighter jet unit was organized in that same month.[16]

By July, 1944, Army Air Force intelligence was producing magazine articles containing very good illustrations and relatively detailed air crew descriptions of the ME 163 rocket fighter as well as both the Me 262 and He 280 jet fighters – that was well before actual photographs of the new aircraft were available. Combat photos of the new craft in action did not appear in print until January, 1945.[17] In regard to jet and rocket fighters being misidentified as mystery nighttime lights, as previously mentioned, the Me 163 Komet was not known to have been used in night operations and, officially, Me 262 jet night fighter operations were limited in both time and geography.

One of the major challenges for military field intelligence is the quick identification and technical analysis of enemy weapons, not only of the weapon's specific characteristics but its deployment, the tactics of its use and its support and maintenance requirements. It is also vital to understand when a new weapon is moving from test and development to actual combat operations. During the early years of World War II, American technical air intelligence was taken by surprise by the high performance Japanese Zero fighter aircraft, which proved deadly in air combat and superior to anything the U.S. was flying at the time. Field intelligence teams raced to recover crashed Japanese aircraft and reassembled them as quickly possible for detailed study.

While the Japanese initially surprised Army Air Force Technical intelligence, the Germans continued to provide surprises throughout the war, fielding new and advanced technology weapons up to the final days of combat. Before the war ended the Arado Ar 234 jet bomber made some of the last German reconnaissance flights flown over England – in April, 1945. The Ar 234 was capable of a cruising speed of 435 miles per hour and had an operational service ceiling of over 30,000 feet. In its few actual combat missions as a bomber it had proved virtually impossible to intercept. Effective field intelligence provided sufficient data on the German jet designs to influence the development of early American Cold War warplanes such as the F-86 Sabrejet and the B-47 bomber.

However, it was the tailless, flying wing aircraft, including the prototype Horten Ho 229 and the jet powered, six engine, Horten VIII long range bomber which proved to be of exceptional interest to American technical intelligence. There was a concern that the Russians might capture the designs and personnel necessary to allow them to proceed to immediate development of such advanced aircraft.[18] An Army Air Material Command report cited an initial 1945 estimate of the long range Horton flying wing's performance – describing a potential cruising speed of up to 750 miles per hour, with a full weapons load, and an operational altitude of 20,000 feet.[19]

Rapid identification and analysis of new German technology weapons was a major focus for Allied technical intelligence in Europe. Dealing with a broad variety of new German missiles and rockets was especially challenging, especially considering that the new weapons ranged beyond jet and rocket aircraft, to a variety of tactical and anti-aircraft rockets and missiles. What is particularly important for our subject is that virtually all the new German devices were quickly and accurately described in Allied aircrew observations, significantly aiding the field intelligence effort. German jet aircraft and rockets such as the V-1 and V-2 were observed and accurately reported by Allied airmen – weeks and months before their observations were verified by photographs or recovery of actual devices. Beyond that experience, there is further war time proof that both military and civilian observers can be relied on to accurately describe unconventional aerial objects.

One of the most ambitious and unconventional weapons fielded during World War II came from the Japanese and was used directly against the continental United States. The Japanese developed and launched a unique weapon – stratospheric balloon bombs. Initially several hundred of the carrier balloons were made of rubberized silk, but with increasing materials shortages, the Japanese soon turned to paper. Some 9,000 very high altitude, trans-Pacific balloon bombs were released by a special Japanese Army Regiment during the first six months of 1944.[20] Due to the limited size of the balloon's payload, the devices could only carry relatively small explosive devices. The first choice for weaponizing the balloons was to place incendiary charges in them, with the hope of starting large scale forest fires in the Pacific Northwest. For practical purposes the very long range balloon project was primarily a device for psychological warfare, demonstrating to America that it too could be attacked at home.

Joel Carpenter's work, *Paper Threat – The first intercontinental weapon system: Japanese Fu-Go balloons,* provides a comprehensive study of the stratospheric balloon bomb project and is highly recommended. There are also a number of Internet and print resources available on the Fu-Go balloon attacks.[21] Carpenter describes the fact that the Fu-Go devices were unique in many ways. Their innovative ballast control systems allowed them to take advantage of strong west to east winds at high altitudes, making trans-Pacific flights possible.[22] In post-war years, the Fu-Go balloons would be extensively studied by American scientists as part of the American development of very high altitude "constant level" balloons – ultimately used both for scientific purposes and for covert, high altitude photo reconnaissance across the entire Soviet Union.

The weaponized Fu-Go balloons incorporated devices for self-destruction by burning, however that measure sometimes failed and eventually trans-Pacific balloons were recovered by both military intelligence organizations and the FBI. In later years, when the initial American "flying saucer/disc" reports began to appear during 1947, some of the same personnel who had been involved in the early 1945 Japanese balloon recoveries responded to reports of crashed discs. FBI special agent Guy Banister participated with the Army Air Force in examining a crashed Fu-Go in Montana in December, 1944 and later was involved in a "flying disc" recovery (the object turned out to be a hoax but initially received national media coverage) in July, 1947.[23]

For our purposes, the most important take away from the Fu-Go balloons relates to the accuracy of observations of unconventional aerial objects. Joel Carpenter provides examples of civilian reports from Wyoming and Montana which included descriptions of flames seen high in the sky and afterwards something seen floating downwards toward the earth. At the time, Dr. Lincoln LaPaz, head of the mathematics and meteoritics departments at the University of New Mexico, was a participant in the American Meteor Society's national observer network. During 1944 he noted a number of new reports describing "point meteors", lights that suddenly flared up but showed no movement. After the Japanese balloon bombs became public knowledge, LaPaz realized that it was most likely that the "point meteor" reports had been of the balloons self-destructing or destroying themselves while dropping their payloads.

LaPaz became personally involved in the secret effort against the balloon offensive, driven by ongoing concerns that the Japanese would use the transoceanic balloons for biological and germ warfare. There was a particular fear that anthrax could be devastating if planted among the western livestock populations. Post-war newspaper coverage of LaPaz's activities noted that the Navy had been particularly concerned about germs and viruses distributed by the balloons as the war was coming to an end.[24]

Daylight aerial sightings of the balloons came from points as far apart as Los Angeles and Chicago. Balloon debris was discovered on the ground in Arizona, Alaska, Iowa and Nebraska. Then unexploded bombs began to turn up, in Idaho, Colorado, Michigan, and Texas. One stratospheric balloon payload dropped near the huge Boeing aircraft plant near Everett, Washington. Soon reports were coming in at the rate of several per day. Bits of metal, fragments of rubber and paper, exploded and unexploded bombs turned up in Washington State, Montana, Idaho, British Columbia, Manitoba, Colorado, Michigan, Mexico, and Texas. Ultimately a few of the balloons were even intercepted and shot down by fighters. Although the balloons and bomb materials did disintegrate over time, the remains remained a threat for decades. Some 300 of the aging weapons had been tallied by 2016, one being recovered in Oregon as recently as 1992.[25]

The military response to the novel Japanese weapons also illustrates how quickly field intelligence can operate and the extent to which quick, positive action follows when sightings prove to involve actual threats. The immediate intelligence estimate of the balloon threat involved the worst possible scenario – which was that the balloons could be used to carry biological warfare agents.[26] A program designated the "Lightning Project," was initiated by the United States Army's Western Defense Command. It began to quietly stockpile decontamination supplies in areas deemed at greatest risk. Farmers' organizations and veterinarians were advised by government agencies, without elaboration, to be particularly watchful for unusual diseases in crops or livestock.

Active defensive measures were immediately initiated to protect the highest priority military targets in range of the balloons.[27] The problem was that with the progress of the war, by the fall of 1944 activities were already underway to dismantle the active domestic air defense that had been initially established on the nation's coasts. Elements of that network such as radars and fighter control centers were increasingly moved from active operations into passive/standby status. The active coastal radar network was further curtailed during 1945, with shipborne radars providing coverage for major ports, especially on the west coast.[28] A number of radar installations were maintained, but by 1945 the integrated air defense networks on both the east and west coast had become considerably fragmented and air defense responsibilities had been assigned to a number of units as a secondary, stand by duty.[29]

Once the Japanese balloon threat was confirmed, the Army Air Force began to set up an integrated radar and fighter defense for the Seattle area (the "Sunset Project"). Limited operations had begun by April and the system was up and running by May 1945. In the interim, fire bomb raids on Tokyo had begun to destroy the infrastructure for balloon production. Military secrecy and appeals to the media had preempted any U.S. media coverage and the Japanese were unable to determine that the weapons were having any psychological impact, consequently they officially terminated the project in May – although few details are available on the last of the Fu-Go balloon launches.

Reports from the Sunset Project confirm that both military and civilian observers reliably reported observations of the unconventional aerial objects, however they also provide a real caution in regard to how much discrimination is possible in ground based sightings of objects at high altitudes. On some sixty-eight occasions, ground observers reported unidentified objects and the Seattle Control Group scrambled interceptors against what turned out to be standard weather balloons. Weather balloons were being routinely launched, on a daily basis, from larger airports in the area. Other non-Fu-Go reports involved the planet Venus and even Navy blimps.[30]

The observer experience with civilian observations of Japanese stratospheric balloons provides additional confirmation that observers can and do provide valid sightings of unconventional objects – even if they cannot actually identify objects seen at a considerable distance. As a corollary, the Project Sunset experience cautions that once "sensitized" to a particular type of "target", observer reports tend to surge, as does misinterpretation of similar but conventional objects.

The World War II experience with observations of anomalous aerial objects provides us with considerable insight into the militaries' response to observations which actually lead to positive threat estimates. In the European theater, when unconventional object reports translated to actual new weapons and active threats, an immediate and ongoing series of communications was initiated. The communications provided guidelines on identifying and reporting the threats and extended to advice on how to actually engage them – including detailed suggestions on tactics and weapons to be used. Certain information was classified, but only at a level which restricted it inside the intelligence and command levels. Extensive details on new enemy weapons were communicated to the field forces who would face them in combat.

The Fu-Go balloon threat to the continental United States gives us even more insight into the military response to an actual and well-defined threat estimate. Classified communications occurred and warnings were issued, however a series of preventative media measures were immediately undertaken.[31] Information management was implemented and resulted in voluntary self-censorship by newspapers and outlets, carried out in response to a plea to the media to avoid potential civilian panic – there was considerable concern in regard to a public panic over fears of the balloons being used to carry biological/plague weapons.

On January 4, 1945, the Western Defense Command issued a "confidential" note to newspaper editors and radio broadcasters (not for publication or broadcast) advising them that any balloons approaching the United States from outside its borders could be enemy attacks and their reporting involved military security.[32] Information that such devices had reached the United

States would be considered information of value to the enemy. The media was asked not to aid the enemy by publishing or broadcasting such information without direct authorization. The memorandum was from the Office of Censorship. The media complied with the request and it was only after actual deaths and injuries related to an unexploded balloon bomb found on the ground occurred that the military issued a general warning and the devices became public knowledge.

When military intelligence concluded unconventional flying objects to be a real or even a potential threat, it turned to preventative media measures – the more well defined the threat, the more stringent the measures. Such measures ranged from simple classification of reports and studies, to much more subtle attempts at managing information going to media outlets. When classification and media management occurs, it is a good indication that unidentified object reports are being taken seriously within the military.

In summary, there are a number of important lessons to be learned from the unidentified and unconventional object experiences of World War II. What is most striking is that military personnel did accurately describe and characterize unexpected and unconventional objects, even while under the stress of combat conditions. When given the opportunity for daylight observations at moderate distances, both British and American airmen sighted and accurately described German rocket powered and jet powered aircraft weeks or months before they became confirmed by photos or in physical collections. In some instances, new German devices were accurately described before they were operationally deployed in combat.

The same can be said for observations of the German radio and wire guided glide bombs. In addition there were accurate in-flight aerial observations of the very first of the German Vengeance weapons, the V-1 pulse jet cruise missile and the ballistic V-2 rocket missile. A British reconnaissance fighter pilot delivered a very accurate observation of a V-2 as it was fired from a tree covered launching mobile launcher, the missile itself still in boost phase with fire and smoke erupting from the rocket motor.[33]

In the early 1950s, during one stage in the U.S. Air Force's effort to deal with the issue of unidentified flying objects, one of its scientific consultants proposed a controlled test – a test in which unknowing observers would be exposed to a series of controlled appearances of aircraft and balloons in order to determine the extent to which the personnel would accurately report and identify objects which were assumed to be routinely generating flying disc reports.[34]

It was an interesting idea, although the test was never conducted. In reality, the history of World War II observations and its experience with accurate description of unconventional enemy weapons had already demonstrated that Army Air Force personnel could be accurate and reliable in their descriptions. In short, when confronted with unknown aerial objects during daylight, at close to moderate viewing distances and when consistently and intelligently debriefed, experienced military personnel do indeed provide extremely accurate and credible observations.

There certainly are limits to observer abilities – primarily in regard to nighttime observations – but it seems rather amazing that in later years some senior Air Force officers, themselves with war time experience, would become publicly dismissive of the observational abilities of their own pilots and aircrews. On the other hand, the mystery nighttime light experience produced considerable frustration within intelligence groups, frustration extending to headquarters levels. Nighttime mystery lights also proved to have a seriously negative psychological impact on Allied flyers, affecting morale sufficiently to be referred to in intelligence reports as "nightmare devices".

To more fully appreciate that area of the unidentified object intelligence problem – and the limitations of technical intelligence – we need to dig more deeply into the military response to the nighttime mystery light reports. Reports which dramatically escalated in both the European and Pacific theaters during the final two years of the war.

Chapter One Endnotes:

1. Keith Chester, *Strange Company*, Anomalist Books, New York, 2007, 36

2. Ibid, 40

3. David Clarke and Andy Roberts, "Foo Fighters and the RAF Experience", *UFO Magazine*, 9; British UFO Research Association files – "UFO Sighting from an Aircraft – Report Form", provided by Jan Aldrich

4. Keith Chester, *Strange Company*, Anomalist Books 2007, 32-334.

5. Ibid, 37-38

6. *British Pathfinder Operations as of March, 1944*, issued by Luftwaffenfuhrungsstab Ic/Fremde, Luftwaffen West. Cited from the 146 RAF Night Fighter Squadron website http://www.156squadron.com/about_pathfinders2.asp

7. J.E. Kaufman, *Fortress: Third Reich; German fortifications and defense systems win World War II*, De Capo Press, 2003, 142-147. It should be noted that many of the more easily identifiable targets such as factories, bridges and transportation hubs were protected not only by night fighters but by tethered barrage balloons intended to obstruct low level attacks.

8. Keith Chester, *Strange Company*, 32

9. Keith Chester, Sighting Index, *Strange Company*, 281 – 296

10. Confidential Memo, "Attention: A-2 Duty Desk, First Bomb Wing; Subject: Additional information on the observation of silvery colored discs on mission to Stuttgart", 6 Sept, 1943. Report in National Archives. Also, Keith Chester, *Strange Company* 43-44.

11. Keith Chester, *Strange Company*, 46-47. The similarity in these two sightings, their proximity in time and geography both argue for some test of a new weapon. The possibility that the reports were of a weapons test is supported by the observations of debris fields in conjunction with the discs, suggesting the explosion of a "bomblet" dispersing package from either an aircraft or possibly even anti-aircraft weapons. Walter Dornberger, *V2 The Nazi Rocket Weapon*, Ballantine Books, New York, 1954, 235. These advanced weapons had been designed for use with the jet Me 262's. Air to air bombing was first tested with Me 262 jet in December, 1944 and air to air bombing tactics were implemented using an echelon of four of the jets with special Zeiss optical sights. However, time had run out and operational deployment never occurred. Walter Boyne Messerschmitt *Me 262 – Arrow to the Future* Smithsonian Institution,

1980, 44 For further details and analysis of this particular observation see Andy Roberts: http://www.project1947.com/articles/foosolv.htm

12. Walter Dornberger, *V2 The Nazi Rocket Weapon*, Ballantine Books, New York, 1954, 235

13. *Impact*, Vol. 1, No. 8, November, 1943, Squadron distribution by the office of the Assistant Chief of Intelligence, Washington, D.C. 7. The article also described a new barrage rocket weapon deployed on both single and multi-engine German fighters. Those rocket weapons had first been observed in action in October, 1943, over Schweinfurt, Germany.

14. *Impact*, Vol. 2, No. 7, July 1944, 26

15. Absolute identification of this particular aircrew sighting as a German jet is virtually impossible. As of November, 1943 only one developmental Me 262 was available for testing even though the airplane had been released for production in June, 1943. But pre-production aircraft were being taken into testing in the winter of 1943-44. Luftwaffe Me 262 general pilot training would not begin until June, 1944, but the first operational unit was formed in December 1943 and had begun combat operations in April, 1944 using pre-production aircraft. The first fully confirmed Allied aircraft combat encounter with the Me 262 occurred in July, 1944 over Munich. Walter J. Boyne, Messerschmitt Me 262, *Arrow to the Future*, Smithsonian Institution Press, Washington DC, 1980, 35-38 and 41.

16. Ibid, 158-159

17. *Impact*, Vol. 2, No. 7 July, 1944, p. 26 and "Impact", Vol. 3, No. 1, January, 1945, 40-41

18. Two Allied intelligence studies focused on the Horton aircraft. A 26 page 1945 report was produced by the U.S. Army Air Material Command (Technical Report No. 76); the report used information collected by the U.S. Naval Technical Mission in Europe and was based not only in captured documents but in interviews with a Horton draftsman who had spent a considerable time on the craft's development and in contact with the Horton brothers up to the time of his capture. At the time of the draftsman interview the single flying prototype of the Horton 9 was still in active flight testing. In addition the British Aircraft Authority produced a 75 page report on the Horton Tailless Aircraft.

19. The Allies did seize the parts from one Horton 9 still in construction but not the flying prototype – one of its engines had failed on a test flight and it crashed in landing. It is known that the prototype was flown only at 75% engine thrust due to the fact that it was a design model and the airframe had been heavily modified with multiple cuts and re-welds during production. Since the aircraft had never been rebuilt and operationally tested, its exact characteristics remain a matter of speculation – however the information in the 1945 technical report put its capabilities significantly beyond any of the Allied aircraft then under development. We will see

that in the years immediately after the war, U.S. Air Intelligence at the Pentagon was extremely concerned that the Russians had begun mass production of Horton flying wing combat aircraft. We will also find that when the first UFO reports of 1947 and 1948 began to draw serious intelligence attention, the first thought was that the Russians had indeed stolen a march using German technology. Horten Ho 229, *Hitler's Stealth Fighter/Bomber & Other Horten Aircraft American & British Intelligence Documents*, BACM Research – Paperless Archives http://www.paperlessarchives.com/FreeTitles/HortenHo229.pdf

20. Allan T. Duffin, *Project FU-GO; the Japanese Balloon Bombs*, Warfare History Network, November 17, 2016 http://warfarehistorynetwork.com/daily/wwii/project-fugo-the-japanese-balloon-bombs/

21. "Fugo balloon attacks on North America", *Project 1947*, http://www.project1947.com/gfb/fugolinks.htm

22. In the 1920's a Japanese meteorologist, Wasaburo Oishi, had launched pilot balloons from near Mount Fuji and tracked their movements eastward as they entered the high altitude wind streams. In 1939 a German meteorologist used the term "jet current" to describe the phenomena and over time the wind currents became generally known as "jet streams".

23. Joel Carpenter, *Guided Missiles and UFOs: A Tangle of Fear, 1937-53*. The Joel Carpenter chronologies and commentary may be found at the Project 1947 website, courtesy of Jan Aldridge: http://www.project1947.com/gr/grchron1.htm

24. *New Mexican Had Lookout Job for Japanese Germs*, University News Bureau, University of New Mexico, Albuquerque, New Mexico, undated; late 1945. http://www.project1947.com/gfb/lapazfugo2.htm

25. Allan T. Duffin, *Project FU-GO; the Japanese Balloon Bombs*, Warfare History Network, November 17, 2016. http://warfarehistorynetwork.com/daily/wwii/project-fugo-the-japanese-balloon-bombs/

26. Joel Carpenter, *Paper Threat – The first intercontinental weapons system: Japanese Fu-Go balloons*, http://www.project1947.com/gfb/fugo.htm

27. Ibid.

28. *The Army Air Forces of World War II;- 1942-1945, Volume VI, Men and Planes*, Chapter 3, Air Defense of the United States, https://www.ibiblio.org/hyperwar/AAF/VI/AAF-VI-3.html

29. The figure given for the number of radar installations in place at war's end varies, but the maximum number given for both east and west coast sites is 99, Forth Air Force Historical Study 1941-1945, No. III, Volume 1, 146

30. Joel Carpenter, *Paper Threat – The first intercontinental weapons system: Japanese Fu-Go balloons*

31. On January 4, 1945, the Western Defense Command issued a "confidential" note to Editors and Broadcasters (not for publication or broadcast) advising them that any balloons approaching the United States from outside its borders can be enemy attacks and involved military security. Information that such devices had reached the United States would be considered information of value to the enemy.

32. "Confidential Note to Editors and Broadcasters, Western Defense Command", January 4, 1945, http://www.project1947.com/fig/1945a.htm#fugo

33. Raymond Baxter, *V2 Launch Experience.* http://en.wikipedia.org/wiki/Raymond_Baxter For details of V2 launches: http://www.v2rocket.com/start/deployment/denhaag.html

34. Dr. Howard Cross, Battelle Memorial Institute, January 9, 1953

Chapter 2

Nightmare Devices

In this chapter

- Unidentified aerial object reports in both theaters of war were taken very seriously due to the constant testing and introduction of radically new and innovative enemy aircraft and anti-aircraft weapons.

- Air crews in both theaters became seriously concerned about mysterious nighttime lights which seem to stalk and observe them – apparently under intelligent control and capable of dramatic maneuvers.

- Field intelligence valued detailed daylight descriptions of unidentified aerial objects, using them to characterize and even develop tactics against new enemy weapons – even before full identification.

- In contrast both field and staff intelligence groups became increasingly frustrated by growing numbers of mysterious nighttime light reports, especially as press and political attention demanded answers they could not provide.

- When conventional intelligence didn't work, and Pentagon pressure was on – the answer was to hand it off to the scientists.

- The real UFOs ....profiles and signatures.

During the final two years of the war the introduction of a host of radically new enemy aircraft and weapons added considerably to the challenge of dealing with unidentified and novel aerial object reports. By the end of 1944 Allied intelligence was facing an increasing number of new and ambitious German anti-aircraft weapons, some operational and many more in test or early production. The unguided German R4/M air to air rocket (Hurricane) was mass produced and introduced into combat with elite German air squadrons in 1944 and distributed to regular Luftwaffe units by March of 1945. These rockets (with a 1,000 plus meter range) were produced and used for both air to air and air to ground attack. They were particularly deadly when deployed for Me 262 jet fighter attacks on American B-17 formations. When used during the day, the R4/M produced a characteristic smoke trail and generally the attacking planes would have been seen; identification of the rockets in night attacks would have been much more difficult.

A similar identification problem existed in regard to night fighters with a variety of upward firing automatic cannons. The fighters could attack Allied bombers from outside their crew's normal field of vision. In the final year of the war, German fighters were being equipped with an increasing variety of more powerful upward firing cannons; an advanced system (Jagerfaust) was optically activated, requiring the fighter to simply fly under the target aircraft.

New and novel German anti-aircraft weapons presented an ongoing problem for Allied intelligence, especially so as many of them appear to have been tested towards the end of the war but never came into full operational deployment. Technical intelligence personnel focused on the jet/rocket fighters and long range rockets which became operational with regular German units, however there were also a number of unconventional devices going into prototype testing or limited deployment during the final months of combat. Apart from the new jet and rocket aircraft, the Germans were prototyping, testing and beginning to field a wide variety of guided aircraft missiles.

In his book on the development of the long range "vengeance" rockets (V-2/A-4) German General Walter Dornberger described chairing a meeting on anti-aircraft missiles in January of 1945. A number of independent groups at different locations had been working on guided anti-aircraft rockets of both ground and air launched varieties. For most, the combat use of remote control was still in the future – visual guidance was still the rule in testing. Operational use of the devices at night or in overcast weather would have been months away at best. That immediately forced cuts for most of the projects. Dornberger focused on those with the most potential for early use combat – the Henschel Hs 117 "Butterfly" air to ground missile, the Kramer X 4 air to air missile, and the Wasserfall high altitude anti-aircraft rocket.[1]

The X-4 wire guided rocket, had a tapered, cigar-shaped fuselage, with four small swept wings and four smaller tail fins. It was designed to be air launched and steered with a small joystick from the cockpit of the launch aircraft. Because of the limitations of wire guidance in air combat, it was equipped with a type of acoustical proximity fuse tuned to the frequency of a B-17 bomber's engines operating at cruising speed. The rocket's maximum speed was 1,152 km/h (716 mph) with a range of over three kilometers. Officially it never became fully operational but hundreds were produced for testing and some of the test rockets were reportedly been fired against Allied aircraft towards the end of the war.

Ground launched anti-aircraft rockets were also being rushed into use. The Taifun, an unguided ground to air rocket was tested, accepted and scheduled for mass production in 1945; the initial order was for some 2 million of the anti-aircraft barrage rockets but engine problems and air raids handicapped production. With an acceleration of up to Mach 3 the Taifun could reach altitudes of 15,000 feet. Another anti-aircraft rocket, the Henschel Hs 117 Schmetterling (Butterfly) was successfully tested in spring of 1944 with some 23 units launched. It was ready for mass production in March of 1945 but was canceled before production began.

The Schmetterling was shaped like a small aircraft and used two boost engines and a sustainer rocket engine. With a range of 32 kilometers (19 miles) it could attack targets to 10,000 meters. Targeting was a problem at the highest altitudes because aiming was visual, using a radio command link for steering; it was equipped with both acoustic and photoelectric proximity detonators. An even more ambitious anti-aircraft rocket, the Enzian radar guided weapon, was based on the Me 163 rocket plane and had a strike capability of over 15,240 meters (32,000 feet). Technical intelligence following the German collapse established that 60 Enzians had been produced and some 40 had actually been launched.[2]

There was a level of talk about the new and advanced German aerial weapons, however intelligence studies downplayed the threat, not because of their capability but because it was increasingly unlikely they could be produced in quantities sufficient to actually impact the Allied bombing effort, which was constantly increasing in both size and frequency of raids. Yet as Allied ground advanced across France, the issue of mystery nighttime lights returned to plague field intelligence units. In December 1944, immediately prior to the final German counteroffensive in Europe – the Battle of the Bulge – strange night time lights began to be reported by both ground and air units. Anti-aircraft units were the first to encounter and attempt to engage the mystery lights. American Army XX Corps' units detected two objects on radar, traveling slowly with no noise, first reported by ground observers. They were tracked, fired upon and one seemed to disintegrate while the other appeared to fall to the ground…although nothing was recovered. The following night more objects were detected, fired upon and appeared to disintegrate.[3]

During the next few weeks the Luftwaffe launched one of its last major air operations, committing all its resources in support of Hitler's desperate effort to blunt the Allies' drive towards Germany. Dozens of Allied air crews encountered mysterious lights while hundreds of German aircraft were in action and a massive V-2 rocket attack was being directed towards the Allied supply ports, especially towards the huge port facilities of Antwerp, Belgium. The missile blitz against Antwerp was actually greater than the much better known V-2 campaign launched against London, England.[4]

Allied night fighters had begun to report more frequent observations of unidentifiable nighttime lights in the fall of 1944, but by early spring 1945 they began to be increasingly reported by air crews on night bombing missions. In some cases the lights were fired upon and either showed no effects or appeared to disintegrate – much as the lights which had come under anti-aircraft fire at the Battle of the Bulge. Some of the new reports sounded much like earlier year's descriptions of light phenomena – red balls of fire hanging in the air for ten seconds, followed by yellow streaks of flame – but others were more mysterious because they appeared to be pacing particular aircraft, virtually flying in formation with them, maintaining speed and countering evasive actions. The sightings became so widespread that they began to receive media coverage and even headline level attention in the American and British press where they ultimately were tagged with the name "foo fighter".

These new "nightmare devices"[5] were reportedly maintaining formation with aircraft, seemingly observing them, and coping effortlessly with even with the most strenuous evasive actions. There were no reports of attacks on either Allied night fighters or bombers but airmen had the definite impression that the lights were intelligently controlled and capable of dramatic maneuvers in response to the aircraft observing them. On a number of occasions multiple lights were observed flying in apparently controlled formation. Pilots used to daily combat missions became especially wary of the balls of light. If nothing else the lights definitely began to have a psychological and morale impact, with air crews increasingly nervous as to when the shadowing would turn into something much more threatening.[6] In a number of instances air crews felt that they were encountering the new and dangerous German rocket or jet fighters and observing their exhausts as the mystery lights.[7] That only added to their concern as to when the unknown lights would move to actual attacks.

Research in the decades following the war has largely negated the possibility that any physical devices precisely maneuvering alongside Allied aircraft would have been German jet or rocket night fighters. The only operational German jet night fighter unit (10/NJG/11) went into operation in October

1944 and continued combat into February 1945. It was located 50 miles south of Berlin and assigned strictly to the defense of Berlin. The Me 262 jet fighters in the unit were not equipped with radar and relied on ground searchlights for targeting incoming bombers; radar equipped jets only arrived in spring of 1945. As far as is known no night missions were ever flown by German jets in the Italian theater.[8]

As to the Me 163 rocket interceptors, no records indicate that they were ever tested for night combat and the only operational unit was initially deployed in the Netherlands, being withdrawn into Germany near Leipzig in July 1944. Its combat operations strictly involved daylight attacks on bomber groups and its operational range was limited to approximately 25 miles. Interviews with operational pilots confirm that it would have been suicidal to attempt to land the craft at night.

Although very much on the mind of Allied air crews and increasingly reported to field intelligence units, it appears that German jet and rocket aircraft were apparently not behind the increasing number of "nightmare device" reports, which described highly maneuverable objects approaching and capable of remaining in apparently close contact during bombing missions – although not actually firing or otherwise attacking.

Germany had begun building and testing a limited number of helicopter prototypes, including a jet engine powered rotor design. German helicopters included the extremely agile Flettner Fl 265, capable of outmaneuvering German fighters even in its early flight tests. An improved version, the Fl 282 *Kolibri* ("Hummingbird."), actually went into production and saw use by the German Navy beginning in 1943, flying protective reconnaissance for convoys in the Baltic, Mediterranean and Aegean seas. Only a few dozen were built before large scale Allied bombing destroyed the production lines which had been set up to fulfill an order for a thousand of the small helicopters.[9] The second operational German helicopter, a larger two rotor machine (Fa 223 Drache) was also built in small quantities beginning in 1943; it proved itself as an Army transport, even lifting artillery pieces during fighting in the Austrian mountains.

While potentially having the maneuverability demonstrated in some mystery light reports, German helicopters had neither the service ceilings nor speeds necessary to reach the British and American bombers flying at mission altitudes and cruise speeds. The manufacturing issues which held back their deployment in the desired numbers also illustrate the immense limitations on production of even proven German aircraft during the last year of the war.

Faced with the lack of any specific, identifiable weapon which would match the ongoing reports of maneuvering nighttime lights, intelligence groups were forced to speculate based on descriptions from aircrews as well as information obtained from prisoners of war and escapees. Given the fragmentation of German research and development and the breadth of independent developments by its various military branches and aircraft manufactures, there were ample rumors of truly amazing new weapons. The actual development of extremely novel designs and technologies clearly provided a stimulus for such rumors.

The Focke-Wulf aircraft company was developing a jet powered interceptor which would have been able to take off and ascend at very high speed to defend factories or installations with no adjacent airfields. Proposed in 1944, the cylindrical aircraft was to be propelled by a jet powered rotating propeller – for takeoff the craft would have lifted as a helicopter and in flight functioned as a very high speed propeller driven aircraft. But the craft was only being concept tested at the end of the war; the test units were used only in wind tunnel experiments and no operational prototypes were ever built. Referred to as a "tailsetter" the craft would likely have suffered the same considerable problems in landing that similar American designs, using standard propellers and wings, faced in the years following the war.

Another German vertical takeoff interceptor was rocket powered; the "Natter" air defense fighter project begun in August, 1944. With great interest by the SS (the SS "protective squadron" had increasingly become involved in novel projects), the Natter was flight tested and rushed towards production; some 30 were built. As far as is known, they were used in unmanned launches and glide tests but never became operational.

A more conventional aircraft design, although rocket powered, was pushed into development by the Zeppelin Company. Referred to as the Zeppelin "Rammer" the aircraft was intended to be towed or carried to altitude; aerial towing was an increasingly common German practice towards the end of the war, used with a variety of guided weapons including the V-1 cruise missile. Once at intercept height the Rammer would fire its own rocket motor to achieve a very high speed in attacking bomber formations. It was to attack in two phases, first with nose mounted, unguided rockets and then by actually ramming bombers with specially strengthened wings. As of January 1945 a production build of 16 Rammers had been ordered – but shortly afterwards the factory was destroyed in a bombing raid and further work cancelled.

With rumor and gossip about such novel craft constantly circulating and with Adolf Hitler's public pronouncements about amazing new German "wonder weapons", the mystery light phenomenon was taken quite seriously by Allied intelligence groups, especially as reports appeared to spread across a broad geographic region, with sightings over occupied France, Germany and Italy. A British Bomber Command Operational Report of December 1944 discussed careful "re-interrogation" of flight crews. It commented on the fact that a number of the mystery lights had been fired upon and apparently destroyed, that when fired upon most of them seemed to burst into flames or explode, and some appeared to have exploded spontaneously or were suddenly seen to dive into the ground. Yet no British planes had been damaged or seemingly attacked in any manner.[10] Once again the field intelligence reports were accompanied by complaints by unit personnel that the mystery light investigations continued to be a distraction and were making it difficult to estimate the actual strength and tactics of enemy night fighter operations.

With intelligence about sensational new German weapons coming from voluntary defectors and prisoner interrogations and with the chaos of the last year of fighting in Europe it's little wonder that an evaluation of German capabilities issued in 1945 ranged across flying bombs, bombardment rockets, even noting suspected "phoo bombs" thought to be in development. The phoo bombs were described as jet propelled, radio controlled short range weapons, to be used in ramming attacks on bomber formations. The report noted that reported air encounters cast doubt on the effectiveness of these suspected weapons as no actual damage had been reported, their inflight maneuvers appeared more like "antics" than attacks. The report concluded that such devices would have to be deployed in attacks involving a minimum of one hundred devices to have any real effect on a bomber formation and that such numbers would be unlikely given German production limitations.[11]

Any discussion of phoo bombs and mystery lights has to note that circa 1950, well after the initial era of "flying disc/flying saucer" sightings which followed the war, a handful of anecdotal reports describing German "flying discs" began to circulate. The claims were from individuals claiming to have worked on prototypes of novel aircraft powered by jet turbines used to drive a disc shaped airframe. Those individuals described prototypes and even test flights in the last months of the war – flights with truly amazing performance claims, including supersonic speeds. Research has shown that these German flying disc claims emerged locally and were linked to media stories about flying saucers. Years of dedicated research by a host of interested parties have failed to provide any substantive confirmation that such craft were actually flown.

Another argument against the German flying disc stories relates to the amazing performance reported for the craft. One source described disc flights at supersonic speeds well over Mach 1.[12] Such claims can be compared to the real world work on turbojet, ducted disc aircraft prototypes developed during the 1950's. The concept of a vectored thrust turbo disc was proposed by Nathan C. Price as early as 1953; it was actually filed as a patent by Lockheed Aircraft in 1957.[13]

In 1952 a project to design and prototype a similar craft was actually initiated by A.V. Roe (AVRO) of Canada. The AVRO concept designs were ultimately funded by the US Air Force as Project 9961/ Y and Y2 ("Silver Bug") during the years 1954 through 1958. The goal for that project was to develop vertical takeoff craft capable of very high speed, high altitude flight. The designs called for a large, flattened jet turbine which would be housed in a disc shaped fuselage and propelled by exhaust gasses directed through slots around the rim of the disk. Directing the jet using a full 360 degree ring of exhaust channels was to provide extreme maneuverability.[14]

In the real world, even with ample funding and a concerted design effort, the Silver Bug project came nowhere near expectations, mired in a variety of engineering issues. Ultimately the U.S. Army took over the project in hopes of fielding a "flying jeep", operating over rough terrain. Even that effort, an air cushion, ground effect device (the AVRO Canada VZ-9 Avrocar) fell far short of expectations and prototypes experienced stability and control issues while even a few feet above the ground.

Over the years other German air devices have been mentioned as candidates for the nightmare device observations. One such purported anti-aircraft weapon found widely discussed in print and on the Internet is referred to as the kugelblitz. While the Germans did field a few prototypes of an advanced mobile anti-aircraft system named "kugelblitz", it was a gun system, not an aerial device.[15] The variants and related devices found discussed in the UFO kugelblitz literature remain undocumented and remain highly controversial – to say the least.[16]

Ultimately, field intelligence units grew so frustrated by the mystery lights, the rumors and the gossip that led nowhere, that they simply followed what we will come to recognize as standard practice in such situations – certain of the more significant observations were simply noted in reports, batched in with a much larger quantity of unit paperwork and sent up the chain of command, leaving the unit personnel focused on more critical, tactical intelligence issues. One of the chief complaints seen in the initial field/unit intelligence studies of the mystery lights is that dealing with the reports on them was diverting personnel from focusing on very real threats, such as the evolving German tactics in the combat use of their new and confirmed rocket and jet fighters. The mystery light inquiries were also complicating technical assessments of the newer German weapons such as the air to ground rockets and particularly the new Vengeance/V-series cruise and ballistic missiles.

The reality is that operational intelligence groups focus on known threats to their units, the things that are likely to be shooting at their people or dropping bombs on them. If field reports do not develop into actual dangers/threats, the unit intelligence staff simply pass the reports to headquarters and let the staff guys worry about them. In other words, unit and field intelligence is tightly focused on its own mission and what is immediately affecting it.

Of course the air crews themselves remained very concerned, they continued to talk and as the talk about the mysterious lights spread, the press picked up on it – even the domestic American press. In January of 1945, Newsweek magazine headlined an article on "Foo fighters" (the name was derived from a comic strip of the period), describing them as balls of light which were reported to fly in front of, alongside or trailing Allied aircraft. As would be expected, that sort of media attention led to questions for the Pentagon, and interest by Congressmen. And when the Pentagon received questions about the unidentified devices, it immediately moved to request answers from its headquarters commands.

In January, 1945 the American War Department sent a request to Headquarters, Allied Air Intelligence (SHAEF / Supreme Headquarters, Allied Expeditionary Forces in Europe) for information on the "foo fighters" being reported the media. In turn SHAEF initiated its own inquiry, citing the issue that reports were "agitating and keeping crews on edge when they encounter them, mainly because they cannot explain them."[17] The headquarters inquiry immediately ran into difficulties, apparently based on the fact that in general reports of unidentified lights had been filtered out of intelligence summaries being sent to SHAEF headquarters. The field was focused on combat issues and since the mystery lights had not proved dangerous they had not been elevated as a military concern to SHAEF.

The British Air Ministry responded to the SHAEF inquiry, stating that British crews had certainly been reporting mysterious lights but that the most likely explanation was a mix of jet aircraft and anti-aircraft guns or rockets. These views were supported by a number of reports which did indeed include observation of spurts of gunfire, either from the ground or aircraft, followed by the appearance of "balls of foo fire" becoming visible for periods ranging from seconds to several minutes and which briefly seemed to follow aircraft. In one instance a yellowish red glow was observed; it followed the bomber within machine gun range but did not fire and after closing was seen to be in the shape of a flying wing. The British bomber engaged with machine guns and observed it fall in flames.[18]

By February, 1945 SHAEF still had nothing substantive with which to respond to the War Department, Congress or the media. Its response the high command turned to an option which we will see become a standard practice in regard to dealing with press and public concerns about unidentified aerial objects. The mystery light issue was handed off to scientific advisors and consultants. If field intelligence couldn't resolve the issue, perhaps the scientists could provide an explanation.

Scientists were available as staff support for SHAEF, specifically individuals within the recently organized Scientific Intelligence Advisory Section (SIAS), headed by Dr. Victor H. Fraenckel.[19] SIAS personnel were tasked with a scientific review of reports on the mystery lights in regard to possible association with new German weaponry. In addition, a special scientific group from Washington reportedly made a personal visit to the German front and flew on a couple of bombing missions – in which none of the mystery lights were observed. Names of that team are not on record; the team members apparently expressed serious skepticism and seemed to feel that the aircrews making such observations were suffering from war nerves and simply in need of rotation.

Given that the scientists were from the War Department, the group may well have included David Griggs, one of the senior technical members on Edward Bowles' staff. Bowles was serving as a consultant to the Secretary of War and had brought in Griggs as the War Department's leading expert on radar.[20] It should also be noted that Howard Robertson appears to have been the SHAEF contact for a number of organizations and was playing a key role in the assessment of information on German guided anti-aircraft weapons. Certainly he was in a key position to evaluate reports in terms of what was being learned about the newest generations of German weapons.

Robertson and Griggs were involved with virtually every military and civilian intelligence collections group operating in Europe during the war, including the Office of Scientific Research and Development (OSRD), which had the responsibly for research on radar and radio countermeasures for German weapons. They had broad access to all military reports on suspected and actual weapons development and developed impeccable reputations within both the military and scientific communities.[21] Following the end of combat in Europe, Griggs also performed a similar role, including investigation of mystery lights, in the Pacific theater.

There is no sign that Robertson and the Scientific Intelligence Advisory Section were able to give SHAEF or the War Department any definitive explanation of the "foo lights". Robertson himself continued to be heavily involved in the evaluation of unconventional German technology which was the subject of intense technical collections efforts (operation LUSTY) at the end of the war. He became chief of Field Information Agency – Technical (FIAT) at SHAEF. FIAT was responsible for directing, coordinating and integrating the exploitation activities of all the various technical collection missions. It seems likely that his exposure to the breath of pilot–less, remote controlled and guided weapons under development by the Germans helped convince him that any of the mystery sightings not due to misinterpretation of conventional devices, atmospheric effects or misidentified astronomical objects had been caused by a variety of new and unconventional German technologies and weapons, many of which never came into general production or operational deployment.[22]

Mystery lights proved not only to be an intelligence problem in the European Theater but as large scale bombing raids against the Japanese home islands began, mysterious ball shaped lights also began to be reported in significant numbers in the Pacific. Japanese theater air crews reached the conclusion that the lights posed a potential threat, quite possibly being manned rocket propelled bombs such as the MXY7 Ohka (nick named the "BAKA"/"fool" by American personnel). The BAKA was a glide bomb developed for use against surface naval vessels.[23]

BAKA glider bombs carried a human kamikaze pilot and over 2,500 pounds of explosives; they were equipped with three small solid rocket engines which could be fired individually. The rocket propelled bombs were carried to within two to three miles of a target by a manned bomber and released into a rocket assisted descent at a maximum speed of 500 miles per hour. The rocket powered glide bombs were initially used against the American Navy at Okinawa and records show that up to 800 of the devices were built during the last year of the Pacific war. There were also rumors that BAKAs had been flown against American bomber groups but air to air use was never confirmed.

In the Pacific mysterious fire balls were reported following even the newest B–29 bombers. The B–17 crews reporting them in Europe were flying aircraft which when loaded with fuel and bombs during attacks were operating at altitudes of 20,000 to 25,000 feet. B-29 crews reported mystery lights at altitudes ranging from their service ceilings of 30,000 feet to the much lower altitudes used for actual bombing runs. During April and May, 1945 literally hundreds of "BAKA bomb" and "balls of fire" sightings were reported by the 499th Bomb Group, as well as all the other groups in the American XX (Twentieth) Bomber Command.

One of the best historical studies on the World War II mystery balls of fire has been performed by Jeffery Lindell, a former Air Force Electronics Warfare Specialist. His research at the national archives and oral history work with aircraft crew members is exceptional. Lindell's work with Pacific command records is unique and readers are referred to his monograph "A Historical and Physiological Perspective of the Foo Fighters of World War Two".[24] The following examples are excerpted from the more detailed material in Lindell's paper.

In one incident the commander and crew of the "Southern Belle" B-29 bomber reported several foo fighter type lights, apparently chasing their aircraft. In another incident, a large ball of light approached a B-29 from the nose, only some five hundred feet above and no more than a hundred feet to the right of the aircraft. The approach occurred just before the aircraft released its bombs and no overt action was taken against the bomber during the passage of the light.[25] In another report, a crew observed a ball of fire "about the size of a basketball". The B-29 took a series of evasive maneuvers and each time the ball of fire fell behind the aircraft, only to catch up again during straight flight.

Given the apparent controlled flight of the fire balls, a report was sent to Bomb Wing Intelligence and on to XX Bomber Command Headquarters. Headquarters produced an evaluation which focused on the sighting reflecting the possible introduction by the Japanese of jet craft based on German technology. Jet and rocket designs were indeed being shared with Japan (largely via submarine shipments of documents, technicians and actual engines). Lindell's research found that the headquarters assessment did not make it back to the air groups themselves.

Instead, the unit level intelligence officers were sent extensive information on the BAKA glide bombs captured during the invasion of Okinawa. That information included interrogations which suggested that a new variant had been developed which could be used against B-29 bombers. Prisoners of War had described the new weapon as equipped with a 20 mm cannon, rocket propelled and having characteristics similar to the Me 163

German rocket interceptor. Following the war it was learned that there had indeed been Japanese work on such a weapon, designated as the Okha 22. Development was a matter of simply duplicating the German rocket fighter – but only two experimental craft were built. The first actual rocket flight test resulted in a crash on take-off and the program went no further before the Japanese surrender.

There is absolutely no doubt that military intelligence – both field and headquarters units – in both the European and Pacific theaters definitely did take note of reports of unidentified and unconventional flying objects. In a number of instances daylight sightings were successfully correlated to a mix of German anti-aircraft defenses and to the emergence of a variety of truly unconventional new weapons systems, including not only jet and rocket fighters but a broad range of glide bombs and rocket weapons. It can also be said that virtually all the new German weapons which did become operational were reported and accurately described by Allied pilots, even under combat conditions.

In contrast, intelligence groups at all levels remained totally frustrated by the nighttime sightings of mysterious and apparently guided balls of fire. Allied units in both theaters reported them and it was later determined that both German and Japanese personnel had also seen similar mystery lights. General Curtis LeMay's intelligence staff produced a report on "Japanese Air Defense – Balls of Fire"; the report anticipated that at least some of the German unconventional weapon types would be introduced by the Japanese. In the end it appears that Pacific air intelligence, and likely General LeMay himself, took a pass on the subject, considering the reports as indicating nothing more than a patchwork, last ditch effort (possibly involving some limited introduction of unconventional weapons, derived from German devices) to forestall the American advance.[26]

When the Pacific theater reports are included, the totals for mystery light reports run into hundreds of sightings, something far beyond the scope of any realistic assessment of new weapons available to the Germans or the Japanese in the last year of the war. Based on Lindell's extensive oral history interviews, often with multiple members of the same aircrew, he determined that there were often considerable differences in descriptions of the light's appearance and maneuvers – even from observers on the same aircraft. Some crew members reported single lights while their crewmates described "formations" of lights. Most of the observations were by multiple personnel, however they were clearly highly subjective, not only in description but in interpretation of what the light might actually represent.

His in-depth study of the mystery lights led Lindell to observe that the aircraft crews had faced a chaotic night combat environment, with lights from multiple ground and sky sources, other aircraft and both active and passive air defenses. He noted that the crews had been sensitized to the appearance of new enemy rocket, missile and jet weapons which were being widely reported in the press and wide-spread barracks talk. His conclusion was that under certain conditions individual crew members had begun to experience auto-kinetic illusions in the darkness. Such illusions have become increasingly well documented in regard to pilots and aircrew, affecting both new and experienced flyers. Given the extensive history of such illusions (even on the ground at night) and given the speed at which the reports of potentially dangerous fireballs had spread, Lindell felt that auto-kinetic illusions – combined with actual anti-aircraft defenses – provided the most reasonable explanation for the overall fireball phenomena.

There certainly are a host of natural phenomena which can also confuse observation of lights at night. Meteorological effects and astronomical misidentification add confusion factors. Atmospheric effects can complicate identification and distances are difficult to judge – different members of one aircrew remarked that the object sighted was either big and close or little and far away. Such subjective descriptions illustrate the difficulty of judging actual distance and size of nighttime lights. Unless an actual object came close enough to determine some physical structure, identification of nighttime lights proved to be largely impossible. The nighttime identification problem would continue plague intelligence groups through decades of post war unidentified flying object reporting.

There is no doubt that war time intelligence investigations of daylight sightings of unconventional and initially unidentified aerial objects produced accurate descriptions and valuable information on what to prove to be new enemy weapons and defensive devices. It is equally clear that the widespread reports of nighttime mystery lights largely resulted in frustrating the intelligence and scientific personnel who dealt with them.

For future reference, it also needs to be noted that a detailed study of war time observations also leaves us with a small group of observations to be filed away and reserved for later consideration. Those observations involved discrete and well defined objects seen at relatively close range, and the descriptions involved reflect performance and maneuvers which appear totally unrelated to what we now know of German or Japanese unconventional weapons, even those strictly in the developmental stage at the end of the war.

Actually there appear to have been a very limited number of such sightings; they never became the topic of any specific intelligence inquiry nor were they separately investigated as the "mystery lights" or "foo fighters" were. They received no general media coverage but were clearly not just lights or balls of fire – yet they remained buried within the much greater dialog over mysterious nighttime lights. When assembled as a collection they appear uniquely anomalous, providing a profile (including both physical appearance and behavior) which may be relevant to post-war events. Specific examples of such anomalies include the following:

> **May 1943**, the Captain and crew of a British Halifax bomber reported observing a well-defined, silvery-gold, cylindrical object, seen as they entered their bomb drop zone near Essen, Germany. The object was larger than their aircraft (the Halifax was approximately 80 feet in length), was not in motion and appeared simply to be suspended in the air, at a 45-degree angle to the ground. It also appeared to have several portholes spaced along the visible side. After approximately half a minute, it began to climb at an incredible speed and vanished from sight.[27] This observation was simply collected as part of mission debriefings and reports and lumped together with all the other unknown aerial phenomena.
>
> **August, 1944,** a British Lancaster bomber crew returning from a mission over southern France had a close encounter with a very large disc shaped object. The object was first seen as a string of very bright yellow (changing to white) lights but as the aircraft closed to within a thousand yards, its overall structure became visible. The gunners held their fire and the disc stayed in view, motionless, for no more than three minutes before it suddenly shot ahead of the aircraft and disappeared from view.[28]
>
> **May, 1945**, the crew of a B-24 bomber, flying over Truk atoll in the mid-Pacific observed two objects which flew separately off each wing of the aircraft, following the bomber through a variety of evasive actions on the pilot's part. The lights changed color from red and orange to white. These objects stayed near their aircraft for over an hour. One object departed while the other continued alongside the B-24 during sunrise and into daylight – never approaching close enough to be within machine gun range. At that point the object was seen to be bright silver in color.[29]

Spring, 1945, the "father" of Swedish aviation, Albin Ahrenburg, and six crew members of a transport plane had a daylight encounter with an oval/cylindrical object approximately 40 feet long. The object appeared to have windows along its side. This object "paced" their transport aircraft for something on the order of an hour and a half before departing.[30]

July, 1945, interceptor pilots based at the Naval Air Station in Pasco, Washington were scrambled in response to a radar track on an unidentified object, moving at a high rate of speed (World War II radars generally had an operational height ceiling of around 30,000 feet). That was acceptable for spotting Fu-Go balloons which had a normal cruising height of 30,000 feet and a ceiling of around 40,000 feet. The object then seemed to go stationary over the Hanford atomic materials processing plant. When the interceptors arrived, they at first saw nothing but eventually sighted an oval shaped object estimated to be twice their altitude. The F6F Hellcats had an operational altitude of some 37,000 feet, enough ceiling to catch a Fu-Go. But even though they pushed their aircraft to almost 42,000 feet, the object remained far above them –and far above the ceiling for any aircraft prior to the mid–1950s. All they could do was to watch it, until it disappeared from view at an even greater apparent height. Fu-Go's had been sighted over the Hanford atomic plant reservation prior to the incident but this observation matched none of the balloon experiences.

Finally, circa **May/June of 1945**, the crew of a US Marine transport plane flying east of Okinawa and through a cloudless sky observed a very large, cylindrical-shaped object approximately a quarter mile from them. Upon closer observation they noted that the cylinder was being followed by three, much smaller, metallic looking "discs". The discs were then observed to enter the cylinder after which the cylinder moved off at extreme speed.[31]

The individuals involved in these particular incidents were experienced, competent observers; they provided specific observations of shape, structure, appearance and movement. In addition, the reports came from primary sources – the observers themselves. Most importantly there seems to have been no obvious bias in the reports – none of the observers were expecting or anticipating the encounters.

In military intelligence work, especially technical intelligence, the term "signature" is sometimes used to describe the distinctive characteristics of both fixed and dynamic intelligence "targets". The term "profile" has become common in more contemporary, nonmilitary use. Based on the anomalous observations listed above, the World War II experience leaves us with an initial profile for a target set of exceptionally interesting objects. That profile characterizes objects which are relatively large (bomber sized or larger), "guided" craft, which appear cylindrical or oval depending upon the viewing angle. The objects sometimes display apparent "portholes" and are capable of excessively high accelerations and speeds. On occasion the objects are able to serve as a carrier, discharging smaller disc shaped objects capable of independent flight.

Exploring World War II intelligence work related to unidentified aerial objects has given us background and context which should be useful in evaluating how intelligence groups would cope with observer reports of unknown objects in the future. In several instances such war time observations had proved to be extremely valuable, leading to the identification of new and novel weapons. In other instances, in particular in regard to nighttime light reports, they simply generated intense frustration and became to be viewed as diversions. With this benchmark for both success and failure, as well as a reminder to keep a particular, anomalous "signature" in mind, we now proceed to the military and intelligence community's first post-war unknown aerial object challenge – that of the "X-flyers" and "Ghost Rockets" over Scandinavia in 1946.

Chapter Two Endnotes:

1. Walter Dornberger, V2 - *The NAZI Rocket Weapon*, Ballantine Books, New York, 1954, 229–231

2. Wolfgang Samuel, *American Raiders*, University of Mississippi, 2004, 138

3. Ibid, 99

4. Ian Hoag and J.B. King, *German and Allied Secret Weapons of WWII*, Chartwell Books, Secaucus New Jersey, 16. Some 1,341 V-2s were fired at Antwerp, with an additional 100 plus launched into other Belgian cities.

5. The term used in a XX (20th) Air Force report of orange balls which traveled at high speeds as well as both green and red balls which were seen floating down. Mysterious night lights were widely reported in the Pacific Theater as well as over Europe. Keith Chester, *Strange Company; Military Encounters with UFO's in WWII*, Anomolist Books, San Antonio, Texax", 2007, 156

6. Observations were described and reported under many different designations, ranging from "foo lights", "foo fighters", "foofighter", "balls of fire", "phoo bombs", "night phenomenon" and even "nightmare lights".

7. Jeffery A. Lindell, *A Historical and Physiological Perspective of the Foo Fighters of World War* http://greyfalcon.us/foos.htm

8. Op cit,

9. Mike Markowitz, *World War II German Helicopters - Flettner Fl 265 and Fl 282*, Defense Media News, July 23, 2014 http://www.defensemedianetwork.com/stories/nazi-rotors-german-helicopter-development-1932-1945-flettner/

10. Keith Chester, *Strange Company*, 106–107

11. *An Evaluation of German Capabilities in 1945* United States Strategic Air Forces in Europe, Office of the Director of Intelligence

12. Henry Stevens, *Hitler's Flying Saucers*, Adventures Unlimited Press, Kempton, Illinois, 2003, 42–45

13. Publication number US3066890 A http://www.google.com/patents/US3066890

14. Joint ATIC/WATC Report on Project Silver Bug, Project 9961, Air Technical Intelligence Center, February 15, 1955 http://www.foia.af.mil/shared/media/document/AFD-090218-169.pdf

15. A broad contextual background on purported German flying discs and the numerous topics that have developed around them, including extraordinarily advanced anti-aircraft devices, can be reviewed on the Internet at http://www.german-discs.net. Brad Turner, copyright 2003

16. Op cit, May 6, 2007 also http://www.german-discs.net/saucers/kugelblitz.php

17. Keith Chester, *Strange Company*, 126–127

18. Ibid, 147, 150, 149 One fact that must be considered is that at that stage of the war, even operational weapons and aircraft often failed due to hurried manufacturing, much of it performed in slave labor factories, a desperate shortage of materials (with questionable substitutions), little quality control, untrained maintenance crews etc. The failure of many of mystery lights to successfully engage may not indicate that they were not indeed weapons but rather weapons that failed due to a host of difficulties in actually making them effective weapons in those final months and days of the war.

19. Ibid, 127–128 and 251

20. Ibid, 134–135

21. Ibid, 62–63

22. Ibid, 174–175

23. The Funryu 2 ground to air missile had a maximum speed of 525 mph and could reach an altitude of three miles. The proposed Funryu 3 was to have a speed of 650 mph and operational ceiling of 20 miles. Unguided Japanese air-to surface missiles were simply standard bombs with attached rocket motors, having a maximum range of three miles.

24. Jeffery A. Lindell, *A Historical and Physiological Perspective of the Foo Fighters of World War Two*. http://jeff.lindell.home.comcast.net/~jeff.lindell/The%20Sparticani.htm

25. 20th Air Force, Consolidated Mission Report, 499th Bomb Group, April 20, 1945

26. Keith Chester, *Strange Company*, 162–166

27. Ibid, p. 40

28. Ibid, 75–75. At the time of this encounter, the Lancaster's radar set had just stopped operating so no radar confirmation could be obtained.

29. Michael Swords and Robert Powell, *UFO's and Government, A Historical Inquiry*, 7

30. Jerome Clark, *Strange Skies – Pilot Encounters with UFO's*, Citadel Press., 2003, 14

31. Ibid, p. 17

Chapter 3

Fear Factors

In this chapter

- The Soviet Union is declared to be the major strategic threat to the United States – a 1946 report to President Harry Truman calls for immediate American preparation for a war involving atomic and biological weapons.

- Concern over Soviet actions in occupied Europe and Joseph Stalin's decision to maintain the Red Army at wartime strength leads to a directive from Joint Chiefs of Staff on preparation of plans for a preemptive American atomic strike on the Soviet Union.

- American reconnaissance and electronic intelligence missions begin against the Soviet frontiers in the Far East and Europe – B-29 reconnaissance squadrons are established to map the Arctic for atomic strikes across the Polar Regions.

- A wave of unidentified aerial objects over Scandinavia is widely interrupted as the beginning of Soviet intimidation targeting neutral nations being courted by the emerging Western Bloc.

- America's new Central Intelligence Group is tasked with evaluating a wave of "ghost rocket" unidentified aerial object reports from Scandinavian countries as possible Soviet psychological warfare.

As World War II ended, senior American military officers had begun to take the view that the Soviet Union was replacing the Axis (Germany/Italy/Japan) as the major challenge to the security of the United States – posing an immediate threat in both Europe and the Balkans. In October 1945, the Joint Intelligence Committee of the Joint Chiefs of Staff (JCS) had begun drafting plans for an American preemptive first strike on the Soviet Union, an attack which would have involved something on the order of 20-30 atomic bombs. That was considered a realistic estimate of the atomic weapons which could be immediately constructed given available uranium ore and isotope production facilities. Such a plan was consistent with a JCS document issued on September 20, 1945 which endorsed a "first strike" strategic atomic policy and directed that during a crisis, even as diplomacy proceeded, preparations to strike a "preventative" first blow should be taken.[1]

Based on the JCS planning directive, General Lauris Norstad's Air Plans staff began to expand on the initial planning which had been done in August – that work had produced "A Strategic Chart of Certain Russian and Manchurian Areas" which targeted 15 key Russian cities. An appendix listed the number of bombs required to destroy each city – six each for Moscow and Leningrad. Plans included B-29 staging areas and flight paths.[2]

The final draft of the expanded 1945 strike plan called for the destruction of some 66 Soviet cities considered to have strategic importance. Both conventional and nuclear bombing as well as a broad range of conventional military attacks were to be used. The plan also called for stockpiling 466 Nagasaki class atomic bombs. Because of its general lack of knowledge of atomic bombs and their effective employment by air forces, the Board decided to add this as a priority project for its Air Research and Development staff.

The Joint Chiefs' focus on atomic warfare was reinforced by the results of the first American peace time atomic weapons tests in 1946. The test series (Operation Crossroads) involved over 80 war surplus target ships. Both the Army Air Force and the Navy were involved with the test, which was considered essential to determining the future survivability of Navy surface ships during an atomic attack. The bomb tests received a huge amount of international media coverage, firmly establishing perceptions of American military preeminence in the post war era – but they also led the Joint Chiefs to conclude that the aggressor in any surprise atomic attack would win. There simply was no effective defense against atomic weapons.

As part of their evaluation of the atomic bomb as a military weapon, the Joint Chiefs stressed that in an age of atomic weapons the nation was going to need an intelligence service and collections effort with a far greater effectiveness than the nation had ever had either in either peace or war.[3] That report, submitted to President Harry Truman in June, 1947, supported ongoing calls for a dramatic expansion of American intelligence. In response President Truman approved an extensive restructuring of the military and intelligence services, effected by the National Security Act of September, 1947. That act included authorization for both the Central Intelligence Agency and the National Security Council.

With the Soviets perceived as the nation's primary threat, and with concerns that Stalin might begin to move the Red Army further to the west in Eastern Europe at any time, the U.S. military embarked on an increasing level of aerial surveillance of Soviet territory in the years immediately following the war. That surveillance had actually begun as early as six weeks after the Japanese surrender with a Navy Mariner patrol bomber flying within a mile of Russian forces at Port Arthur in Manchuria.

As the Navy bomber turned for home, it was attacked by a Russian fighter. The Mariner made it back to base safely and four months later the Navy sent another patrol bomber over Darien, near Port Arthur – the site of a large Russian radar installation. That flight was intercepted by two Soviet fighters which again attacked the American aircraft. It also made it home and the Navy issued the first of what was to become a long line of claims that its pilots were simply disoriented and off course.[4] Navy "ferret" flights continued during 1946 and early 1947. The flights were initiated to obtain electronic intelligence (Elint) on the capabilities of the large Russian radar installations on Big Diomede Island. Those Soviet radar installations covered the airspace across the Bering straits, between Russia and Alaska.[5]

The Soviets quickly evaluated the rather obvious patterns in those Navy flights, as well as similar missions conducted around the Soviet frontiers in Europe and the Mediterranean beginning in 1946. They easily tracked the aircraft by radar and quickly concluded that American and British military intelligence groups were at work – with the obvious intent of collecting information on defenses which would need to be penetrated in any attack against the Soviets. This led to an ongoing series of even more aggressive intercepts of the flights and attacks on American aircraft – which the U.S. military continued to explain by reference to navigational difficulties.[6]

The American activities also seem to have encouraged the Soviets to begin a series of intelligence collections missions of their own, with Soviet aircraft flying from Vladivostok to Tokyo frequently departing their designated corridors to reconnoiter military installations and the U.S. Seventh fleet. The same tactics were used by the Soviets in Germany and over Sweden; Soviet aircraft penetrated Swedish air space on apparent ferret missions in both 1946 and 1947.[7]

Having fought back from the successful surprise attacks on Hawaii and the Philippines in 1941, America's senior military leaders had vowed that they would never again run the risk of being surprised. It was anticipated that any Soviet air attack would come against America over the Arctic, the same route which would be used for American interdiction attacks. The U.S. Air Force had much to learn about operating over the Arctic, including details of the geography, weather systems and magnetic phenomena of the airspace over Canada, Alaska and Greenland. It was also desperate for information on Soviet defenses on the polar routes into Russia. This led to the 1946 formation of one of the first units in the newly created Strategic Air Command.

The unit was not a bomber group, but rather a reconnaissance squadron. The B-29 equipped Forty-Sixth Reconnaissance Squadron was established at Ladd Field, outside Fairbanks Alaska in June, 1946. Project Nanook was initiated, with the objective of mapping the Alaskan, Aleutian and Siberian regions as well as northern Greenland. That would allow SAC bombers to strike into Soviet Siberian bases and to operate out of a major strategic American base at Thule, Greenland. The Forty-Sixth would later be expected to prepare and train SAC strike groups – beginning with the original 509th Bomb Wing – for "war day" over the Arctic.[8] As of 1946, in support of its strategy to respond to any Soviet military action by direct attacks on the Russian homeland the U.S. Army Air Force was increasingly committed to conducting ferret and reconnaissance flights into Soviet territory.

The view that the Soviets – under Joseph Stalin's rule – represented a very real threat extended far beyond the American military. The U.S. State Department and senior military leaders began to take the position that the Soviets had already begun the run up to an actual "offensive". The first stage in that territorial advance had been in Poland at the end of 1945. That move had been a surprise, but Stalin had shown his true colors by declaring the Communist position in a radio speech on February 9, 1946.[9] In that speech Stalin had warned that no peaceful international order was possible in the face of a "capitalist-imperialist monarchy."[10]

Tension was further increased by the hostility evident in other areas of Soviet influence. Anglo-American forces faced what appeared to be open aggression in the Soviet zone of occupied Yugoslavia. In August 1946 the Yugoslav's first forced down and later shot down unarmed American transport aircraft. The Soviets also began to forcefully back regimes in Yugoslavia and Bulgaria in efforts to detach the northern provinces of Greece. In addition Stalin demanded that Turkey allow Russia to occupy certain Turkish territory in order to "defend the straits" and ensure Russian access through the Bosporus and Dardanelles.[11]

At the highest levels of American government, the perception of imminent Soviet military moves continued to gain traction. In 1946 President Truman received a 100 page report from two of his presidential staff. The report summarized their fact finding with the Joint Chiefs, the Secretary of Defense, the intelligence community, the State Department and other key sources. That report minced no words, calling the Soviet Union's foreign policy "a direct threat to American security...designed to prepare the Soviet Union for war" and recommending that the United States immediately begin preparations for atomic and biological warfare.[12] Truman found the report so volatile that he had the 20 copies confiscated and locked up in the White House safe.

As 1946 progressed, it was increasingly felt that the Soviets had moved into a mode of full scale political and military confrontation – and that even neutrals would be placed under increasing pressure to declare themselves for either the "East" or the "West". Given this state of affairs, a series of unidentified aerial object sightings across neutral Scandinavian nations quickly became a major point of intelligence interest and concern. Low key and covert inquiries were begun by both British and American military intelligence – as well as American State Department officers – in the neutral countries. The unidentified aerial objects reported first over Sweden and then other Scandinavian nations symbolized the fears of the earliest days of the Cold War, secretly viewed by both British and American intelligence groups as representing aggressive Soviet psychological warfare.

Initially the unidentified objects were reported as relatively small devices, apparently rocket powered and with either very small wings or no wings at all. Newspaper articles described a number of reports from multiple observers, with some observations made at a very close range:

Dagens Nyhete / May 24, 1946: Two night watchmen in Landskrona-Pasten sight "wingless, cigar-shaped body of dimensions of a small airplane, which at regular intervals spurted bunches of sparks from its tail." Estimated altitude at only 100 meters and moving at "ordinary airplane speed" to southwest.[13]

The immediate media response to the reports was that the objects were likely to be German devices, being launched by the Soviets.

Dagens Nyhete May 26: "Even if reports of a wingless aircraft spurting fire over Landscrona are to be treated with a certain reserve, it is very possible that what people saw were V-1 bombs fired by the Russians from some experimental station on the Baltic Coast. This statement was made by an air expert, to whom 'Dagens Nyheter' submitted the reports in yesterday's telegrams. The experts state that the whole of Germany has been fine-combed by the occupying powers for robot bomb material and experiments are being carried out zealously. The observations made by the inhabitants of Landscrona, namely that the sparks from the tail come at intervals, agrees with the V-1 bomb's manner of operation. It is true that the witnesses have given the length of the projectiles now seen as considerably less than the V-1 bomb's 6-7 metres but it is easy to err on such points."[14]

During the spring of 1946, Swedish newspapers began to carry more reports of unknown objects, objects which continued to be described as similar in physical characteristics to the V-1 and V-2 missiles introduced by the Germans at the end of WW II. Within weeks, and with continual broad media coverage, those reports blossomed into a wave of similar sightings across Scandinavia. An excellent, detailed study of this wave of sightings can be found in part four of a series of extensive, illustrated chronologies by Joel Carpenter, *Guided Missiles and UFOs: A Tangle of Fear - 1937-53*.[15] Carpenter's detailing of the Scandinavian reports is extensive, containing primary materials including newspaper articles, photos and government documents. In addition, the Project 1947 website contains an extensive series of Scandinavian reports for this period, provided by Dr. Thomas Bullard.[16]

Both the British and U.S. militaries took an early interest in the sightings, a message from the British Air Attaché in Stockholm on June 1, 1946 stated that the matter had already been discussed with the Swedish Air Force – which had not yet been able to officially confirm any sightings but had agreed to pass on related information of interest. There is additional evidence that American Army Intelligence was also concerned that the Russians had pushed ahead in exploiting German technology. On June 24, the Pentagon requested that German rocket scientist Werner Von Braun be interviewed; it needed an immediate evaluation of the German technicians who had been left in the Soviet zone and an estimate of how long it might take for them to perfect an intercontinental missile.[17]

The British Air Attaché began to include Swedish newspaper clippings which discussed the unidentified objects along with their reports and routinely forwarded similar material to the Air Staff (Intelligence) of the British Air Ministry:

> Morgon-Tdningen / June 1, 1946: "It seems as if the mysterious flier, which was observed in Osternarks at the beginning of the week, was not altogether an illusion. Yesterday the same thing was reported in fact in Katrineholm. An object which can be compared to a silver-glistening rocket, in the shape of a giant cigar, was noticed in the east on the horizon. The time was 11:43 a.m. in the morning. The

'ghost airplane' had no hint of wings, but on the other hand some thought it that had the semblance of a stabilizer or the like. It traveled very rapidly through the air and many observers pointed out that not even the fastest fighter plane would be able to keep pace. A light rumble was heard, near the object after it had made a turn toward the west, in a diving continued trip toward the south....The projectile, or whatever it might be, was as long as an ordinary training plane and went at 300 meters altitude..."

These Scandinavian sightings came to be generically referred to as "Ghost Rockets". As the public increasingly followed the reports, misidentification of astronomical phenomena began to occur; photographs from the period show both nighttime and daytime meteors (bolides) being reported as mysterious aerial objects.[18] As with the unconventional object reports from World II, observations ran the gamut in terms of quality, including numerous long distance and nighttime sightings as well as a number of very credible close range, daylight reports.

Following the June 12 report from Eskilstuna , the Swedish defense ministry issued orders to all its personnel to report such observations to its headquarters and requested that its military attaches in Norway and Denmark also collect and forward reports from those countries. At that point in time several sightings clearly seemed to be describing objects similar to the German V-1 "flying bombs". Newspaper reports of two objects sighted in Norway – the Norwegian newspaper was referring to such objects as "Flier X's" – illustrate the similarity:

"The two "Flier X's" were sighted in daylight by a number of individuals. At one location four family members (Sigvart Skaug, his wife and grown son and daughter) had observed one from two separate locations. Mrs. Skaug and her daughter saw them first from the top of a high ridge at a place called Badstuakeren. They heard a loud noise in the air and believed at first there was a plane coming. But the sound did not resemble plane noise; it was more like a powerful whistle. Right afterwards they caught sight of two plane-like objects which came from over the edge of the woods at a tremendous speed and so low that the two women involuntarily threw themselves down on the ground. The air current was so strong that the treetops swayed.

Farmer Skaug and his son observed the objects from the side, at a height of around 50 meters....Mr. Skaug said they were like pictures of V-1s he had seen in newspapers. In any case they could not have been ordinary planes. They were cigar-shaped, approximately 2 ½ meters long, with approximately

1 meter long wings. The wings were set about 1 meter from the nose, and the fore and after parts had a metallic gleam, but the midsection with the wings was black. It looked as if there was attached an apparatus, perhaps a steering device, in the rear. The objects both described a slight arc, about the way a stone is cast, and fell together into Lake Mjosa so the water plumes rose many meters high in the air. No explosion was heard. They sky was completely clear, and Mjosa lay still again in a moment."

In July and August the *Aftenposten* newspaper reported that the "flying bombs" continued to be sighted and that the Swedish defense staff did not believe that the sightings were astronomical. They also noted that there clearly seemed to be two general types of sightings, those which appeared cigar shaped, often seen with flames and smoke coming out the rear and those which seemed identical to the well-known V-1 pulse jet flying bombs.

The U.S. State Department actively followed the ghost rocket reports and speculated that the Soviets might be trying to intimidate the Swedes. There were critical loan negotiations underway and the Soviets were also known to be concerned that Sweden was leaning to stronger western ties, influenced by American military power and by the recent atomic tests at Bikini Island. Soviet political pressure on Sweden in regards to refugees from the Baltic had also recently been reported. State Department communications underscored the belief that the Soviets were actively involved in putting intense diplomatic pressure on the Scandinavian countries, in particular Sweden, in order to preserve Russian influence and encourage them to maintain a position of neutrality rather than move to the Western alliance.

Both British and American military intelligence groups joined in the effort to identify the ghost rockets as reports spread across Scandinavia during the summer of 1946 but it appears that little information on the rapid development of American and Soviet V-1 derivative missiles was shared with the Swedes. By late 1944 the U.S. Army Air Force had quickly decided to move to mass production of an exact V-1 copy (designated the JB2).[19] The missiles had been rushed into production in anticipation of their use in the anticipated invasion of the Japanese home islands.

The basic V-1 copy was also adapted to "zero-length" launching by the use of a solid fuel rocket booster for the missile. The first Republic aircraft MX-544/JB2, a reverse engineered V-1, launched from Elgin Army Air Force base in Florida in October, 1944. By May of 1945 the Army had conducted some 97 successful launches of the V-1 duplicate. The zero-launch capability developed by the Army was especially attractive since it made the weapon far more mobile, allowing the missile to be fired off very short ramps and eliminating the need for construction of fixed launch sites. That capability also paved the way for the launching of such missiles from ships; the U.S. Navy quickly became interested in a submarine-based version of the weapon. A Navy version of the V-1 cruise missile was developed, named the Loon. Follow-on versions of the early V-1 derivatives would later be deployed on Navy carriers.

The Germans had developed the equipment and techniques for launching V-1's from aircraft during the war. In fact German air launches had become standard combat operations, with over a thousand V-1 attacks staged from Heinkel He 111 bombers – even though a number of carrier aircraft had been destroyed during launching accidents. The U.S. Army was quick to adapt its V-1 derivative to be carried by aircraft and during 1945 several of those new U.S. Army missiles were launched from a modified B-17 bomber.[20][21]

As part of their development work, in 1945 the Army tested an improved radio command controlled guidance system for the missile. While the original German uncontrolled V-1 had been extremely inaccurate, with radio control the missile could be directed to make course changes and corrections as well as to initiate a controlled terminal dive to impact.

Radio control led to a considerable improvement in accuracy with an average error of a quarter mile at a distance of 100 miles. It was that type of radio control – for both course changes and targeting – which was considered in American military investigations of the mysterious "ghost rockets" of 1946. That degree of advance in guided missile control and accuracy in targeting was apparently not shared with either the Swedes or the British.

As early as 1943 Russian engineers had already begun testing an experimental cruise missile, launched from a plane and with a range of several hundred kilometers.[22] Provided with information from the British on German V-1 missiles, the Soviets work on their own derivative version in October, 1944. Their first step was to design a new autopilot and magnetic compass for course control. Initial Soviet tests of the new designs were all conducted with aircraft launched rockets. By December, 1944, dozens of flight tests had been conducted with the new guided rocket designs and they were declared ready for full scale production by early 1945.

Records show 100 rockets were built in February, another 300 in March and following that some 15 units a day.[23] "Officially" the Russian versions of the V-1 were only tested in central Asia, in preparation for anticipated Russian engagement with Japan. An early end to the war resulted in their not being introduced into a Japanese campaign. Records show that the next steps in Russian development involved an effort to extend the missiles' range as well as to further refine remote control guidance. In addition to radio control, the new developments included radar guidance control from the launch aircraft and final targeting through the use of a rocket based television camera. By 1948 that development had produced a version with a speed over 800 kilometers per hour and accuracy of better than three kilometers at the final target.[24]

As the 1946 summer months proceeded, more and more Scandinavian sightings involved what appeared to be very high speed rocket shaped craft, devices with no wings and with shapes very similar to the World War II German V-2 ballistic missiles. Those sightings were also of great interest to the British and American intelligence groups – but once again information about British, American and Russian testing of V-2 missiles appears not to have been shared – in fact it is also appears to be missing from the ghost rocket intelligence reports being circulated in both Britain and America.

By the summer of 1945, the British military had gained considerable firsthand experience with German ballistic rocket weapons. As British forces advanced on the continent, their 21st Army Group had captured a number of abandoned V-2s as the German forces withdrew from their firing sites in the northwestern Netherlands. While the Americans were capturing the German rocket designers and scientists, the British were capturing the field personnel who actually knew the practical drill of preparing and launching the rockets.[25]

In the spring of 1945, the British proposed and organized a V-2 firing project (approved by SHAEF; the Allied high command), code-named Backfire. The British War Department and General Staff were enthusiastic and British officers were delegated responsibility for the project. In May of 1945, Brigadier L.K. Lockhart was assigned logistics support and began site survey and selection. One requirement was that the launch corridor would have ample radar sites for tracking of the rockets. The Schleswig peninsula was chosen and a former Krupp naval gun range south of Cuxhaven, on the North Sea, was selected for operations. As work began on the Cuxhaven firings, the United States began its own plans for V-2 launches at White Sands, New Mexico – those would begin in 1946.

The British managed to recruit a substantial German military contingent to support the Backfire project; the head of the German group had formerly been the commander of the V-2 experimental firing unit established at the Peenemunde rocket development facility in 1944. He had gone on to command a tactical group, his unit had launched their last German V-2 only four months before he began work with the British Backfire team. Although the Allied high command was dissolved in July, 1945, the Backfire group continued on with the project, designated as the Special Projectile Operations Group, reporting to the British War Office.[26]

In determining specifics for the launches, the decision was made to limit the firings short of the full 200 mile range of the missiles because that would have taken them too far off the Danish coast for complete camera and radar tracking. Instead the missiles were set for 150 miles and launched into the North Sea at a target point 46 miles southwest of Ringkoebing, Denmark. Shipping and aircraft were warned away from a 30 mile radius of the aiming point. During October, 1945 a series of V-2 launches were conducted. A group of Russian observers were invited to attend the final launch.

We now know that the Russians themselves were aggressively working with V-2s. One of their immediate goals had been a pilot production line for the missiles. To do this they reestablished engineering and production facilities inside Soviet Zone of occupied Germany and by September 1946 some 30 flight worthy V-2s had been produced.[27]

While observing the project Backfire British V-2 launches in 1945, Russian observers had offered to trade a closer view of the launch activities for a British and American visit to the Peenemunde. The offer suggested, as Allied intelligence already suspected, that the Peenemunde facility had been at least partially reactivated by the Soviets. In addition to V-2 production, the Russians had developed two special trains of between 80 and 100 cars with full facilities for transporting V-2s, their launchers and all required personnel – the trains were designated as "mobile meteorological stations".

Available reports from German rocket scientists conscripted by the Russians record no actual launches of the V-2s inside Germany; they do discuss static firings at German facilities, recorded as early as September, 1946.[28] But by mid-1946 Russian scientists, unknown to the Germans who had volunteered to assist their development, were already involved in enhancements to the V-2 design which would stretch its range to 400 miles. The Russians had, within one year, become almost totally independent of the Germans in terms of further missile development. Relatively few German rocket personnel were transported to Russia and in the main served as a resource for ideas and a cross check for Russian designs; Russian teams siphoned off German knowledge, allowing them to work on independent projects.[29] Any Soviet launches conducted from former German facilities, or new rocket bases, would very likely have been kept secret from the Germans, who were totally compartmentalized from Russian developments.[30]

Beyond American and British suspicion of Russian psychological warfare in Scandinavia, there was an additional military concern. If the Soviets had become confident enough in working with new types of advanced cruise missiles or guided rockets to use them for psychological warfare, they might also be moving towards operational deployment. That would have added a significant long range bombardment capability to their already huge standing army, an army which was not being hurriedly demobilized as were the Allied forces, but rather being maintained in place in Soviet occupied territory across Eastern Europe.

Determining what was actually going on with the "ghost rockets" was a definite American intelligence priority – a major challenge for the new Central Intelligence Group headed by General Hoyt Vandenberg. But with the old war over and a new period of confrontation with the Soviet Union beginning, intelligence collections were moving into a new era. Peace time technical collection and analysis was going to become covert and largely deniable, conducted out of the public view.

Chapter Three Endnotes

1. Richard Rhodes, *Dark Sun*, Simon and Schuster, New York, 1996, 225. Rhodes notes that the neither the US government nor any of its presidents ever formally endorsed the preventive war concept but that the extreme convictions of military, and in particular, Air Force leaders led to decades of military planning and preparation for either preventive or preemptive attacks against the Soviet Union.

2. Ibid, 23-24

3. *The Evaluation of the Atomic Bomb as a Military Weapon*, Truman's Papers, President's Secretary's file, Atomic Test – Crossroads, June 30, 1947.
https://www.trumanlibrary.org/whistlestop/study_collections/bomb/large/documents/index.php?documentid=81&pagenumber=12

4. William Burrows, *By Any Means Necessary*, Farrar, Straus and Giroux, New York, 2001, 93

5. Ibid, 94

6. Ibid, 94

7. Ibid, 95

8. Ibid, 95-96

9. Dean Acheson, *Present at the Creation – My Years in the State Department*, W.W. Norton and Company, New York, 1969

10. Ibid, 150-151

11. Ibid, 190-195

12. James McGovern, *Crossbow and Overcast*, William Morrow, New York, 281

13. Swedish *Ghost Rocket* reports for 1946, provided by Dr. Thomas Bullard, for reference see: http://www.project1947.com/fig/1946a.htm

14. Op Cit

15. These Joel Carpenter chronologies and commentary may be found at http://www.project1947.com/gr/grchron1.htm on the highly recommended Project 1947

website operated by Jan Aldrich. The Carpenter essays are essential reading in regard to the Ghost Rocket phenomenon.

16. Swedish *Ghost Rocket* reports for 1946, provided by Dr. Thomas Bullard, for reference see: http://www.project1947.com/fig/1946a.htm

17. McGovern, *Crossbow and Overcast*. On June 23, 1946 Maj Hamill (US Army Ordnance) was sent an urgent and confidential message for Werner Von Braun. The Pentagon (War Department) wanted "an immediate evaluation of the German rocket technicians left in the Soviet zone of occupied Germany and how long it might take such experts to perfect an intercontinental missile." Von Braun responded, "There is no doubt that the bulk of the most capable members of the Peenemünde group are in the United States now. There are, however, many very good former Peenemünde experts working for the Russians too… the two most capable of these men…are: Dipl. Ing. Helmut Grottrup…and Engineer Martin. These two men are, according to the best available information, in charge of the Russian project – new development projects (Grottrup) and A-4 manufacture in Nordhausen (Martin). As regards future developments such as A-9, A-10, and A-11 Grottrup is a very able and clever leader of a development group.

18. Michael Swords and Robert Powell, *UFO's and Government / A Historical Inquiry*, Anomalist Press, San Antonio, Texas, 2012, 12-13

19. In August of 1943 British technical intelligence learned that the Swedes had recovered a new type of small pilotless rocket which had crashed on the island of Bornholm in the Baltic, about half way between Germany and Sweden. The device's apparent warhead section was filled with concrete. Two other crashed V-1's were recovered in Sweden in 1944. Although Sweden had been operating as a neutral country the apparent shift in the war towards a victory of the allies apparently led to the Swedes sharing information about the German device with British technical intelligence starting in May of that year. One of the missiles was recovered largely intact due to an aerial explosion in its fuel tank and the failure of its warhead to detonate, that missile had traveled approximately 350 kilometers from its launch site at Peenemunde.

20. Andreas Parsch, *Directory of U.S. Rockets and Missiles*, Copyright 2001-2014, Appendix 1, http://www.designation-systems.net/dusrm/

21. Ibid. A JB variant (JB-4) was an air launched glide bomb fitted with a Ford pulsejet engine (the same type as used in the JB-2). The JB-4 was equipped with an AN/AXT-2 TV transmitter, sending an image to an operator in the launching aircraft who could send radio commands to change the course of the missile. The JB-4 was tested in 1945, but the program was cancelled as WWII ended.

22. Wilfred Kopenhagen, "The V-1 And Its Soviet Successors", *Schiffer Military History*, Schiffer Publishing, September 30, 2000. 20-21

23. Ibid. With the help of an original crashed V-1 supplied by the British and other material captured in German territories, the Russians also began development of the German "Butterfly" guided anti-craft missile in the same time frame.

24. Ibid, 24

25. Ordway and Sharp, *The Rocket Team*, The MIT Press, Cambridge, Massachusetts, 1982, 294-297

26. Ibid, 298-299

27. In October, 1946 the Moscow *New Times* had harshly criticized rumors that "mysterious kinds of weapons" were reportedly being manufactured in the Soviet Zone of Germany. The article declared all such remarks to be blatant propaganda. That Soviet statement was totally false as the Russians had indeed done extensive rebuilding of German V-2 missile facilities and by September, 1946 they had produced at least 30 operational V-2's at these facilities.

28. Ordway and Sharp, *The Rocket Team*, 320-322

29. Ibid, 322-324. It certainly is true that the V-2 itself was actually in firing, boost phase for no more than a few minutes. A burn time of 67 seconds allowed a V-2 to reach an altitude of 113 miles. Seeing an actual rocket flame at high altitudes would not be consistent with a V-2 (smoke and condensation trails might be seen during daylight) but at twilight it was possible to see the white hot control vanes in the rocket engine section even at very high altitudes. Dornberger, *V-2 – The Nazi Rocket Weapon*, 199-200.

Chapter 4
Weight of Evidence

In this chapter

- Swedish, British and American investigators all covertly investigated the "Ghost Rocket" reports over Scandinavia and selectively withheld information from each other due to diplomatic and security concerns.

- Britain and the United States each independently carried out covert technical collections activities with the Swedes from 1946 into 1948.

- The Swedes compartmentalized joint technical intelligence work with the British and Americans, shielding their confidential conclusion of Russian involvement in certain of the unidentified aerial object / "Ghost Rocket" incidents.

- The United States Central Intelligence Group reported to President Harry Truman that the "weight of evidence" pointed to Russian involvement and to a psychological warfare operation conducted by the Soviet Union against the neutral Scandinavian nations.

- More "anomalies"….profiles and signatures.

In terms of intelligence concerns and challenges, the Ghost Rocket sightings of 1946 must be viewed in context of the emerging Cold War. The Scandinavian experience is especially educational in that it provides considerable insight into why military intelligence would take a very low profile, even covert approach to investigating unknown aerial objects. It also illustrates the degree to which security concerns and compartmentalization of information complicates such investigations.

With documents now available we can see that Swedish officials went to considerable lengths to shield certain information about their initial joint investigations with the British from the Americans. Later, photo reconnaissance missions performed with American support were not fully shared with the British. In turn, British and American intelligence contacts did not share information (testing, range extension and advanced remote control) about their own new weapons developments related to derivatives of the German V-1 and V-2 weapons.

The challenges of "ghost rocket" identification also highlight many of the issues which would become ongoing in unidentified aerial object inquiries over the following decades. As noted in the previous chapter, with extensive press attention, the limited number of initial "wingless aircraft" and "flyer X" reports mushroomed into a broad wave of "ghost rocket" sightings, with well above a thousand reports. The Swedish scientific committee appointed to study the phenomena determined that the great majority of the newer sightings were night time observations of lights, often with fiery tails. In some cases smoke and occasionally a rumbling or whistling noise was associated with the observations. Some of these lights were extremely bright and on occasion "stars" or sparks were seen falling from them. Others were silver colored, described by observers as descending stars.

Under normal conditions, such observations would most likely have received little attention, readily accepted as normal astronomical phenomena. The more vivid sightings of nighttime or daylight fireball class meteors (bolides) would have been noted, perhaps in small news articles. Bolides are very large meteors and do often leave smoke and debris trails; such trails are normally brief but can last up to several minutes.[1] Observers have also reported associated sounds with such bright daylight meteors.[2] These bright meteors are often large enough so that some remnants may reach the ground, resulting in physical impressions and leaving debris.

It is very difficult for untrained or inexperienced observers to estimate the actual distances to either meteors or their debris falls. Fireballs in particular are often felt to have fallen a great deal closer than they really are – people often race to recover the object they saw fall, only to learn later that the actual impact was hundreds of miles away. Bolide class meteors actually stop burning when they are at an altitude of ten to twenty miles, fragments from those that appear to fall at the horizon hit the ground something on the order of three hundred miles away from the observer. If they seem to drop behind a hill or trees, the distance is most likely at least fifty miles. In some cases it can take more than five minutes for fragments to actually reach the ground after the fireball explodes or burns itself out.

While "normal" meteors are generally seen only for a second or two, bolides which enter the atmosphere in a relatively flat trajectory can be observed for 40 seconds to a full minute. On rare occasions fireballs also result from objects which have moved into temporary orbits at relatively low altitudes. One famous low earth orbit observation over Canada was made by Professor C.A. Chant, of the University of Toronto, in 1913. Chant provided the following description of a suddenly appearing fiery red object which "seemed to be followed by long trail….it resembled a rocket, the body showed no sign of dropping to the earth. On the contrary it moved forward on a perfectly horizontal path… without the least apparent sinking towards the earth."[3]

In the Toronto observation, the first bolide was followed by others, giving the appearance of a formation; in some locations a sound like distant thunder was heard during their passage. Individual meteors were seen in flight for up to a minute, all with seemingly horizontal paths. In comparison, the more familiar and well observed Peekskill fireball of 1992 was green and as bright as the full moon. That bolide descended over a ground path of some 600 miles; its shallow trajectory and in-flight disintegration also created the impression of multiple objects traveling in formation with each other.

The following observations from Sweden and Norway illustrate how both astronomical and aircraft misidentifications can become additions to a general wave of unidentified object sightings.

July 15, 1946 – Many people felt they had seen a "ghost plane" over the Oslo area last night at 23 o'clock (11 pm). It was described as a large luminous star. The "star" had a yellow-white dazzling color and became visible on the horizon in a southerly direction. The luminous object held a completely straight course at a great height and had such speed that it did not take much over a minute from its appearance on the horizon until it disappeared in the north-northwest over toward Oslo.

July 16, 1946 – A "ghost flier" seen over Norway was described as a large bright star which came from the south and disappeared northward, changing color to a bluish light before as it moved away. Its speed was very great and the height was estimated as about 1000 meters. The mystery light was identified the following day when the pilot of a private plane reported that at the exact moment the bright light was observed he was testing his landing lights while in flight. After the test he had turned the landing lights off until making his final approach and actually landing.

July 17, 1946 – A luminous orange object traveling at great speed and height over Sweden appeared to maintain a level flight path while it quickly traveled across the sky. Observers felt that because the object had not appeared to be descending it could not have been a meteor.

August 26, 1946 – Two individuals separately reported a brightly lit nighttime object passing over Oslo, Norway. It traveled at the speed of a fighter plane, was larger and brighter than an ordinary star and left a small smoke trail. Because its path was horizontal observers felt that it could not have been a meteor.

Sustained by intense press and media coverage, such reports diverted and frustrated the Swedish "ghost rocket" investigation in much the same way that "foo fighter" reports had diverted Allied intelligence during the recent war. But other, much more concrete, reports convinced the Swedish Ghost Rocket committee that there was something very real in play in a limited number of the sightings. Their attention focused on a core of close range, daylight observations – including cylinders, both with and without wings.

Some of the objects had been seen to crash into lakes, visibly impacting the water. Fragments had been recovered both on land and from beneath the surfaces of the lakes. Available documents show us that Swedish, British and American military sources reached the same opinion. All parties initially concluded that a number of the reports actually did represent guided missiles and rockets, very likely launched by the Russians.

The Swedish military came to believe that at least a few of the sightings related to V-1 type cruise missile technology and that the objects were subject to some sort of remote control using narrow, high frequency radio beams. Potential control centers were calculated and there was also speculation that ships might have been used as control stations.[4] On July 16 a British diplomatic officer in Stockholm cabled the Foreign Office to report that he had met with the Swedish Chief of Combined Intelligence. The Swedes were definitely worried that the Soviets were behind the ghost rockets but that Swedish officials would not make a public statement because of "the vital importance of utmost secrecy and delicacy of the position regarding other nations."[5]

On July 18, the British sent a representative from the Air Ministry (an expert in artillery and rocket intelligence) to Stockholm for a briefing; he traveled in civilian clothes at the request of the Swedes and reported that there was an insistence on the "utmost secrecy". Information pertaining to his mission was to be confined to selected members of the British and Swedish General Staffs.

By the end of July, the British Air Attaché in Stockholm telegraphed the British Foreign Office that he had been asked by Swedish Air Staff to take all possible measures to prevent the Americans from finding out the full cooperation between the British and Swedes in investigating the mystery missiles. Leakage of the cooperative investigation was seen as potentially embarrassing to Swedish authorities.

The following week, a memorandum to the British Air Ministry reported that the Swedes had reactivated their wartime radars and immediately began tracking the unidentified objects.[6] Such radar tracks suggested devices similar to the V-1 cruise missile or some type of glide bomb. The devices traveled at aircraft class speeds, rather than the German V-2 ballistic missile which traveled at over 3,500 mph during its trajectory and impacted with a speed of 1,800 mph.

Knowledge of their own highly secret missile developments, as well as of Soviet seizure and development of both German rocket and jet technology, was definitely a factor in focusing western intelligence groups on the Soviets as a source for at least some of the Scandinavian sightings. On July 19, a new memorandum was prepared for the commanding general of the American Army Air Force; it estimated that a rocket seen over Helsinki, Finland had been fired from the Porkkala area, 20 miles southwest of Helsinki on the Baltic. That territory was on the Finnish mainland but belonged to Russia. The idea was beginning to solidify that the rockets might well be a form of psychological warfare / intimidation – in support of either pending Russian territorial claims or in an effort to force the Scandinavian countries into a political position of neutrality.

In August, public media in Sweden began to report that the Swedish defense staff had recovered pieces of rocket projectiles. No details were available but reportedly writing had been found on one piece of recovered metal. By this point the Swedish military had issued orders that place names of reported impacts were not be made public – an indication that the situation was viewed seriously enough to put a level of media security in place. A serious effort to locate impacts and recover materials was definitely underway.

The Swedes did have a limited radar capability and their Air Staff attempted to track the unidentified objects. The initial equipment used was the British Ames 66 – Mark II (the RAF designation for the US Army Signal Corps SCR 615 ground control intercept set). That unit has a range of only 25 miles for objects at 1,000 feet altitude and 50 miles up to 10,000 feet.[7] In late July, the Swedes reportedly obtained a four minute radar plot of an object approaching from northwest of Uppsala. The plot showed the object executing a turn of something like 120 degrees and returning back in the general direction from which it had originated.

Whether or not such a turn was actually within the capabilities of both the remote control and maneuvering capabilities of the V-1 derivatives of that time remains an open question. A related issue would be whether or not the Soviets might have been using captured German jet aircraft in reconnaissance or "spoofing" flights – certainly there are records of incursions by conventional Soviet aircraft during the period.

Given the range limitations of the SCR 615 radar it would have been impossible to pinpoint the object's point of origin, especially if it were outside of Sweden. At the time the observed speed and guided flight were felt to be consistent with an enhanced V-1 class cruise rocket of the type both the U.S. and Soviets were working with during that period. Clearly, to obtain fully documented evidence of the device's origins, a more elaborate radar tracking network needed to be established.

The Swedish and British militaries reached the tentative conclusion that certain of the observed objects were most likely Russian rockets. Based on that assessment the British moved to send in an RAF technical party, under a "technical cover", to expand radar tracking of the objects – with the obvious intention of documenting their origin. The cover provided was that of an invitation from the Swedish Air Force to assist with radar and signals equipment for the British Vampire jet aircraft being purchased by Sweden.

One of the British team members made two visits to Sweden and recommended locations for the tracking radar. The full British party was to depart for Sweden on August 22 but the whole project was blocked at the last minute by order of the Swedish Prime Minister. No grounds were given for the order but news of the mission and its cancellation did leak to the Swedish media.

Within days the British Prime Minister demanded an explanation of the cancellation of the covert radar mission – no formal Swedish reply was received, leaving the British legation in Stockholm making extensive speculation about possible motives. If any answer was provided to the British it was done secretly. In turn, internal communications reveal that British scientists and Foreign Office personnel were increasingly frustrated by the lack of any definitive physical evidence.[8]

The Swedish Ghost Rocket committee was able to provide no absolute, physical evidence relating the objects to the Soviets – they felt that some sort of cruise missile was in play but were also skeptical that any nation had the technology which would have enabled the 1946 sightings.[9] It appears that the Swedish committee was totally unaware of the rapid and significant cruise missile development work being carried out by the British and Americans – they had even less understanding of the true state of Soviet air launched and radio guided V-1 derivatives.

By September, 1946 British intelligence fell back to treating the whole affair as a social phenomenon, the sort of scare any country close to Russia might suffer. In Sweden, although impossible to officially document, it appears that the initial political concerns in regard to "secrecy and delicacy" in international relations may very well have overridden any decision to publicly name the Russians in regard to certain of the reports.

The release of British military documents from this period now makes it clear that the Swedish military had been very aggressively investigating the unidentified objects with the help of the British, while holding the U.S. military at arm's length. In contrast, American intelligence reached a very different conclusion, and initiated contacts which allowed it to work secretly with the Swedish military over some two more years, searching for evidence of Russian involvement.

The official American intelligence assessment of the ghost rockets is found in a top secret memorandum from the Director of the Central Intelligence Group[10] (CIG) to President Harry Truman. Director Hoyt Vandenberg reported that his Central Intelligence Group had concluded that the "weight of evidence" pointed to Peenemunde as the launch point for the missiles and stated that they had information that Swedish radar course-plotting had also led the Swedes to the conclusion that Peenemunde was the launch site.[11]

CIG speculated that the missiles were extended-range developments of V-1 devices being aimed for the Gulf of Bothnia for test purposes. It felt that they were not over-flying Swedish territory specifically for intimidation. The devices were considered to be capable of self-destruction, implemented by small demolition charges. Another American study, prepared in January 1947 by the War Department's Intelligence Division, also concluded that a core of the most credible Scandinavian sightings involved very real devices – devices of Russian origin.

The American assessments seem to be consistent with findings in the final Swedish Ghost Rocket committee report of December 1946. That memorandum stated that nearly one hundred impacts had been reported and that thirty pieces of debris were recovered. The reports of objects seen in daylight were considered to have been "real physical objects." There was also mention of "unspecified" information obtained from radio and radar tracking as well as from "special sources."[12] A reference to radar, echo and other equipment observations had been contained in a Swedish Defense Staff statement of October 1946. It seems likely that technical intelligence had confirmed the physical nature of the devices, if not their exact origins.

Certain follow-on actions also suggest that the Swedes and Americans had secretly concluded that the core sightings in the wave of "ghost rockets" had indeed been Soviet devices. In July, 1947, U.S. Naval Intelligence began conducting electronic intelligence flights focused on Peenemunde. During those flights, radio guidance and control signals were detected, at 14.5 megacycles, with durations up to 14 minutes. Swedish officers also reported radio interception of long-wave, guided missile control signals. Intelligence assessment concluded that the signals suggested experimentation with either radio-controlled aircraft or enhanced V-1 type cruise missiles.[13]

Researcher Jan Aldrich has written about several 1948 communications relating to an ongoing American interest in Russian "ghost rocket" activities.[14] An Air Force document from August, 1948 noted a personal report by the Swedish Armed Forces Commander in Chief, who had observed an aerial explosion which was felt to be due to some sort of guided missile originating from the Estonian Islands (Dago or Osel).

The Swedes proceeded to conduct aerial reconnaissance over suspect Baltic islands during both 1948 and 1949, using a specially equipped F-51 Mustang which carried a K-22 high resolution camera supplied by the United States. The goal of the flights was to locate suspected Russian missile sites which were thought to have been associated with the ghost rockets and suspected to have been V-1 type devices.[15]

The 1946 activities of all the intelligence agencies responding to the Scandinavian sightings illustrate that when unidentified object reports are viewed as potential threats or national security issues, they are investigated – but investigated initially as quietly and covertly as possible. The rapidly escalating wave of ghost rocket sightings also provides us with the caution that with broad media coverage, even a small number of credible initial sightings quickly breed many times their number. There is a temptation to evaluate the importance of such sighting waves in terms of total numbers, including relatively questionable nighttime phenomena and daylight, long distance observations. Giving in to that temptation violates the basic intelligence guideline of separating the wheat from the chaff.[16]

The 1946 Scandinavian sightings also reinforce a truly important lesson learned in studying the reports of unidentified aerial objects during World War II. Observers can and do provide very concrete and valuable descriptions of objects which they see at relative close range, especially under daylight conditions. Certain of the Scandinavian sightings provided useful and specific details in regard to shape, performance characteristics and other observable "signatures" which could be used to profile the most credible core sightings in the incidents being reported. Examples of such profiles include:[17]

> "...wingless, cigar-shaped body of dimensions of a small airplane, which at regular intervals spurted bunches of sparks from its tail." Estimated altitude at only 100 meters and moving at "ordinary airplane speed" to southwest."

> "They heard a loud noise in the air and believed at first there was a plane coming. But the sound did not resemble plane noise, it was more like a powerful whistle. Right afterwards they caught sight of two plane-line objects which came from over the edge of the woods at a tremendous speed and so low that the two women involuntarily threw themselves down on the ground. The air current was so strong that the treetops swayed. Farmer Skaug and his son observed the objects from the side, at a height probably around 50 meters....Mr. Skaug said they were like pictures of V1s he had seen in newspapers. In any case they could not have been ordinary planes. They were cigar-shaped, approximately 2 ½ meters long, with approximately 1 meter long wings. The wings were set about 1 meter from the nose, and the fore and after parts had a metallic gleam, but the midsection with the wings was black. It looked as if there was attached an apparatus, perhaps a steering device, in the rear. They described a slight arc, about the way a stone is cast, and fell together into Mjosa, so the water plumes rose many meters high in the air. No explosion was heard."

With knowledge of the actual state of Soviet rocket and missile capability at the time – including Russian aircraft-launched V-1 derivatives becoming operational as early as 1945 – it is easy to follow the official American intelligence assessment that a limited number of Soviet actions were at the heart of the "ghost rocket" wave. Some may have been actual test failures, missiles malfunctioning or failed guidance tests. It is also possible that some of the reports of large "rockets", moving at great speed and altitude may have been secret V-2 test launches.

The earliest and best documented reports of the "ghost fliers" seem most likely to have been remotely guided V-1 cruise missiles – equipped for self-destruction and used for intimidation. It would have been a message to both the Swedes and the British that they were within range of quite accurate, long range rocket weapons. That was a very real and practical military concern for the Swedes regardless of America's atomic weaponry. The wide spread damage resulting from German rocket bombardment of both England and Belgium were still fresh on the public's mind. The Scandinavian countries were also quite familiar with the Russian history of intimidation. From that perspective the "ghost rockets" of 1946 may well have served as a very pragmatic and effective example of "realpolitik" communication.[18]

In summary, the Scandinavian experience reveals a great deal of the complexity of unidentified object investigations – as well as the extent to which intelligence collections can become complicated and even compromised by security and public relations concerns. Perhaps most importantly the experience illustrates that without absolutely conclusive physical evidence, internal intelligence assessments may be quite different from public pronouncements. As we will find in following decades, internal analysis and public positions can be two very different things, subject to high level factors such as geopolitics and national security concerns.

Before we leave 1946 entirely, it is again important to note certain anomalous reports which also stand out during the "Ghost Rocket" period. Two particular observations provide highly credible descriptions of unconventional aerial objects which match the "signatures/profiles" first noted in a limited number of World War II reports. The 1946 observations – one from Sweden and one from the United States – described large, elongated objects with no conventional wings or control surfaces such as tail fins. The objects were cigar/torpedo shaped and moved at speeds well beyond those of conventional propeller driven aircraft.

The first such incident occurred with a daylight sighting on April, 1946, when Army Air Force Captain Jack Puckett (then Assistant Chief of Flying Safety for General Elwood Quesada) was piloting a C-47 Army transport on descent into Tampa's McDill Air Base. During his descent Puckett's co-pilot noted a bright, shining object, apparently very close to his aircraft, and moving at high speed.

The object was pointed out to Puckett, who had no time to respond before the object had passed them. Puckett stated that the object was cylindrical, and metallic in appearance, something like twice the size of a B-29 bomber and with luminous portholes. What appeared to be a stream of fire came out of the rear of the object. It was on a collision course with his aircraft and at a distance of approximately 1,000 yards it had veered to cross the C-47's path. The cylindrical object remained in view for two to three minutes, becoming lost to sight beyond the horizon. Based on reference points and duration, the pilots estimated its maximum speed at something on the order of 2,000 miles per hour.[19]

The second observation came from a Swedish air crew in August, 1946. The Swedish bomber crew, flying on a daylight training mission with good visibility, observed a cigar/torpedo shaped object of some 50 feet in length at a distance of approximately 3,000 feet. It was clearly no conventional aircraft – it lacked any control surfaces – and the pilot moved to a parallel course for closer observation. At that point he realized that he would be unable to gain on it and the object pulled away from the bomber at a speed estimated to be around 400 miles per hour.

Gunnar Irholm, the pilot of the Swedish bomber, was extremely experienced, at the time commanding a Swedish air group. Irholm was later assigned to lead the group flying the first British Vampire jets acquired by Sweden and he was later promoted to head the Swedish military testing grounds for new aircraft, missiles and rockets.[20]

In terms of shape and basic appearance, the objects described in both the Puckett and Irholm sightings were similar to certain of the anomalous cylindrical objects reported by British and American aircrews during the war years – the difference being that in 1946 both objects were observed in independent, transiting flight, not shadowing or pacing the observing aircraft.[21]

We will continue to track that signature as we move on to 1947, the year in which unidentified aerial objects began to be reported not only overseas but across the continental United States itself.

Chapter 4 Endnotes

1. Luminous fireball trains are actually composed of ionized gas and occur very high in the atmosphere, higher than 65 miles. Smoke trails associated with fireballs occur at much lower altitudes and are more often seen in the daytime; they can appear similar to the condensation trails made by high flying aircraft. Fireballs have been reported in a wide variety of colors – blue-white, yellow, green – and the literature suggests that both composition and velocity may contribute to the color seen, with slower meteors appearing red or orange while faster ones being blue or blue-white. American Meteor Society, Fireball FAQ's http://www.amsmeteors.org/fireball/faqf.html#1

2. Ibid, both sonic boom and a more mysterious type of sound (electrophonic) have been reported in conjunction with fireballs. The sonic boom seems to be caused by the explosion of the fireball at lower altitudes (30 – 50 miles) and seems to be associated most often with a 45 degree viewing angle. The noise normally arrives from around two to five minutes after a fireball explodes/disintegrates. The electrophonic noise occurs simultaneously with the observation of the fireball and is not fully understood; it is heard as a hissing or sizzling noise or as popping and may be induced by very low frequency radio waves. During the Leonid meteor shower of 2001 there were numerous reports of both green colored fireballs and fireballs associated with hissing and crackling. This is similar to the noises often reported with the more dramatic aurorae displays. Controlled sound recordings related to fireballs were made during a 1998 Mongolian expedition. The expedition was led by Slaven Garaj, a Swiss physicist, and support the conclusion that fireballs do indeed create audible noises.

3. John O'Keffe, "Tektites and the Cyrillid Shower", *Sky and Telescope* magazine, January 1961, Volume XXI, No. 1, 4-8

4. High frequency radio control had in fact been one of the major goals of German missile development. It was a major priority for increasing the accuracy of the V-2 rocket. Radio guide beams had been tested which allowed a lateral dispersion of approximately one and a half miles. Their goal was less than a thousand yards. One radio beam guided V-2 unit did become operational before the end of the war. Radio control was also in development for other guided weapons including the rocket propelled glide bombs. There appears to be far less detail available on success with those devices, however, we do know that the V-1 missile could be programmed to make a number of course changes during flight in order to confuse tracking stations and complicate counter measures. Dornberger, V-2 : The NAZI rocket weapon, 122 –125 and Ordway and Sharpe, *The Rocket Team*, 181-182 and 201 Both the US and the Russians tested guidance systems in their derivative versions of the V-1.

5. PRO FO371/56988, quoted in David Clarke and Andy Piatkus, *Out of the Shadows: UFOs, the Establishment and Official Cover Up*, London, 2002

6. Ibid, cited in 22 Aug 46 Group Captain Simpson memo; PRO Files

7. Reference SCR 615 technical specifications at: http://ibiblio.org/hyperwar/USN/ref/Radar/Radar-7.html

8. David Clarke and Andy Roberts, *Out of the Shadows; UFO's, The Establishment & The Official Coverup,* Judy Piatkus Publishers Limited, London, 2002, 32-35

9. Op Cit, 36

10. E.K. Wright, Colonel, Executive to the Director, Central Intelligence Group, memorandum "Ghost Rockets over Scandinavia"; Michael Swords and Robert Powell, *UFOs and Government,* Anomalist Books, 2012, 22-23

11. The Central Intelligence Group came into place following the disbanding of the Office of Strategic Services (OSS) at the end of WWII. In June 1946, General Vandenberg became its chief, with a staff of some 100 persons. Vandenberg had been serving as the Army Director of Intelligence. He grew the new CIG organization during 1946, being succeeded by Rear Admiral Roscoe Hillenkoetter for a few months in early 1947 – before the CIG was superseded by the creation of the Central Intelligence Agency. The formation of the CIG had been given special impetus by a Joint Chiefs report on the evaluation of the Atomic Bomb as a weapon. In its report the Chiefs stated that the "protection against the catastrophic consequences of an atomic bomb surprise attack will require an intelligence service with a far greater effectiveness than any such agency this country has ever had in peace or war. Such an agency, charged with the duty of constant, world-wide scrutiny to determine whether atomic weapons (or other weapons of mass destruction) are being manufactured or readied for use must be our first bulwark of national defense. "The Evaluation of the Atomic Bomb as a Military Weapon", *The Final Report of the Joint Chiefs of Staff Evaluation Board for Operation Crossroads,* 30 June 1947

12. Jerome Clark, *The UFO Book,* Visible Ink, 1998, 247

13. Joel Carpenter, *Guided Missiles and UFOs: A Tangle of Fear – 1937-53 –* Part Three http://www.project1947.com/gr/grchron3.htm

14. Jan Aldrich, "EARLY TOP SECRET UFO DOCUMENT DISCOVERED", Project 1947 Article available in 1948 Document area of the Project 1947 website.

15. "Bortom Horisonten", July 18, and November 12, 23, 1948. Operation "Falun"

16. Cynthia M. Grabo, *Anticipating Surprise; Analysis for Strategic Warning,* University Press of America, New York, 2004, 131

17. Article excerpts from http://www.project1947.com/fig/1946a.htm

18. Op Cit

19. Letter from Jack E. Puckett to Maj. Donald Keyhoe, USMC ret., NICAP head, on July 24, 1957, CUFOS file. Also "Statement submitted to the House Committee on Science and Astronautics at July 29, 1968, Symposium on Unidentified Flying Objects", Rayburn Bldg., Washington, D.C., by James E. McDonald, 1968.

20. Michael Swords and Robert Powell, *UFO's and Government; A Historical Inquiry*, Anomalist Books, San Antonio, Texas, 2012, 15-16

21. A number of issues are immediately raised by the characteristics described in Puckett's report, which described an object traveling at supersonic speeds. Perhaps the most obvious is that with known technology any object of the reported size would be producing a highly noticeable sonic boom as it traveled above the speed of sound – a sonic boom which should have been heard on the ground all along its path. In addition, the reported flame trail, although suggestive of rocket power, could not be maintained over any long distance flight path by any known single stage rocket, especially one of the described size. If the object reported by Puckett and his crew was indeed a craft of some sort, it would be unlikely to have been a conventional rocket.

Chapter 5

Something Real

In this chapter

- Multiple, detailed reports of flying discs from government weather observers before the "flying saucer" sightings of summer made it into the press.

- UFOs reported over strategic American bases and facilities overseas and across the United States.

- Disconnects between dismissive Army Air Force public statements on UFOs and the actual intelligence investigations of 1947.

- UFO investigations as an Army Air Force priority due to the almost total lack of a continental air defense following the end of World War II and the shocking news - known only the AEC, President Truman and the Air Force senior commanders - that the nation had no inventory of functional atomic bombs.

- The initial Air Intelligence flying saucer opinion of fall 1947 that certain sightings involved "something real and not visionary or fictitious" – most probably advanced aircraft involving extensions of German wartime developments by the Russians.

As 1946 gave way to 1947, the American public remained exuberant, celebrating the end of rationing, welcoming home discharged military personnel, buying up newly available consumer products and adapting to a new role – that of a global military super power, the sole possessor of atomic weaponry. Worries about wartime mystery lights and foo fighters were already ancient history, the ghost rockets over Scandinavia made little media impression in the United States. What public concerns there were largely focused on what Joseph Stalin might choose to do with the Red Army in Europe. International news centered on fears that the Soviets were expanding their influence in Europe, aiding communists in gaining control over nations in their zones of occupation. There was also extensive reporting on the struggles of Britain, France and other colonial powers to regain control over their far flung territorial possessions. The Cold War was on the horizon but for the moment "war nerves" seemed to be a thing of the past for the general public.

Behind the scenes, known only at the highest levels of command, the American strategic military situation was considerably less comfortable. The U.S. atomic advantage was so tenuous that the 1946 Bikini atom bomb demonstration had used two of only three operational atomic bombs. The third weapon had been scheduled for use in the testing but was held back specifically out of concern for potential military conflict with the Soviets.[1] In January 1947, the new U.S. Atomic Energy Commission (AEC) began to take control of atomic development from the WW II Manhattan project. The Manhattan project had produced the atomic bombs used on Japan and seven Mark III bombs were supposed to be in inventory in a storage vault at Los Alamos, New Mexico. In reality, there were no assembled and functional bombs at Los Alamos, there were only parts.

In April 1947, after a personal inspection at Los Alamos, members of the AEC returned to Washington D.C. to verbally advise a shocked Harry Truman that America actually had no atomic bomb inventory. Parts were available and possibly a few functional bombs could be prepared – but only if assembly teams could be reformed and retrained.[2] As it turned out, even with the maximum effort possible, no more than 13 operational weapons would go into the American inventory by the end of 1947.[3] Truman held no atomic "hole card" in 1947 and in terms of troops he was left with little more than a single standing U.S. Army division in Europe to oppose the 260 Russian divisions available to Stalin – in any confrontation Stalin might choose to precipitate.[4]

Worse yet, the Hanford atomic reactors had suffered an unanticipated contamination which delayed production of both plutonium and polonium. Delays in plutonium production were going to slow the creation of a weapons stockpile. Without polonium operational weapons could not be "recharged" – they would have a life span of only a year. The Soviet Union was aware of the reactor contamination issue and had actually learned a great deal more about American atomic weapons development. During 1947 and 1948 the U.S. would learn just how successful Soviet espionage against the Manhattan program had truly been. The only thing the Soviets seemed not to have known in 1947 was that the United States did not actually have a significant atomic weapons inventory.[5]

The fact that America's plutonium production reactors were concentrated at Hanford, Washington was also of strategic concern. A successful bombing strike against those facilities would have been devastating - and Hanford was directly on the trans-Arctic strike path the United States itself was preparing to exploit in its planning for interdiction attacks against Russia.[6] It was feared that the Soviets had, or would soon have, the means for a surgical, if suicidal, strike on the Hanford reactors. They had confiscated three American B-29 bombers which had landed in Manchuria following an attack on Japan and it was known that they were rushing to copy the aircraft. Working under the highest priority the Tupolev aircraft group did just that and by 1948 were able to put the Russian version, the Tu-4, into mass production.[7]

Intelligence estimates were that the Russian Tu-4 bombers flying from airfields in Siberia would be capable of missions against both the Northeast and Northwest American coasts. Based on its knowledge of the B-29's capabilities, in 1946 the Army Air Force had already identified the polar routes over Alaska and the North Atlantic as a priority for both offense and defense. The use of one way attacks was accepted as a military reality. In 1947 the U.S. Army Air Force had no operational European bases for its B-29 heavy bombers - and would have no in-flight refueling capability until the very end of 1948. In fact, one way missions for the next generation heavy bomber, the B-50, would still be in the Air Force plans as late as 1953.[8] If the United States was willing to plan one way strikes to attack Russia, it was assumed the Russians would be willing to make the same commitment to remove the existential threat of American atomic weapons.

Worse yet, along with the reality of limited American strategic bombing capability, its continental air defenses were equally lacking – even for its atomic warfare complex. The Hanford atomic facility was the first site to have at least some minimal level of air defense, beginning during the final year of the war.[9] Pasco Naval Air Station was located just to the southeast of the Hanford reservation, and its primary war time mission was to train pilots for aircraft carrier operations. Beginning in December, 1944 and extending into early 1945, Pasco field radar had tracked a number of unidentified aircraft, generally flying at low speeds and producing radar returns similar to those from light civilian planes, equivalent to a Piper Cub. Given the critical security nature of the Hanford complex, Pasco pilots were tasked with intercepting and shooting down the unidentified aircraft. On a number of occasions intercepts were attempted, but no contacts were made and the effort faded away as the war ended.

Radars and interceptors deployed to deal with the Japanese Fu-Go balloons also offered some protection for Hanford. Hanford would become the first of the atomic war complex sites to have an active air defense, part of the focus on protecting against Russian strikes across the polar routes. Given the fear of Soviet air raids, a newly reactivated, post-war Air Defense Command established airspace surveillance radar stations at Half Moon Bay near San Francisco and Arlington in Washington State. Similar radars were to be deployed in New Jersey and Montauk, New York.

In June, 1947 the Atomic Energy Commission (AEC) requested that the Secretary of War review military protection at all its key atomic weapons development and production facilities.[10] They had good reason for concern, since none of the critical facilities other than the Hanford plant had been brought into an air defense network. That included the radioactive materials production facilities at Oak Ridge, Tennessee, the design and engineering complex at Los Alamos, New Mexico, and the new atomic weapons assembly site going into place in Albuquerque, designated as the Special Weapons Command at Sandia Base. There was also no wide area air defense radar in place and no interceptor group available to protect Walker air field near Roswell, New Mexico. Walker was home to the 509th Bombardment Group, flying the only B-29 aircraft with the capability for atomic bombing.

There were ground control approach radars in operation at military air fields and civilian airports across the nation, using radar equipment designed for locating and tracking multiple aircraft at relatively short distances – on the order of 40 to 50 miles. In contrast, search/surveillance radars are designed for detecting aircraft at much longer ranges, earlier versions sacrificed some ability to discriminate multiple targets in return for increased distance. Typical search radars available at the end of the war offered detection ranges of from 60 to 200 miles depending on terrain and the altitude of the aircraft to be tracked. Search radars of the period required separate height finder radars to actually determine the height of a target, a critical factor for guiding fighter aircraft to actually intercept "bogies". Circa 1947/1948 working ceilings for the best World War II era height finder radars were in the range of 40,000 feet - sufficient for air defense against the anticipated Soviet heavy bombers, whose service ceilings were anticipated to be comparable to the American B-29, at just above 30,000 feet.[11]

Specialized instrumentation radars, with very narrow beams capable of tracking rockets and missiles at very high altitudes, were in use at research and development sites such as the Holloman test range at White Sands, New Mexico.[12] Those radars had been developed as high altitude anti-aircraft gun pointing systems and had a very limited field of "view", some four degrees. They were turned on only during tests of missile launches and directed towards calculated trajectories; in some instances emitters were placed on the devices being tracked, to allow the instrumentation radar to home in on the target. Those radars were used for very specific periods of time in support of scheduled tests and not operated in a general search mode or for extended periods. The Army 8th Air Force actually had to schedule access to the White Sands radar equipment (which was normally staffed by civilian Signal Corps Laboratory personnel) for radar counter-measures training in 1947.[13]

Air Combat command records show no air defense radar deployment in New Mexico in either 1947 or 1948; it would not be until 1950 that a minimal air defense capability went in place for the numerous atomic warfare sites in New Mexico as well as the Oak Ridge plants in Tennessee.[14] While war surplus radar equipment was available for a continental defense network, a much more fundamental challenge was finding sufficient technicians and operators. The dramatically downsized Air Force faced a major manpower shortage. In March of 1948, when a Soviet air attack was felt to be imminent, General Carl Spaatz, commanding general of the Air Force, ordered the vital radar stations in the northwest to 24 hour operation. Even with the threat of immediate attack, the Air Force was unable to muster enough trained personnel to staff even those sites on an around the clock basis.[15]

The lack of air defense radars was mirrored by a major shortage of interceptors. Only two interceptor groups were operational in 1947, a single P-61 night fighter group had been deployed to a base near Tacoma, Washington, and one P-47 daylight only group was positioned at Dan air field in Maine.[16] Those two units had been relocated to defend against attacks over the polar routes. General Spaatz was determined to deploy whatever defenses could be brought into action against the anticipated Soviet air strikes coming across trans-Alaskan and Northern Atlantic flying routes into the continental United States.[17] Despite his deep concerns over the Soviet threat, Spaatz was left with the hard fact that the rush to post war demobilization had gutted all the armed services. The Air Force in particular had only 18% of its aircraft at combat readiness and only 2 of the 18 air combat groups left were considered combat ready.[18]

Strategic disagreements and political wrangling - combined with President Harry Truman's push to cut defense budgets - slowed moves to a true continental air defense. In April, 1947 the Army Air Force proposed an integrated network of air defense radar stations and control centers. Such a network did not become operational for some six years. In the interim, the Air Force continued to deploy war surplus radars. The first airspace surveillance radar network was known as "Lashup" since in many instances equipment literally had to be lashed to poles and towers.[19]

The Lashup network started to come on line in June of 1948; it was completed in 1949.[20] At that point General Whitehead of the Continental Air Command reached an agreement with the Civil Air Agency to coordinate information on commercial flights into the northwest and the east coast. Up to then there had been no controlled flight zones and no standing interception directive or rules for engagement. Whitehead issued orders to intercept and shoot down suspected hostile aircraft in the vicinity of Hanford and Oak Ridge; that order was temporarily rescinded in January 1950 but went back into place in April of 1950.[21] By 1950 air defense radar sites were set up at 44 sites in the industrial northeast, the Great Lakes, Washington state and California. Lashup continued in place and at least minimally operational until the new, integrated system started to go into service in 1952.

In short, when a wave of sightings of unconventional and unknown aerial objects began to hit the American media in the summer of 1947, the Army Air Force was in an exposed position in regard to detecting and dealing with them. Worse yet, if the Soviet threat was imminent, as many believed, and the sightings represented some sort of pre-strike Soviet reconnaissance, the U.S. would have been facing Russian military action with virtually no atomic war fighting capability and no means of defending the majority of the facilities that could resolve that weakness.

The military reality of 1947 was that the United States had no continental radar surveillance network[22], extremely limited interceptor resources[23], no special air or ground defenses for its atomic facilities other than the Hanford complex[24], no significant inventory of operational atomic weapons and very limited delivery capability for those few atomic weapons it did hold.[25] Only the nation's highest levels of military and national security command were aware of its limitations in responding to what might potentially turn into an imminent threat.

When "flying saucers" entered the American national news scene and the American conscious in the summer of 1947 the average citizen may have felt secure enough, focused on a return to normalcy, with servicemen back in the civilian economy, consumer product production booming and rationing a thing of the past. In contrast, senior military leaders were preoccupied with fears of Soviet military action and the Army Air Force was struggling with more crash defense projects than it could possibly deal with – public and media questions about possible foreign intrusions into American air space, apparently undetected and unchallenged by the military, would have been embarrassing. If the dialog went too far and the media inquiry became too deeply involved in investigating the state of the nation's air defense it could well become a true national security problem – exposing American weakness to the Soviets.

The arrival of unidentified aerial objects over America in 1947 was widely covered in newspapers, with national, regional and local stories about civilian sightings of "flying discs" and "flying saucers. Initially factual and somewhat concerned in tone, the reporting quickly turned from simple news coverage to something more in the nature of popular entertainment. Excellent studies of the overall 1947 flying disc/flying saucer sighting wave are found in the in depth field work done by Ted Bloecher in his *Report on the UFO Wave of 1947*, the collection of original articles and news reports available on the Project 1947 website organized by Jan Aldridge, and the excellent work of Mike Hall and Wendy Connors, published in Alfred Loedding and the Great Flying Saucer Wave of 1947 – Loedding was a key scientific investigator in the Air Force's first investigations of the unidentified object reports.

It was in late June 1947 that flying discs exploded into the American media. The first widely covered sighting came from private pilot Kenneth Arnold. On June 24, 1947 Arnold reported seeing a line of nine shiny, silver objects flying at very high speed in the vicinity of Mount Rainer, in Washington State. Arnold's story was picked up by all the national press services and appeared in some 150 papers (generally with banner headlines) the following day. Arnold himself did not describe the objects as "saucers" but rather as being "disc" shaped. The "saucer" term came from the press:[26]

> "ARNOLD: These objects more or less fluttered like they were, oh, I'd say, boats on very rough water or very rough air of some type, and when I described how they flew, I said that they flew like they take a saucer and throw it across the water. Most of the newspapers misunderstood and misquoted that too. They said that I said that they were saucer-like; I said that they flew in a saucer-like fashion."

Almost immediately the press began to receive dozens and then hundreds of sightings of objects which became tagged in the headlines as either "flying saucers" or "flying discs". The ensuing wave of summer "flying saucer" reports presented the same sort of public relations challenge to military intelligence as had the "foo fighters" of World War II. The Army Air Force, immediately began to be questioned about the unknown objects apparently moving at will above the nation. The number and pace of the inquiries were overwhelming

- too many reports from too many places, all at once. The service's senior leadership, quietly preparing for possible attack by the Soviets, quickly became both concerned and to some extent diverted from its primary priorities.

In later years, researcher Ted Blocher scoured the nation's newspaper collections in off hours during his working travels around the country. Bloecher's newspaper research developed a catalog of 853 UFO media reports for the months of June and July of 1947 alone – while the currently available Air Force archives list only 59 reports for the same period.[27] The virtual flood of sightings during the summer months of 1947 meant that even key observations were only reviewed months or years after the actual events.

In addition, at the beginning of the 1947 summer "saucer" wave, there was no procedure for centralized reporting of sightings either for civilians or within the military – in fact there were no standing military orders in place on the subject, nor any directives for classifying reports.

If observations were reported to a local military base it was entirely up to the base commander or his headquarters to determine if any investigation would be performed. When military personnel or civilians working on military projects happened to talk to a reporter about a sighting, it ended up in the newspapers. There were no orders and no policy relating to press comments by base or headquarters representatives. In the days and months following the Arnold sighting and its broad press coverage, a number of military sources were quoted in the local and national press (via the Associated Press news wire service) – almost universally with negative remarks about the sightings and the individuals making the flying saucer reports.

A study of those remarks reveals that the statements from base public information offices, base staff officers, and even headquarters personnel often bore little connection to the actual Army Air Force intelligence investigations which had begun by the end of July. An early example can be seen in a statement from a lieutenant colonel at White Sands test range in New Mexico. In responding to an Associated Press story on the Kenneth Arnold sightings, the colonel stated to the media that Arnold might have been fooled by the exhaust pipe glows from jets, giving the illusion of discs. The colonel seemed to be unaware that Arnold had first seen the objects approaching him rather than from the rear. The following day the colonel changed to new explanation - Arnold had most probably seen meteorites, which "appear much larger and are apparently coming closer to Earth than usual". In contrast to such dismissive remarks, the Army Air Force was actually taking the unidentified aerial objects quite seriously, conducting its own very low profile field investigations and beginning consultations with a professional astronomer.[28]

For a time the negative remarks from seemingly official sources faced contradiction in comments from highly credible civilian observers. Just as the White Sands' colonel was offering his explanations for the Arnold sighting, several unidentified object reports began coming in from personnel attached to the White Sands test range. One of the most significant, which did get into the Air Force files, was a report from three specialists working on a project related to some of the early V-2 test launches.[29] Dr. C.J. Zohn and two other individuals who were working for the Naval Research Lab on rocket projects were driving to the test grounds early on the afternoon of June 29, when their attention was attracted by a "glare" in the sky. Upon closer observation the glare was seen to come from a "silvery disc whirling though the unclouded sky". They quickly stopped their car and got a good look at the object, noting that it was either disc-shaped or spherical; it had no appendages and was moving in a straight course at a rapid rate of speed. One individual also reported a short vapor tail, not noted by the others.

A detailed report was made to officials at White Sands, it apparently received little response. Newspaper interviews with the observers state that they received only "fishy eyed stares" and "smiles". The observation is carried in Air Force files as having been identified as a balloon; there is no indication that the identification was discussed with the individuals making the report.[30]

Following on the heels of the White Sand's colonel's statements to the press, an intelligence officer for the Eighth Army Air Force was asked to comment on UFO sightings in Texas. He was blunt in his assessment - "they might be true but I doubt it." Two days later he was quoted in the Houston Post as being more definitive – saying that flying saucer reports were nothing more than "an interesting study in human psychology." Within a week his view was supported by a United Press International interview with an Army Air Force spokesman at Wright Field, the location of the Army Air Force Technical Base. A major was quoted as saying that a preliminary investigation of unidentified object reports had been dropped "because of lack of concrete evidence". In reality the investigations in progress were being done by field commands and no formal, Army Air Force wide intelligence study had yet been ordered or formally authorized.

In Washington D.C. the media was citing an unidentified source as saying "the Air Force people are inclined to believe that the observers just imagined they saw something or that there are some meteorological explanations for the phenomenon." One of the possibilities mentioned was that large hailstones could have flattened out and glided for some distance. The Washington source advised that the Army Air Force investigations had been dropped due to the lack of any facts. That position seemed to be confirmed in a report from the Army Air Force Technical Base in Dayton Ohio (the base would be renamed as Wright Patterson AFB in January 1948).[31] Reportedly the Air Material Command had been asked by the commanding General of the Army Air Force, General Carl Spaatz, to check into the unidentified object reports. The base's public information officer stated that investigations had found nothing to show that the discs actually existed and that as things stood they were a "phenomenon" or a figment of somebody's imagination.[32]

Those initial position statements appear to have been little more than a "knee jerk" public relations response to the surge in flying disc sightings which occurred during the first week of July, 1947, with a dramatic peak on July 4. Many of the July 4 sightings were made by large numbers of people at sporting events and picnics – 60 people reported three formations of discs at Twin Falls, Idaho, 200 individuals watched a disc near Spokane, the entire crew of a United Airlines flight observed two groups of discs near the Idaho-Washington border, dozens of reports came from Portland, Oregon, and a newsman and friends observed a speeding disc near Boise, Idaho. While the July 4 sightings were national in scope, the Pacific Northwest was producing a noticeable concentration. It also lead the nation in numbers of reports throughout June and July.

As the first week in July ended, there still had been no formal orders issued for any general Army Air Force investigation, intelligence collection or technical study. Some bases and commands had begun local inquiries that were being directed at a base or numbered Air Force command level.[33] None of the public information officers, Pentagon spokespeople or official sources would have had any actual studies or intelligence assessments as support for the remarks they were giving to the press and wire services. Fortunately for the Army Air Force spokespersons, any general media discussion of American air defense or broader issues of national security was quickly coopted by a number of widely reported misidentifications and outright hoaxes. By August press skepticism had become common and flying saucer sightings began to be treated more in the nature of opportunities for humor or entertainment than news.[34]

UFO historian Jan Aldrich provides examples of this media transition in an article on the "UFO Summer of '47".[35] As early as the second week in July a story by a popular columnist ran in over 1,000 papers – describing someone in Oklahoma being kidnapped by a big, hairy Martian. In a follow-on article the hero of the story escaped his captors and managed to return to earth, in the end pondering the effects that beer might have had on his imagination. A Catholic Priest's experience was also widely quoted in regard to his flying saucer experience, the unidentified object landing near him had turned out to be a saw blade.

During July, press coverage turned to unidentified objects which were actually recovered on the ground. Stories about misidentified weather balloons, weather kites and radar tracking devices associated with weather balloons became routine. Mysterious devices from "crashes" turned out to be scientific equipment - radio transmitters (radiosondes) and radar tracking devices (rawinsondes) used with meteorological balloons.[36] One newspaper printed a letter to the editor, from a former army weather service member, reassuring readers that some of the mysterious flying saucer wreckage being discovered was nothing more than foil and craft paper, used to construct radar reflectors attached to meteorological balloons to allow them to be used in plotting wind direction and velocity during cloudy weather.

One particular crash recovery of July 1947 did receive national press attention, although only for a short time. It proved especially embarrassing for the Army Air Force although it did seem to reinforce the point that pretty much anybody could make a mistake in regard to flying saucers. The story originated in a press wire out of Roswell, New Mexico – with the announcement that Air Force personnel in New Mexico had recovered a "flying saucer". The following day newspapers such as the Las Vegas Review-Journal followed up with a story explaining that the Air Force personnel in New Mexico had already been sternly rebuked for failing to realize that the material in question - shown to reporters as pieces of foil, sticks and rubber – was nothing more than the remains of a radar target which had been attached to a meteorological balloon.[37] At the time the apparent misidentification in New Mexico served simply as one more caution to the public, appearing to support both Army Air Force spokespersons and scientists who continued to bemoan flying disc reports as a combination of misidentification and hoaxes.

And hoaxes were definitely in play. The early July reports of misidentifications had almost immediately been followed by even more entertaining stories about actual hoaxes, ranging from advertising slogans on paper plates dropped from an airplane and tossed garbage can lids to more elaborate "contraptions" with a variety of mismatched motors, propellers and electronic components.

While the larger 1947 flying saucer story is fascinating, our focus will be on the very low key but intense intelligence response to unidentified objects reported by military personnel and commercial air crews. In their initial public comments Army Air Force spokespeople openly downplayed flying saucer and flying disc reports, actively reassuring the public that the sightings were simple misidentifications or actual hoaxes. Internally, the Air Force (which became a separate service in September of that year) was most definitely concerned and seriously investigating flying disc observations – and as the first internal intelligence assessments would state, the actual working assumption was that military personnel were providing reliable observations and reporting actual craft of unknown origin.

Indeed the first documented daylight observations of flying discs over the United States had occurred with no media coverage at all. The observers were members of a meteorological team working out of a Richmond, Virginia, weather station. Their work of daily wind measurements involved launching and tracking special weather balloons (pi-ball balloons). Each balloon's altitude and speed were visually tracked and measured with the use of a specialized optical instrument (a theodolite).

On at least three occasions the team observed unidentified objects (silver, ellipsoid in shape) maneuvering in the vicinity of the pi-ball balloons. Their final observation, in mid-April, 1947, was made by the team leader, Walter Minczewski. Using the team's theodolite, Minczewski was able to describe the object's shape as flat with a dome on its upper side. At that point the balloon was at 15,000 feet and he was able to keep the object in view for some 15 seconds. The other sightings had occurred at even higher altitudes, up to 27,000 feet.

Minczewski reported the incidents to the Weather Bureau and in some fashion the reports eventually made their way to the Air Force, where they were mentioned in one of the appendices to a Top Secret 1948 Air Force Intelligence Directorate, "Analysis of Flying Object Incidents in the U.S."[38] Strangely, neither Minczewski nor his team appear to have been personally interviewed about the sightings. According to Air Force documents, the weather team observations were highly rated, yet listed as unknown with no explanation offered. The experience of the observers was also noted - as well as the fact that the theodolite observation allowed a solid size comparison between that of the object and the known size of the weather balloon. In 1967, UFO researcher Ted Bloecher discovered that at some point the Minczewski observations had somehow found their way into the Air Force UFO (BLUE BOOK) archived files.[39] The report summary itself is extremely minimal and verifies that no follow-up was done with any of the actual observers.

That first series of 1947 disc sightings was repetitive, consistent and came from multiple, and experienced, sky observers. No media conditioning can be associated with them, as flying discs had received no press coverage at all as of April, 1947. The known weather balloon altitude and size provided a reference for accurately estimating the height and relative size of the unidentified object. In addition, the use of the telescope on the theodolite allowed for an accurate description of the object's disc shape and general physical characteristics even though it was not a close range sighting.[40]

While the Minczewski weather team was not interviewed, even quietly, it appears that it was the concentration of early flying disc reports from the Pacific Northwest which was of particular concern to General Carl "Tooey" Spaatz, the Chief of Staff for the Army Air Force. Both the vital Boeing aircraft plants near Seattle and the Hanford atomic complex had already led to his designation of the northwest as a primary Soviet target. The rash of unidentified aerial object sightings from the Pacific Northwest dovetailed with Spaatz's fears of a surprise Russian air strike over the pole, one which might well be preceded by reconnaissance flights over the key military/industrial facilities and/or by efforts to create confusion prior to and during such a strike.

If any of the unidentified objects being reported from the West Coast were indeed of Soviet origin it might well be an indicator of impending military action, at a minimum it would confirm the worst fears of a Soviet threat to the continental United States. In response, Spaatz directed the 4th Air Force, responsible for West Coast Air Defense, to assign intelligence resources to an investigation of flying saucer sightings. Reports were to be forwarded to the Air Material Command in Dayton, Ohio.

Two officers from Hamilton Air Base in California were assigned a B-24 for the use in field investigations. The officers conducted a number of interviews and inquiries, including meeting with Kenneth Arnold on multiple occasions. While returning from one of their field investigations their plane suffered an engine problem and crashed; both officers were killed in the accident. The plane crash occurred while they were returning from making inquiries into a sighting (Maury Island) - which ultimately was determined to have been a complex hoax.

Beginning in mid-July the Pentagon's Air Intelligence Collections group began building case files of credible sightings. General Spaatz also involved General Schulgen (Assistant Director of Air Intelligence Requirements Division) in the flying disc inquiry. In turn, Schulgen contacted General Twining (Chief, Air Material Command/AMC) to request an initial technical assessment of the objects being reported. Twining assigned that activity to General Howard McCoy, head of the Air Material Command's technical group. On August 22, 1947 the Collections Branch of Air Intelligence Requirements issued an advisory based on its initial study of the most reliable reports.[41] The advisory stated that it was "apparent that several aspects of their appearance (flying saucers) have a common pattern" and provided a listing of common characteristics as reference for further investigation.

The following incidents provide an insight into the reports that Air Intelligence had available as background for its initial collections guidance:

June 24 - Mt. Rainer, Washington State / afternoon. Kenneth Arnold, an experienced private pilot, observed 9 brightly scintillating disc shaped objects in a chain-like formation, flying at a speed which he estimated to be well above 1,000 mph. The objects swerved round the mountain peaks in their path and flipped from side to side, flashing in the sunlight Due to the media attention attracted by this incident, Fourth Air Force officers were assigned to investigate and were impressed with Arnold and his report. Dr. Allan Hynek, an astronomer, was consulted by the Air Force on the sighting. His analysis brought Arnold's speed estimate into question; however, the question remained open as to whether Arnold had misestimated the speed of the objects or their size.[42]

Arnold's basic observation was corroborated by other sightings. The Army Air Force received a report from a prospector, Fred Johnson, who described seeing six objects at the same time as Arnold, the objects were oval shaped, tapering at the forward edge. Investigators determined Johnson and his report to be credible (his report is listed as the first unexplained/unknown report in the Air Force files). The Army Air Force investigation turned up additional corroboration from a forest service employee who reported having seen "flashes" near Mount Ranier at the exact time of Arnold's sighting. The flashes appeared to him to be moving in a straight line.[43] It should be noted that the Mt. Rainer area is only some 100 miles west of the Hanford atomic materials production complex.[44]

June 29 – White Sands test range/ early afternoon. Dr. C.J. Zohn (a member of the V-2 testing project) and three other individuals observed a "silvery disc whirling though the unclouded sky". Their attention had been drawn to it by a "glare" in the sky. They quickly stopped their car and got a good look at the object, noting that it was either disc-shaped or spherical, had no appendages and was moving in a straight course at a rapid rate of speed. One individual also reported a short vapor tail, not noted by the others.

July 1 - Chitoze Army Air Base, Mokkaido, Japan/evening. Chitoze Air Base was within some 230 miles of an operational Russian air base at Ostov, on Sakalin Island. A GCA (ground control approach) radar operator at the base tracked a target moving at speeds in excess of 600 miles per hour. During the observation it made four different changes in heading with one course reversal of 360 degrees immediately following a GCA radio challenge call from the Chitoze tower. After the course reversals it departed the area, fading out of range. This incident caused considerable interest in Washington D.C. and personnel from Wright Patterson, including AMC engineer Alfred Loedding.[45]

July 3 - Harborside, Maine / 2:30 pm – Astronomer John Cole was alerted by a roaring noise overhead, he then observed approximately 10 round objects traveling in a loose formation. Two of the objects appear darker than the rest with projections which were somewhat wing-like. They were observed for 10-15 seconds, traveling extremely fast. Their estimated size was 50-100 feet in diameter, and a loud roar was associated with their passing.

July 3 – San Diego Naval Air Station, 9 pm – Two Navy Chief Petty officers observed a three disc, triangular formation coming into the base area from the west (ocean), circling to within some 20 miles of the base and then banking to reverse course and head back west, out over the ocean. The objects' speed was moderate, estimated at 400 mph.

July 4 - at 7,000 feet over Emmett, Idaho / 9:12 pm – The three person crew of a United Air Lines DC3 (flight 105) observed five evenly spaced discs with flat bottoms as silhouettes. The discs climbed and merged in a loose formation and outpaced the plane, going out of sight in some 5 min. A few minutes later, the aircraft again encountered four of the discs, with three in line. The discs were at a slightly higher altitude than the DC-3 and again outdistanced the aircraft (which had a top speed of 185 mph), disappearing in the western sky.[46]

July 6 - Fairfield-Susisan Air Base, San Francisco / daytime – An Army Air Force officer and his wife reported one round, flat object, highly reflective and about the size of a C-54 transport moving at a high rate of speed. It remained in view for approximately a minute, being estimated at 10,000 feet altitude. Fairfield-Susisan Air Base (later renamed Travis AFB) is located in the San Francisco Bay area and is America's largest military cargo and transportation hub on the west coast; it handles more traffic than any other Air Force facility, being known as the "Gateway to the Pacific."

July 8 – Pearl Harbor Naval Base/5:30pm – Some 100 Navy personnel observed a silvery, oblong object passing over the base, zigzagging, speeding up and slowing down. The object was at high altitude as it passed over the base.

July 8 - Muroc Air Test Center, California/ daytime - A number of objects were observed by different sets of witnesses during the day. Sizes of the objects ranged from five to ten foot diameters to larger but un-specified. Speeds were estimated to be in a range from 200 to 300 mph. The reports included an afternoon observation by a pilot flying an P-51 aircraft 40 miles south of Muroc. He encountered a "flat object of light reflecting nature" at 20,000 feet. The object was some distance above him and he was able to observe that it had no wings or other structures such as fins. Unfortunately he could not get his aircraft up to an altitude which would allow him to approach it closely.[47]

July 10, 1947 – Harmon Field, Newfoundland/ daytime. Two Pan-American Airways mechanics and a third individual reported a circular object flying at high velocity, paralleling the ground, leaving a trail and apparently "burning" a path through a cloud formation. Two other individuals also saw the object's trail, which remained in the sky for almost an hour. The trail was also photographed by another airline employee and those photographs substantiated the observations. The men estimated the objects size as approximating that of a C-54 transport plane and its trail was several miles in length.

The trail passed over Harmon Air Force Base (a critical Air transportation link on the trans-Atlantic route and in the 1950s a major SAC bomber base) and was compared to the afterglow of a powerful searchlight when the light is switched off. Several personnel at the base also confirmed observing the trail.

This series of observations in Newfoundland led to an intense round of study by engineering staff and intelligence officers from AMC.[48] There was a definite concern that if at least some of the unidentified aerial objects being reported were Soviet reconnaissance flights, they were passing over areas of the far north, possibly charting the same polar routes that Army Air Force was investigating for its own Arctic strike missions. Sightings in Alaska and Newfoundland, within days of each, other seemed to support that concern.[49]

A detailed account of the Newfoundland incidents is contained in an excellent piece of research by Michael D. Hall and Wendy A. Connors - *Alfred Loedding & the Great Flying Saucer Wave of 1947*. Hall and Connors relate that by July 21st a preliminary report of the initial sightings had been filed with the Pentagon, resulting in General Schulgen's orders for a team to leave to Newfoundland "immediately." [50] The intelligence team's report drew immediate and serious attention from the engineering staff at AMC. Their findings excluded the object as being a daylight meteor (fireball) and commented that its trail suggested a powered craft propelled by a turbo-jet, an athodyd motor (ramjet) or some combination of such power plants. The absence of noise and the apparent dissolving of the clouds suggested a large airflow and considerable heat. In short, their assessment was that some advanced foreign aircraft had passed over Harmon field. [51]

The early Harmon Field reports were a major stimulus for the military to take flying disc reports seriously. At the same time General McCoy at AMC was sending personnel to Nova Scotia, he was also pushing his staff to interview a captured German scientist in regard to German developments using blimps or similar lighter than air devices as "piggy back" carriers, having the potential for carrying smaller craft over long distances.[52]

July 29 - Hamilton Air Force Base, California / 2:50 p.m. The Assistant Base Operations Officer and an experienced B-29 pilot both observed two round, shiny, white objects. The first object was sighted as it headed right over a P-80 jet fighter coming in on a preliminary landing – in an approach at around 6,000 feet. A second object then appeared, flying a left to right "protective" maneuver over the first craft until they each passed southward toward Oakland and then out over the ocean. Both officers estimated the objects to be 15 to 25 feet in diameter, shiny white in color, and circular-shaped. The total duration of their sighting lasted about fifteen seconds, as the craft sped by in a clear sky. The objects appeared to be traveling 3-4 times the apparent speed of the P-80 fighter which they overflew. One of the objects flew straight and level while the other seemed to be weaving from side-to-side as if it were providing escort.[53] [54]

August – Rapid City Air Force Base. An intelligence officer with the 28th Bombardment Wing reported that a major in the command had observed (from the flight line of the base) a group of twelve discs, flying in a tight formation, "stacked down" from the lead object. They approached from the northwest, descended to approximately 5,000 feet and made a shallow, wide radius turn over the base, departing to southwest and accelerating as they departed. Their apparent speed was 300-400 mph and size approximately that of a B-29 aircraft. No sound was heard but the objects did appear to have a type of luminous glow around them.[55]

On August 11, General Spaatz's office directed the Air Material Command (AMC) to send an officer interrogator to Fort Bliss to interrogate German scientist Gerhard Riesig. He was to be questioned about a book on "distant control of rockets", written by him and believed to be in Russian hands. He was also to be specifically interrogated about an unspecified project named ABSTRACT.[56] Based on further messages, it appears that ABSTRACT related to the combination of rocket missiles with atomic energy. AMC was directed to locate and interrogate an extended list of Germans who were felt to have been associated with the project. Reportedly key documents on the project had been secretly buried both in Germany and Italy.

August 14 - Harmon Field, Newfoundland / 10:30 a.m. Three airmen with the 147th AACS (Airways and Air Communications Service) squadron observed two small crescent-shaped objects pass over them at approximately twice the speed of the jets with which they were familiar. The objects were flying a zigzag path heading west and were relatively low, at an altitude estimated just above 1,000 feet. Both objects disappeared into the clouds and a few seconds later one of them emerged and continued on west.

With such observations in hand, it is not surprising to find that as of the end of August, the initial Army Air Force internal memoranda describe the flying disc/flying saucer issue as involving a core of very real sightings. At that point in time the Collections Branch of the Air Intelligence Requirements Division provided an initial assessment, titled "Flying Saucer Phenomena", to the Deputy Chief of Staff for Air Force Research and Development.[57]

"From a detailed study of certain reported observations on the flying saucers, selected for their veracity and reliability, it is apparent that several aspects of their appearance have a common pattern...Surface is metallic-- indicating a metallic skin, at least...When a trail is observed, it is a lightly colored blue-brown haze, similar to a rocket engine's exhaust. Contrary to a rocket of the solid type, one observation indicates that the fuel may be throttled, which would indicate a liquid type rocket engine...as to shape, all observations state that the object is circular, or at least elliptical, flat on the bottom and slightly domed on the top...Size estimates place it somewhere near the size of a C-54 or Constellation as they would appear while flying at 10,000'...Some reports describe two tabs located at the rear and symmetrical about the axis of flight motion...Flights have been reported containing from three to nine objects, flying good formation on each other, with speeds always above 300 knots... The discs oscillate laterally while flying along, which could be snaking."

At his own initiative, Schulgen also contacted the Federal Bureau of Investigation, informing them that the Army Air Force would be actively investigating the flying saucers/discs and that it was using its scientific assets to evaluate the reports as to whether they represented some celestial phenomenon or were actually foreign, controlled mechanical devices. Schulgen specifically expressed concern that the sightings might be a Communist-orchestrated effort to create fear of a Russian secret weapon. It appears that he hoped the FBI might help determine if key reports might be coming from or seeded by enemy agents. Director Hoover's initial response to the request was to note that the Bureau would only cooperate if given access to any objects actually recovered.[58]

For a period of less than 90 days, the FBI did become actively involved with flying saucer reports. A policy statement was issued that directed field offices to investigate any sighting which was brought to their attention and to ascertain whether it was bona fide, a prank, a publicity stunt or possibly a subversive act. While some reports did prove to be hoaxes, the Bureau also received and documented some highly significant observations, including the previously mentioned airliner crew observations made near Emmett, Idaho. The FBI did extensive interviews and background checks on the pilots involved in that sighting and found them to be quite credible.[59] That incident, along with a number of pilot observations, became key support for the initial Air Force intelligence assessment that those very real sightings were occurring.

As it turned out, FBI interest and involvement proved to be short lived. FBI personnel became aware of an internal Air Force communication letter which they felt implied that the FBI was being used simply to filter out pranks while the Air Force concentrated on serious reports. When this was brought to the attention of Director J. Edgar Hoover, he quickly advised the Army Air Force that he could not permit the personnel of his organization to be used in such a matter and issued a directive advising that all flying saucer reports be referred to the Army Air Force - with no investigations to be performed by the Bureau.[60] The FBI's longer term involvement would only be with reports relating to security at vital installations such as atomic facilities.

Schulgen's concerns about the unidentified aerial objects potentially being part of a Soviet psychological warfare initiative was an obvious extension of the earlier War Department Intelligence Division report which had concluded that a "hard core" of the Scandinavian ghost rocket sightings did involve real devices which were of Russian origin. The Air Force also began receiving confidential information concerning a series of British observations suggesting that England was being targeted by high altitude, high speed Russian reconnaissance. Their radar tracking showed objects at a very high altitude (35,000 feet plus) and at high speeds (450 miles per hour). The British had become so concerned that they established a project ("Operation Charlie") to detect and, if possible, intercept the unidentified objects involved in the radar tracks and sightings.[61]

Given the widespread concerns over possible Russian military moves in Europe or the Far East, the worries about possible Soviet reconnaissance and/or psychological warfare seem quite reasonable. But the AMC staff was facing a major challenge - obtaining solid information on the physical nature and type of propulsion system being used by the discs. The characteristics of the reported objects could be studied, but the real specialty of the technical personnel at AMC was aeronautical and engineering analysis. Their primary missions were to support the national intelligence effort to avoid technological surprise, to advance Air Force technology and accurately describe the weapons capabilities of potential enemies through a study of their technology. At the end of World War II technical intelligence had begun to focus its efforts on "exploitation", the acquisition of enemy technology and science.[62] The key element of fulfilling that mission was to obtain actual samples of enemy weapons or at least portions of the hardware associated with those weapons.

The Army Air Force Directorate of Intelligence had been in charge of the World War II Operation "LUSTY" field teams, responsible for the collection of as much advanced Luftwaffe technology and science as humanly possible. As a result of that effort over 1,000 tons of technical papers had been brought to AMC in Dayton, Ohio by the spring of 1947 and approximately 100 German scientists were in residence there – all part of an effort to jump start the American aeronautical industry in the fields of jets and rockets.[63] It was only beginning to become clear that the pragmatic American focus on optimizing existing aircraft designs had left the U.S. behind in the science and technology required for supersonic flight and as well as long range ballistic rocket weapons. The engineers and aircraft specialists at AMC faced a huge task in reviewing and capitalizing on the captured German technology and devices - but at least that work offered the study of actual, physical hardware.

In contrast, the data available on the new flying saucer/flying disc problem was strictly a matter of observations and reports, there was no hardware and no actual physical evidence available for analysis or hands on study. Worse yet, there was virtually no true technical intelligence at all, not even a comprehensive set of radar tracks – and no obvious way to acquire them given the lack of an American radar network. The lack of air defense resources was so dire that even in 1948 when officers involved with the flying saucer inquiry asked for fighter aircraft to be assigned to intercept unknown objects for the purpose of obtaining radar data or photographs their request was refused – there simply were no available aircraft.

As the huge number of summer sightings began to fade in late summer 1947, the Army Air Force continued to reassure the public that the flying saucers represented no reason for concern, they were simply misidentification of various conventional objects – balloons, flights of birds, weather anomalies such as lenticular clouds or astronomical phenomena. Internally, the official intelligence assessment was something quite different. In late September the Air Material Command produced the Air Force's (now an independent service) first opinion paper on "flying discs":[64]

The stated opinion was that there were indeed objects being reported which were "something real and not visionary or fictitious."[65] The next step was obvious, a concrete identification of the devices including both their origins and the technology involved. Only then could an actual threat assessment proceed. In pursuit of that end, the commonalities of the objects in question were defined – essentially a "profile" of the intelligence target. The following excerpts from that paper define the objects to be investigated, offer insights into the possible technology involved and present possibilities for their origin:

- A relatively flat bottom with extreme light-reflecting ability.

- Absence of sound except for an occasional roar when operating under super performance conditions.

- Extreme maneuverability and apparent ability to almost hover.

- A form approximating that of an oval or disc with a dome shape on the top surface.

- The absence of an exhaust trail except in a few instances when it was reported to have a bluish color, like a Diesel exhaust, which persisted for approximately one hour. Other reports indicated a brownish smoke trail that could be the results of a special catalyst or chemical agent for extra power.

- The ability to quickly disappear by high speed or by complete disintegration.

- The ability to suddenly appear without warning as if from an extremely high altitude.

- The size most reported approximated that of a C-54 or Constellation type aircraft.

- The ability to group together very quickly in a tight formation when more than one aircraft are together.

- Evasive action ability indicates possibility of being manually operated, or possibly by electronic or remote control devices.

- Under certain power conditions, the craft seems to have the ability to cut a clear path through clouds -- width of path estimated to be approximately one-half mile. Only one incident indicated this phenomenon."

The incident relating to the last item (k) in the Air Intelligence profile was in reference to the Harmon field observations previously discussed.[66] Copies of two photographs from that sighting did eventually end up in Air Force files and confirmed the witnesses' observations.[67] Consideration of Soviet adapted German technology was very strong at this phase of the early technical analyses and the bluish-black trail from Harmon field suggested some novel combination of jet, turbo-jet, or ram-jet power plants.[68] The absence of noise and apparent dissolution of clouds was also suggestive of advanced technology.[69]

The Air Material Command paper also called out specific characteristics of the unidentified objects being described in the most credible reports and commented on the possible German technological origins of such a craft:

- This strange object, or phenomenon, may be considered, in view of certain observations, as long-range aircraft capable of a high rate of climb, high cruising speed (possibly sub-sonic at all times) and highly maneuverable and capable of being flown in very tight formation. For the purpose of analysis and evaluation of the so-called "flying saucer" phenomenon, the object sighted is being assumed to be a manned aircraft, of Russian origin, and based on the perspective thinking and actual accomplishments of the Germans.

- There is also a possibility that the Horten brothers' perspective thinking may have inspired this type of aircraft - particularly the "Parabola", which has a crescent plano form. Records show that only a glider version was built of this type aircraft. It is reported to have been built in Hellegenberg, Germany, but was destroyed by fire before having ever been flown. The Horten brothers' latest trend of perspective thinking was definitely toward aircraft configurations of low aspect ratio. The younger brother, Riemar, stated that the "Parabola" configuration would have the least induced drag - which is a very significant statement. The theory supporting this statement should be obtained if possible.

- The German High Command indicated a definite interest in the Horten type of flying wing and were about to embark on a rigorous campaign to develop such aircraft toward the end of the war. A Horten design, known as the IX, which was designated as the Go-8-229 and the Go-P-60 (night fighter) was to be manufactured by the Gotha Plant. It is reported that a contract for fifty such aircraft was planned, but only three or four were built. This plant is now in the hands of the Russians. A recent report indicates that the Russians are now planning to build a fleet of 1,800 Horten VIII (six engine pusher) type flying wing aircraft. The wing span is 131 feet. The sweepback angle is 30 degrees. The Russian version is reported to be jet propelled.[70]

By the end of September 1947, the internal Air Force view was that a core of flying saucer/flying disc observations represented something real and that the characteristics of the objects in question suggested extensions of German wartime developments, most likely by the Russians. By October, 1947 intelligence collections requests with considerable detail were distributed to American military attaches in England, France, Sweden, Finland, USSR, Turkey, Greece, Iran, China, Norway, Philippines, as well as to the Commander-in-Chief, Far East, the Commanding General, United States Air Forces in Europe, and through the Commanding General, EUCOM. The European command was specifically directed to pursue all leads which might tie the objects to the Horton brothers, their designs, and any sign that they the Russians were pursuing their work. It intelligence collections document was quite definitive:[71]

a. What German scientists had a better-than-average knowledge of the Horten brothers' work and perspective thinking; where are these scientists now located, and what is their present activity? Should be contacted and interrogated.

b. What Russian factories are building the Horten VIII design?

c. Why are the Russians building 1,800 of the Horten VIII design?

d. What is their contemplated tactical purpose?

e. What is the present activity of the Horten brothers, Walter and Riemar?

f. What is known of the whereabouts of the entire Horten family, particularly the sister? All should be contacted and interrogated regarding any contemplated plans or perspective thinking of the Horten brothers, and any interest shown by the Russians to develop their aircraft.

g. Are any efforts being made to develop the Horten "Parabola" or modify this configuration to approximate an oval or disc?

h. What is the Horten perspective thinking on internal controls or controls that are effective mainly by streams of air or gas originating from within the aircraft to supplant conventional external surface controls?

The Air Force very quietly embarked on a new hunt for unconventional German aircraft/propulsion technology, adapted and being used by the Soviets. According to Edward Ruppelt, (who would head the official Air Force UFO investigation in the early 1950's), there was no question among the Air Force investigators that very real devices were being reported – and it was felt to be only a matter time before their true nature and origins would be determined. The intelligence specialists were confident that they would resolve that question within a few months, certainly in no more than a year.[72] There also seems to have been little doubt that when that identification was finalized, the objects would be of foreign origin and the Soviets would be found to be involved.

Chapter 5 Endnotes

1. Norman Polmar. *Strategic Air Command – People, Aircraft and Missiles*, Nautical and Aviation Publishing Company, 1979, 9. A full (and un-sanitized) picture the immediate post-war American atomic capability has only emerged in recent years. In 1979, a history of the Strategic Air Command described the Bikini tests as so successful that the third bomb did not need to be dropped.

Richard Rhodes, *Dark Sun - The Making of the Hydrogen Bomb*, 261-263. A very conflicting view is offered by historian Richard Rhodes, including the fact that the primary target, the battleship Nevada, was left afloat and that the B-29's bomb sight was later determined to have been mis-calibrated. General Groves proposed to the Joint Chiefs that it would be best to save the single remaining weapon in inventory and they agreed.

Richard Hubler, *SAC - The Strategic Air Command*, Van Rees Press, 1958, 66. Another book on the Strategic Air Command remarks that future historians will record that the supply of primitive nuclear weapons in the Marianas available following the atomic bombings of Hiroshima and Nagasaki was enough to "effectively destroyed in a single day every Japanese city with a population in excess of 30,000 people." In dramatic contrast, an early SAC history records that there were no additional bombs available at all at that time.

2. Richard Rhodes *Dark Sun - The Making of the Hydrogen Bomb*, Simon and Schuster, New York, 1996 281-284

3. William Boyne, *Wild Blue – A History of the US Air Force 1947-1997*, St Martins Press, New York, 1997, 28 In addition the atomic weapons were not under Air Force control, only the AEC actually knew the number and types of weapons available.

4. The Soviets would be starting up their first reactor just as the U.S. had to shut down its Hanford weapons reactors due to an unanticipated radioactive contamination side effect. The problem affected not only plutonium production but the production of polonium, required to "charge" any devices which could be built. The Hanford problems had a significant impact on bomb production – some 40 to 50 devices would be all that could go into the stockpile for 1948.

5. William Boyne, *Wild Blue – A History of the US Air Force 1947-1997*, 295

6. Stripped down B29 bombers could operate at 35,000 feet and were selected to form the 46th Reconnaissance Squadron, organized in June, 1946. The 46th was based in Fairbanks, Alaska and its mission was to survey strike routes into Russia. *Any Means Necessary*, William Burrows, p. 96.

7. Robert Kilmarx, *A History of Soviet Air Power*, 1962, 230

8. Walter Boyne, *Wild Blue- A History of the US Air Force 1947-1997*, 40

9. UFOs Over Hanford: Commander R.W. Hendershot, Project 1947 http://www.project1947.com/fig/hendershot.htm

10. Kenneth Schaffel , *The Emerging Shield, The Air Force and the Evolution of Continental Air Defense, 1945-1960*, 68-69

11. The war-time surveillance and height finder radars were replaced as quickly as possible with equipment capable of dealing with jet aircraft, including the new jet interceptors which were coming available. By 1950 new sets with height finding capability up to 60,000 feet were being deployed.

12. Jim Eckles, *Pocketful of Rockets; History and Stories Behind the White Sands Missile Range*, Fiddlebike Partnership, Las Cruces, New Mexico, 2013, 154-155

13. http://www.project1947.com/roswell/baindoc.htm

14. *Searching the Skys; The Legacy of the United States Cold War Defense Radar Program*, Air Combat Command, United States Air Force, June 1997, 16-20

19. Kenneth Schaffel, *The Emerging Shield, The Air Force and the Evolution of Continental Air Defense, 1945-1960*, 78-80. A crisis atmosphere existed in the spring of 1948 and was reflected in a Joint Chiefs meeting with Defense Secretary Forrestal. The Air Force commander in the Far East had reported strange incidents and excursions over Japan and was concerned about the outbreak of war within a few months. General Stratemeyer ordered an immediate implementation of an Alaskan air defense as well as a functional air defense for Seattle and the Hanford plant. These orders were issued on March 27 and were to be implemented by April 3, 1948.

20. Ibid, 59; Pursuit (P) designations were used for Army Air Force fighter/bomber aircraft up to and during World War II. As an independent service, the Air Force began the use of Fighter (F) nomenclature for new fighter/bomber aircraft, beginning with the F-84 Thunderjet introduced in the fall of 1947.

21. Ibid, 57-58

22. Walter Boyne, *Wild Blue- A History of the US Air Force 1947-1997*

19. Kenneth Schaffel, *The Emerging Shield – The Air Force and the Evolution of Continental Air Defense, 1945-1950*, 70-72. The "Lashup" first generation Air Defense radars (AN/CPS5) sweep radar used in conjunction with an AN/TPS10 height finger) which would go into service in

1948/49, they had a normal range of only 60 miles (and a maximum approaching 100 miles with a target at maximum altitude) and an altitude limitation of approximately 25,000 feet. They were especially limited at low altitudes with a range of 35 miles with the target at 1,000 feet and less if the target were lower. Follow-on radars would come into use in the 1948-51 period but they would still be limited to a range of something like 200 miles and an altitude of 40,000 feet – just enough to track the highest performance WWII fighters such as the P-51 Mustang and P-82 Twin Mustang amd the first operational American jet fighter, the F-84 Thunderjet. More importantly, they would have the necessary altitude capability to track the B-29 and the Russian TU-4 ("Bull") derivative.

20. Ibid, 23 and 95

21. Ibid, 126

22. David Winkler, *Searching the Skies – The Legacy of the Cold War Radar Defense Program*. In 1947 only two Air Defense search radar stations were operating - one at Arlington, Washington and one at Half Moon Bay near San Francisco. It would not be until March, 1948 that similar sites would be ordered set up for Los Alamos, Kirtland Air Force Base (which hosted the Sandia atomic weapons facility) and Roswell Air Force Base. also see: http://www.pinetreeline.org/articles/resartj.html

23. Ibid, 77 In 1946, the Army Air Force's sole US based operational night-fighter unit had been temporarily deployed to McCord Field, Washington. In November of 1947 it was relocated to Hamiton Field, California. The unit consisted of 13 P-61 "Black Widow" night fighters, the only unit of its type at the time. The Air Force's only day-light pursuit squadron, with P-47 aircraft had been moved to Don Field in Maine. Neither unit had actually gone fully operational during 1946.

24. Ibid, 68-60. In June, 1947, the AEC requested that the Secretary of War review military protection at key facilities. The review determined that no special protection was in place for any AEC facility as of the end of the review in July, 1947.

25. Richard Hubler, *SAC, The Strategic Air Command*, 75-76. At the time of its official organization, in 1946, the Strategic Air Command (SAC) had only 250 heavy bombers (B017, B-24 and B029). It was incorporated into the 8th and 15th Air Forces in early 1947 and in May, 1947 was officially designated as the organization to deliver the nation's atomic weapons. At that point SAC had only one full strength operational B-29 unit (a number of its groups were of "paper" units with only a few planes) and a "handful" of atomic weapon capable B-29's.

Norman *Polmar, Strategic Air Command – People, Aircraft and Missiles*, 8-17. During 1947, SAC was devoted to increasing both its aircraft and manpower strength and began rotations overseas to develop its ability to stage units to advance bases in Asia and Europe; its first overseas deployment in 1946 had been to Alaska. SAC also began the ongoing practice of staging mass training flights against major American cities such as Kansas City, Chicago, St Louis and NYC, simulating conventional B-29 attacks. The fact that much work remained to be done was reflected in a "maximum effort" mission against New York City in May, 1948. One hundred and one aircraft practiced bomb drops but another 30 had scrubbed the mission, remaining at their home bases due to maintenance and supply problems. SAC was continuously confronted with serious manning, supply and administrative problems during its first two years, those problems significantly reduced its ability to practice its main mission, strategic bombing.

26. "Transcript of Edward Murrow-Kenneth Arnold Telephone Conversation", CUFPS Associate Newsletter, February-March 1984, 3, Project 1947. http://www.project1947.com/fig/kamurrow.htm

27. Ted Bloecher, *Report on the UFO Wave of 1947*, Section 5 and the online *Project BLUE BOOK Archive* provided by Tom DeMary: http://www.bluebookarchive.org/default.aspx

28. Ibid, I-6

29. F. Zwicky, *On the Possibility of Earth Launched Meteors*, The Astronomical Society of the Pacific, Volume 48, 1946. A number of very prominent scientists including not only rocket specialists but also well-known figures in atmospheric and astronomical research were involved with projects at White Sands, including an extended series of V2 launches as well as other projects by both the Army and Navy. One night time V2 launch in December of 1946 involved an experiment to create and track artificial meteors. http://ufxufo.org/gfb/artifmet.htm, http://ufxufo.org/gfb/zwickoralhist.htm

30. Ibid, III-18

31. Wright field and Patterson field had seen independent use for a number of years before World War II, as had Dayton Army Air Field. In 1945 they were operationally merged as the Army Air Forces Technical Base. In 1947, with the designation of the Air Force as a separate service the installation was named the Air Force Technical Base and in 1948 re-designated as the Wright Patterson Air Force Base. To avoid confusion, the installation is most commonly referred to as Wright Patterson or Wright Patterson AFB.

32. Ibid, I-6 – I-7

33. Early examples involve a Tinker Air Force Base investigation of a report from Oklahoma City. Both the Air Force and FBI followed up on press coverage of Byron Savage's observation; Savage was considered credible based on his being a private pilot as well as a local businessman. A May 19 multiple disc report by several observers near Manitou Springs, Colorado was investigated by 15th Air Force on June 29 – after appearing in the local press (reported to the press only after the Arnold sighting coverage).

34. Blocher's research demonstrates that positive media coverage of the "flying saucers" quickly soured - within no more than two weeks. During the first week of July reports were presented factually, with little commentary. By the second week in July, news coverage usually contained both skepticism and often outright ridicule. In some cases reporters began adding their own details in order to create a more impressive and sensational story, Blocher demonstrated this by comparing the news stories with interviews and local reports. In many cases incidents reported factually in local papers became laughable when remarks were added for national wire service distribution. The flying saucer "treatment" was even worse among national columnists, who felt free to add creative material and considerable humor to their remarks. Unfortunately, as early as the second week of July, a series of simple mis-identifications, outright hoaxes and practical jokes began to provide ample material to use in humorous stories about UFO's.

35. Jan Aldridge, "The UFO Summer of '47", Project 1947, http://www.project1947.com/roswell/ufo47.htm

36. Radiosondes are battery powered instrument packages which transmit instrument readings such as altitude, pressure, temperature, and humidity to a ground receiver. When equipped with radar reflectors to allow tracking and distance measurements, such meteorological packages are referred to as rawinsondes.

37. "Flying Disc Tales Decline as Army, Navy Crack Down", *Las Vegas Review Journal*, AP Wire Service, July 9, 1947

38. Analysis of Flying Saucer Incidents in the U.S./Summary and Conclusions, United States Air Force, Directorate of Intelligence, April 28, 1949, Appendix C, 8, http://www.project1947.com/fig/1948air.htm

39. Despite any indication of Air Force follow up with the actual observers, this incident was specifically cited as highly credible in the December, 1948 Pentagon Air Intelligence Analysis of UFO's.

40. Ted Bloecher, "Report on the UFO Wave of 1947, I-1" also Mike Hall and Wendy Connors, "Alfred Loedding and The Great Flying Saucer Wave of 1947". http://www.nicap.org/comments.htm.

The existing report can be found in the Project Sign Collection, Page ID USAF-SIGN8-358. http://www.bluebookarchive.org/page.aspx?PageCode=USAF-SIGN8-358&tab=2

41. "Flying Saucer Phenomena", Collection Branch, Air Intelligence Requirements Division, August 22, 1947

42. Ted Bloecher, Report on the UFO Wave of 1947, I-3

43. Loren E. Gross , UFOs: A History 1947, Fremont, CA, 1991, 8 as referenced in Mike Hall and Wendy Connors Alfred Loedding and the Great UFO Wave of 1947, 26

44. In 1948/49 the Air Defense Command established an interceptor group at the Larson Air Force Base near Moses Lake Washington. The interceptors and associated radar equipment provided air security for the Hanford Complex and for Grand Coulee Dam. In June, 1947, neither radar nor interceptors were operating in the region of Mount Ranier.

45. Michael Hall and Wendy Conners . Alfred Loedding and the Great UFO Wave of 1947, Chapter 3. Also NICAP Report Summary. http://nicap.org/docs/loedd/loedd_contents.htm, http://www.nicap.org/waves/1947fullrep.htm

46. Op Cit, http://www.nicap.org/waves/1947fullrep.htm

47. Jerome Clark, "The UFO Book", 1997, 407 It is worth noting that the first head of the Air Force's "Project BLUE BOOK" observed that it was the Muroc sightings which first provoked a deep interest in UFO's; the Muroc witnesses were extremely credible, independently confirming each other and the observing conditions were clear and sunny. Ultimately the Air Force recorded all the Muroc reports as weather balloons – apparently ignoring several of the specifics cited by the witnesses in their reports.

It should also be noted that the Muroc test center served as the test and demonstration point for all the major US advances in aircraft technology following WW II. The X Plane program began there in 1946 and all the early high speed and supersonic aircraft were developed with testing at Muroc; the sound barrier would first be broken at Muroc in October, 1957. It was also the test site for a wide range of prototype aircraft including the Northrup flying wing aircraft. In January 1950, Glen Edwards died while testing a prototype of the Northrop YB-49 flying wing and Muroc was designated as Edwards Air Force Base and U.S. Air Force Flight Test Center in June, 1951.

48. These images are available for review online in the NICAP collection. http://www.nicap.org/images/harmon1, http://www.nicap.org/images/harmon2

49. American reconnaissance of the summer of 1947 is reflected in the following message from Air Force of Chief of Staff Spaatz to the 46th Reconnaissance Squadron in Alaska: 19 Aug 47 – Alaska (TS) War Dept outgoing msg to Alaskan Air Command Fort Richardson Alaska, "From AFACC signed Spaatz A 16856. "Sufficient priority should be given to primary mission FERRET flights by 46 reconnaissance. Squadron to insure minimum of 1 flight south of Bering Strait and 1 north each month. No geographical restrictions except aircraft must remain at least 15 miles from non-United States territory. Your theater will effect normal coordination with FEAF on any flights into that area. Consistent cover story should be arranged in case of forced landing on foreign soil and every precaution taken to maintain security of operations.

Intelligence requirements as forwarded for operations PASSIONATE and FLOODLIGHT still in effect. End" http://www.project1947.com/gr/s92.htm

50. Michael D. Hall and Wendy A. Connors, "Alfred Loedding & the Greatest Flying Saucer Wave of 194, 90

51. Ibid. References cited by Hall and Connors include: "*Project BLUE BOOK* Files", Roll No.1, Case 59, listed as Incidents 26-27 in 1947 era documents; Gross, "UFOs: A History 1947", pp.44-45, and *Project BLUE BOOK* Files, Roll No.2, Case 63, listed as Incident 41 in 1947 era documents as well as Michael D. Swords, "Project Sign and The Estimate of the Situation" and "Project BLUE BOOK" Files, Roll No.2, Case 60, listed as Incident 27a in 1947 era documents.

52. Michael Swords and Robert Powell, *UFO's and Government / A Historical Inquiry*, Anomalist Books, San Antonio and Charleston, 2012, 39. It should be noted that McCoy's request occurred immediately after what was initially reported as the crash of a flying disc near Roswell New Mexico. The incident was initially reported by an air base press release describing the recovery of a flying saucer, quickly followed by an official statement that what had really been recovered were materials from a downed weather balloon. Air Force archives contain no record of the Roswell incident; no base records on the handling of the recovery, the materials themselves or the issuance of the press release can be located, even by an official Air Force inquiry.

53. Ted Bloecher, *Report on the UFO Wave of 1947, 1967*, I-14 Note: Hamilton AFB would soon undergo expansion to serve as a major Air Defense Command fighter base during the 1950's.

54. Michael Hall and Wendy Conners, *Alfred Loedding and the Great UFO Wave of 1947*, Chapter 5.

55. J. Allan Hynek , *The Hynek UFO Report*, 1977, 40-41

56. Joel Carpenter, "Guided Missiles and UFOs:A Tangle of Fear - 1937-53 - Part Three" http://www.project1947.com/gr/grchron3.htm

57. Michael Swords and Robert Powell, *UFO's and Government / A Historical Inquiry*, Anomolist Books, San Antonio, Texas, 2012, 40

58. Lawrence Fawcett and Barry Greenwood , *The UFO Cover-Up, 1984*, 147-148. It should be noted that Director Hoover annotated a memo relating to Schulgen's request with a remark that an object recovered in Louisiana by the Air Force had not been shared with the Bureau. That may have been true but the object in question was definitely determined to have been a crude hoax. That incident is documented in Blue Book files for July 7, 1947.

59. Ibid, 151-156

60. Ibid, 156-159

61. Dr. David Clarke, "UFO's in History; Operation Charlie", *The Real UFO Project*. After some months, the British concluded that the majority of the reports, especially those from January of 1947, were probably produced by British launched weather balloons encountering some extremely unusual weather and wind patterns. However, there remained a series of very high altitude (35,000 feet plus) and high speed (450 miles per hour) tracks which were not so easily explained. Although the Russians had no aircraft of their own which could achieve those figures it was known that the Russians had captured and were working with the German JU 287 which had a 612 mile range, ceiling of 30,000 feet and speed of over 600 mph. In addition, the Americans had captured German Arado jet bombers with a 967 mile range, a 32,000 foot ceiling and a speed of 461 mph. There are no records of Russian seizure of Arados, but some 210 had been produced including 14 four jet versions. The Arado had been fully operational and used by the Germans for high speed photo reconnaissance over England during the war. The updated version of this article was published in 2004 by Project 1947 http:www.project1947.com Also available at: http://www.uk-ufo.org/condign/histcharlie.htm

62. Wolfgang Samuel, *American Raiders; The Race to Capture the Luftwaffe's Secrets*, University Press of Mississippi, 2004, 95-99

63. Ibid, 401-411

64. Ibid, 479-484

65. "AMC Opinion Concerning Flying Saucers", Memorandum from Air Materials Command to Commanding General Army Air Forces, September 23, 1947 Richard Hubler. SAC – The Strategic Air Command, Van Rees Press, 1958, 66.

66. Harmon Field had been an extremely active base during WW II and was one of the largest U.S. military airfields outside the continental US. It could handle the largest aircraft in service and was a vital trans-Atlantic refueling stop.

67. "*Project BLUE BOOK*" Files, Roll No.1, Case 59, listed as Incidents 26-27 in 1947 era documents see also U.S. Air Intelligence Report No. 100-203-79, "ANALYSIS OF FLYING OBJECT INCIDENTS IN THE U.S." http://www.nicap.org/harmon.htm

68. *Britannica Concise Encyclopedia*. Copyright © 1994-2008 Encyclopedia Britannica, Inc. Athodyd – "A ramjet is an Air-breathing jet engine that operates with no major moving parts. It relies on the craft's forward motion to draw in air and on a specially shaped intake passage to compress the air for combustion. After fuel sprayed into the engine has been ignited, combustion is self-sustaining. As in other jet engines, forward thrust is obtained as a reaction

to the rearward rush of hot exhaust gases. Ramjets work best at speeds of Mach 2 (twice the speed of sound) and higher.

69. Michael D. Swords, "Project Sign and The Estimate of the Situation", first draft of unpublished article written for 1998 issue of *Journal Of UFO Studies*

70. An online copy of the full collections document, as well as many key Air Force documents of the period may be viewed, courtesy of Jan Aldrich and the Project 1947

71. Michael Swords and Robert Powell, *UFO's and Government / A Historical Inquiry*, 479-485

72. Edward J. Ruppelt, *The Report on Unidentified Flying Objects*, Doubleday and Company, Garden City, New Jersey 1956, 26

Chapter 6
Foreign Origins?

In this chapter

- The Air Force Flying Saucer response – publicly dismissive but internally concerned.

- The Air Material Command requests initiation of an official study of the "discs" based on observations of high speeds, formation flight, evasive maneuvers and the possibility of advanced propulsion, "possibly nuclear".

- A formal intelligence investigation – Project SIGN – is authorized, based on the possibility that the discs represent unconventional devices of foreign origin.

- A December 1947, Air Intelligence summary states that it has reports from competent observers including USAF rated officers and notes that the "flying discs" may be conducting reconnaissance, ferreting out defensive capabilities or conducting a psychological tests of public reactions.

- Scientific analysis of recovered fragments generates speculation that "self-destructive" artificial devices are involved in at least some of the unconventional object reports.

While the public was receiving dismissive remarks from Air Force officers and even public relations spokespersons, Air Intelligence groups were actually taking certain flying disc/saucer reports quite seriously. At the end of July 1947 Brigadier General George Schulgen, head of the Air Intelligence Requirements Division, requested an opinion on flying disc sightings from the technical specialists at the Air Material Command. In response there were urgent and frequent technical meetings of AMC staff and personnel were dispatched on field assignments, including an in depth investigation of the Harmon field, Newfoundland observations.

In September, Pentagon intelligence officers traveled to AMC for a meeting with the technical experts. Following that meeting, on September 23, Lieutenant General Nathan Twining (AMC Chief) endorsed a joint intelligent assessment in a letter to Schulgen. Twining included a summary of the initial AMC findings and requested that Air Force Headquarters authorize a numbered, security-designated project for an ongoing study of what were felt to be very real unconventional devices, devices of foreign origin.

It needs to be noted that tracing internal Air Force communications such as the Twinning letter is a major historical challenge and that effort has involved numbers of dedicated researchers over decades. We can only deal with the highlights of their work here, but readers who are interested in examining primary source materials should refer to the extensive research collections available on the National Investigations Committee for Aerial Phenomena (NICAP) and Project 1947 websites. The work on the Twinning AMC letter by Jan Aldrich and his Project 1947 "A-Team" illustrates the depth of research which is now available.[1] Readers are also encouraged to consult Brad Sparks' overview of the various Air Force investigations, the groups involved and the personnel involved with them.[2]

In his call for an official Air Force study, Twining noted that the "discs" had been observed to climb at high speeds and demonstrate maneuvers which could be construed as "evasive" action in response to aircraft and radar tracking. In several instances numbers of these discs had been observed in a "well-kept formation", suggesting manual, automatic or remote control. Their performance also suggested the possibility that a foreign power had developed a form of propulsion, "possibly nuclear", which was beyond current American technology.[3]

Twining qualified that point by noting that the observed performance of the discs was not totally outside the scope of anticipated aircraft designs. He felt it likely that a piloted aircraft could be developed which would have the general characteristics of the objects being reported, craft with a range of 7,000 miles at subsonic speeds.[4] In regards to high speeds, the United States itself was beginning to test rocket propelled aircraft capable of supersonic speeds and extreme rates of climb to very high altitude. The Bell X-1 rocket plane flew for the first time in October 1947, reaching a speed of 800 mph and an altitude of 42,000 feet; the X-1A would soon do 1,700 mph and reach 90,000 feet.[5] As early as 1945 work had begun on the X-2 which, within a few years, would travel at over 1,800 mph (beyond Mach 3) at an altitude of 126,000 feet.[6]

In terms of the flying discs' unconventional shapes (with no extended wings or tail structures), the American military had begun work on "flying wing" fighters during the war, based on the designs of Jack Northrup. The XP-56 interceptor was a "flying wing" with no horizontal tail. It went into initial flight testing in 1944, at a site near the Muroc test center in California.[7] Northup's flying wing designs were also tested with rocket motors and turbojet engines. The turbojet version flew for the first time in September 1945. An unmanned cruise missile variant (JB1) of the Northrup flying wing, powered by twin turbojets, had begun flight testing in December 1944. Allied intelligence collection on the German V-1 resulted in a redesign, with power provided by a Ford company version of the German pulse jet engine. The JF-1 was launched from a rocket sled and dozens of 1945 trials were carried out from sites near Muroc and Elgin Field in Florida. The JB-10 was capable of carrying two tons of high explosive at a cruising speed of 425 miles per hour.[8]

Following the war, the "flying wing" design emerged as a serious contender for the next generation of American long range bombers. The Northrop XB-35 flying wing began test flights in 1945. During 1946 the propeller driven flying wing was flying from Muroc; in October 1947 a jet powered version (YB-49) began flying out of the Muroc facility. By 1948 the Northrup bomber would be capable of 500 mph speeds on 9 hour plus flights.

The flying wing (a huge aircraft with a wing area of almost 4,000 square feet) was extremely difficult to see from a distance due to its lack of extended wing or tail structures; it was almost invisible in any view other than full cross section. Its shape also made it difficult to detect by any of the radars of the period.[9] Not only was the huge flying wing difficult to spot visually and extremely hard to track, it was so maneuverable that the XB-35 could both turn inside the first operational American jet fighter (P-80 Shooting Star) and out-climb it! At the time stability problems with the flying wing as a bombing platform (as well as certain performance issues compared to competitive aircraft) led to the Northrup design not being selected as the Air Force's bomber of choice. The advent of computers and computerized flight control would change that in time and Northrup flying wing designs would become the choice for the America's late 20th Century and early 21st Century strategic bombers

While the Navy's World War Vought XF-5U (the "flying flapjack"), propeller driven test aircraft was mentioned for comparison purposes in certain of the Air Force's flying disc studies, great care seems to have been taken to avoid mentioning the capabilities of the new rocket planes and in particular the Northrup flying wing. The Northrup flying wing bomber had a projected range of almost 10,000 miles with full bomb load and a maximum speed of just under 400 mph. There is also no mention of the early American projects focused on atomic propulsion. As early as May, 1946 the Army Air Force had initiated a program to apply atomic energy to aircraft. The NEPA (Nuclear Energy for the Propulsion of Aircraft) program opened a facility at the Oak Ridge atomic energy complex and began studies on shielding for aircraft; it was re-designated as the Aircraft Nuclear Propulsion program in 1951.

In 1947 hopes for an atomic powered bomber visualized an aircraft with unlimited range and, if applied to the Northup flying wing design, would have resulted in a craft similar to that which Twining referenced in his comment on achievable technology. In reality it would be more than two decades – in 1979 – before a proposal for an Advanced Technology Bomber produced a new round of designs reminiscent of the Northrup flying wings. A next generation Northrup design was selected in 1981 and by 1989 the "flying wing" B-2 Spirit bomber, capable of subsonic flight (at over 600 mph) and with a range of some 6,000 miles began testing – an aircraft very similar to that visualized by General Twining in 1947.

While the B-2 lacks the ability for the extreme speeds mentioned in several of the early flying disc reports, twenty-first century unmanned combat air systems such as the Northrup Grumman X-48B UCAS are now demonstrating both high maneuverability and the ability to perform totally autonomous, unmanned operations, including formation flight and even mid-air refueling.[10] In 2016, the Air Force announced that its next generation long range strategic bomber, the B-21, would be coming from Northrup-Grumman; yet another Northrup "flying wing" design.

Twining's flying disc technology comment was also consistent with both the Air Force's own advanced project studies and the most advanced thinking in the American aircraft industry at the time. General Curtis LeMay, appointed Deputy Chief of Staff for Research and Development at the end of World War II, had publically declared that the next war would be fought with "rockets, radar, jet propulsion, television-guided missiles, speeds faster than sound and atomic power". LeMay had been active in supporting the "paperclip" project which brought German scientists and engineers to Wright Patterson and White Sands. He had also commissioned a number of advanced technology studies, including the "Preliminary Design of a World Girdling Spaceship".[11]

Only a few years later, in 1953, Lockheed Aircraft Company filed a patent on a disc shaped aircraft design which incorporated a huge and novel turbo-ramjet power plant. The craft was to be 50 feet in diameter and weigh in at approximately 55,000 pounds. Specifications called for a vectored engine thrust which would be directed towards the ground for take-off and then rotated to the rear for a gliding climb. At some 50,000 feet it would transition from turbojet to ramjet and eventually comb to an operational ceiling of 100,000 feet where it would be capable of a supersonic cruise speed of over four times the speed of sound, at almost 3,000 mph.[12] Ultimately such ambitious concepts were overwhelmed by engineering challenges – as demonstrated in the previously discussed failure of Air Force Project 9961 / Project Y (Silver Bug). However it would take the better part of a decade to fully understand and accept that reality.

Twining and the Air Force's technical specialists viewed the devices being reported in the most credible of the unidentified aerial object observations as being both real and even feasible within the developmental scope of known technologies. Given that viewpoint, it's somewhat strange that no comparative estimates of advanced Soviet aircraft development appear in any of the early intelligence studies. The Soviets had flown their MiG-9 jet fighter in 1946, at a speed over five hundred miles per hour; they were testing the MiG-15 in late 1947. The MiG-15 had a speed of over six hundred miles per hour and a range of over 700 miles.[13]

Russia had been especially fortunate in obtaining most of the surviving German jet and rocket fighters (eighty percent of the German aircraft industry had been in areas occupied by the Russians) as well as prototypes for very advanced German jet bombers.[14] The Junkers Ju-287 four engine jet bomber prototype had been captured by the Soviets and flown in May, 1947. It was capable of flying at speeds over six hundred miles per hour and at heights up to 30,000 feet. With a range just short of a thousand miles, certain of the mystery objects tracked over both Britain and American overseas military installations were within the capability of the captured German aircraft.

What American intelligence actually knew about Soviet developments circa 1947 is unclear but what it most certainly did know about was the war time work on German flying wing aircraft.

The wartime Project Lusty collections effort had acquired considerable detail on the German Horton flying wing aircraft, that material had been collected and archived within the Foreign Equipment Branch of the Air Material Command at Wright Patterson AFB in Ohio.

The first German jet flying wing aircraft, the Horton Ho-229 fighter/bomber flew in 1944 and did not become operational during the war. In the last year of the war, a long range bomber version of the craft, designated Ho-IX was being designed – with a projected range of almost 1,200 miles and a speed over 600 mph.[15]

Although also not discussed in the Air Force flying saucer studies, it was well known that both the Germans and Russians were experienced in the practice of extending the range of their jet and rocket craft by carrying them to launch points on long range bombers. There also appears to have been some early Air Force suspicion that high altitude balloons might also have been used as carriers to add to the operational range of unconventional craft. In pursuing that possibility, Air Material Command personnel conducted interviews with a former Nazi scientist working at Goodyear as to German war time use of blimps or other lighter than air devices to serve as "carryalls" for smaller craft, specifically small disc craft.[16]

Conceivably an aircraft or balloon carried launched variant of the Ho-229 could have been responsible for certain of the 1947 flying disc reports; covert flights of captured German jet aircraft could have been responsible for others, especially those within range of operational Soviet airfields:

- Japan / a radar target tracked at 600 mph; within 230 miles of an operational Soviet air base

- Guam / crescent shaped, estimated flying twice the speed of a contemporary fighter aircraft

- Japan / radar tracking over some 70 miles at speeds above 800 mph

- Harmon field, Newfoundland / observations indicated a combination of turbojet and ramjet type propulsion

- Harmon field, Newfoundland / two crescent shaped objects estimated flying twice the speed of a contemporary jet aircraft

In December 1947, Air Intelligence at the Pentagon prepared a summary on the subject of "flying discs", citing key sightings and the various activities that had been taken to pursue explanations – including contact with the FBI on the possibility of at least some reports being related to a "subversive" effort by foreign powers. The paper noted that an alleged flying saucer type aircraft or object approximating the shape of a disc, had been reported by many observers from widely scattered places, such as the United States, Alaska, Canada, Hungary, the Island of Guam, and Japan. "The objects have been reported by many competent observers, including USAF rated officers. Sightings have been made from the ground as well as from the air."[17]

The report also emphasized the urgency of investigating foreign aircraft projects, specifically stating that one of the Horton flying wing designs would be a match for certain of the flying disc observations. The possibility that the devices represented a national security threat was clearly stated; while no hostile actions had been noted, the flying discs could be in use "for photo reconnaissance purposes, or to ferret out our defensive capabilities, or to test the American psychological reactions". [18]

Air Intelligence did qualify its summary by stating that it was "difficult to conceive why any foreign nation, if it possessed such an unconventional aircraft or missile, would risk sending it near or over the United States for anything short of an attack. Even if the disc contained a self-destructing device, any crash landing would disclose a certain amount of information which the nation possessing such an aircraft or missile would desire to keep secret. This would be particularly true if the form of propulsion was outside American knowledge".[19] It was also noted that there appeared to have been no strikingly significant number of reports from the most strategic American military or national security facilities during 1947.

Given that the Horton flying wings (much like the Northrup aircraft) matched the "low aspect ratio" profile of the flying disc reports, a major intelligence collection effort was launched in Europe. Its mission was not only to learn more about the Horton wartime developments but to what extent the Russians might have obtained the services of German scientists or technicians familiar with the flying wing technology. Suspicions that the Russians were involved appear to have been fed by the intelligence that the Soviets were in the process of actually building a fleet of some 1,800 Horton-VIII six-jet bombers. The collections document specifically called for locating the factories being used in the Russian effort and developing information on their projected tactical mission.[20]

The next Air Force move was to authorize an official investigation; that technical intelligence project (SIGN) was to focus on discovering whether key flying disc reports reflected a breakthrough in Soviet military capability. SIGN had been authorized with the stated purpose of "collecting, collating, evaluating, and distributing to interested government agencies and contractors, all information concerning sightings and phenomena in the atmosphere which could be construed to be of concern to the national security." [21] The project (unofficially known as Project Saucer) was assigned a 2-A priority (A priorities were the highest available for an Air Force project), a RESTRICTED classification, and a code name of "SIGN".[22] Although SIGN held a high priority, its security classification was relatively low, reflecting the need for its personnel to communicate widely in collecting and distributing information, including working with the Army, Navy, Coast Guard and FBI.

In exploring the SIGN effort, it is critical to keep in mind that its high priority reflected a sense of military urgency; it was not due to either simple curiosity or scientific interest. The presence of unidentified objects over the continental United States was being viewed strictly in context of the assumed Soviet threat and the nation was far from ready to counter such a threat with atomic weapons.

In February 1948 the Soviets occupied Prague, Czechoslovakia. In turn the Western bloc nations moved into a series of high profile confrontations with the Russians over Berlin and access to the city through the Berlin corridor. The Russians had walked out of an arms control meeting and began obstructing Allied rail access to the city. The American commander had threatened to meet further attempts to block land access with force. However given the extreme disparity in conventional forces in Europe, the only credible counter force was SAC and the threat of atomic weapons. During the Berlin crisis SAC did deploy some sixty B-29s to bases in Britain; the move was done publicly and received extensive media coverage. What was kept extremely secret was that the bombers were not actually accompanied by atomic bombs.

Actually 1948 had begun with only 13 atomic bombs in the American inventory and no teams were available to assemble bombs for an actual stockpile. Major General Nichols, acting head of the Armed Forces Special (Atomic) Weapons Project, advised that his civilian weapons assembly teams were in the Pacific, preparing for the spring Sandstone series of atomic bomb tests which would begin in April at Eniwetok atoll. There simply were no civilian personnel available to assemble new weapons and military assembly teams had yet to be trained.[23] Nichols received orders directly from the President to accelerate training and prepare for the transfer of weapons to the military.[24]

It was in that atmosphere of military confrontation that the activities of the new SIGN project were being conducted. While both conventional human intelligence work and technical collections moved forward, it was initially felt that the most likely path to quickly resolving the origin of the unidentified aerial objects would be through an investigation of advanced German aircraft technology and it's adaptation by the Soviets. AMC seemed well positioned to pursue that avenue; a number of its key research and development personnel had been involved in the technical missions to collect, study and exploit German air and rocket technology. The overall SIGN effort was led by Colonel Howard McCoy, and the technical group worked under William Clingerman in the Intelligence Analysis Division. McCoy had been a participant in the German technical exploitation (LUSTY) during World War II and was very involved in collecting and building an archive of German air and rocket technology; he worked with Albert Deyramond in that effort.[25] Alfred Loedding and Albert Deyarmond were assigned as engineering team leaders.

Deyarmond, a reserve Air Force Colonel, had been called back to active duty from his civilian job specifically to participate in SIGN. Deyarmond was personally close to Major General George McDonald in the Pentagon Air Intelligence Directorate and to former LUSTY team leader Colonel Harold Watson. In 1948, Colonel Watson was serving in the Pentagon's Air Estimates branch, focused on Russian target selection and applying the results from atomic bomb tests to the Air Force's highly secret atomic warfare plans.

The story of the SIGN investigation of 1948 is important not simply for what it reveals of the complexity of the real world intelligence process but its lessons on the extent to which attitudes and even career considerations can affect the process. Fortunately we have considerable insight into the individuals and personalities involved, much of it based on Michael Hall and Wendy Connors' historical research – including their study of Alfred Loedding, one of the engineering leaders of the AMC study group assigned to project SIGN.[26]

General Twining's initial AMC response had called for the creation of an EEI document (Essential Elements of Information) – such documents are essentially a checklist for collecting important details of any technical topic. That had been a standard procedure during wartime technology exploitation operations. Reportedly, Alfred Loedding and Pentagon consultant Dr. Charles Carroll drew up the EEI to be used in the SIGN intelligence collection. It was then sent to all Air Force commands to serve as a basis for investigating unidentified object sightings. One of the SIGN team's main Pentagon connections was to the intelligence collections division via Lt. Colonel Garrett. Loedding himself maintained a close connection to Garrett, and had already focused on the Horton flying wing collections work in Germany. One of the first actions in the new inquiry was to call for and review the Pentagon's entire intelligence collection on the "ghost rockets" in Scandinavia.[27]

Unexpectedly, even as project SIGN was just getting organized and underway, early feedback from the European collections effort had already begun to undermine the assumption that Russian development of the Horton brothers flying wing aircraft was the most likely source for the flying discs. The Horton brothers were located, along with key draftsmen and assembly personnel who had worked on the German flying wing projects.

Excerpts from the following European Command report of December, 1947 illustrate how quickly the European collections effort had concluded that the flying saucers were not the result of a crash Soviet development of flying wing type aircraft:[28]

Subject: Horten Brothers (Flying Saucers)

To: Deputy Director of Intelligence

European Command, Frankfurt

APO 757, US Army

1. The Horten brothers, Reimer and Walter, are residing in Goettingen at present. However, both of them are travelling a great deal throughout the Bi-Zone. Walter at present is travelling in Bavaria in search of a suitable place of employment. It is believed that he may have contacted USAFE Head-quarters in Wiesbaden for possible evacuation to the United States under "Paper Clip". Reimer is presently studying advanced mathematics at the university of Bonn, and is about to obtain his doctor's degree. It is believed that when his studies are completed he intends to accept a teaching position at the Institute for Technology (Techniscbe Hochechule) in Braunschweig sometime in February or March 1948.

2. Both brothers are exceedingly peculiar and can be easily classified as eccentric and individualistic. Especially is this so of Reimer. He is the one who developed the theory of the flying wing and subsequently of all the models and aircrafts built by the brothers. Walter, on the other hand is the engineer who tried to put into practice the several somewhat fantastic ideas of his brother. The clash of personalities resulted in a continuous quarrel and friction between the two brothers. Reimer was always developing new ideas which would increase the speed of the aircraft or improve its maneuverability; Walter on the other hand was tearing down the fantastic ideas of his brother by practical calculations and considerations.

3. The two men worked together up to and including the "Horten VIII" a flying wing intended to be a fighter plane powered with two Hirt engines (HM-60-R) with a performance of approximately 650 horsepower each. After the "Horten VIII" was finished, one of the usual and frequent quarrels separated the two brothers temporarily. Walter went to work alone on the "Horten IX", which is a fighter plane of the flying wing design, with practically no changes from the model VIII except for the engines.

After extensive tests, the Horten IX was accepted by the German Air Force as represented by Goering, who ordered immediate mass production. The first order went to Gothaer Waggon Fabrik, located in Gotha (Thuringia) in January 1945. Goering requested that ten planes be built immediately and that the entire factory was to concentrate and be converted to the production of the Horten IX. The firm in question received all the plans and designs of the ship. In spite of this explicit order, production of the Horten IX was never started. When US troops occupied the town of Gotha, the designs of the Horten IX were kept in hiding and not handed over to American Military authorities. The original designs in possession of the Horten brothers were hidden in a salt mine in Salzdettfurt, but the model tested by Eugen was destroyed in April 1945. The original designs were recovered from Salzdettfurt by British authorities in the summer of 1945.

The Horten brothers, together with Dr. Betz, Eugen and Dr. Stueper (the test pilot of the aerodynamic institute in Goettingen), were invited to go to England in the late summer of 1945 where they remained for approximately ninety days. They were interrogated and questioned about their ideas and were given several problems to work on. However Reimer was very unwilling to cooperate to any extent whatsoever, unless an immediate contract was offered to him and his brother.

In the spring of 1947 Walter Horten heard about the flying wing design in the United states by Northrop and decided to write Northrop for employment. He was answered in the summer of 1947 by a letter in which Northrop pointed out that he, himself, could not do anything to get him over to the States, but that he would welcome it very much if he could come to the United States and take up employment with the firm. He recommended that Walter should get in touch with

USAFE Headquarters in Wiesbaden in order to obtain necessary clearance.

As can be seen from the above, most of the Horten brothers work took place in Western Germany. According to our source, neither of the brothers ever had any contact with any representative of the Soviet Air Force or any other foreign power.

As far as the "flying saucer" is concerned, a number of people were contacted in order to verify whether or not any such design at any time was contemplated or existed in the files of any German air research institute.

The people contacted included the following:

Walter Horten, Fräulein von der Groeben former Secretary to Air Force General Udet, Guenter Heinrich former office for research of the High Command of the Air Force in Berlin, Professor Betz former chief of Aerodynamic Institute in Goettingen and Eugen. All the above mentioned people contacted independently and at different times are very insistent on the fact that to their knowledge and belief no such design ever existed nor was projected by any of the German air research institutions. While they agree that such a design would be highly practical and desirable, they do not know anything about its possible realization now or in the past.

Given the negative results from intense field intelligence work in Europe, it became increasingly clear that SIGN would be forced to rely on technical intelligence collections to determine the true nature of the unknown object's propulsion and their flight capabilities – including rates of acceleration, turning ratios, maximum speeds, operating altitudes as well as their reported ability to remain virtually motionless, hovering like some sort of helicopter. Beyond that, close range visual observations were critical to actual identification and radar tracking was vital in order to establish their flight paths and origins. SIGN needed concrete data if it was going to provide answers that would be acceptable to the Pentagon – and ultimately the public.

But it was 1948, the nation was still in transition from a war time economy, President Truman wanted to reduce military spending, the Air Force was establishing itself as a newly independent service and SIGN had to operate within the limitations of a post-war America. Specifically that meant within the capabilities of a virtually non-existent continental air defense. When SIGN generated a request to task Air Force alert aircraft to respond to unidentified object reports, the request was denied by Air Force Plans and Operations – based on both resources and priorities.[29] Operations felt that there were not enough available alert aircraft and that radar limitations meant that ground controlled interception would not be feasible. Even at the limited number of radar sites, few height finder radars were in place and there were very few ground controllers with experience in directing aerial intercepts. It would have been an exercise in futility, simply tying up both aircraft and personnel.[30]

The deeper reality – not just a denial of resource but a wholesale lack of them – was highly classified at the time. The true lack of air defense resources is illustrated by the fact that a major Air Force air defense exercise, planned for May, 1948 was cancelled at the last moment. The exercise had been organized to pit the new Strategic Air Command against a hopefully rejuvenated Air Defense Command. Mock attacks were planned against targets from Maine to Virginia. In preparation, the 505th Aircraft and Control Warning Group (the only such existing unit in the Air Force) had been ordered to the East Coast.

With no warning or explanation, the exercise was called off and the air warning group was relocated to the Pacific Northwest and Alaska. In addition, all fighter units were moved to alert status. We now know that those actions were taken in response to Lieutenant General George Stratemeyer's (Chief of the Air Defense Command) urgent order to augment Alaskan air defense and establish at least a minimal defense for strategic targets including the Boeing Aircraft plants outside Seattle and the Hanford atomic complex in eastern Washington State.[31] Putting even a limited effort in place meant shifting the few assets available all the way across the continent.

As 1948 continued, Generals Stratemeyer and other senior Air Force staff remained sincerely concerned that the Soviets were preparing to launch an air attack across the Arctic. Air intelligence estimates projected that the Soviets had some 300 long range Tu-4 (B-29 equivalent) bombers available for a first strike, it would be a one way mission for them but could eliminate the American atomic advantage by taking out the Hanford complex. America's Far Eastern Air Force commander had reported a series of strange incidents and incursions over Japan (an apparent follow-on to the mysterious radar track incursions of 1947) and a Joint Chiefs meeting chaired by Defense Secretary James Forrestal had taken place in an atmosphere of virtual crisis.

Such fears explain the priority given to project SIGN and the pressure it faced to quickly provide an explanation for the flying discs/saucers. If the Soviets were indeed conducting reconnaissance and/or ferret flights against overseas bases and atomic facilities, it could have been a critical warning that they had obtained intelligence on the true limitations of the American atomic capability. Given the rapidly emerging evidence of successful Russian atomic spying, that possibility seemed very real. If so, the Soviets might have well have been willing to take advantage of a window of opportunity for a surgical strike, leaving the United States at the mercy of the huge Soviet advantage in ground and tactical air forces.[32]

Denied interceptor aircraft for its work, SIGN was equally constrained in regard to its other main resource for technical intelligence collection – radar. It was only in June, 1948 that elements of a new Lashup air defense network began to go into limited operations. The surveillance radars were World War II era AN/CPS5 search units, working in combination with AN/TPS 10 height finders. Those radars set the standard for aerial object tracking in 1948 and had a normal range of 60 – 150 miles up to 20,000 feet altitude, with some reach to 30,000 feet and minimal performance above 35,000 feet. At low levels, around 1,000 feet, their range was 35 miles and their general performance in controlling interceptors was rated as poor.[33] In addition to the limitations of individual radars, there was no integrated communications network in place which would have allowed tracking objects for any real distance.

Without such a network, there was simply no chance of estimating the actual origins of unidentified aerial objects. They simply showed up as they happened to come within range of either the few surveillance radars, or more frequently the very range-limited ground control access radars associated with commercial or military airfields. Worse yet, tracks which suddenly disappeared could be equally interpreted as either the result of temporary atmospheric phenomena such as temperature inversions – or as indications of intelligent evasive maneuvers by objects making either rapid descents or ascents to take themselves outside the radar's capabilities.

Project SIGN needed technical data to come up with an intelligence estimate that would satisfy the Pentagon. Yet it was being forced to rely almost entirely on visual reports, with little to no confirmation from either ground based or airborne interceptor radar. The lack of gun camera photographs from interceptors left it to turn to images obtained from civilian photographers. One set of photographs which initially proved to be of considerable interest to the AMC staff had first appeared in the Arizona Republic on July 9, 1947, taken by William Rhodes of Phoenix, Arizona. Following publication in the newspaper, Rhodes had received multiple visits from intelligence officers and his photographs and negatives had been voluntarily turned over to the Army Air Force.

The photographs were especially interesting in that they appeared to show an object virtually identical to one particular description provided by Kenneth Arnold, taken from Arnold's early report of a formation of unidentified flying objects near Mount Rainer, Washington. Rhodes claimed to have taken two separate photographs at relatively close range (an estimated 2,000 feet at the closest) as the object circled near his home in Phoenix on July 7 1947.[34] Author Kevin Randle notes that Rhodes' photographs gained additional credibility because they were taken before public disclosure of Arnold's description and illustration of a "heel shaped" object being among the disc shaped objects he had observed, If Rhodes had faked the photographs he would only have had the newspaper descriptions of "flying saucers" as a reference.[35]

On February 19, 1948 an intelligence officer prepared a preliminary evaluation of the images which found them to be "of true photographic nature", consistent with the camera, film and other descriptive information provided by Rhodes. Several senior AMC personnel subsequently traveled to Phoenix to interview Rhodes and were apparently impressed in their initial contact. The object in the photographs reinforced the then current concept that the unidentified objects were indeed some type of flying wing. SIGN had even obtained a photo of a German "lenticular" model craft which appeared quite similar to both the Rhodes photo and the description that Kenneth Arnold was then providing for one of the craft he had sighted.[36]

An April progress report from SIGN contained the Rhodes photos alongside descriptions of German "lifting bodies". It seemed the Horton brother's work might not be the specific source of the flying saucers, but flying wing designs were certainly not unique to them and it is clear that as of April, 1948, AMC still felt that it was dealing with very real aerial technology, with actual objects with distinct shapes, flight characteristics and capabilities.

The longer term Air Force experience with the Rhodes photos proved less encouraging. In time the photos and the entire incident would be classified as a "possible hoax", not due to the images themselves but apparently due to Rhodes lack of verifiable academic credentials and his self-employment. Kevin Randle's research on the photographs has uncovered the handling of the photographs over time, the changing view of Rhodes and the eventual loss of his photographs by the Air Force.[37] In the end it appears that the photographs themselves, while legitimate, could not stand as independent proof – certainly not proof that was sufficient for formal scientific acceptance. The incident provided an early indication of just how difficult it was going to be to obtain evidence that would be sufficient to make the argument that flying saucers were actual craft, regardless of the issue of their origins.

The lack of corroborative technical data from radar or military photographic sources was compounded by issues of centralized control and reporting. Even though Air Intelligence had developed a very solid set of collections guidelines, a number of independent organizations were involved in investigating flying saucer reports. Some of the general Air Force investigative reports apparently never went through AMC at all, but were transmitted directly to the Pentagon Air Intelligence staff. Navy intelligence did its own investigations, not necessarily sharing them with either AMC or Air Intelligence.

The Air Material Command personnel did know of the large balloon trains being launched into the troposphere from White Sands (that program was a designated AMC project). Balloons from those launches generated sightings across New Mexico and into the Midwest. Yet whether the SIGN personnel were briefed on details of all the very high altitude balloon projects that were in progress or under development is unclear. It certainly seems that they were not aware of the details or launch schedule of the huge and highly visible Skyhook balloons being sent up in early launches by teams in Minnesota, teams working for the Navy in atmospheric research.

During 1948, the project SIGN team turned to a variety of channels to collect unidentified object reports. Air Force Intelligence officers stationed at the nearest air base to a sighting usually conducted the first investigations. Some field investigative work may also have been conducted by military units designated Air Intelligence Detachments 1, 2, and 3. These were classified units which had been established during World War II to recover Japanese Fu-Go balloons. After the war several of the teams were apparently kept in place in the event other countries might try to threaten North America with similar balloon warfare. Air Force Colonel Robert Friend is on record stating that the units were also used to conduct unidentified object investigations through 1953. In the often compartmentalized web of military reporting, their findings went to an intermediate office in Virginia and the investigative reports did not go directly to the SIGN project or to follow-on unidentified flying object projects at AMC.

Reports which did end up at the Air Materials Command were handed down to AMC technical groups and a SIGN investigator or staff person might then be dispatched to a sighting location if it was felt that further investigation was warranted. At times the FBI performed an initial interrogation of witnesses and it appears that portions of FBI reports made it into many of the SIGN case files. Other investigative reports were written up by field unit intelligence personnel closest to a given incident report. Those reports were filed locally and shared with whatever government agencies were felt to be most relevant to the incident.

The AMC group proactively solicited new reports from Air Force field level intelligence officers and spread a wide net among other services and agencies. In April, Colonel William Clingerman (AMC's Intelligence Analysis Division) submitted a request to news services for photos of the smoke cloud produced by a dramatic meteor fall in Kansas. The smoke cloud had started over Nebraska and ran south into Kansas, making a highly visible and unusual trail. There had been media concern that a spectacular exploding fireball over Kansas might have been a Russian "ranging shot" to the center of the country.[38] Clingerman's request noted that his command was engaged in an intelligence study involving the identification of meteors and meteorites. Dr. Lincoln LaPaz, of the University of New Mexico meteoritics institute investigated the Kansas meteor reports and was able to plot its course and eventually recover fragments; Dr. LaPaz's work in meteoritics continued to involve him with such reports, particularly in the "green fireball" sightings which began late in 1948.

The SIGN project faced not only limited technical resources but in its earliest months other issues began to surface. In retrospect they can be seen as early indications of a very fundamental intelligence problem. What soon became painfully obvious was that SIGN was able to produce little hard technical data beyond photographs and reports from experienced observers.[39] The Harmon Field incidents had produced multiple observations from Pan-American employees – of an object "flying at high velocity, paralleling the earth's surface and leaving a trail which appeared as a 'burning up' of the cloud formation" – the trail had been photographed and clearly supported the description of the path through the clouds. The problem was that whatever was making the path could not be determined from the photographs.

The Rhodes photograph, according to the initial experts consulted by the Air Force were "true photographic images and do not appear to be imperfection in the emulsion or imperfections in the lens".[40] When enlarged, they showed "a disk-like object with a round front and a square tail in plan form." But like other photographs which would follow, even those taken by military personnel, they were not sufficient to allow incontrovertible estimates of distance and size. Scientists reviewing the Rhodes photograph commented that it might be showing something as simple as windblown debris – there were no other witnesses to corroborate Rhode's descriptions. Time would prove that fake photographs could often be discerned through image analysis. Yet those determined to be legitimate still did not provide conclusive proof as to the nature of the object photographed – at least as far as the scientific community and the Pentagon was concerned.

Even with multiple, experienced witnesses, no incontestable proof of actual craft was forthcoming – even in reports from knowledgeable technical observers. In April of 1948 three scientists, working with the Watson Laboratories team at Holloman AFB in New Mexico, reported two irregular, round, white or golden objects, one-fifth the size of the full moon, estimated to be 100 feet in size. They were flying very high and very fast. One made three loops then rose and disappeared rapidly. The other flew in a fast arc to the West. The sighting time was approximately 30 seconds. The following day the same three individuals observed a large disk/sphere moving over the White Sands test range at high speed and an altitude estimated at 10,000 feet. It was in sight for some sixty seconds.

Civilians and scientists were not the only observers who had produced such detailed reports. An intelligence officer observed twelve oval-shaped disks flying in formation over Rapid City Air Base. The formation descended to approximately 10,000 feet before executing a turn and climbing rapidly out of sight. Another formation of some seven objects was described in a report out of Kirtland Air Force Base in Albuquerque. The objects circled before proceeding and appeared to be flying at very high speed.

Individuals from AMC/ project SIGN had personally investigated and interviewed individuals involved in the Harmon Field, Holloman/White Sands and Rhodes incidents, interviewing witnesses and verifying their reports to the extent possible. As a body of evidence the photographs and observations were all suggestive – but individually none of them absolutely confirmed that a foreign craft had been involved, much less provided information as to origins.

SIGN was going to have to produce data that would stand up to scientific confirmation as well as convince senior officers to put their careers on the line – endorsing not only the reality of foreign craft but acknowledging that they were operating unchallenged over American military facilities. And it was clearly facing academic skepticism by the scientific community. In January the prestigious Joint Research and Development Board had issued a public statement that flying saucers were purely optical illusions, magnified by a form of observer self-hypnosis. The statement also claimed that Army and Navy experts had already "closed their books" on the whole subject.[41]

Of course the final part of that statement was totally untrue, and there is no evidence that the board as a whole was involved with project SIGN or the actual AMC technical inquiry into the subject, especially as early as the date of their statement – January, 1948. The Board itself had been a major force during World War II, with its head – Vannevar Bush – pursuing a relatively conservative course of improving and optimizing known weapons technologies rather than pursuing grand leaps forward (the opposite of the path taken in German weapons development). The Board was in flux following the war, its impact being diluted by the emergence of individual service scientific advisory groups. The reason for the Board's going on record about flying discs at such and early point in time is unclear, it may simply have been part of widespread institutional effort to reassure the American public. Whatever the cause, such pronouncements from individuals with the reputation and scientific eminence of Bush were indicative of the challenge SIGN was likely to face in taking its work to the academic community for scientific scrutiny.

Yet incidents had occurred (and would occur during following years) that went beyond witness observations and photographs. Certain of those incidents dealt with actual "remains" and produced concrete technical data. In a handful of cases there was intense scientific study and even evidence of actual physical devices associated with unknown aerial objects.

On July 6, 1947 a daylight sighting was made of an aerial object disintegrating in flames near a Dow Chemical plant near Midland Michigan. Chemical analysis at Dow labs determined that the recovered remains included a "sizable amount of magnesium" as well as some thorite, which was determined to be moderately radioactive. The FBI performed a very basic inquiry on the incident but the Air Force was initially not involved. In depth research by Joel Carpenter has revealed the much more complex story involved with the Midland fireball. His work is described in an essay titled "The Midland Fireball: Dow Chemical's Early Involvement with UFO's".[42] Readers are encouraged to study the entire essay; the following provides a synopsis of Carpenter's research. It also highlights his discovery that the senior Dow analyst performing the initial materials study was a highly renowned chemical specialist, one of the key scientists responsible for much of Dow Chemical's technical success in new product development.

His name was Hans Grebe and he was considered by colleagues at Dow to be a genius; his early work led to such commercial success that Dow gave him broad leeway in his researches. Grebe established the companies' Physical Research Laboratory – producing an ongoing stream of valuable inventions including "Styrofoam" and a type of synthetic rubber highly valuable to the U.S. military during World War II. He also developed a process for extracting magnesium from seawater; it became Dow's main source for that metal. Grebe's role with the military was extensive; he served as an observer at the 1946 Operation Crossroads nuclear tests and worked closely with the Army Chemical Corps on highly classified chemical warfare projects. In 1948 he was named as chief technical advisor for the Army's Chemical Corps. In September of that year, while working at Edgewood Arsenal, Grebe requested an update on the aerial fireball investigation conducted at Dow Chemical.

After reviewing the recovered material and considering all the available data, – including the fact that the sand from the July "fall" had a different spectrum analysis than sand from the surrounding area — Grebe wrote a memorandum to his Army superior, expressing his feeling that the incident should be taken very seriously. There was every indication that the object might have been a "self-consuming missile, capable of producing considerable smoke and leaving behind only the minimum residue". The chemical composition of the residue could be interpreted to suggest that a battery and radio transmitter had been included with the device. In short, Grebe's note presented the possibility that the Midland fireball had been some sort of self-destructive device, not unlike those which had been discussed in certain of the Scandinavian reports.

Grebe pursued his concerns by personally visiting Colonel Holger Toftoy of Army Ordinance, the commander of Project Hermes. Hermes was the Army's comprehensive missile development program. The project was based at White Sands; it involving a variety of both ground tests and actual rocket launches, including both German V-2 missiles and a variety of derivatives based on the V-2 concept. In an October 18, 1948 conference with Toftoy, and officers from the Army Chemical Corps, Grebe reviewed the reported analysis of fragments picked up from a "flying saucer" (quoted from Toytoy's log) which had vanished with a brilliant flash with remains falling onto a sand bank near Midland, Michigan.

Soil materials recovered from the area included nuggets of "fairly pure" silver and some thorium. The thorium produced detectable radioactivity some ten times that of natural background and possibly could have been attributed to thorium coated filaments in electronic equipment although it appeared to be excessive for standard usages in such applications. There was also evidence of magnesium, which had been completely oxidized.

Grebe advanced the hypothesis that at least some of the reported flying discs/saucers might be small magnesium based devices capable of being propelled over several thousand miles but designed to be largely self-destructive. The traces of silver and thorium might have been the remains of a control system. Grebe's concept may well have been based in his wartime work for Dow, which had involved building a special, shock resistant housing for the highly miniaturized and ruggedized vacuum tubes which were part of the Proximity Fuse developed by the United States, one of the most closely guarded secrets of the war.

Such devices were capable of surviving acceleration of some several thousand g's (the gravitational constant), orders of magnitude beyond standard electronic devices. Generally speaking, Grebe envisioned something very much like a small artillery shell, but one with an aerodynamic design and internal electronics which would allow some degree of flight at the end of its trajectory.

His concept is especially interesting given that two years later, during a 1949 conference on "green fireballs" at Los Alamos, Dr. Edward Teller would mention the possibility that the reported fireballs could be generated by the final stage of a long range artillery device, fired from the Soviet Union. In side comments, Dr. Teller mentioned that the best answer he could come up with was a multistage shell fired from what he referred to as a "pencil gun".[43] During World War II the Germans had experimented with such weapons and actually developed "multi-chamber" guns using rocket assisted shells – as well as special designs based on the "Peenemunde Arrow Shell"[44] It seems that either one of America's most prominent physical scientists, Dr. Teller, had independently come to the same speculation as Dr. Grebe – or that Grebe's hypothesis had been very quietly circulated to some key people within the American scientific/defense community.

During the White Sands meeting with Toftoy, there was agreement to generate a memo to a Bureau of Standards group, asking them to investigate mechanisms which could propel devices of the general type envisioned by Dr. Grebe. That group, essentially hidden within the standards agency, had worked closely with the Army on highly secret war time projects – including an American television-guided bomb, a passive radar homing glide bomb and a radar guided anti-ship glide bomb. The Bureau's engineers had invented a process for "painting" electrical circuits, a forerunner to modern day printed circuits.

Carpenter reports being unable to find any details confirming that the proposed approach to the special Standards group actually occurred. However, there is evidence that the Dow/Michigan incident was known to the Air Force during its initial inquiries into the flying discs/saucers. On December 2, 1947 General Hoyt Vandenberg (Air Force Chief of Staff) had inquired of AMC in regard to their investigation of the Midland, Michigan fireball. Carpenter notes that on December 21, AMC responded that its personnel had no details on the incident and requested copies from the Chief of Staff's office. Unfortunately there is no further evidence that AMC actually pursued an investigation into the actual physical remains from the incident.

Surprisingly, we now know that the Midland, Michigan debris study was not unique. In November, 1947 Director Hoover had sent a note to the Air Force's Director of Special Investigations. It related details about another July, 1947 incident, occurring only two days before the Midland, Michigan "fall". In this second incident, hot metal fragments which had apparently fallen from the sky landed near West Ridge, New Hampshire. Fragments had been obtained when witnesses observed wisps of flame and smoke rising from a circular area, as well as individually burning patches of grass. The smoke and flame appeared to have been caused by extremely hot debris, from an object which had exploded in the air, scattering material across a circle at least two hundred feet in diameter.

The main witness turned over several fragments of debris to Professor Rentges of MIT; he conducted a detailed analysis using MIT laboratory facilities. An FBI document dated July 29, 1947 notes the analysis and comments that the incident was not widely known since few instructors remained on campus during the summer session. After study, Rentges determined that the metal had been subjected to "terrific heat"; he had seen similar effects in the linings of German V-2 missile rocket engines during a stint at Army firing range at White Sands, New Mexico.

Four of the fragments, when pieced together, appeared to have been part of a hollow cylinder some 8 inches in diameter and with a wall thickness of three-sixteenths of an inch. The material itself was ordinary cast iron but it had been subjected to a very high degree of heat. The debris seemed to be a portion of thin-wall cylinder 8 inches in diameter and Reintjes described it as resembling V-2 engine linings he had seen at White Sands.[45]

These two 1947 materials studies become even more interesting when referenced to a comment Joel Carpenter makes in his study of the Midland Fireball case. He notes that in 1952, the Bureau of Standards was involved with a study of material which had reportedly fallen near Washington D.C. during a wave of UFO sightings there. Commander Alvin Moore, of the U.S. Navy, had recovered the fragments and turned them over to the National Bureau of Standards for analysis. The testing revealed that the fragment was from an artificially produced artifact, composed primarily of magnesium (filled with millions of microscopic iron particles).

The scientists reported that the fragments appeared to have been a section of a cylinder, some 10.4 inches in diameter. Commander Moore sent the report to Captain Edward Ruppelt (in 1952 in charge of the Air Force Project BLUE BOOK UFO investigation) who forwarded it to the Battelle Memorial Institute. At that point in time Battelle was beginning a contract study of UFO reports for the Air Force. It appears that the fragments received only cursory attention from Battelle, perhaps understandably since the Battelle study was focused on other areas than physical evidence.[46]

Why Ruppelt appears not to have pursued the details of the actual recovery of the material or why it allegedly came from a Navy source is hard to fathom – especially since he himself was so involved with the Washington D.C. UFO incidents. It is equally hard to understand why he appears to have been so casual in regard to what would have been hard physical evidence of an anomalous nature.

Even in isolation the recovery of an actual fragment in 1952 would seem to have been extremely important, but when combined with its similarity to both the Midland/Grebe study and the MIT incident/study it seems of considerable importance. The remarks about small guided missiles and self-destructive designs again bring to mind the explosions and fragments observed during the 1946 wave of undefined aerial objects over Scandinavia. It seems at least suggestive that we find three independent fragment studies that appear to support the possibility of "self-destructive" artificial devices as a source for at least some of the unconventional object reports. Carpenter's research also reveals that anomalous physical materials associated with unidentified aerial objects were actually being recovered and studied during 1947 – without seemingly making any real impression on the Air Force unidentified object inquiry, even when brought to AMC's attention by the Air Force Chief of Staff.

In the context of national security it's difficult to understand the apparent lack of follow up in regard to the two 1947 incidents which could have involved some sort of self-destroying missile. Air Force intelligence seems to have had no proactive involvement with either of those incidents, which could have indicated a true security issue – leaving us to speculate about the equal lack of interest in a SIGN era file on the New Hampshire / MIT investigation which notes that the material recovered in New Hampshire was determined to contain "metallic fragments similar to the lining of V-2 bombs"?[47]

Military intelligence is devoted to identifying and characterizing threats, as well as determining enemy capabilities and intentions. The Air Force had initiated Project SIGN to determine if the flying discs/flying saucers were real devices operated by foreign powers. Beyond that the single most important question was whether or not they indicated that the Soviets were performing either reconnaissance or targeting of American military assets in preparation for a hostilities.

The alternative was that they were advanced aircraft/missiles being used in some type of Russian psychological warfare effort, something similar to that which the Central Intelligence Group found to have occurred over Scandinavia in 1946. SIGN had been assigned an extremely high action priority, indicating the Pentagon wanted answers and it wanted them quickly. Was it the Russians, was it advanced technology, and were the Soviets actually engaged in operations over American overseas bases or over the continental United States – Yes or No? AMC and Project SIGN had been given a significant priority, and with priorities come expectations.

Chapter 6 Endnotes

1. Jan Aldrich, "Secret Twining Letter – The reported phenomena are real", *Project 1947* http://www.nicap.org/twining_letter.htm

2. Brad Sparks, *List of Projects and BLUE BOOK Chiefs, Work in Progress* (Version 1.26, Jan. 31, 2016), Compiled by Brad Sparks © 2001-2016, NICAP http://www.nicap.org/bb/BB_Unknowns.pdf

3. AMC Opinion Concerning *Flying Discs,* September 27, 1947 http://www.nicap.org/twining_letter.htm

4. Brad Steiger, *Project BLUE BOOK*, Ballentine, New York, 1976, copy of Hynek Incident #17 report, 34-36. As part of its investigation of the Arnold sighting, AMC contracted with an Astronomy professor, Dr. J. Allan Hynek to evaluate Aronold's (and other) sightings. Hynek's study took into consideration the structural detail reported by Arnold and highlighted the several points in regard to the eyes capability for resolving such detail. His analysis led him to conclude that Arnold had mis-estimated the distance of the objects and that to show the details Arnold had recorded, the objects could have been no more than six miles away from him. Hynek's adjusted distance led him to calculate an actual airspeed for the objects of approximately 400 miles per hour, definitely subsonic.

5. Walter Boyne, *Beyond the Wild Blue*, St Martins, New York, 1998, 368-372. The proposal for a "transonic" aircraft had first been made in March of 1944 by the National Aeronautical Council and in July of that year the first US rocket plane, the Northrop MX-324 had made its initial flight. Also in July, 1944 the first wrecked but captured German "buzz bomb" had been delivered to Wright field and within 17 days Ford motor company had completed a copy of its pulse jet motor.

6. Jim Winchester, *Concept Aircraft: Prototypes, X-Planes and Experimental Aircraft*, Thunder Bay Press, 2005, 30-35

7. Graham M. Simons, *Northrup Flying Wings*, Pen and Sword Books, London, England, 2012, 45

8. Ibid, 55-64

9. Ted Coleman, *Jack Northrop and the Flying Wing*, Paragon House, NY. 1988, 121-129. The six jet Northrup XB-35 flying wing first flew in June, 1946 and would later set both speed and distance records; in 1948 and 1949 it cruised coast to coast across the United States at 511 mph. During a test flight from the West Coast, the flying wing returned across radar test stations and was never detected; its visual profile was such that indeed it could only be seen directly

overhead in virtually its full cross section. Later tests confirmed that the radars of the period simply could not see it.

10. X-47B fact sheet, Northrup Grumman, 2015 http://www.northropgrumman.com/capabilities/x47bucas/documents/ucas-d_data_sheet.pdf

11. Richard Rhodes, *Dark Sun*, 227-228 One commentator reports that the US Navy was already discussing the use of earth satellites and LeMay did not want the Navy to supersede the Air Force in any such endeavor. Later, LeMay became very negative in regards discussion of satellites, not even permitting them to be discussed for planning purposes – until the Soviet launch of Sputnik forced him to change that position.

12. Patent for the Lockheed design http://simszone.org/area-bebas-hambatan/lockheed-ufo-patent-in-1953/ A craft with many of the design and performance characteristics noted in the Lockheed patent was put into development in the Air Forces Project Y2; Silver Bug. That effort revealed a number of fundamental issues with the concept and after a number of years the project was discontinued. http://www.project1947.com/fig/sb/head3.htm

13. Robert Kilmarx, *A History of Soviet Air Power*, 228

14. Ibid, 214-216

15. Jim Winchester, *Concept Aircraft, Prototypes, X-Planes and Experimental Aircraft*, Grange Books PLC, 2005.

16. Michael Swords and Robert Powell, *UFO's and Government; A Historical Inquiry*, 39

17. This collection initiative was ordered by General Schulgen of the Air Intelligence Requirements Directorate. Schulgen and the Directorate reported to General Cabell, head of the USAF Directorate of Intelligence.

18. Michael Swords and Robert Powell, *UFO's and Government; A Historical Inquiry*, Anomalist Books, San Antonio, 2012, 486-491

19. In some respects, McDonald's comment might seem somewhat controversial since there had been a number of observations at over and the skies around the Muroc air development base and the White Sands rocket and missile test facility, as well as in the area of the giant Seattle and Los Angeles aircraft manufacturing complexes. Still, in terms of true American strategic targets it is important to note that the Air Force considered those to specifically include the Hanford works (the first plutonium reactor complex), the Oak Ridge, Tennessee, atomic facility and the Los Alamos atomic weapon assembly plants as well as a series of underground atomic weapons storage facilities just going into construction in 1947 – the first of those facilities would

become operational at the Manzano mountains outside Albuquerque, New Mexico (adjacent to Kirtland AFB) and in the tunnel system in Killeen base in Texas. In 1947, no weapons were actually stored at Roswell AFB, the base for the only atomic weapon capable B-29 squadron. The General's observation may also include the fact that the Air Force's listing of flying disc sightings was extremely limited in regard to the totals reported in the media. On the other hand, there is no indication that either Project SIGN or the Pentagon Intelligence groups actively solicited, collected or studied civilian/professional or military staff observations at the strategic atomic facilities during 1947.

20. Michael Swords and Robert Powell, *UFO's and Government; A Historical Inquiry*, Anomalist Books, San Antonio, Texas, 2012, "Air Intelligence Guide for Alleged "Flying Saucer" Type Aircraft", 480-484

21. Jan L. Aldrich, Project 1947, *1949 UFO DOCUMENTS*, Report by the Director of Intelligence, USAF to the Joint Intelligence Committee on Unidentified Aerial Objects http://www.project1947.com/fig/jic.htm

22. Op cit.

23. Richard Rhodes, *Dark Sun*, 321. The US was continuously revising and updating its war plans. In early 1948, BROILER was proposed in March, modified to FROLIC and finally approved as HALFMOON in May. An Air Force atomic annex to the plans included dropping 50 atomic bombs (the total arsenal) on some 20 Russian cities, paralyzing Soviet industry but failing to stop the Russians from overrunning Europe.

24. Ibid, 320-321

25. Wolfgang W.E. Samuel, *Watson's Whizzers; Operation Lusty and the Race for NAZI Aviation Technology*, University Press of Mississippi, 2004, 125-127; 366-368; 401-410 and 423. One of the general points of contention between AMC staff and Colonel Watson at Pentagon Air Estimates may have been a disagreement on AMC's initiative in obtaining both a German technology data collection and a staff of German engineers (something advocated and supported by AMC staff at Dayton). In his role with General Eisenhower's Scientific Advisory Group at the close of WWII, Watson had played a key role in leading technology exploitation field teams. However, he reportedly was adamantly opposed to bringing German scientists to the United States, feeling that their advanced expertise would somehow stifle American developments already in progress. Clearly the Germans were much more advanced and had superior facilities (such as supersonic wind tunnels), being perhaps two to four years ahead in supersonics alone. The Scientific Advisory Group had been working extensively with personnel from major aircraft and scientific corporations including Lockheed, Boeing, Curtis-Wright, Bell, GE, Sperry and Bendix. Apparently the opinion has been expressed that "the return of a number of imminent German scientists may jeopardize their own professional status." Watson and Putt had both been

stationed at AMC immediately following the war, building a German intelligence collection with over 1,000 tons of documents. However, the AMC technical intelligence staff took the initiative in lobbying to bring in actual German scientists. Watson and Putt's opposition slowed down that process initially but by March of 1947 some 100 Germans were working at facilities across Wright Field at AMC.

26. Hall and Connors, *Alfred Loedding and the Great Flying Saucer Wave of 1947*, 1998, Chapter Six.

27. Michael Swords and Robert Powell, *UFO's and Government / A Historical Inquiry*, 52

28. Horton (sic) Brothers (Flying Saucers), S-2 Branch, Headquarters Berlin Command, Office of Military Government for Germany (US), December 16, 1947 http://ufologie.patrickgross.org/aircraft/horten.htm

29. Letter from Hq AMC, Wright-Patterson Air Force Base, Dayton, Ohio

30. TO: Commanding General, Air Defense Command, Mitchel AF Base, Mitchel Field, New York NOV 30 1948 http://www.nicap.org/waves/1948amcreqradar.htm

31. Anderson memoranda http://www.project1947.com/fig/anderson.htm

32. *The Emerging Shield: The Air Force and the Evolution of Continental Air Defense 1945-1960*, Kenneth Schaffel, 77-78

33. In the summer of 1948, when the Russians blockaded Berlin from ground access, the Soviets had 400,000 troops available in Europe; the United States had 60,000.

34. *The Emerging Shield: The Air Force and the Evolution of Continental Air Defense*, 1940-1960, Kenneth Schaffel, 45-48

35. Memorandum for the officer in charge, "Investigation of Flying Discs", September 2, 1947 http://www.theufochronicles.com/2010/06/counter-intelligence-report-photographs.html

36. Kevin D. Randle, *The Government UFO Files; The Conspiracy of Cover Up*, Visible Ink Press, Detroit, Michigan, 2014, 59-60

37. Michael Swords and Robert Powell, *UFO's and Government / A Historical Inquiry*, 53-54

38. Kevin Randle, Alien Mysteries, *Conspiracies and Cover-ups*, Visible Ink Press, Canton, Michigan, 2013, 84-88

39. http://www.nicap.org/papers/swords_Sign_EOTS.htm

40. *Analysis of Flying Object Incidents in the U.S.*, Top Secret Directorate of Intelligence, Headquarters of the United States Air Force, *Top Secret*, April 28, 1959, 8-12 http://www.project1947.com/fig/1948air.htm

41. Daniel Wilson, Phoenix Arizona Rhodes photographs, document collection, NICAP http://www.nicap.org/docs/470707phoenix_docs1-27.pdf

42. Michael Swords and Robert Powell, *UFO's and Government / A Historical Inquiry*, 52-53

43. Joel Carpenter, *The Midland Fireball*: "Dow Chemical's Early Involvement with UFO's" Carpenter, http://www.project1947.com/articles/dow.htm

44. *Sign Oral History Project* interview with Doyle Rees, Col. USAF retired Thomas Tulian, Copyright © 1999 AFS/Dialogue Productions LLC, 2545 Pillsbury Ave. S., Minneapolis, MN 55404. http://www.project1947.com/shg/sohp/dreesint.html

45. Ian Hogg and J.B. King, *German and Allied Secret Weapons of WWII*, Chartwell Books, 1976, 12-22

46. Joel Carpenter, *Guided Missiles and UFOs: A Tangle of Fear – 1937-53 – Part Three* http://www.project1947.com/gr/grchron3.htm

47. Kevin Randle, *When UFO's Fall From the Sky*, New Page Books, 2010, 92-93. It should be noted that in 1960, Elroy John Center, formerly a research scientist at Battelle, privately commented that while at Battelle he had analyzed material from a fallen UFO. Some researchers have speculated that his remark related to material ("memory metal") from the Roswell crash but it seems probable that Center was actually speaking of the Washington DC material which was officially given to Battelle for study, especially since it has been shown that Center worked on that study in the mid-1950's.

48. Michael Swords and Robert Powell, "UFO's and Government/A Historical Inquiry", *57*

Chapter 7

Failure to Identify

In this chapter

- Anomalous object profiles and signatures remain constant from 1945-1948.

- Interplanetary origins scenario for flying discs proposed by technical staff from Project SIGN.

- Air Intelligence explores the possibility that unidentified objects may be experimental space ships or tests of long range missiles launched by a foreign power.

- Project SIGN chided for failure to identify or determine origin of the flying discs in the face of "inescapable evidence" of unknown objects being sighted.

- Pentagon Air Intelligence tasked with conducting its own alternative study of flying discs/saucers.

- Press challenges are met by a new Air Force strategy to focus on sightings which have been identified and provide responses illustrating misidentification of conventional aircraft and natural atmospheric/astronomical phenomena.

- Pentagon Air Intelligence report – supported by the Office of Naval Intelligence – concludes that a core of credible sightings support the contention that "some type of flying object" has been observed but offers no identification or explanation for their appearance.

It is hard to overstate the level of air defense concern under which Project SIGN was operating. In March, 1948 Air Intelligence warned that the Soviets were preparing a surprise attack and Air Force Chief of Staff, General "Tooey" Spaatz, ordered the Air Defense Command to operate its northwestern radar sites around the clock – only to find that there were not sufficient personnel to do so. The Air Force was all too aware that it possessed no national early warning network – its Project Supremacy proposal

(November, 1947) would have positioned over 400 radar sites in Alaska and the continental United States, with 18 control centers to consolidate warning data and deploy interceptors which would then be guided to final engagements by the individual radar sites.[1]

With that project stranded in national budgetary battles it had stationed a small number of World War II radars in Albuquerque, New Mexico and in another dozen sites in the Northeast. That "Lashup" radar deployment could do little more than provide a minimal warning against Soviet aircraft approaching the vital northeastern corridor over the polar routes.[2] When the Supremacy proposal eventually foundered, the Air Force turned to a much more limited plan – for some 75 radar sites, designated as the "permanent network". That proposal found little more acceptance than Supremacy and the plan faded away; Secretary of Defense Louis Johnson kept it out of both the fiscal year 1949 and 1950 budgets.

AMC and the SIGN staff were very much aware of the air defense aspect of their mission; they addressed that in an initial response to Air Intelligence Director Charles Cabell in April of 1948. The report made positive reference to actual objects being involved in the flying disc/saucer sightings; objects with well-defined shapes, patterns of flight and advanced propulsion.[3] Physically the craft appeared to be disc shaped, in the lenticular or flying wing class of aircraft, similar to developments by the Horton brothers in Germany or the Northup aircraft in the United States; Northrup flying wing aircraft were discussed and pictured in the first SIGN paper.

The initial SIGN response also noted that "cigar, or pencil-shaped objects have been sighted in fewer numbers…..a few accounts tell of the disks having a rough cigar-shape when viewed while maneuvering…therefore is possible that a single type of object may be involved in all sightings, and differences in description may result from viewing the objects at various angles and under differing conditions of visibility."

The early SIGN assessment confirms that the descriptions of the most anomalous and truly unconventional aerial objects reported in 1947 remained quite consistent. The most close range and credible observations are virtually identical with the anomalous object profiles we summarized from the World War II observations as well as in a handful of incidents from 1946. In terms of the signature/profile of unconventional physical objects, the commonality in observations is evident in these first years – and we will find it continuing during 1948 and over the following two decades.

As discussed in the preceding chapter, early hopes for a quick solution to the flying disc problem had proved to be overly optimistic. First the hope for a quick identification of Soviet origins had failed to come about and then efforts at technical collections were constrained by available Air Force resources. And for some reason actual physical evidence and the technical data/evaluations from its scientific analysis appear not to have made any real impact on the AMC technical investigators. Instead SIGN became largely focused on observational reports. Certain of those incidents were sufficiently anomalous to move some AMC staff members beyond the scenario of unconventional Soviet aircraft and rocket adaptations to speculation on another – much more sensational – possibility as to the origins of the unknown objects.

Anecdotal reports suggest – with later confirmation from future Air Force UFO program head Edward Ruppelt – that by the end of summer, 1948, certain staff members at SIGN were proposing an interplanetary origin for some of the most credible reports. Ruppelt described a document he had seen during his own tenure with the later *BLUE BOOK* investigation, circa 1952/53. His speculation was that the document had been part of a preliminary finding that the craft were not of earthly origin. He also felt that such an assessment could have been heavily influenced by the intensive SIGN investigation of the Chiles-Whitted aircrew sighting of a very high speed, cylindrical craft – described as having lighted windows down its length.[4]

The Chiles-Whitted sighting provided a description of an object closely matching the public conception of a "rocket ship"; it also resonated with the initial military development work on very long range ballistic rockets - the first tests of such a device were underway at White Sands in the summer of 1948. The possibility that certain unidentified aerial objects might be advanced rocket propelled craft may have helped sway several of the SIGN team members towards the interplanetary conclusion.

Such thoughts were not unique to the personnel at Project SIGN. At Air Intelligence, Major General Cabell had requested a study by the RAND consulting group on space ship propulsion. In his request to RAND, Cabell stated that Air Intelligence was considering whether certain sightings could be due to experimental spaceships, or test vehicles of a foreign power. He also noted that Intelligence felt it was probable if the objects were rocket ships that they were from earth rather than being interplanetary. Cabell was looking for specific parameters which could assist his intelligence collections staff in profiling sightings against space rockets or long range missiles.

In November, Brigadier General Donald Putt, Director of Air Force R&D also requested that RAND provide special design and performance characteristics of such devices and RAND's official report would eventually be included as an appendix in a later Air Force UFO report (Project GRUDGE). RAND's response pointed out that long range rockets would only generate massive rocket flame trails during their launch/boost stage, making them a poor candidate for pilot sightings over the continental United States.

In retrospect, and with far more data now available, a strong case can be made that the observations in the Chiles-Whitted incident are a good match for the passage of a nighttime bolide meteor. Decades long studies of such fireballs - supplemented with real time digital video recordings only possible within the last decade – emphasize the point that very short duration sightings of nighttime bright lights can be very misleading as to both size and distance. Beyond that, the video records show a number of actual incidents where meteor observations come very close to matching the exact description provided by the pilots in the Chiles-Whitted sighting. Readers are referred to Kevin Randle's analysis of the bolide explanation and the related images in his blog post at "A Different Perspective"[5]

In his own book, Ruppelt cited rumors still circulating during his tenure that an interplanetary scenario developed by SIGN had gone all the way to Air Force Chief of Staff Hoyt Vandenberg, who had ordered it destroyed. Extensive research over a number of years has been unable to confirm that speculation – including the idea that Vandenberg ordered the actual destruction of a formal SIGN estimate of the situation. In retrospect it appears that what Ruppelt had seen was a preliminary assessment prepared by certain members of the SIGN technical team. The paper may have been circulated among their contacts at the Pentagon to "test the waters" in regard to higher headquarters' acceptance of such a sensational finding.

Such a paper could have been shown to sympathetic intelligence contacts in the Pentagon, such as Lt. Colonel Garrett in the Collections branch. Collections would likely have been heavily involved along with SIGN in the Chiles-Witted study. The scenario of an interplanetary origins working paper being circulated for comment within Air Intelligence is reinforced by the research of Hall and Connors. They report that in early August, individuals within the SIGN project, who were leaning towards an extraterrestrial source for at least some of the objects being sighted, had reached the tentative conclusion that certain sightings - including the Chiles-Whitted incident - were interplanetary in origin.[6]

Hall and Connors describe a classified document, created under Alfred Loedding's authorship, which traced the history of unidentified objects back through the ghost rocket sightings of 1946. They note that SIGN team members Loedding, Deyarmond and Truettner made a special trip to the Pentagon in support of an interplanetary estimate.[7] Reportedly the Loedding document concluded by recommending that the military move into a state of alert. It is unknown whether AMC Commanding General Joseph McNarney was aware of the document and also unclear whether or not AMC intelligence chief Colonel Howard McCoy specifically endorsed such an assessment at that point in time. McCoy's later communications to the Pentagon certainly do not suggest that. In his own correspondence he simply mentioned that certain of his staff had considered the possibility of interplanetary origins.

It is understandable that a copy of such a working paper could have remained in Pentagon files to be viewed by Ruppelt and Pentagon public information officer Major Dewey Fournet as late as 1952. The interplanetary origins premise undoubtedly generated considerable reaction among various individuals and groups within Air Intelligence but it would have been extremely difficult to support at higher levels of command without solid technical corroboration. Who saw that document, who commented on it and whether or not it ever made it to Vandenberg will remain a matter of debate - what is known is that several of the AMC personnel who apparently supported that view did not continue with the Air Force flying saucer/disc study when it when it was reorganized and renamed early in 1949.

What is absolutely certain is that something prompted Major General Cabell, Director of Air Force Intelligence to issue his own August directive for a separate Pentagon Air Intelligence study of flying discs/flying saucers. Whether or not that directive was prompted by the material being circulated by the SIGN personnel or by other factors, by August 1948 the Air Force had been dealing with the subject for over a year and to that point no positive identification was in hand. Specifically, AMC/SIGN had not been able to provide absolute proof that the objects were physical craft, much less tie them to the Soviet Union. In response to Cabell's directive, Pentagon Intelligence, in conjunction with the Navy, moved to prepare its own estimate and did so within a matter of months – a draft was submitted to Cabell's office during November.

While Pentagon Air Intelligence was responding to Cabell, apparently his office received no progress reports from either SIGN or AMC. On November 3, 1948 Cabell sent a short and direct letter to the Commanding General of AMC, on the subject of "Flying Object Incidents in the United States". It began with a reminder that AMC had been directed to initiate a study of the subject at the end of December, 1947. The letter reaffirmed the point that it was "inescapable" that some type of flying object had been observed – and that no identification or knowledge of origin had yet been provided to Air Force headquarters. The point was made that efforts must be increased, conclusive evidence must be obtained – evidence was required in order to implement appropriate national defense measures. The letter's final point was that the press was in the process of taking matters into their own hands and the Air Force clearly needed something to share with them – "silence on our part will not long be acceptable."[8]

In reading the letter from Cabell's office to the AMC commander, it seems clear that the Director of Intelligence was not happy with the lack of progress from AMC on the SIGN project; that impression is reinforced by the fact that the letter was not copied to the head of SIGN and that it was personally signed by Cabell himself. That sort of communication clearly demanded a response and on November 8, Colonel McCoy replied (for AMC and SIGN as well) with a detailed synopsis of the work conducted to date.[9] It was a comprehensive reply, as would be expected given Cabell's remarks – but it provided nothing concrete on either identification or origins.

What McCoy did do was to affirm that there were a "certain number of reports for which no reasonable everyday explanation is available" and state that no physical evidence had been obtained. The only conclusion reached to that point was that the objects were not domestic. It was in this communication that McCoy noted that his staff had considered the possibility that the objects were "vehicles from another planet" but that there was "no tangible evidence" to support such a possibility.

McCoy's letter also stated that a full report on the SIGN study was in preparation and would shortly be available; however with no physical evidence in hand it was going to be impossible to provide conclusive evidence that the objects were real and not simply misidentifications.

McCoy also offered the opinion that the press should not be given information on unidentifiable/unknown objects but rather that they be informed in regard to how many of the incidents had been identified (balloons, planets, stars, etc.). That suggested approach appears to have taken hold at headquarters and would become the ongoing Air Force mantra with the press – talk about what we have identified, stress the misidentifications and close with the point that investigations are still in process to determine reasonable explanations for the rest.

With McCoy's response in hand but an official estimate still pending from AMC/SIGN, on December 10, Cabell received the official Pentagon Air Intelligence analysis which he had requested - with its conclusions supported by both the staffs of the Air Force Directorate of Intelligence and the Office of Naval Intelligence.[10] The Air Intelligence study was extensive, containing a number of appendices. Upon circulation and review it (rather than the eventual AMC/SIGN estimate) would provide the primary support for the official Air Force assessment of the flying saucer phenomena.[11]

Perhaps surprisingly, a close reading of the report reveals that Air Intelligence maintained that there was a core of credible sightings of unknown and unconventional flying objects – "The frequency of reported incidents, the similarity in many of the characteristics attributed to the observed objects and the quality of observers considered as a whole, support the contention that some type of flying object has been observed. Approximately 210 incidents have been reported. Among the observers reporting on such incidents are trained and experienced U.S. Weather Bureau personnel, USAF rated officers, experienced civilian pilots, technicians associated with various research projects and technicians employed by commercial airlines."

In particular the study commented that the very early reports from the U.S. Weather Bureau observers were compelling – "During observations of weather balloons at the Richmond Bureau, one well trained observer has sighted strange metallic disks on three occasions and another observer has sighted a similar object on one occasion. The last observation of unidentified objects was in April, 1947. On all four occasions the weather balloon and the unidentified objects were in view through the theodolite. These observations at the Richmond Bureau occurred several months before publicity on the flying saucers appeared in a U.S. newspaper." The report also pointed out that the descriptions of the flying objects fell into three configurations – disk shaped, cigar shaped and balls – but that differences in visibility and observer angles of sight left open the possibility that a single type rather than three different types of object might be involved. In addition to the weather team observations, the report cited certain highly credible 1947 observations:

> On 1 July 1947, twelve disks were reported over the Rapid City Air Base by Major Hammer. These disks were oval-shaped, about 100 feet long, flying at a speed estimated to be in excess of 500 mph. Descending from 10,000 feet, these disks made a 30-degree to 40-degree climbing turn accelerating very rapidly until out of sight.

On 4 August 1947 -, the pilot and co-pilot of a DC-3, in flight near Bethel, Alaska, reported a flying disk larger than their aircraft. This disk crossed their path at about 1,000 feet and they turned to give chase. The DC-3 was flying at 170 mph, but the disk flew out of sight in four minutes.

On 16 September 1947, a radar at Fukuoka, Japan, picked up a target at 89 miles distance and trailed it to 19 miles, where it faded. Its speed was 840-900 mph. The speed measurement, made by a good crew through a full 70-mile track, was believed accurate.

On 12 November 1947, two flying disks trailing jet-like streams of fire were reportedly sighted from the bridge of the tanker Ticonderoga, according to the ship's second officer. The Ticonderoga was 20 miles off the Oregon shore. This officer said the disks were in sight 45 seconds, moving at a speed estimated at 700-900 mph, traveling in a curving, long, low arc.

The Air Intelligence paper also maintained a focus on possible Soviet involvement, with a mention of hypothetical tactics and the possible reasons for the Soviet use of unconventional aircraft over the United States. The report concluded with the view that "some type of flying object has been observed over the U.S. seems to be substantiated. It is not known at this time whether these observations are misidentifications of domestically launched devices, natural phenomena, or foreign unconventional aircraft." However since nothing concrete could be said in terms of identification, the report declared it "impossible to make any reliable explanation for their appearance over the U.S. or the tactics which they may employ if the objects observed include any foreign developments in aeronautical fields."

In short, at the end of the end of 1948, neither AMC/Project SIGN nor the Pentagon's Directorate of Air Intelligence were able to provide explanations – much less positive identification - for a number of highly credible observations of anomalous aerial objects. The best they could do was verify that "some type of flying object has been observed." The level of Air Force consensus extended only to the point that something real was being seen - but whatever the objects were, it was impossible to positively identify them, much less intercept and deal with them. The Air Force simply did not have a good answer (or a reassuring one) for the American public. A statement confirming that something was being observed (and might be observing us), that it could not be identified, and that its source and intent was not known, was definitely not something to hand out to the press.

And the press remained very interested in the subject of unidentified flying objects apparently moving at will over the United States. In the late fall of 1948, the Saturday Evening Post had launched development of a major article on flying disc incidents and was asking for Air Force at the Pentagon level to become involved with the article – and to provide some answers for the public. That media pressure had been reflected in Cabell's November letter to McCoy in regard to obtaining a position to be shared with the press. Yet McCoy's reply had not focused on "unidentified objects"; he preferred to focus on reports which had produced actual identification's.

General McCoy was very specific about that in his communications with Major General Cabell - "It is not considered advisable to present to the press information on those objects which we cannot yet identify or about which we cannot present any reasonable conclusions. In the event that they insist on some kind of a statement, it is suggested that they be informed that many of the objects sighted have been identified as weather balloons or astral bodies, and that investigation is being pursued to determine reasonable explanations for the others."[12]

General Cabell seems to have concurred with Colonel McCoy's suggestion. That comes across in his staff's own media recommendations, drafted for forwarding to Defense Secretary Forrestal:[13]

"The U.S. Air Force collects and evaluates all information on flying saucers. A special project has been in progress since early 1948 wherein a detailed, technical analysis on all data is being made to ascertain origin and identification of "flying saucers." Meanwhile the Directorate of Intelligence has completed a preliminary analysis of flying saucer incidents to establish possible explanations. At the present time evaluation of these reports has progressed only to the extent that we must accept that some type of flying objects have been observed although their identification and origin are not yet discernible. We, therefore, conclude that insufficient data is available to date to warrant any further action except continuing attempts to determine the nature and origin of these objects."

The recommendation to Forrestal continued, noting: "increasing pressure on the part of the U.S. Press to publicize flying saucer incidents. The Director of Intelligence, USAF, has attempted to dissuade the Press from publishing articles of this nature. It has also been pointed out to the Press that these articles would necessarily be speculative in nature and would probably result in a flood of reports, making the problem of analysis and evaluation of flying saucer reports increasingly difficult. Despite efforts to limit this publicity, the Saturday Evening Post has directed a member of their staff, a Mr. Sidney Shallet, to write an article dealing with flying saucer incidents. Mr. Shallet has approached the Directorate of Intelligence for assistance in the preparation of this article. It is believed that an article of this nature would be less harmful to the national interests if the Directorate of Intelligence assists in its preparation."

After analyzing the McCoy/Cabell exchange and Air Force Office of Information UFO files, respected UFO historical researcher Jan Aldrich is of the opinion that Cabell's recommendation was never actually approved for submission to Secretary of Defense Forrestal. That would have left the Air Force with no sanction for a formal Air Force media policy – and Cabell unhappy about it.[14]

To maintain perspective, it is important to recall that Project SIGN had been initiated as part of the overall Air Force responsibility for the air defense of the United States – and with the strong suspicion that some sort of Russian activity might be involved in the flying saucer sightings. As 1948 ended, the Air Force still faced two inter-related problems, it obviously did not have the resources to deal with possible foreign craft operating over the continental United States and at any time the ongoing press attention to the flying saucer story might shift to an expose of the nation's actual air defense weakness.

In December, 1948 General Vandenberg wrote to Vannevar Bush, acting head of the United States Research and Development Board; the Board had been created under the new National Security legislation of 1947 and reported to the Secretary of Defense in the new Department of Defense. Vandenberg wanted advice on air defense planning, especially advice on new air defense technologies. Bush referred the query to the R&D board's Early Warning/Radar subpanel. In general terms the reply to Vandenberg was that a lot more could be done, new technology was available for an improved radar detection system – but it would require serious project funding.[15]

While the Air Force continued to lobby for that funding, its own science consultants, the members of its Scientific Advisory Board (headed by Theodore Von Karman) began to focus on defining an effective air defense for the coming decade - when jet bombers, guided missiles and very likely Soviet atomic weapons would represent a new level of threat to the nation. One member of that group, George Valley of MIT, became especially active in regard to developing a new air defense initiative. Given that interest, Valley soon became directly involved with the Air Force unidentified object inquiries.

As 1948 was ending, it was clear that the public and media attention given to the flying discs/saucers was simply not going away – high profile sightings continued to catch the interest of regional and national press and neither SIGN nor the Air Intelligence Directorate had offered any practical suggestions for an Air Force media response other than the suggestion not to discuss observations which allowed for no "reasonable" explanation and focus the press on misidentification of "weather balloons and astral bodies".

Although not officially acknowledged, that approach appears to have established the context for a reset and restart of the Air Force unknown aerial objects inquiry in 1949. On December 16, 1948 with the final, official AMC/SIGN report still in preparation, Project SIGN was re-designated as Project GRUDGE – the "Detailed Study of Flying Discs."

Within days a new a new direction began to evolve within the renamed GRUDGE effort. It began on December 18, 1948, with a high level meeting held at the National Bureau of Standards. The meeting involved Air Intelligence Collections staff, National Bureau of Standards personnel and representatives from the Air Materials Command/Technical Intelligence group. At that meeting copies of the complete SIGN case files were given to both Pentagon Air intelligence and to MIT Air Defense expert George Valley.

Dr. Valley had been specifically involved at the request of Theodore Von Karman; his involvement represented a move to integrate the observational and radar data from the flying disc report collections into plans for an ambitious new, automated air defense system.[16] Valley's participation was actually the first serious involvement of scientists outside the AMC technical intelligence group. With the ongoing failure to actually identify the flying discs/saucers, there was a move to garner a broader scientific opinion on the subject, very probably with the unstated intent of increasing the number of conventional explanations for the sightings.

Project GRUDGE was underway and the Air Force inquiry was already in the process of moving forward even before the appearance of the final SIGN study report. That report finally appeared in February, 1949.[17] It was submitted under the signature of Colonel W.R. Clingerman as Chief of the Technical Intelligence Division and Colonel H.M. McCoy as Chief of the Intelligence Department – with Clingerman signing for both himself and McCoy

The report described SIGN's work as being primarily the collection of data, stressing that "insufficient information was available to either confirm or disprove the actual existence of unidentified objects as new and unknown types of aircraft." It also took the position that no preliminary estimate of the situation could yet be made and that the report itself was simply a description of the work done to date, providing information to "higher echelons" where decisions would be made on the possible threat to national security presented by the "large numbers of unidentified flying objects."

In general the SIGN report was a recap of the investigations, contacts and opinions which SIGN had collected during 1948; it did not go into the level of analysis seen in the Air Intelligence report submitted to General Cabell the proceeding December. Given the lateness and relatively inconclusive summary from SIGN, it appears that the Air Intelligence report rather than the SIGN summary of February, 1949 served as the basis for the overall Air Force position going forward.

Perhaps "frustration" is the best description of the internal Air Force attitude towards flying discs and saucers which had set in by early 1949. However, General Cabell clearly felt that the fundamental air defense issue of responding to unidentified flying objects remained a matter of concern. He took the matter seriously enough to report on it to the military Joint Intelligence Committee, which he chaired. Cabell also circulated a Top Secret eight page summary report from his Pentagon intelligence staff to the Joint Committee; that memorandum contained far more reservations and concerns than the Project GRUDGE based reassurances which were being provided to the press in Pentagon media briefings.[18]

Cabell's intelligence staff assessment outlined how difficult "positive identification" had proved to be and attributed many sightings to misidentification. However it also stated that there were consistent physical descriptions of spheres, discs and cylinders. It concluded that a number of reports from "reliable and credible" observers simply could not yet be explained.

There was also an acknowledgement that Air Force consultants at RAND (a consulting group spun off from Douglas Aircraft in 1948, heavily used by the Air Force in post-War decision making related to military use of engineering research and development) had concluded that certain of the observations simply had no "rational explanation", suggesting something other than simple misidentification was in play. And there was mention of several credible observations which suggested the possibility of atomic powered craft – it recommended serious study by leading aerodynamic experts and the Atomic Energy Commission.[19]

At General Cabell's level the issue of unidentified objects was far from resolved and Cabell intended that there should be ongoing, serious investigations of flying disc/saucer reports. But as far as the public and media were concerned, there was a very different story line in play. On April 29, the Directorate of Air Intelligence issued a very positive and upbeat memorandum on Project Saucer on April 29, 1949.[20] That particular Air Force media release was a virtual work of art from a public relations standpoint. The release - "Project Saucer" and the "Saucer Story" - reads a good bit differently than the internal Air Force letters, reports and summaries that were being presented inside the Air Force at the same time.

The media release begins with the Project SIGN's "birthday" in January 1948 and refers to the investigation of 240 domestic and 30 foreign incidents as well as the help provided from several government and private agencies. As of the date of the release, personnel at AMC technical intelligence were said to have already identified 30 percent of the reports as conventional aerial objects. It was expected that at least another 30 percent would be resolved with further investigation. However no further mention is made of the 40% remaining – a percentage of true unknowns that would have been anathema in reports of unidentified and unknown objects during the years to come.

Instead, the release related that answers to the flying saucer quandary had been found in "guided missile research activity, weather and other atmospheric sounding balloons, astronomical phenomena, commercial and military aircraft flights, flights of migratory birds, shots from flare guns, practical jokers, victims of optical illusion, the phenomena of mass hallucination, etc." It continued by noting that "question marks" remained in the saucer story but wrote off unconventional aircraft using nuclear power as "highly improbable" - and visitations form Mars, Venus or distant planets in other star systems as an almost complete impossibility. Reassurance was also offered that while the existence of unknown aircraft has not been completely ruled out, there is no cause for worry – "exhaustive investigations have turned up no alarming probabilities."

The Army, Navy, FBI and agencies such as the AEC appear to have fallen in line with the proposition that the Air Force was continuing its inquiry and as more data was obtained, all the unknown object reports might well be fully and scientifically explained, with no reason to focus on any foreign threat. The shift towards conventional explanations had been evident in the Air Force's comments that misidentification and natural phenomena were widely involved in the flying saucer sightings - and Navy Intelligence had even concurred with that assessment.

A more aggressively negative view of the intelligence problem of unknown flying objects was being expressed inside the Central Intelligence Agency. In March, 1949 the CIA's Office of Scientific Investigation originated its own internal memorandum in regard to the subject of flying discs/saucers, based on reports apparently shared from the SIGN records.[21] The CIA's comments on the subject of unidentified objects were extremely dismissive and skeptical – "a rapid perusal of your (Air Force sourced) documents leaves and inclined to supineness (sic)".[22] Certain of the comments suggest the CIA reviewer had not even read the Air Intelligence report – the remark that "No suggestion is noted that there is a possibility that many of the objects may be 'free' meteorological sounding balloons" was simply incorrect if he had.

A negative observation on the possibility of remotely controlled devices scoffed at the concept, stating that the idea of "guided aircraft at a range of several thousand miles are beyond any known capabilities, including ours". Such remarks appear a bit naïve in view of the frequent and well documented use of guide aircraft to perform remote control for both rockets and pilotless airplanes during the war – efforts conducted against targets hundreds of miles if not thousands of miles distant. The limitation had to do with deployment of the weapons and guide aircraft, not the total distance to target. Those same techniques were undergoing further, rapid development by both the United States and Russia.

Given the extreme negativity and blunt sarcasm evident in the CIA commentary, it seems worth questioning why the Office of Scientific Investigation (CIA/OSI) was so overwhelming negative and dismissive. Part of the answer may lie in the fact that the CIA itself had been in existence for less than a year. Its Office of Scientific Investigation had no direct experience with the subject of flying discs, its personnel had performed no field investigations, it had no direct exposure to observers or radar data, had performed no field collections and had no direct contact with SIGN technical personnel, much less Air Intelligence staff.

In addition, from its very formation the CIA was in something of a hostile relationship with the military service's intelligence groups, jockeying for position and competing for resources. The national security legislation of 1947 had inserted the CIA in a position to pass judgement on and filter the intelligence assessments of the individual services. Intelligence historian Jeffery Richelson provides excellent insights into the early contention between the military (each service and the Department of Defense with its own groups of scientific advisors) and the CIA - in particular the Office of Scientific Investigation.[23] In turn, even non-service organizations such as Vannevar

Bush's Joint Research and Development Board felt "stymied" in their efforts to obtain information which was being assembled by the CIA. Bush complained to the Secretary of Defense that the CIA was "highly inefficient, particularly in its scientific intelligence area".[24]

In January, 1949 a highly critical National Security Council assessment of CIA technical intelligence had been sent to President Truman and as of the first quarter 1949, the CIA's technical intelligence group was removed from its role as the primary scientific advisor to the President, as well as serving as the clearing house for information to be channeled to the Joint Research and Development Board or the Atomic Energy Commission. Given that loss of stature and the CIA's overall birthing struggles, it seems reasonable to speculate that some of the brevity, and even surliness, evident in the initial CIA/OSI response to the Air Force's flying saucer intelligence work may have contained a bit of "attitude" generated by inter-agency rivalry and conflicts.

As the reconstituted GRUDGE project proceeded, General Cabell remained open-minded on the issue of unknown object reports and the possibility that they might indicate some type of national security threat. He supported broadening the inquiry, involving other agencies and obtaining extended scientific participation in the studies. In contrast, a strikingly different attitude was coming into being at AMC and within the GRUDGE personnel. Certain of the officers within the Pentagon intelligence groups had been fiercely skeptical of unknown aerial object reports from 1947 forwards – viewing the whole subject as a diversion of critical intelligence resources, much as "foo fighters" and nightmare lights had been regarded as diversions during the recent war. With the assignment of one of those officers, Colonel Harold Watson, to command of the technical intelligence functions at the Air Material Command (including oversight of Project GRUDGE), the attitude within the project became increasingly skeptical.

Watson was the same individual who had previously told the press that flying saucers were "all a bunch of nonsense" and that people who reported them were jokers, crackpots or publicity hounds, with the exception of airline pilots who were "just fatigued"; they were simply misinterpreting windshield reflections as flying saucers.[25] To some extent those personal opinions may have been carry overs from his experiences in intelligence work in Europe during World War II. The mystery lights – foo fighters – had become the bane of many intelligence officers in the European theater where Watson had served. Whatever the cause, beginning in 1949 and continuing until September, 1951, the personnel working at Project GRUDGE appear to have increasingly turned away from ambiguous evaluations in favor of definitive, conventional explanations.

The most obvious practical result of the transition from SIGN to GRUDGE was that beginning in the spring of 1949, the GRUDGE staff appear to have become focused on taking each individual report and if at all possible, offering a simple explanation for it – explanations based in misidentification of balloons or other conventional objects, atmospheric or astronomical phenomena. AMC/GRUDGE became known for quick explanations and reassurance rather than broad investigation or alternative scenarios.

That approach certainly demonstrated a lack of attention to (or acceptance of) the remarks in the Pentagon Air Intelligence staff report - which had advised General Cabell that certain sightings could relate to "photographic reconnaissance missions", "familiarization flights" and psychological warfare activities intended to produce public concerns about America's defenses. With the detection of the first Russian atomic explosion in August, 1949, that threat and the associated concern over a potential Soviet air attack were certainly on the increase at Air Force headquarters.

The Air Force's problem remained fundamental, unidentified flying objects were being reported on an ongoing basis and unidentified objects were, in and of themselves, an air defense concern that could not simply be abandoned. Cabell himself was deeply involved in a new Air Force initiative to launch an extensive series of electronic and photographic intelligence missions to monitor Soviet air defenses in support of planned American attacks over the Polar Regions. Watson may not have related the unidentified object reports to the confrontation with the Soviets; in contrast Cabell appears to have regarded the reports as directly related to possible Soviet activity.

The irony of those concerns is that the Air Intelligence report of late 1948 noted that its study had found no evidence of any pattern reconnaissance of strategic American targets. Further investigations were left to Project GRUDGE, which was focused on individual explanations for reports and sightings, not patterns.

It was at exactly that point in time, the winter of 1948/49, that the first indications of unknown objects targeting high security national security facilities began to emerge. Beginning at the end of 1948 and continuing throughout the majority of 1949, personnel at atomic/nuclear warfare complex sites across the Southwest, from New Mexico to Texas, began reporting a series of what could only be described as incursions over and around the nation's most critical and secure strategic military facilities.

Chapter Seven Endnotes:

1. *Searching the Skies; The Legacy of the United States Cold War Defense Radar Program*, Air Combat Command, United States Air Force, June 1997, 16

2. Ibid, 17

3. *Initial Report on Unidentified Flying Objects*, Project Sign, April, 1948 http://www.nicap.org/docs/PrelimSignRpt23Apr1948.pdf

4. Jerome Clark, *The UFO Book*, Visible Ink Press, Detroit Michigan, 2008, 178

5. Kevin Randle, "A Different Perspective"http://kevinrandle.blogspot.com/2010/04/meteorite-men-and-ufos.html

6. Hall an Connors, *Alfred Loedding and the Great Flying Saucer Wave of 1947*, 1998, 140-141

7. Ibid, 144.

8. "Flying Object Incidents in the United States", letter to the Commander Air Materials Command, 3 Nov. 1948 http://www.project1947.com/fig/1948b.htm

9. Basic Letter for Headquarters USAF, AMC, "Flying Object Incidents in the United States", from Headquarters AMC to Chief of Staff, United States Air Force, 8 Nov 1948 http://www.project1947.com/fig/1948c.htm

10. "Analysis of Flying Saucer Incidents in the U.S.", Air Intelligence Division Study No. 203, 10 December 1948 http://www.nicap.org/docs/airintelrpt100-203-79.pdf

11. "Analysis of Flying Saucer Incidents in the United States/Summary and Conclusions", Top Secret, Directorate of Intelligence, Headquarters United States Air Force, April 28, 1949 http://www.project1947.com/fig/1948air.htm

12. Michael Swords and Robert Powell, *UFO's and the Government; A Historical Inquiry*, Anomalist Books, San Antonio, Texas, 2012, 494-496

13. As we will detail in a following chapter, Air Force assistance with the Saturday Evening Postarticle was quite effective. Unfortunately for the Air Force, the article did not have the desired effect in winding down future UFO reports. Experience over some 50 years indicates that while negative press may tend to close down "waves" of sightings, it has never prevented further "waves" from occurring.

14. Jan Aldridge, "1948 UFO Documents: Background", Project 1947 http://www.project1947.com/fig/1948back.htm

15. Kent Redmond and Thomas Smith, *From Whirlwind to MITRE; The R&D Story of the SAGE Air Defense Computer*, The MIT Press, Cambridge, Massachusetts, 2000, 12-13

16. Project 1947, 1948 Document collection, reference: http://www.project1947.com/gr/nbsconference.htm

17. "Unidentified Aerial Objects", Project SIGN, Technical Report, Air Material Command, Wright Patterson Air Force Base, February 1949 http://www.nicap.org/docs/SignRptFeb1949.pdf

18. Jan Aldrich, *Top Secret 1949 Document, CUFOS* http://www.nicap.org/papers/ciaufo.htm

19. Op Cit

20. Air Force press memorandum, "Project Saucer", April 29. 1949 http://www.project1947.com/fig/projsauc.htm

21. Lawrence Fawcett and Barry Greenwood, *Clear Intent*, Prentice Hall, Englewood Cliffs, New Jersey, 1984, 113-114

22. "Flying Saucers", Office of Scientific Investigation, Central Intelligence Agency, March 15, 1949 http://www.foia.cia.gov/sites/default/files/document_conversions/89801/DOC_0000015337.pdf

23. Jeffrey Richelson, *The Wizards of Langley; Inside the CIA's Directorate of Science and Technology*, 1-8

24. Ibid, 3

25. Ibid, p. 83

Chapter 8

Security Concerns

In this chapter

- High security atomic weapons facilities in New Mexico and Texas experience periods of intense unidentified flying object activity during 1949 and 1950.

- Nighttime sightings of mysterious "green fireballs" receive extensive press coverage and divert Pentagon level headquarters from responding to ongoing security concerns of local and regional AEC, Air Force and Army security groups.

- Regional Army headquarters advises Pentagon of serious, even "grave" security concerns – including the possibility that "some foreign power is making sensing shots with some super-stratosphere device designed to be self-disintegrating".

- During a Los Alamos security meeting Doctors Edward Teller and Stanislaw Ulam (nuclear physicists formerly with the wartime Manhattan atomic bomb project) speculate that certain of the mystery lights could be stratospheric shells ("pencil rockets"), fired by a foreign nation.

- Local AEC, Army and Air Force security concerns are rejected at Pentagon level based on Air Force dismissal of sightings being misidentifications and atmospheric/astronomical phenomena.

- Instrumented and triangulated measurements of unidentified object size, distance and speed are repeatedly made by teams of trained military observers and provided to the Air Force UFO project – only to be filed away with no further investigation or analysis.

The Air Intelligence studies of both 1947 and 1948 confirmed credible reports of unknown aerial objects, but noted that the sightings did not indicate any particular focus on the nation's strategic manufacturing and military assets. There were regional variations in numbers but no concentrations specifically associated with strategic "targets". Even through foreign reconnaissance and target mapping were mentioned as potential motives for the appearance of unidentified aerial objects, the absence of such a pattern argued against Soviet involvement.

Yet even as that assessment was being circulated, reports from New Mexico signaled the beginning of a trend which would emege during 1949 and 1950 - concentrations and patterns of sightings which suggested that some sort of strategic reconnaissance might very well be in play. The change involved multiple waves of seemingly focused sightings, each lasting over three to four month periods. The sightings involved strategic facilities of a very particular type - the sites constituted the heart of the nation's atomic warfighting complex.

The first such concentration of reports came from Atomic Energy Commission (AEC) sites in New Mexico. They began at the AEC Los Alamos atomic weapons design and development complex, with a September 23, 1948 morning sighting by several Scientific Labs personnel. While waiting for their plane at the local airfield, the individuals noticed a glint in the sky – which upon further observation appeared to be a circular, metallic object, high in the north. That same day, an AEC security guard at Los Alamos reported an oval orange object, highly luminous, crossing the sky in level flight and trailing flame. The object was seen to disappear into a cloud.

Those first Los Alamos reports seem to have drawn little attention, but they were only the beginning of a wave of sightings which quickly spread across strategic facilities in the Southwest. That regional wave of sightings began in earnest in early 1949 and moved across three AEC facilities during the year. It included clusters of observations around the restricted atomic development complex at Los Alamos (northern New Mexico), the Sandia Base weapons design and assembly facilities near Albuquerque (central New Mexico) and the new Q site atomic bomb depot (Site B) being built adjacent to Fort Hood and Gray Air Force Base (Texas). The sightings involved a large number of nighttime mystery light observations but there were also a considerable number of the reports involving daylight sightings, with descriptions of physical objects matching the characteristics called out in the first Air Force intelligence assessments of 1947.

Surprisingly, this regional wave of strategic facility observations triggered virtually no security response, either at the Pentagon or from the Atomic Energy Commission headquarters. Several factors appear to have contributed to its being largely ignored in terms of any immediate physical security measures. The primary factor which argued against it being taken seriously was one familiar to us from the intelligence experience with World War II "foo fighters" – mysterious nighttime lights tend to draw a lot of attention and create considerable local concern, but are virtually impossible to concretely identify. And across the Southwest, it was the mysterious night lights that literally stole the show, not just with the press and public but also with Project GRUDGE and the Air Force.

During 1949, the sudden appearance of bright green lights passing through the night skies over New Mexico created constant press headlines and in effect diverted everyone's attention from the less spectacular but frequent daytime sightings of unidentified flying objects. The mysterious lights became referred to as "Green Fireballs"; they quickly gained the attention of both the press and local military field intelligence personnel. When reports of these new and anomalous types of aerial sightings did begin to draw attention outside New Mexico, the primary response was not that of increased security or even an air defense response – instead the green fireballs were left to the attention of scientific consultants, ultimately resulting in record levels of frustration for all the field intelligence and local AEC personnel directly involved with the observations.

The much more concrete unknown object reports from the atomic weapons sites – all of them involving restricted and classified areas – became submerged in the green fireball mystery. When the matter was ultimately deferred to Air Force scientific consultants, they focused strictly on providing an explanation for the green fireballs. The ongoing daylight observations of well-defined physical objects received no overall attention, instead each report was simply tucked away in individual incident files or simply noted within the "green fireball" summary reports.

From a national security perspective it's important to differentiate the individual clusters of sightings at strategic facilities from the much broader green fireball experience. In retrospect the atomic weapons complex observations certainly seem to suggest that something significant to the intelligence problem of unidentified object was occurring. Equally importantly, certain organized technical observations which were undertaken at one of the military facilities produced the hard observational data – instrumented measurements including triangulation and calculation of height and size – which Project SIGN had been desperate for in 1948. Yet when such observations were actually made, documented and transmitted to AMC/GRUDGE only a year later in 1949, they seem to have been simply filed away with no comment!

During 1949 and well into the following decade, the state of New Mexico contained several of the primary bases and facilities which were vital to America's atomic warfare capability. The Hanford, Washington and Oakridge, Tennessee plants produced the actual nuclear materials, but the bombs themselves were conceived and designed at Los Alamos, assembled and stored by personnel at Sandia Base near Albuquerque and, if released by the AEC at the president's order, handed over to SAC B-29 bombers flying into Kirtland Air Force Base (AFB) outside Albuquerque.

Sandia Base housed the Armed Forces Special Weapons Project (formerly the Manhattan Project) and in 1949 the Department of Defense established the Armed Forces Special Weapons Command there. The first atomic bombs, built during World War II, had been assembled by project W-47 Z-Division personnel in Utah and flown out of Wendover Army Air Base on special B-29 aircraft. The Z-Division was relocated to Sandia Base during 1947.[1] By 1949, Sandia Base and Kirtland AFB respectively served as the single weapons assembly and the sole distribution pickup point for American atomic weapons.

Going forward, Sandia Base (Sandia Labs as of November, 1949) would serve as the nation's atomic weapons ordinance facility, designing and producing the non-nuclear elements (arming, fusing and firing systems) of atomic weapons, while Los Alamos designed the high explosive/nuclear package.[2] Sandia Labs also oversaw atomic weapons storage in a special secure area adjacent to Kirtland AFB.

Initially the assembled weapons were housed in concrete "igloos" in Tijeras Canyon, just south of the Kirtland runways.[3] Strategic Air Command bombers flying out of Roswell, New Mexico had to make an intermediate stop at Kirtland when on atomic missions. Later Sandia Base was assigned to establish and operate a limited number of distributed atomic weapon storage facilities, known as Q Areas – Site A was located in the Manzano mountains beyond Sandia Base and Site B was located in central Texas, at Killeen Base, adjacent to Fort Hood, in Texas.[4] For all practical purposes, from 1949 and into the early 1950s, these Southwestern sites constituted the nexus of American atomic war fighting capability.[5]

Generally speaking, unidentified aerial object reports from New Mexico were nothing new; we previously reviewed several New Mexico sightings including those from the White Sands test range. Scientists and technicians performing rocket, missile and stratospheric balloon launches from Holloman/White Sands continued to report discs and globes maneuvering over the range during

1948 and into 1949. Anomalous nighttime lights had also been reported previously, in both January and August 1948.

But beginning during the winter of 1948/49, local security concerns began to develop at both the Los Alamos and Albuquerque atomic facilities, triggered by a burst of reports of what appeared to be relatively low altitude, rapidly moving green balls of fire.[6] The first reports came from central New Mexico - over Albuquerque, the Sandia Mountains to the east, northeast to Las Vegas and southeast to Vaughn, New Mexico. Ten separate observations were reported on November 5. One observation described a light larger than a basketball descending slowly and exploding about 400-500 feet above the ground. The pilot and copilot of an Air Force transport reported a green fireball which appeared to have shot up from the ground to approximately 500 feet; that sighting occurred east of the Sandia Mountains. The pilot and copilot of a Pioneer Airlines flight reported a pale green fireball approaching them head on at 9,000 feet; after taking evasive action the object dropped to ground level.

During the following three days, green flares/fireballs were observed and reported by security personal at Kirtland AFB, Sandia Base and Los Alamos. The Sandia Base sighting was directly over the atomic weapons assembly site, a huge fireball observed arching downwards. Security at Los Alamos described a brilliant, rapidly flickering light low enough so that the Sangre de Cristo Mountains were visible behind it. On December 8, two Air Force Special Investigations (AFOSI) officers, flying a light plane on an investigation of the lights, observed a green fireball which appeared to be under ten thousand feet altitude; it suddenly appeared to burn up, producing reddish-orange glowing fragments.[7]

The OSI's primary role was that of independent criminal investigation within the Air Force, however it was also given duties related to facility security and counter intelligence, particularly the investigation of what might be Communist activities related to spying or even potential sabotage. Each military service has an investigative service with similar duties; the Navy has the Office of Naval Intelligence (ONI) and the Army the Counter Intelligence Corps/CIC (later re-designated as the Army Intelligence and Security Command, INSCOM). In 1949 and 1950 both Air Force OSI and Army CIC investigators became involved with reports of unidentified objects sighted in the vicinity of security facilities in the southwest, and later at Oak Ridge, Tennessee. OSI reports including UFO inquiries were normally transmitted from their District offices (District 17 at Kirtland AFB covered New Mexico and Texas) to OSI headquarters in Washington, D.C. and copied to AMC's technical intelligence group at Wright Patterson AFB for scientific analysis.[8]

The green flare/fireball sightings received special attention as several of the objects appeared to be at far lower altitudes than could be explained by meteors, several moving in seemingly flat trajectories. In Albuquerque, Air Force Special Investigations reached out to Dr. Lincoln LaPaz of the University of New Mexico Institute Of Meteoritics. LaPaz had previously worked with the military during World War II, in the efforts to track and locate Japanese Fu-Go balloon weapons.

On December 5, 1948, a meeting between Office of Special Investigations (OSI), Los Alamos Security, Army Counter Intelligence (CIC) and the Department of Justice (DOJ) was held at Sandia Base. The Los Alamos Chief Inspector summarized elements of the fireball phenomena including remarks by Dr. LaPaz and his mention of similar green fireballs in the area of the Hanford atomic materials production facility. The FBI was copied on the meeting memo and reports were sent to respective headquarters; a follow up conference was scheduled on Sandia Base for December 13.

With the participation of Dr. LaPaz, two simultaneous observations of a December twelfth fireball were documented and analyzed. Calculations determined the path of the fireball to have been some twenty five miles in length, passing almost directly over the Las Alamos complex at a height of some eight to ten miles (40,000 to 50,000 feet). That altitude was far below the height at which meteors normally burn during atmospheric entry. Dr. La Paz offered an initial opinion that the fireballs was not of meteoritic origin.[9] Within days another triangulated observation indicated a similar flight path, directed towards Los Alamos.

On December 20, Dr. LaPaz sent details on the observations to the Air Force Office of Special Investigations District 17, located at Sandia Base. He summarized several of the incidents of the previous weeks and provided commentary on observational data and the significant difference between the observed fireballs and typical meteors – including their extremely low calculated altitudes, relatively low velocities, significantly longer durations and vivid green color. LaPaz expressed his conclusion that the fireball he had personally observed, as well as others being described, were not meteoritic in nature.

On December 21, the Chief Inspector for AEC Security at Los Alamos advised his Area Manager of continuing reports of rapidly moving, high intensity blue green lights – observed by night security personnel in the vicinity of the Los Alamos facility. At least one observer commented that he felt the "gaseous appearance" of the light to be the exhaust from some sort of engine. A letter of that same date from the Director of Military Applications of the Atomic

Energy Commission noted that AEC headquarters was aware of numerous Las Alamos security team observations and of Dr. La Paz's evaluation as well as of the OSI's intent to investigate. The AEC recommendation in the letter was limited to a call for monitoring the situation and coordination with the military and Air Force Intelligence in Washington.

With the green fireball sightings continuing, Air Force OSI (AFOSI) personnel in Albuquerque attempted to get AMC's attention but with SIGN focused on providing a summary of its work to the Pentagon, no interest was immediately evident. However in January, Dr. LaPaz made personal contact with Dr. Joseph Kaplan – an atmospherics specialist from UCLA, serving on the Air Force's Scientific Advisory Board. Kaplan was impressed enough by the anomalies in the reports to take the matter to Dr. Theodore Von Karman, chairman of the Board. In turn Von Karman raised the matter with Air Force Intelligence at the Pentagon.[10]

Army security personnel with responsibilities for New Mexico were also concerned about the sudden appearance of mysterious nighttime lights. On January 4, 1949 Fourth Army G2 (Intelligence) reported to the Army Director of Intelligence that there had been some 20 reports over the prior six weeks of intense, white or greenish lights at an altitude of 5,000 to 7,200 feet, (far too low to be meteors), traveling at what appeared to be supersonic speed but with no noise registered. Headquarters Forth Army also requested (on January 3, 1949) that a thorough investigation be conducted, reflecting the fact that at the field level Army Intelligence was fully aware of the phenomena and its possible security implications.[11] That memorandum was accompanied by a detailed report containing information from ongoing meetings at Kirtland and Sandia Base.

A follow-on Army memo of January 13 expressed the view that local agencies considered these sightings to be of "great importance" and recommended that a scientific board be convened to evaluate them. As a follow up to the January meetings, on February 2, the AEC Security Director at Los Alamos proposed a meeting of investigators and scientists to discuss the lights/fireballs. Fourth Army responded positively to the proposal, with Army Intelligence expressing its intention to participate.

On February 18, Fourth Army transmitted an update on the subject of unconventional aircraft to Army Intelligence at the Pentagon. The Summary of Information in the update reflects the degree of concern shared among the various local and regional security groups; it also illustrates the differences in attitude regarding unidentified aerial objects which were developing between the field commands and the Pentagon. The Army memorandum stressed that local agencies were greatly concerned over these phenomena and noted that there is an opinion that "some foreign power is making sensing shots with some super-stratosphere device designed to be self-disintegrating". The memorandum noted concern that once the targeting is perfected, an actual strike might be conducted against the key facilities in New Mexico. Another expressed concern was that some form of "radiological" warfare might be in preparation.[12]

The Army communication stressed that the incidents were felt to be of "great importance" as they were occurring in the vicinity of sensitive installations and that the matter should be addressed with the least possible delay. Such concerns over radiological warfare were actually quite realistic – any of the key American atomic faculties could have been taken out of action by low flying aircraft simply "dusting" them with radioactive materials. The United States military had investigated weaponizing radioactive materials during World War II. There had been a worry that the Germans might deploy "dirty bombs", even if an actual nuclear explosive was beyond them.[13] The idea of "death dust" was discussed in the popular press and in fiction stories throughout the 1940's. Yet in 1949 serious local security concerns over "targeting" or the use of radioactive dust to neutralize American atomic weapons facilities seems to have gained no traction at all with higher commands at either the Air Force or Army.

Given that Pentagon level Army Intelligence actually had no independent data on the incidents being reported, Army Headquarters' responses to Forth Army was surprisingly dismissive. A "corrective" letter was sent to Fourth Army advising them that the subject of unidentified aerial objects remained under study and strongly suggested that such sightings were only unexplained due to lack of sufficient data. The letter stated that Army headquarters ("this office") did not believe that there was any "unnatural or hostile basis" for the sightings and that they were not due to "unconventional aircraft." A separate letter from the Pentagon stated that after consultation with the AEC, Army headquarters did not believe the matter was sufficient to justify a "formal meeting as proposed" but that if an informal meeting was held, the Army representative should convey the official Army position cited in the previous communication.[14]

AEC headquarters demonstrated an equal lack of interest, however an "informal" regional meeting was permitted and convened at Los Alamos, on February 16, 1949. Attendees included Fourth Army, AEC Security, the FBI, Dr. La Paz and six scientists from the University of California, including Dr.

Edward Teller (a key figure in America's atomic bomb development effort). AMC had been advised of the meeting and a representative was expected - but failed to appear.

Numerous reports were discussed at length, with extended exchanges between the scientists attending. When one of the scientists inquired about National Defense Establishment interest, the Army representative stated that the general impression of the regional security personnel was that they were being perceived as "crackpots", and that it would be easiest if the scientists verified that the objects were actually meteors. Towards the end of the meeting, Dr. Teller commented that the lack of any sound associated with the phenomena suggested to him that there was no physical object involved and that it must be purely an electrical phenomena. Shortly afterwards the meeting concluded - with no stated consensus or recommendations.[15]

Following the initial Los Alamos meeting on February 16, a Fourth Army Intelligence liaison report noted that there had been some ten incidents (since December, 1948) of "green fireballs" following essentially horizontal flight paths, with a constant velocity and a duration of approximately two seconds. Some twenty more reports were similar, with "minor deviations", and during that period several "normal" shooting stars and meteors had also been observed. The memo reported Dr. Teller's tentative conclusion that the objects could not be regular rockets or other physical objects due to the lack of any reported noise.

Actually Teller had offered an alternative possibility, speculating that the fireballs could be the result of tiny stratospheric "shells". Teller concurred with a possibility expressed by his colleague, Dr. Ulam, that the fireballs could have been produced by what was termed a "pencil rocket", fired from a special gun – with the intent of either scientific research or if from a hostile nation, for psychological effect.[16] It was later learned that there had been experiments attempting the creation of artificial meteors, conducted from the Holloman, New Mexico test range. An effort was made to determine if any of those tests had recently occurred but it was found that the projects - of earlier years and known to Dr. La Paz - could provide no explanation for the 1948/49 "green fireball" sightings. That line of inquiry suggested that artificial meteors were actually one possible explanation, but if so they were not being produced by American experiments in New Mexico.[17]

Finally, on February 24, AMC technical intelligence (responding to unknown object reports under the newly designated Project GRUDGE) responded to the District 17 OSI investigation, sending a Captain from Wright Patterson to a meeting at Kirtland. The meeting included OSI and Fourth Army Intelligence as well as Dr. La Paz. A report on the meeting noted that the Army representative commented on the perceived lack of Air Force interest and recommended that OSI discontinue its investigation. One OSI representative expressed a lack of understanding of Air Material Command role and noted that without some higher level directive, their office would be reducing its own investigative efforts.

Based on further remarks from the AMC attendee, the Army representative left the meeting (apparently in frustration). The AMC attendee also informed Dr. La Paz that the lack of statistical data in his reports on the subject "precluded proper evaluation by interested personnel in other branches of science and engineering." He also noted that Dr. Hynek, the Project GRUDGE astronomical consultant, was leaving his duties with the project in the near future. At the conclusion of the meeting, Kirtland OSI personnel requested that AMC initiate a study of the fireballs and enlist their help in the investigation – no such inquiry or request was forthcoming from AMC or specifically from Project GRUDGE.

By spring 1949 a serious gap had obviously developed between field intelligence and higher headquarters. Personnel at AMC/GRUDGE were becoming increasingly dismissive of unidentified object reports - while security personnel at some of the nation's most critical atomic centers continued to worry about sightings occurring over and around their facilities, even considering the possibility that the facilities were being targeted for attack.

At the same time, the high visibility and press coverage of the green fireball reports seem to have diverted attention from a number of much more concrete, close range sightings. An especially dramatic observation had come from Sandia Base in an incident on February 17, 1949 when a University of New Mexico Professor (who had trained with Dr. La Paz in meteor tracking) described observing a round object about a third the size of a full moon. Upon closer approach to the base the light became much more distinct, looking like a bent pipe and with well-defined edges.[18] The object made a slight climbing turn and changed to a yellow-orange color as it turned more sharply and disappeared in the distance in a cloudless sky. This seven minute sighting was independently corroborated by a large number of base security guards including the Officer of the Guard, who reported a yellow orange cigar shaped object also seen for some seven minutes at the same approximate time.[19]

On March 13, two military police at Sandia Base reported a spherical object with a flaming tail twice its length. The object appeared to be quite large, half the size of a full moon. Within days, on March 21, a number of witnesses at both Albuquerque's Sandia Base and Kirtland AFB made daylight reports of multiple aerial objects between 1:00 and 1:30 in the afternoon – they were described as round, silver colored and silent. And on March 24, three Sandia Base military police reported a hovering, round silver colored object which departed first in level flight but then straight up at high speed. Minutes later yet another MP reported four similar objects flying at high speed several thousand feet over the base.[20]

When a report summarizing some 150 sightings near New Mexico atomic sites was later compiled in the summer of 1950, discs and flat shaped objects constituted a significant proportion of the total.[21] Yet higher level Air Force interest, as minimal as it was, was characterized totally in terms of mystery lights, the "green fireballs".

Local and regional security concern about the "green fireballs" continued throughout 1949 and into 1950, but it had become clear that higher headquarters of both the AEC and the military services were simply not interested in actively joining field investigations. Left to his own devices, LaPaz managed to obtain air samples from at least one of the green fireballs. The sample contained debris which showed evidence of copper, an element not found in meteors. That evidence solidified his opinion that missiles of some sort were involved with the fireballs.[22] But as the summer months ended, the frequency of the green fireball sightings began to decline. By the end of August Dr. La Paz found that the trajectories of the fireballs had noticeably changed, the early sightings had displayed very uncharacteristic (for meteors) flat trajectories while by August virtually all the fireballs sighted were descending, several almost vertically.

Eventually, in October of 1949, the Los Alamos facility security director chaired a second regional security meeting, involving District 17 OSI, Fourth Army, a number of Los Alamos personnel, Dr. La Paz and two Air Force representatives - a major from the Air Force Geophysical research division and Dr. Joseph Kaplan. Dr. Kaplan (formerly of the operational analysis branch of AMC/technical intelligence) represented himself as simply an Air Force scientific consultant.

Dr. Kaplan presented the proposition that the green fireballs were actually natural phenomena, not meteors but geophysical in nature, more on the order of aurora. That view was rejected by virtually everyone else in attendance.[23] It should be noted that follow up geophysical research project (TWINKLE) and some six decades of general scientific studies have failed to provide evidence of atmospheric phenomena which would substantiate Kaplan's premise. Beyond that, the following decades have produced no comparable, geographically focused "wave" of anomalous low altitude, flat trajectory green fireball sightings – anywhere.

Green meteors do continue to be reported periodically, images of the more recently observed green fireballs are easily found with a simple Internet search, but the ongoing reports and images illustrate the characteristics of normal bolides, including a broad geographic dispersion, debris trails, and clearly descending trajectories. As recently as 2004 and 2005, the author observed two spectacularly brilliant, intense green fireballs over Oklahoma. The first had a dramatic, sparkling orange-gold trail and the second descended relatively slowly, almost appearing to be drifting downward, with no trail at all. Both were unquestionably meteors and other than color and brightness were totally unlike the types of observations which puzzled Dr. La Paz during the New Mexico wave of early 1949.

Following the October, 1949 meeting, Los Alamos personnel remained very interested in the subject of the fireballs but expressed the position that they had done what they could.[24] Dr. Kaplan's view of the mystery lights as aurora type natural phenomena was officially taken as a position by the Air Force and accepted by the AEC and Army Intelligence. A Pentagon Intelligence memo of November 30, confirmed the Air Force's "tentative" acceptance of that explanation and a separate memo from Pentagon Army Intelligence advised Fourth Army of Kaplan's evaluation, stressing that Army Intelligence had consistently held the view that the fireballs were natural phenomena - essentially telling Fourth Army to drop the issue of unexplained light phenomena.[25]

Yet behind the scenes there was less than unanimous agreement that the issue of the green fireballs had indeed been scientifically resolved, despite Kaplan's assertions. In his paper, The White Sands Proof, long time researcher Bruce Maccabee relates that in 1952, during a controversy over press articles about sightings at White Sands, the Air Force Scientific Advisory Board had recommended that information on fireball studies not be declassified "for a variety of reasons, chief among them is that no scientific explanation for any of the fireballs and other phenomena" had been revealed by a 1950 Air Force sponsored geophysical photography study (TWINKLE).

The recommendation on classification noted that "some reputable scientists still believe that the observed phenomena are man-made." A follow-on memo from the Air Force Directorate of Intelligence to the Directorate of Research and Development supported the opinion that no release should be made – based on the likelihood that releasing information "would cause undue speculation and give rise to unwarranted fears among the populace" since there actually had been no validation of Kaplan's theory.[26]

Kaplan had also failed to convince a number of the Los Alamos scientific personnel who were not easily dissuaded from further study of what they felt was something very real, and very possibly man made. A facility security memo of November 30, 1949 notes that a group of scientists and technicians from the Los Alamos Scientific Laboratory (all cleared under AEC security) were working independently and outside their normal duties to observe and record data on the unidentified aerial objects being sighted there; it notes that several observations had already been made and data recorded. The scientific personnel involved were trained in astronomy, physics and meteoritics. Other agencies including AFOSI at Kirtland had been advised of the ongoing studies but no further memoranda on these independent efforts has been located.[27]

The de facto Pentagon acceptance of Kaplan's opinion on green fireballs as atmospheric phenomena seems to have been used to dismiss any extended examination of other, extremely detailed unidentified object reports from across the Southwest, including those from AEC and Army facilities in Texas. During 1949 such observations, involving both night and day time sightings, had senior Army personnel at Killeen Base/Fort Hood, Texas extremely concerned - due to fact that they were occurring in the vicinity of a new, highly secret and restricted special (atomic) weapons storage facility (Q site).

AEC Q sites were being constructed to distribute the atomic bomb stockpile in order to more effectively allow the new Strategic Air Command to assert American deterrence against any Soviet military ambitions. The sites contained weapons under the custody of the AEC, with oversight by the Armed Forces Special Weapons Project. The "Q" designation for the sites related to the level of AEC security required for access, which required a complete FBI background check. Q sites were used for stockpiling atomic weapons, testing high explosive detonators and performing assembly and disassembly of training weapons for SAC. They were heavily guarded, located adjacent to major Army bases and SAC air bases. The Killeen site was one of the first four to become operational, providing stockpile storage remote from the initial operational/alert weapons housed under the control of Sandia Base outside Albuquerque.

A detailed study of the 1949 experience at Killeen Base reveals a far more sensational series of sightings than those of the green fireballs, with many of the observations being of objects at very close range - and with ground level incursions of a provocative, if not actually threatening nature. The sheer number of incidents, concentrated over a relatively small area, allowed the Army time to set up instrumented observation posts, producing very specific and concrete estimates of size, distance and speed - exactly the sort of information that Project SIGN had needed but itself failed to obtain. Ultimately the reports ended up in the Air Force files, however GRUDGE apparently failed to make any use of them. Strangely, while key reports demonstrating actual triangulation and determination of location, altitude and size of the objects have been discovered in the Air Force files, Edward Ruppelt (head of a reinvigorated Air Force UFO inquiry, designated *BLUE BOOK*) would later write that such instrumented observations were proposed but actually never conducted.

Ruppelt wrote about the unidentified objects at Killeen Base (without naming the base or giving its location) in some detail in his book *The Report on Unidentified Flying Objects*. He discussed formations of lights seen more and more frequently, until they became a nightly occurrence – once observed by a full parade ground formation of troops. He discussed the plan by the base commander to set up a series of radio linked observation stations, with optical fire control equipment routinely used in artillery observations. Four man teams were to be used, with observer, communications, timing and recorder personnel. Ruppelt describes it as the ideal plan for obtaining concrete data – but then states that the Air Force never approved the observations so the plan was dropped.[28]

Yet we now have an extensive set of Army documents on the Killeen Base experience, with exceptional observational detail. Researchers have located actual artillery team observations, with specific measurements within the Air Force *BLUE BOOK* project files.[29] Those reports confirm that the observation plan was executed, carried out on multiple occasions and produced hard data on the objects being observed. UFO historian Francis Ridge and the Nuclear Connections Project have compiled a detailed listing of the sightings at Killeen Base/Camp Hood (later designated Fort Hood) as well as other sightings near Texas air bases during the same period. Several of the following incidents and reports are excerpted from that work, which includes links to the original source documents.[30]

The Killeen Q Site story began on March 6, 1949 when a patrol in the Special Weapons Project reported a small, blue-white, oblong object traveling above the site. Other Army patrols also observed unidentified lights/objects over the period of 8:30 pm to 2 am in the morning. The following day, at 1:30 in the afternoon, an Army private observed an orange teardrop-shaped object descend vertically, directly in front of him.

On March 17, an Army captain serving as assistant intelligence officer was preparing to fire flares to prove that recent sightings had been simple misidentifications. While making preparations for the test, he and his men observed a series of unidentified lights which clearly were not Army flares. And at the end of March, another Army lieutenant on patrol duty observed a reddish white ball of fire pass horizontally over the base airstrip; he also noted interference on his field telephone while he was reporting the sighting.

Sightings continued in both the Q area and across Fort Hood. On April 27, southeast of Killeen Base, at 9:20 pm a two man Army patrol reported a small, blinking, violet object only a dozen feet or so away from them, passing through the branches of a tree before disappearing. Only five minutes later, four soldiers sighted a small light which appeared to have a metallic cone trailing behind it. The object was several hundred feet from them and about six to seven feet off the ground. Approximately ten minutes later the same four men observed a small white light appear about one hundred feet from them and move away in zigzagging flight some six feet above the ground - before suddenly disappearing. Less than an hour later they saw another light to the west- southwest of them.

While the green fireballs had been sensational, they were observed at considerable distance from observers. Something much different occurred in and around the Killeen Q site. The sightings there were more in the nature of encounters, occurring at ground level, with lights and objects passing directly by military and security personnel in both nighttime and daylight sightings.

The following day, April 28, twelve guards and other personnel reported 9 different sightings in the area of Killeen base, one an object with a metallic cone similar to the object which had been independently reported the previous evening. Groups of lights moving in formation were described in multiple instances, one a formation of four, another of up to ten lights. Over two nights, the incidents had essentially blanketed the entire facility.[31]

The mysterious nighttime sightings were accompanied by daylight observations. In early May at 11:30 in the morning two Army majors and a captain observed two oblong, highly reflective white discs, flying at an altitude of approximately 1,000 feet at an estimated speed of some 200-250 miles per hour. Both objects then made a coordinated, shallow turn. On the same date a small (three inch) object passed through a field of fire during live artillery firing exercises on the Waco #4 range.

With Army concerns growing due to the frequency and quality of sightings, a network of artillery observers, with their ranging and plotting equipment, was organized and put into place.[32] In early May, multiple network stations began making coordinated, measured/triangulated observations. On May 6, a brilliant light, changing from pinkish to green, was seen at 4,000 yards. It was in view for almost an hour.

On May 7, two sites (the Army triangulation network plotting center command post and another observer at a second network site) observed a brilliant, white diamond-shaped light at a relatively low altitude. Their triangulation calculations placed the unidentified light at 1,000 feet in height and at a distance of 15,000 feet (2.8 miles). The light was tracked for 57 seconds and traveled approximately 3 and a half miles during the observation. No sound was heard.

The following day, May 8, three observation posts observed a similar brilliant diamond-shaped light at an altitude of 1,600 feet, slowly descending for some 9 minutes. Senior officers form the agencies involved in Killeen base security reviewed the progress on the observations and concluded "agencies were unanimous in agreeing that the new observation system instituted by Fourth Army provided precise results and definitely indicated that the unknown phenomena in the Camp Hood area could not be attributed to natural causes."[33]

The early May sightings had caused the Fourth Army to approach Air Force intelligence at San Antonio for help in investigating the lights, however the AFOSI commander at that base declined, stating he was still awaiting direction from his headquarters in Washington. Unwilling to accept such a reply, Fourth Army convened the first of a series of weekly meetings with representatives from Army CIC (intelligence), Navy Intelligence, the FBI and Armed Forces Special Weapons Project (AFSWP) personnel. The Army and Navy personnel agreed that the reports were "a source of grave concern", the AFSWP attendees felt that someone would come up with a natural explanation - the FBI and AFOSI offered no comments at all.[34]

On May 19, an early morning daylight sighting described a round, silver, thin object seen for some 5 minutes. The object was rocking, giving an edgewise view. It continued irregular motion as it traveled upwards and away at a slight angle. This report is interesting in that it is virtually identical to the object described in flight over Los Alamos – in the initial report made in September, 1948, two months before the beginning of the green fireball wave.

The sightings continued into June, with yet another triangulated/measured observation on the evening of June 6; the aerial object moving within 4 miles of one observation post. Shortly after 9 pm that evening individuals in the plotting network tracked a hovering orange object some 30-70 feet in diameter and one mile in altitude. After 2 minutes and 40 seconds of observation it began moving in level flight and then appeared to explode in a shower of particles.[35]

That night three balls of light were observed and plotted, ranging from 15 to 24 feet in diameter and at a height of some 1,000 to 1,600 feet. The lights were generally stationary although one moved some 120 yards over 40 minutes. Durations of the various observations ranged from 57 seconds to 40 minutes. The lights "bracketed" the restricted Killeen Q-site area. All area aircraft flights, training exercises and other military activity had been eliminated as possible sources. In short, based on several weeks of instrumented field observations, the Army developed and documented an extended set of measured scientific data related to UFO appearances.

By July the Killeen/Fort Hood wave had begun to diminish; an Army report of July 2, 1949 provides a detailed summary of incidents which had begun on March 6.[36] It focused on the ongoing series of sightings of small "fire balls", usually greenish-white but sometimes orange-red in color. The lights were described as having shapes - round, oblong or diamond. Some of them moved but others simply appeared as bursts of light. They had been seen in groups of from 4 to 50. The incidents were frequent and widespread. The report confirmed that the Army had stationed artillery observers and plotting equipment and was able to get a number of concrete fixes and measurements. The Fourth Army summary report was distributed to a variety of agencies including the Air Material Command at Wright Patterson. Based on the July report, the Air Force and specifically Project GRUDGE at AMC was advised that a series of instrumented and triangulated observations had been made and data were available – including those for three separate observations on the night of May 7, 1949. The majority of the Killeen base observations can be found in the Air Force UFO/*BLUE BOOK* files, virtually all designated as BBU, *BLUE BOOK* Unidentified.[37]

Despite the rather obvious lack of interest by Project GRUDGE, an official Air Force response was ultimately provided to Fourth Army, from the Pentagon. In June a letter was prepared by the Air Force Directorate of Intelligence and provided to the Army Director of Intelligence. Air Force headquarters advised the Army that the Air Force Directorate of Intelligence had tentatively evaluated all the southwestern light reports as natural phenomena and was supporting plans for atmospheric/geophysical research to validate that assessment. It further advised that the Air Force had no need for observations from the Army. The Air Force letter was attached to a letter from Army Intelligence at the Pentagon, then transmitted to the Commander General, Fourth Army, in September, 1949.[38] And that – officially – was that as far as the Pentagon was concerned. Local security concerns would remain just that, local.

Yet despite the implications of Air Force letter, the majority of the Killeen/Fort Hood observations were totally distinct from the "green fireball" reports which Air Force consultants had relegated to unknown atmospheric phenomena. The Texas incidents were occurring (confirmed by multiple, triangulated observations) at moderate to low altitudes, in some instances at almost ground level - with many observations lasting for extended periods of time. And the activity was extremely localized, involving a highly secure area. However, both the Air Force and the Army at the Pentagon, seemed to have lumped the "green fireballs" together with the Killeen reports, effectively using Kaplan's "aurora" theory to close off discussion of what should have been a major security issue involving a number of extremely restricted sites. The lack of any serious headquarters response left regional Army personnel in Texas extremely frustrated – sharing many of the same emotions as the personnel at Los Alamos and Kirtland AFB in New Mexico.

In short, months of credible reports, several of them accompanied by instrumented measurements and calculations, of "unusual objects" flying over and through high security areas in two states had been effectively canceled out by Dr. Kaplan's opinion that the green fireballs were a previously unknown atmospheric phenomena, perhaps similar to aurora. That explanation had been rejected by all the concerned parties actually involved with the observations.[39]

It was however, officially – if "tentatively" - accepted by Pentagon staff and other headquarters organizations. Documents from both Air Force and Army headquarters advised local commands that the reports were considered as being due to "natural phenomena" and presented no threat as they did not reflect any signs of being associated with "hostile action" or having caused any "damage".[40] An Air Force Directorate of Intelligence memorandum to the manager of AEC security outlined the Air Force opinion that "nothing would indicate that the luminous aerial phenomena" represented either an "actual or potential" threat to AEC installations. It noted the acceptance of Dr. Kaplan's theory and referred to future scientific experiments, to be conducted by the Geophysical Science Branch, to validate the theory. In conclusion it specifically stated that in the future reports of a similar nature "will be no longer considered by the Directorate of Intelligence."[41]

The Air Force Scientific Board's endorsement of further study did result in a photographic research project – designated TWINKLE – which only became operational well after the wave of anomalous fireball sightings had ceased. Rather than being set up in Los Alamos or Albuquerque areas, the TWINKLE camera equipment was placed near Vaughn, New Mexico, the location of only a few of the earliest fireball reports. TWINKLE produced few photographic records and no validation of Kaplan's theory.[42] Interestingly enough, the project's summary report did note later independent observations of green fireballs during 1950, over the White Sands Missile Range.

Those reports involved a fireball seen during an aircraft missile launching and another following a V-2 rocket launch. However issues of communications - technical difficulties – had precluded the TWINKLE study from obtaining viable data from the missile range technical staff. In summary, the geophysical research project's results were described as "negative" in determining the nature of the green fireballs. No evidence was obtained to support Kaplan's aurora speculation. TWINKLE turned out to be, as Captain Ruppelt later described it, "a bust".[43]

However not all the scientists participating in TWINKLE had been satisfied with maintaining the atmospheric phenomena explanation, one of them would later take his experience and opinions to the public, in the form of a nationally circulated article maintaining that the unidentified objects seen over New Mexico and Texas were most definitely not natural phenomena, and did indeed represent a potential threat to the nation. But that would be a good two years after the fact.

In the end, what could have been interpreted as an extended series of aerial intrusions, targeting key facilities in the southwestern atomic weapons complex, was left unexplained – with no meaningful answers for regional security personnel. The Air Force, above the level of regional AFOSI personnel, had largely refused to engage with the issue, leaving commentary on the observations to a handful of scientists, some of whom offered speculation about long range, self-destructive projectiles. That speculation went nowhere and in the end Dr. Kaplan's tentative answer of unknown aurora phenomena was allowed to stand, even when it failed to be validated or fully accepted by his own colleagues on the Scientific Advisory Board. Worse yet, the Air Force had essentially ignored the completely independent body of observations involving daylight reports of apparently solid objects – discs, round and flat shaped objects – which had constituted a significant portion of the southwestern observations.[44]

As 1949 turned to 1950, a new series of sightings focused around atomic facilities began to emerge. The 1950 incidents involved the nation's radioactive materials production plants and may also have included observation and sampling of the first domestic atomic weapons tests. Local security concerns would continue to be expressed – to the AEC, the FBI, local Special Investigations officers, to OSI headquarters in Washington D.C., occasionally to Air Intelligence and in some cases to the Air Material Command at Wright Patterson AFB. In response, AMC/GRUDGE simply filed the reports and whenever possible offered conventional explanations. The explanations did little to satisfy local security and intelligence personnel, who became increasingly sensitive to security as the nation moved back into full scale warfare in Korea - and ultimately to a state of national emergency.

Chapter Eight Endnotes:

1. Don Alberts and Allan Putnam, *History of Kirtland Air Force Base*, June, 1982, 27

2. Charles Loeber, *Building the Bombs; A History of the Nuclear Weapons Complex*, Sandia National Laboratories, Albuquerque, New Mexico, 2005

3. Don Alberts and Allan Putnam, *History of Kirtland Air Force Base*, 28-29

4. http://www.globalsecurity.org/wmd/facility/q_area-intro.htm

5. Charles R. Loeber, "Building the Bombs; A History of the Nuclear Weapons Complex", Sandia National Laboratories, Albuquerque, New Mexico, 2005, 84-89During 1946-1949, weapons assembly would be carried out first at Sandia Base and later at the Burlington Ordinance Plant in Iowa. In 1949 Sandia's assembly function would transfer to Burlington and in 1951 another assembly facility would come operational at the Pantex Plant outside Amarillo Texas.

6. "1948 UFO Chronology", National Investigations Committee on Aerial Phenomena http://www.nicap.org/waves/1948fullrep.htm

7. Carroll L. Taylor, Area Manager Atomic Energy Commission, "Appearance of Phenomena at Los Alamos Project", December 21, 1948

8. Colonel Edward J. Hagerty, "Air Force Office of Special Investigations 1949-2000", Air Force Office of Special Investigations, 2008, 69-71

9. Lincoln LaPaz, Director of Meteoritics, University of New Mexico, "Anomalous Luminous Phenomena / memorandum to L. Col. Doyle Rees, Commanding Office, District 17, Office of Special Investigations"

10. Michael Swords and Robert Powell, *UFO's and Government : A Historical Inquiry*, 78-79

11. Eustis Poland, G-2, Headquarters 4th Army, "Unusual Incidents", memorandum to Director of Intelligence, General Staff, United States Army, January 3, 1949

12. Atomic bombs were not the only type of nuclear weapon considered during and after World War II. Doctors Conant, Compton and Urey, S-1 Executive Committee, "Use of Radioactive Material as a Military Weapon". National Security Archive http://nsarchive.gwu.edu/radiation/dir/mstreet/commeet/meet3/brief3.gfr/tab_f/br3f1e.txt

13. Doctors James,B. Conant, Chairman, A. H. Compton, and II. C. Urey, "Use of Radioactive Material as a Military Weapon", Subcommittee of the S-1 Executive Committee also Alex Weatherstein, "Death Dust, 1941", The Nuclear Secrecy Blog, March 27, 2014 http://nsarchive.gwu.edu/radiation/dir/mstreet/commeet/meet3/brief3.gfr/tab_f/br3f1e.txthttp://blog.nuclearsecrecy.com/2014/03/07/death-dust-1941/

14. James Ligon, Lt. Col, "Unconventional Aircraft", Intelligence Division, Army General Staff, Washington D.C, memorandum to Commanding General, Fourth Army, February 18, 1949 and George Smith, Colonel, Army Intelligence Division, "Conference for Discussion of Unconventional Aircraft Activities", February 15, 1949

15. "Conference on Aerial Phenomena", Los Alamos Scientific Labs, meeting notes. Extensive notes of the meeting are on record, consisting of 24 pages. A Sandia Base trip report on the meeting is also available on record, prepared by Richard Mandelkorn, US Navy, Research and Development Division, Sandia Base, February 18, 1949

16. Carol Taylor, "Office Memorandum, Joint Meeting Aerial Phenomena", October 25, 1949

17. Michael Swords and Robert Powell, *UFO's and Government: A Historical Inquiry,* Anamolist Books, San Antonio, 2012, 80

18. That particular description, including the "bent pipe" detail, appears in reports from other atomic facilities, including the Oak Ridge radioactive materials production plant.

19. AFOSI Case 24; "Vertical Climb, Then Leveled Off", February 17, 1949, Albuquerque, NM, NICAP UFO Chronologies http://www.nicap.org/albuq490217Bdir.htm

20. Robert Hastings, *UFO's and Nukes*, Author House, 2008, 47.

21. Ibid, 34-35

22. Lincoln LaPaz letter to Colonel Doyle Rees, "Anomalous Luminous Phenomena/Sixth Report", August 17, 1949

23. Dr. Teller and Dr. Ulam had put forth the possibility that the lights might result from a tiny high velocity stratospheric projectile fired from a "needle gun"; the objects mass would be so small that not sound effects would be produced, only light. They felt such a device would be used for psychological effect and that the gun could be positioned offshore on a freighter or submarine.

24. A group of Los Alamos personnel, at their own initiative and on their own time established a series of observation points with equipment and cameras by November, 1949. It appears that by the time they got their project well under way, the fireball "wave" had declined substantially and no significant data was obtained from their effort. Interestingly, the same effect occurred in southern New Mexico, once camera equipped stations were put in place, the fireball sighting wave had already ended.

25. "Aerial Phenomena", memorandum to Director of Intelligence, General Staff, United States Army from Department of the Air Force, June 15, 1949 also "Aerial Phenomena" memorandum from General Staff United States Army to Commanding General, Fourth Army, September 19, 1949

26. "The White Sands Proof", Bruce Maccabee, Copyright 2002 http://brumac.8k.com/WhiteSandsProof/WhiteSandsProof.html

27. Jerome Clark, *The UFO Book*, Visible Ink Press, 1998, 256. The group in question, the Los Alamos Astrophysical Association, was actually permitted to examine certain other fireball reports. Although no official memoranda dealt with their conclusions, the group itself concluded, along with Dr. LaPaz, that a number of the sightings could not have been conventional fireballs/bolides.

28. Edward Ruppelt, *The Report on Unidentified Flying Objects*, 56-57

29. *Fort Hood Sightings 1949*, Texas Museum and Research Library http://roswellbooks.com/museum/?page_id=594

30. Francis Ridge and The Nuclear Connections Project Team, "The Camp Hood Sightings" http://www.nicap.org/texas/texassightings.htm

31. Jerome Clark, *The UFO Book*, Visible Ink Press, 1998, 258-259

32. Ibid, 259-260

33. "Vicinity of Camp Hood/April 22-May 6", conference record, H. L Gandy, Lieut. Col, Commanding Officer, Killeen Base, NARA record locator T1206-88

34. Jerome Clark, *The UFO Book* , 259

35. Ibid, 260

36. Office of the Acting Commander, G-2, Fourth Army Headquarters, Fort Sam Houston Texas, Summary of Observations of Aerial Phenomena, Camp Hood, Texas, July 2, 1948

37. *Fort Hood Sightings 1949*, Texas Museum and Research Libraryhttp://roswellbooks.com/museum/?page_id=594

38. Basic Letter for Headquarters Second Armored Division, Camp Hood, Texas, "Aerial Phenomena", Department of the Air Force. Directorate of Intelligence. Copy for Director of Air Force Intelligence, June 15, 1949 also Concurrence letter by General Staff, United States Army Intelligence, Letter to Commanding General Foruth Army , Fort Sam Houston, Texas, September 19, 1949

39. The activities of those Los Alamos personnel will be discussed in a later chapter, in a detailing of the "radiation story" first revealed in Captain Edward Ruppelt's book on the Air Force UFO investigations.

40. United States Army, General Staff, Intelligence Division, memorandum to Commanding General, Fourth Army, San Antonio, Texas, September 19, 1949

41. John Schweizer, Jr. United States Air Force, Directorate of Intelligence, memorandum to Francis Hammock, Director of Security, U.S. Atomic Energy Commission, November 30, 1949

42. Ephrain Radner, Chief Operations Section, Geophysics Research Division, "Transmittal of Final Report on Project Twinkle", December 11, 1951

43. Edward Ruppelt, *The Report on Unidentified Flying Objects*, 52

44. Ibid, 34-35

Chapter 9
Nuclear Connections

In this chapter

- As Kirtland AFB expands to support the move of atomic testing from the South Pacific to Nevada, the Albuquerque atomic warfare complex continues to report both daytime UFOs and anomalous nighttime lights.

- The Kirtland and Sandia Base sightings receive no special attention from either the Air Force or the AEC – as daylight sightings increase in number and complexity.

- The multi-month 1949 spikes in southwestern UFO incidents end – only to begin again in 1950 at the radioactive materials production facilities in Tennessee and Washington State.

- Radar tracking supports the surge in UFO visual sightings at the Oak Ridge and Hanford facilities.

- An Army intelligence assessment presents the Oak Ridge sightings as involving real objects of a physical nature, possibly electronically guided and with the intent of harassing and demoralizing personnel at the Oak Ridge facility.

- A series of anomalous radiation spikes at Oak Ridge correlate with UFO sightings but the surge ends before plans for a monitoring system are completed.

- Studies of the new Nevada site atomic tests and their airborne radioactive fallout movements correlate the testing with a series of related UFO sightings.

The 1949 unidentified object appearances over and around atomic warfare facilities in the American southwest triggered serious local and regional security concerns – which were officially dismissed at headquarters and Pentagon level. In sharp context to the earlier SIGN investigations, technical intelligence personnel at AMC and GRUDGE simply appeared uninterested. Conventional explanations were provided for reports that did make it to AMC and the "green fireball" question was handed off to scientific consultants.

The lack of any serious GRUDGE interest is particularly notable given that technical data was being collected and forwarded to AMC. First Dr. LaPaz obtained fireball altitude measurements and directional plots showing fireballs moving towards and over Los Alamos. He then provided altitude calculations which showed the fireballs to be moving far too low in the atmosphere to be normal meteors. Later, Killeen base personnel obtained measurements which placed both stationary and moving nighttime lights and objects at low altitudes, some at exceptionally close range.

Unfortunately, technical corroboration in the form of radar tracking was still missing in both sets of incidents. The reason for that was simple – in 1949 the Air Force's plans for a continental air defense network were still years from being a reality. Lashup radars were in place on the vital northwestern and northeastern polar route air access corridors but only the Hanford facility benefited from that coverage (although even the Hanford radar did not offer 24 hour coverage). As for the atomic weapons facilities in New Mexico, Texas and Oak Ridge, Tennessee - air defense surveillance radar and alert interceptors were simply not in place in 1949.

The detection of the first Russian atomic explosion in the fall of 1949 reinvigorated calls for a comprehensive continental air defense but it was only in March of 1950 that the Joint Chiefs were presented with the "*BLUE BOOK* Plan", a proposal to have a truly functional surveillance radar network in place by July, 1952. When North Korea invaded South Korea on June 25, 1950, the Joint Chiefs ordered a continental air defense alert to test the Air Defense Command (ADC) – the exercise uncovered major weaknesses in the existing air defense. A separate SAC exercise demonstrated that it was virtually impossible for ADC to detect low level air space penetrations. Some 60 SAC missions were launched against Seattle and Hanford, but only aircraft flying between 17,000-25,000 feet were detected and challenged.[1]

With the deployment of a true radar defense screen years away, the only alternative was to immediately create a civilian sky watch. A full time Ground Observer Corps was seen as a short term option for putting "eyes on the sky" and achieving some minimal warning of a preemptive Soviet air attack. But once again the Air Force was trapped in a familiar dilemma – not wanting to advertise its weakness but still needing to recruit a large number of volunteers for the program.

It was not until late in 1950, after the nation had become involved in open warfare in Korea that civilians came forward in large numbers. By 1951 over 200,000 volunteers had signed up and 8,000 observation posts had been established along the nations' northern border and its east and west coasts. That year saw the first national test of the spotter network. The series of exercises proved to be less than impressive from an actual defense perspective, but by mid-1952 over 300,000 volunteers were on regular shifts in the ground observer corps and the Skywatch program was fully operational.[2]

But there had been no Skywatch in the Southwest in 1949 and no surveillance radar or alert interceptors to confirm the incursions being reported. No organized air defense zone was in place and the nation as a whole had a very limited number of interceptor aircraft available.[3] Still, the lack of air defense was a priority issue and by 1950 there was an increasing radar and interceptor presence around the nation's atomic weapons facilities.

Four radar sites went into place and became operational near Hanford, one unit covered the Oak Ridge plant and three surveillance radars in central New Mexico covered Los Alamos and Sandia Base.[4] Air Defense fighter groups were also becoming operational. The 93rd Fighter-Interceptor Wing, flying F-86 Sabre Jets, was assigned to Kirtland Air Force Base – with the intent of establishing alert fighters in position to defend both the Sandia Base atomic weapons activities and the Los Alamos facilities. The 81st Fighter-Interceptor Wing was assigned to Moses Lake Air Force Base in Washington State, providing an air defense for the Hanford atomic facilities.

Atomic weapons related activities at Sandia Base/Kirtland AFB had substantially increased by 1950, not only in the growth of bomb assembly and storage but with the activation of the Air Force Special (atomic) Weapons Command and the creation of Air Force units involved in providing logistics support for weapons development and testing. The 4091st Air Support Wing flew both heavy bombers and transport aircraft in support of an extensive series of atomic weapons tests. A special group, the 4925th "Megaton Blasters" were responsible for flight testing all nuclear weapons as well as carrying out live test drops of atomic weapons. Before 1950 atomic devices were exploded in tests on and in the vicinity of various Pacific islands, but in 1951 the Las Vegas Bombing and Gunnery Range began to be used for atomic weapons tests. The first test occurred in January, 1951, with the air drop of a relatively small, one kiloton bomb.

Atomic weaponry was driving the growth at both Kirtland AFB and Sandia Base and despite what the personnel at GRUDGE might have preferred, those installations continued to report an increasing number of daylight sightings of unidentified flying objects. On March 21, 1950 personnel in the Sandia Base ordinance area observed several silver colored objects engaged in what appeared to be aerial maneuvers over the base. Their actions appeared similar to aircraft engaged in "dog fighting". The objects were extraordinarily maneuverable, engaging in right angle turns as well as being able to immediately reverse their direction of flight.[5]

The following day, March 22, 1950 eleven members of the 4925th Atomic Test Group observed an unidentified "flying wing" shaped object in horizontal flight northwest of Kirtland, in full daylight.[6] Unknown objects were also reported over Albuquerque, Sandia base and later the Manzano storage facility; not only did the sightings continue, they actually increased during the early 1950s. Yet until 1952, they received no special intelligence attention other than from local Air Force special investigations personnel.

Unknown object sightings associated with high security areas had become fairly routine in New Mexico by 1950, but few observations had come from the rest of the atomic warfare complex, in particular from the radioactive materials production facilities. The Oak Ridge facility had produced its first shipment of enriched uranium 235 in March, 1944, sending it out to Los Alamos for bomb development. By September of that year it had shipped a full kilogram of material.[7] That month, an unidentified "tube" (cylindrical) shaped object was observed at relatively low altitude, hovering over the Oak Ridge facility. It remained in place until a large crowd had gathered and then departed.

The Hanford complex completed refinement of its first batch of plutonium in February, 1945 and shipped it to Los Alamos shortly afterwards.[8] By April, 1945 Hanford was sending weekly shipments to Los Alamos. Summer, 1945 saw the first reported Hanford UFO visit; with an object being tracked by radar into the Hanford reservation. Piston engine F6F Hellcat interceptors were scrambled but they had an operational ceiling of some 37,000 feet, far below the apparent altitude to which the object had ascended. Even though they pushed their aircraft to some 42,000 feet, the object remained far above them until it finally rose out of sight.

The objects involved in those war time sightings apparently made no effort to conceal themselves or behave covertly. The Oak Ridge object was at very low altitude, essentially hovering directly over one of the radioactive materials buildings. It was observed in full daylight and remained in place long enough to be seen and described by a considerable number of people.

The Hanford object also made no effort to hide itself, however it could be said to have behaved "evasively", moving to a very high altitude directly over the facility by the time interceptors arrived, suggesting the possibility that it had the ability to monitor the aircraft and even the ability to detect that it had been scanned by radar. The incident at Hanford was unique in that both radar and interceptors were involved at that very early date. In fact the only Air Force interceptors on duty in the continental United States had been stationed in the Pacific Northwest, in response to the Japanese Fu-Go high level balloon attacks towards the end of World War II.

From 1945 until 1947 we find no reports of any objects being sighted in the immediate vicinity of the atomic production reservations, much less directly over either the Hanford or Oak Ridge plants. In 1947 a single but credible report placed unconventional objects in the general Hanford security area. A three disc flight of unidentified objects was observed traveling at high speed south/south-west of Hanford.

There were no other reports until May 21, 1949, when an unidentified object was reported hovering within Hanford restricted air space. The object was visually described as silvery and disc shaped; radar confirmed a target at an altitude of 17,000 to 20,000 feet. The silvery, disc-shaped object was confirmed with visual observation by personnel from the Hanford radar station. A call for an interceptor was relayed to Moses Lake air field but before the F-82 fighter was even airborne the disc suddenly took off in a southerly direction at a speed "faster than a jet".[9]

The spot intelligence report states that the pilot of the F-82 was instructed to search for the object and "intercept it in hopes that it might be a disk." However, the object had quickly moved out of the range of ground radar and the pilot of the F-82 was not able to locate it. A short time later, another aircraft was observed on radar in the restricted air space and appeared to behave "evasively", again suggesting the possibility that the intruder had the ability to detect radar scanning or the approach of aircraft. Following that incident, neither Hanford nor Oak Ridge reported unknown object observations until 1950.

Other than those incidents, there were no ongoing or concentrated series of unidentified object reports from ether Oak Ridge or Hanford, not even during the national "flying saucer" wave of 1947. Only one sighting came from Oak Ridge in 1947 (it did produce a photograph) and a report of three objects by two witnesses was made in 1949. The relative dearth of reports from the atomic plants during 1947-1949 seems to argue against the Air Force's stated belief that media coverage was to blame for ongoing flying saucer reports, which are not found at Hanford or Oak Ridge until 1950.

Construction at the nation's atomic materials production sites had escalated dramatically in the years immediately following 1947. Two new weapons material reactors and three new plutonium production plants were authorized at the Hanford site. The Oak Ridge complex was authorized for three new gaseous diffusion plants and new facilities were to be constructed in Paducah, Kentucky and Portsmouth, Ohio. A reactor testing station began construction near Idaho Falls, Idaho and new component and assembly plants were opened at Rocky Flats, Colorado and Amarillo, Texas.

In addition to the ramp up at the Hanford and Oak Ridge radioactive materials production sites, construction began on five heavy-water reactors for producing tritium and plutonium at the Savannah River facility in South Carolina. Initially Savannah River served as a second source – Hanford being the first – for production of plutonium and heavy water. Later Savannah would become a primary facility for producing the tritium needed for hydrogen weapons. The Savannah River plants became operational circa 1952-1955.

In 1950, President Truman announced that the U.S. would develop nuclear fusion weapons (hydrogen bombs), which would have destructive power far greater than the atomic fission bombs currently in production. That year the Y-12 plant at Oak Ridge began to develop the lithium isotope separation process which would be key to development of the hydrogen bombs. Two years later, America tested the first fusion thermonuclear device at Eniwetok Island in the Pacific. Its yield was over ten megatons, some 700 times that of the atomic bomb detonated over Hiroshima, Japan.

During 1950 American atomic weapons production began to accelerate at a fevered pace, with production of both materials and bombs growing exponentially. An inventory of only 13 atomic weapons at the end of 1947 would grow to some 1,100 bombs by 1953 and doubled to over 2,200 by 1955. The growing stockpile was distributed beyond the early Manzano and Killeen base Q sites previously discussed, with other continental storage sites becoming operational – as well as seven storage sites overseas.[10]

It was during the earliest phases of the dramatic increase in materials and weapons production that unidentified aerial object reports at the nuclear materials plants began to dramatically spike.[11] This new series of atomic warfare complex appearances followed hard on the heels of the southwestern sightings of 1949. It began with several June, 1950 sightings, including one of three objects flying over the Oak Ridge facilities in Tennessee.[12]

Hanford was next, with a July 30th encounter between an F-94 jet interceptor, on nighttime patrol in restricted air space over the Hanford reservation, and an unidentified aerial object. The jet was at 26,000 feet when its gun sight radar picked up an object approaching at high speed. A red glow was seen, outlining a very large disc-shaped object. The object approached the jet head on and the pilot banked sharply; at that point the object reversed its direction and headed directly for the F-94 again. The pilot felt that he was under attack and prepared to fire but the object jogged aside at the last moment, again and again approaching the jet and veering off. The pilot described playing "cat and mouse" with the object for some 15 minutes before it stopped, flashed a red light twice and then sped off at very high speed.

This incident represented a new type of encounter, one that would become more common over the next few years. In 1948 an unidentified object had fled at high speed when a jet interceptor was scrambled towards the Hanford plant. But in the 1950 encounter, the "bogie" appears to have actively "engaged" the jet interceptor. From a purely military perception it could have appeared that the unidentified objects had moved from reconnaissance to actively testing the air defense of the nuclear facilities. During the next two years, more and more pilots would begin to feel that they were encountering potential hostiles – "bandits" rather than simply "bogies".

Similar incidents continued at Hanford during August and September. An Army memorandum of August 4, 1950 reported that round objects were being sighted over Hanford at altitudes above 15,000 feet. All pertinent agencies including the AEC, Air Force, FBI and the area air defense units were informed and aware of the observations.[13] Studies of individual reports from both Oak Ridge and Hanford are available in the published research of investigator Bruce Maccabee and in summaries of research done by the National Investigations Committee on Aerial Phenomena (NICAP) Nuclear Connection Project.[14] NICAP's nuclear research project began in 2003 and its extensive work explores a variety of potential connections between unidentified object reports and the overall history of American nuclear research and development.

Following a series of late summer sightings at Hanford, a concentration of incidents began to be reported from the Oak Ridge atomic facilities. An Air Force OSI Spot Intelligence Report of October 20, 1950 itemized and summarized a variety of reports from Oak Ridge. It was circulated to the Air Force OSI Director and AEC offices at Oak Ridge. The document shows no signs of other circulation at the Pentagon or to the Air Material Command/ GRUDGE.[15] It appears that the incidents at Oak Ridge were being treated strictly as a local security issue, rather than in regard to any potential threat to the nation's overall atomic weapons infrastructure.

Observations noted in the Spot Report had begun on October 12, 1950 with a concentrated cluster of reports being generated over and around the Oak Ridge security reservation. On October 12, 1950, at 1:25 pm, ADC radar observers (662nd AC&W Radar Detachment at the McGhee Tyson Airport, Knoxville, Tennessee) detected eleven and possibly more unidentified targets over the Oak Ridge restricted flight zone. An F-82 was scrambled around 9 minutes later and vectored towards two radar targets. The plane arrived over the security reservation but had no visual contact and no visual observations were made from the ground. Further unidentified radar contacts were reported the following day.

It must be noted that such failures to intercept were not uncommon and would remain so over time. Many of the early Lashup radars could only paint a target in terms of distance; they required a complementary height finder radar set to determine the target's altitude. If a height finder was not available, inoperative or unmanned, interceptor pilots could only be given the direction of unidentified object. Only with the advent of improved direction/height guidance from well-trained ground intercept controllers – supplemented by interceptors carrying on board weapons targeting radar – would actual interceptions become common, but generally only then at medium to high altitudes.

The Air Defense Command radars were often unable to effectively deal with targets at altitudes below 5,000 feet. That weakness had become clear as early as 1948 when on one of its early exercises, Strategic Air Command bombers had conducted a simulated attack on strategic sites in the northeast – opposed by a squadron of F-80 Shooting Star jet interceptors. The result was a total air defense defeat. The surveillance radars simply could not effectively acquire and track low altitude targets.[16]

In another SAC penetration exercise the following year, sixty bombers simulated attacks on Seattle area aircraft plants and on the Hanford atomic complex. Surveillance radars detected the high altitude attack (17.000-25,000 feet) but were unable to direct interceptors to engage and block it. The low altitude phase of the attack was a total success for SAC with the defense radar unable to track or successfully direct the defending interceptors.[17]

The known limitations of both air defense radar and interceptor engagement are an important factor to keep in mind in reviewing reports of interceptors being sent to engage unidentified aerial objects. Through the use of effective tactics and with sufficient maneuverability, both propeller driven and jet aircraft were able to avoid ground based radar tracking for decades. Low level attacks became standard practice for SAC by the end of the 1950's. Only with the advent of "down looking" Doppler radar systems in interceptors and aerial surveillance aircraft in the 1970s would relatively low altitude engagements become feasible.

On October 15, 1950, at about 1:30 in the afternoon, John Isabell, a security guard on the Oak Ridge Patrol Force, observed a silver-white spherical object traveling from the southwest to the northeast and passing over the K-25 uranium enrichment area. It was white or silvery and round like a ball. The guard phoned the information on the sighting to his security headquarters; at the same time radar was picking up an indistinct target every third or fourth sweep over the K-25 area. An F-82 interceptor was scrambled. The ground witnesses reported that the fighter plane arrived about 15 minutes after the object had disappeared.[18]

At 3:25 pm, the same day, three security guards and a caretaker visually observed a large object over the security area surrounding the Nuclear Energy Propulsion project (NEPA). The house-sized object was silver in color, and saucer shaped. There was a "blister" on top of the saucer as well as windows on the side. Observed at very low altitude, the saucer rose slowly for some 100 feet, moved forward, rose the same distance and then departed at high speed.

At approximately the same time on that same day, Oak Ridge security personnel and other observers made an extended, low altitude, daytime observation of an unidentified object. In addition to the visual sightings at the Oak Ridge facility, Knoxville Airport Radar reported intermittent, short "paints" of a radar track; the radar returns were brief, quickly disappearing only to reappear at another location.

When first observed, the object was estimated to be approaching from an altitude of some 12,000 – 15,000 feet over the Solway security gate. AEC and FBI reports contain detailed observations and descriptions of the object and its movements:[19] The object first appeared to be an aircraft which was starting to make an outside loop, trailing smoke behind. However the observers soon realized that the apparent smoke behind the aircraft was actually some sort of tail. The object continued to descend in a controlled dive and when it approached the ground it leveled off and flew slowly, parallel to the ground.

The object came within some two hundred feet of the two initial observers, flying some six feet above the ground. One security officer attempted to approach the object but it quickly became smaller as it moved off in a southeasterly direction. As it approached a nine foot chain link fence it moved up, cleared the fence and then maneuvered around a tree and a telephone pole. The pear shaped object then accelerated and moved over a hill approximately a mile distant. As the object gained altitude it appeared to the observers to actually appear larger than at its closest distance.

Approximately five minutes later the object reappeared from the same direction for a few seconds. Overall it was observed for some seven minutes, by four different individuals including both the security officer (Rymer) and the captain of the AEC security patrol (Joe Zarzecki). All the witnesses viewed the object and its maneuvers, later providing consistent descriptions and corroboration of each other's observations:[20]

> a. As first sighted the object appeared to be an aircraft trailing smoke.
>
> b. When the object was approaching the ground in its descent, it took on the shape of a bullet with a tail.
>
> c. When the object was sighted on the ground, at a distance estimated at just over 200 feet, it appeared to be approximately the size of a 2"x5" card, with a twenty foot ribbon tail. The object and the tail were alternately moving up and down, and the ribbon appeared to be waving in the breeze. The color was a metallic gray.
>
> d. When Trooper Rymer came within fifty feet of the object he described it in similar terms, however a portion of the tail seemed more solid to him, but with most of its length transparent, with sections intermittently glowing.

It seem important to note that these very close range Oak Ridge observations are similar in several points to those which had previously occurred in certain of the Killeen Base/Fort Hood sightings – relatively small objects, with flexible tails, flying at extremely low altitudes and maneuvering in and around obstacles at will.

The August ground level observation at Oak Ridge was followed by a continuing series of sightings in September and October. Both the local Army and the FBI offices appear to have taken these reports quite seriously. On October 16, the responsible Army Counter Intelligence Corps (CIC) agent decided it was time to focus some attention on the security situation at Oak Ridge.

He generated a report which noted earlier Oak Ridge sightings in 1947 and 1949 but focused on the recent surge in observations. Beyond his report, Army CIC officers were concerned enough to conduct full background investigations of the current witnesses – examining employment records and FBI reports in order "to ascertain their reliability, integrity and loyalty to the United States Government." No reason was found to discredit the witnesses, many of whom were professional security guards. The CIC and the other security agencies discussed the situation and attempted to arrive at some consensus on the potential threat presented by the incursions.

Bruce Maccabee's study of the Oak Ridge documents notes that the Army Counter Intelligence exchanges were in direct contrast to AMC's efforts to respond to the sightings with simple, routine explanations. In contrast, the local personnel were looking beyond the standard and unsatisfactory conventional explanations – "One gets the impression….when it came to explaining UFO sightings as mundane phenomena, the security officials (at Oak Ridge) who were involved in the investigations had "been there, done that" and now they were looking for something new and convincing to explain these sightings".[21] Maccabee observes that the local security personnel specifically rejected the sorts of routine and trivial explanations being produced by the Air Force personnel at AMC and were not hesitant to state why they had done so.

"The opinions of the officials of the Security Division, AEC, Oak Ridge; Security Branch, NEPA Division, Oak Ridge; AEC Security Patrol, Oak Ridge; FBI Knoxville; Air Force Radar and Fighter Squadrons, Knoxville; and the OSI, Knoxville, Tennessee, fail to evolve an adequate explanation for OBJECTS SIGHTED OVER OAK RIDGE, however the possibilities of practical jokers, mass hysteria, balloons of any description, flights of birds (with or without cobwebs or other objects attached), falling leaves, insect swarms, peculiar weather conditions, reflections, flying kites, objects thrown from the ground, windblown objects, insanity, and many other natural happenings have been rejected because of the simultaneous witnessing of the objects with the reported radar sightings; because of the reliability of the witnesses; because of the detailed, similar description of the objects seen by different persons; and because of impossibility."[22]

The local agencies clearly felt that in view of the quality of the observers and the level of detail provided in their reports, misidentifications and routine explanations were simply not plausible. The Army intelligence assessment was that the objects were actually of a physical nature and that they might very well be electronically guided, possibly for the purpose of harassment or demoralization of personnel at the Oak Ridge facility.

Army CIC was not alone in its concerns, the Senior Agent of the Knoxville FBI office put the local office on record to FBI Headquarters on October 18, 1950 – noting a series of security incidents on October 12, 15 and 16 and mentioning that local Air Force Special Investigations personnel were monitoring the reports at Oak Ridge:[23]

> CONFIDENTIAL
> October 18, 1950
>
> Director, FBI
> SAC, Knoxville
> Objects Over Oak Ridge, October 12, 15, 16, 1950
> PROTECTION OF VITAL FACILITIES
>
> *There is being submitted herewith a copy of two reports made by District Representative of the OSI, 8th District, U.S. Air Force, with regard to the detection of unidentified objects by the means of radar, as set forth in referenced teletype. These reports continue to set forth additional reports concerning unidentified objects in the air space are over Oak Ridge,*
>
> *Tennessee, which to date have not been explained. No investigation is being conducted by the Knoxville Office in this matter, but any further information received from OSI or from CIC representatives will be forwarded immediately.*

Clearly all the local security agencies were concerned, however the best they could do was to express that concern to higher headquarters – and as we have seen previously, AEC headquarters and Pentagon-level Army Intelligence were simply not inclined to challenge the official Air Force position on such sightings.

Activities by unknown aerial objects over Oak Ridge continued and on October 20, the superintendent of security for the X-10 control zone observed a round object, with something hanging below it. The object appeared to be 8-10 feet long and remained stationary as he viewed it briefly from his automobile. Earlier that same afternoon Knoxville radar had detected unknowns in the same area and an interceptor was scrambled. The fighter remained on patrol for an hour and a half, however, it was not observed by the superintendent so there was some doubt that it had been directed into the specific vicinity of the object he had observed.

Sightings at Oak Ridge continued to produce low altitude observations of small objects with complex structures attached to them. By the fall of 1950 similar "devices" had been reported over Hanford, Killeen Base and Oak Ridge. The possibility that such objects were engaged in close proximity radiation/radioactivity technical collections was not mentioned in the Army intelligence reports - however the reports did speculate that the devices could well be unmanned and radio controlled.

For reference, air particulate sampling and radiochemical analysis has proved to be one of the most effective methods for assessing radioactive materials production – providing the ability to differentiate between power plant and weapons class materials as well as between materials related to hydrogen fusion vs. fission weapons.[24] Such sampling was routinely employed by the United States, first in assessing Soviet atomic development and later in intelligence studies of Chinese atomic programs. The significance of possible air sampling reflected in reports such as those from Killeen base and Oak Ridge should not be overlooked - although it appears not to have been a consideration for local security personnel or the AEC at the time.

An Air Force memorandum of October, 1950 does reveal at least some level of Pentagon attention to the ongoing Oak Ridge reports. The brief letter stated that "There is substantial evidence that unidentified objects have been sighted over the AEC installation. It is further evident that officials of the investigative agencies are concerned over the situation and it is not viewed with levity. The possibility of radio controlled objects cannot be dismissed." [25]

Even with such specific concerns, there is no indication of any extended field involvement by personnel beyond those from AMC thorough the July-October wave of Oak Ridge sightings. Visual observations continued throughout the month of October, including the report from the security supervisor of the X-10 facility (Graphite reactor plant) within the security control zone. Following his sighting, similar objects were reported by the assistant security chief of the NEPA Division and an Air Force major assigned to NEPA (Nuclear Energy Propulsion of Aircraft). The NEPA project was a joint AEC and Air Force effort just going into place at Oak Ridge in 1950. NEPA was devoted to applying atomic energy to aircraft propulsion. During the October 20 sightings, radar tracks led to the routing of a patrol aircraft into the area of the initial ground observations but the interceptor was not able to visually acquire any targets.[26]

On October 23, at 4:30 in the afternoon, an Oak Ridge laboratory employee observed a low altitude flash from what appeared to be a metallic object traveling over the restricted area. Following his report it was discovered that a nuclear radiation detection station in the vicinity of the sighting had registered a burst of both Alpha and Beta emissions. The purpose of the station was to detect any leaks of radiation from the Oak Ridge Laboratory but there had been no leak; analysis provided no local explanation for the radiation spike. A note on a related FBI report of the incident states that no intentional or accidental radioactivity releases which would have explained the Geiger counter incident had occurred during the entire month of October.[27]

Sightings continued into November, and on November 5 at 11:55 in the morning an illustrator for Fairchild Aircraft reported a very large object shaped like a pear, translucent but with a dark core, making darting movements around his working area for some 5-10 minutes. Investigation reports are found in both AFOSI and FBI files and the illustrator provided a sketch of the objects appearance and movements.[28]

November saw a further series of daylight visual reports – both astronomical objects and weather balloon sightings were offered as explanations - however after extensive research none of the reports could be coordinated with actual balloon launches. Fighters were scrambled but none of the objects were actually intercepted. The local air defense personnel had become sensitized – and frustrated – by the ongoing reports but it was only at the end of November when a combination of radar tracks and radiation incidents finally forced AMC and its technical intelligence group to truly focus attention on Oak Ridge.

On November 29, 1950, just before 6 pm, Air Defense Command reported a number of radar tracks blanketing the restricted Oak Ridge security reservation. Interceptor aircraft were sent but made no visual contacts. At 7 pm, a Geiger counter in the Oak Ridge area recorded both a spike in Alpha particles and a slight rise in Gamma radiation at the same time – later investigation showed no operational explanation for the emissions. That was the second instance of anomalous radiation detection at Oak Ridge during the tracking of unknown aerial objects, however an extended series of similar radiation incidents had occurred at other locations, including Los Alamos, during the period from 1947-1950.

It would be years before those observations were widely known, discussed in Edward Ruppelt's book on UFOs published in 1956.[29] Researchers have obtained and analyzed several documents which elaborate on the material presented by Ruppelt – who went to considerable lengths in his writing in order to conceal names and locations for security purposes. A portion of that material is available online and we will explore the "radiation story" in more detail in a following chapter.[30][31]

The unidentified Oak Ridge radar "paints" of November 29 continued over a two to three hour period and the Eight District AFOSI took both the radiation and radar observations quite seriously, sending a detailed spot intelligence report to the OSI Director in Washington. That report discussed equipping jet interceptors with Geiger counters in an effort to correlate unidentified object intercepts with radiation detection. Documents do indicate that a technical team from Wright Patterson went to Oak Ridge at that point and performed various interviews and examinations, including a determination that the radar equipment was not malfunctioning and that the operators were competent and followed correct procedures.

In its final summary report on the radar incidents at Oak Ridge, the AMC technical team offered no official conclusion and only expressed personal opinions that the incidents might have been caused by weather conditions and "temperature inversions". In additional memoranda, thoughts were offered on various outstanding questions - including the basic question of why the "chaff" like images only appeared in the Oak Ridge sector of the radar. A variety of explanations including reflections from power wires, towers and other ground structures were presented. Many of those comments sound quite reasonable until the follow on question is raised – why would such reflections not re-occur periodically under similar weather conditions?

The issue of anomalous reflections from such "permanent" structures seems not to have been pursued by the personnel from AMC but on December 14 another "blanketing" of the Oak Ridge radar was observed. This time the radar operators were prepared and performed their own studies. An interesting document discussed by Fawcett and Greenwood in their book *Clear Intent* records that a lieutenant of the 663rd radar group took photos of the radar screen at that time and at a later date. When developed, "the numerous targets could be readily identified from the permanent radar echoes by comparing the photographs."[32]

Those findings appear to negate the only conventional explanation offered by the AMC technical team – but that comparative study was never officially evaluated at higher levels. Readers are referred to *Clear Intent* as well as the entire series of Oak Ridge related documents online at NICAP for a more detailed background on the radiation and radar incidents.[33] Of course even a proven resolution of the "chaff" radar reflection incident would not have resolved the radiation detection issue or the fact that Oak Ridge continued to experience an ongoing series of visual, daylight observations from security and scientific personnel.[34]

Ultimately the AMC conclusion was that all the incidents at Oak Ridge were mundane (radar anomalies, balloons, and aircraft); it left only two of the Oak Ridge sightings listed as unidentified. Yet as with the Los Alamos, Kirtland/Sandia Base and the Killeen/Fort Hood incidents of a year earlier, local military officials and scientists were outspoken in rejecting such "mundane" identifications. Instead of tacitly accepting the Air Force explanations, some of them moved to begin their own scientific investigation. Lt. Col. John Hood, the AEC Field Engineering Officer, outlined a plan in a December 5 memorandum entitled "Technical Approaches to the Problems of UFOs."[35]

He proposed placing radiation counters over a wide area of the facility. With sufficient anomalous object reports to establish a pattern, the data recorded by these counters would then be compared for time and location with the sightings "to see if any change in the background (radiation) occurs with the presence of sighted objects." He also proposed that portable counters be made available which could be taken to the area of a sighting. Along with the counters he proposed that an aircraft with Geiger counters and also a magnetometer be made available. The magnetometer would indicate any fluctuations in the local magnetic field associated with sightings. Hood also suggested more accurate radars capable of measuring height as well as direction and distance. This plan was to begin operating near the end of December, 1950. Yet before it could move forward, the last Oak Ridge sightings were about to occur.

In December, 1950 a number of individuals, traveling to separate work areas at Oak Ridge all reported seeing an unusual flying object over restricted areas. To the Air Force officers in one of the cars it appeared as would a bright reflection from a very distant aircraft. It was southwest of them and they only saw it for a few seconds. At the same time several other NEPA project employees were in another car at a different location. They saw the object for some 30 seconds before it was obscured by the nearby hills. They described it as a bright circular light with an intensity greater than that of the full moon. It was between 15 and 30 degrees above the horizon as it moved in a northwesterly direction. They also observed a strange effect on the circular light: it seemed to "darken, starting at approximately 7:00 to 9:00 o'clock along the perimeter and continuing to darken along the perimeter and inner area until the light was concentrated in approximately 1:00 to 3:00 o'clock position of a very small diameter, at which point it appeared somewhat similar to a large star."[36]

As was common in many of the Oak Ridge sightings, the 663rd Aircraft Control and Warning (AC&W) Squadron at Knoxville Airport had noted a brief target appearance over the Oak Ridge Controlled Area. It was estimated to be at 2,500 feet in altitude and only appeared briefly. A fighter was scrambled but no interception was accomplished.

That incident was the end of the Oak Ridge wave of 1950, there would be no further sightings of devices maneuvering at low levels, jumping security fences and being concurrently observed by numbers of security personnel. The Oak Ridge sightings occurred over some six months, with the greatest density of observations in some four months' time - much the same pattern as the 1949 wave associated with the atomic weapons complex wave in New Mexico and the Killeen base sightings in Texas.

By the end of the year, the Oak Ridge reports were in the AMC files and it was all simply a matter for the record. As in New Mexico, local intelligence and scientific personnel would be left with their own opinions about the matter. Available documents leave no doubt that, just as in New Mexico and Texas a year earlier, Army intelligence and base security personnel appear to have taken the incidents more seriously than the Air Force – which remained committed to the "explanation and reassurance" response that was becoming established at Wright Patterson.

Given the apparent lack of high level follow-up to the local Oak Ridge security concerns, it is surprising to find that on December 10, 1950 a Richmond, Virginia FBI office memorandum reveals that the FBI had been confidentially advised by Army Counter Intelligence that CIC had been placed on "high alert" for any information regarding "flying saucers". There is no indication that the Air Force was informed of the Army alert. CIC advised that information on the alert was to be treated as highly confidential and was not to be distributed to other agencies. There has been considerable speculation about both the motive and nature for the Army alert. Given the incidents at both Hanford and Oak Ridge, one possibility was that the Army – if not the Air Force or the AEC - was reacting to a potential threat of atomic plant sabotage.

Given the international situation, the possibility of sabotage directed against America's atomic facilities was certainly a reasonable concern. By the late fall of 1950 there was a definite possibility that the United States would be forced into atomic warfare in Korea. During October, 1950 U.S. and U.N. forces had advanced beyond the 38th parallel and across North Korea, only to encounter massive Chinese intervention and a series of losses forcing them back into the South. During November U.S. Marines and Infantry had been surrounded by the Chinese Communist forces at the Chosin Reservoir and President Truman publicly acknowledged that the United States might be forced to use atomic weapons. In accordance with the president's warning, the Strategic Air Command began preparations for atomic strikes in Korea. General LeMay issued orders to quietly set up a series of short range radio guided bombing systems (SHORAN) in the event that orders were ultimately received for atomic bombing missions against North Korean targets, potentially even against Chinese forces.[37]

With United States troops at extreme risk, an ongoing advance by massive Chinese forces and the use of atomic weapons a possibly, it would have been perfectly reasonable to be concerned over sabotage or even direct attack against the American atomic weapons complex. Then, on December 10, air defense radar sites detected what appeared to be a number of unidentified objects approaching the northeastern United States. The incident did not appear in the press at the time; it was only later revealed in remarks by President Harry Truman. Truman wrote that early on the morning of December 10, 1950 he was warned that air defense radar was showing large formations of incoming aircraft. Sometime later in the morning he was advised that the radar tracks had been a false alarm.[38] The exact source of the radar tracks remains unknown, speculation centered on atmospheric phenomena, flights of migrating geese, off course military aircraft or some combination of all three.

Given reports of the air raid warning and the match in timing between that and the "high alert" noted in the Army CIC/FBI memorandum, it would certainly appear that the Army had serious concerns about the security situation at the atomic facilities. Such concerns and enhanced protective measures would also have been in line with President Truman's declaration of a state of national emergency on December 15, 1950. Given the fears of Soviet intervention in Korea, Truman's declaration was essentially a call to mobilize for what might turn into a full scale global conflict. The declaration significantly expanded the president's own executive powers in regard to preparing for war and empowered a new mobilization effort to coordinate national defense. It was also followed by Truman's approval of a major increase in military spending, something he had opposed up to that point in time.

The 1950 wave of unidentified object sightings in and around the nation's atomic plants occurred during an extremely sensitive period, one in which

America could well have ended up using atomic weapons for the first time since World War II. Yet at the time neither the press nor the general public made much of any connection between unidentified object reports and the nation's atomic weaponry. The incidents and sightings that did make it into the newspapers simply showed up as part of the general coverage of "flying saucers", with no obvious atomic association. Given certain new research it's possible that both the Air Force and the press missed yet another contemporary link between such sightings and the nation's atomic weapons programs.

It is only relatively recently that a small number of researchers, with access to information which was classified at the time, have done the detail work necessary to propose that a certain group of unidentified object reports might actually have a relationship to the opening of the AEC's Nevada atomic test range - and the extensive program of atomic weapons testing which began in January of 1951. While there had been prior atomic testing in the south Pacific, the number of atomic explosions/tests conducted during 1951/1952 was on an entirely new scale. There had been 9 nuclear detonations during the period of 1945-1949. There were none in 1950 but during 1951/52 a total of 29 atomic devices were detonated in just under two year's elapsed time.

The possible association between the surge in atomic weapons testing and unidentified aerial object reports is not discussed in the majority of UFO literature and not at all in the official Air Force reports which simply list report classifications and totals for those years. The correlation is elaborated in the methodical work of researcher Daniel Wilson. Currently the best overview of Wilson's studies is presented in Robert Hasting's book *UFOs and Nukes*.[39] The following synopsis of the possible atomic testing correlation is based in Wilson's research.

In support of the new Nevada range atomic testing, a radiation monitoring network was set up at 50 sites across the nation, with the goal of capturing particulate matter (fallout), measuring the rate of fallout movement and allowing the development of maps showing fall out intensities and distribution patterns. Wilson focused on mapping the movements of the radiation clouds produced by the various 1951/1952 atomic test detonations (referred to as "shots"), relating the movement of radiation to both UFO project files and newspaper reports of UFO sightings. Wilson found that a high incidence of fireball sightings had been reported within hours or at most a few days after the passage of the test fallout through a given geographic region.

The first series of tests/shots began in January, 1951 and was designated Operation Ranger. Ranger was the fourth series of American atomic tests but the first to be conducted in the continental United States; the explosions in the Ranger tests were all from actual air dropped weapons with bombs dropped from B-50 bombers. Aircraft and logistics support were provided by the new Air Force atomic test squadron based at Kirtland AFB outside Albuquerque.

The Ranger shots occurred during January and February of 1951. On January 28, the second test explosion at the Nevada proving grounds produced a radioactive cloud which deposited fallout as far away as Albany, New York by late the following day. Within 26 hours of that New York fallout, two F-86 pilots at 26,000 feet over Albany reported observing a "ship-like" green flare descending at a steep angle. The pilots estimated that the flare had passed within 200 yards of them, burning up below them at approximately 25,000 feet. If those estimates were correct the fireball was certainly not a typical meteor.[40]

In November, 1951 the Buster-Jangle series of atomic tests were carried out; they were the first to involve not only observers but extended Army maneuvers to evaluate tactical operations in atomic combat – and to study the psychological impact on the Army personnel. The effects on military equipment and fortifications were also studied as part of the Buster-Jangle series. The military exercises were designated as the Desert Rock series. Desert Rock I, was carried out in conjunction with the Buster-Jangle detonations and involved some 2,800 Army participants, with tactical troop maneuvers by 880 personnel. Troops observed the Dog shot from some seven miles south of ground zero.[41]

On November 1, the Dog test weapon exploded and the radioactive debris cloud began to move south-east, first across Arizona and then New Mexico. At that point more westerly winds carried it towards west central Texas and by the end of the day the cloud had passed beyond Texas. Over the next two days, a series of fireball sightings occurred and were reported by Arizona and New Mexico newspapers. Two months later the reports of November were mentioned in a *LIFE* Magazine story on fireball sightings. In one sighting, less than a day after the Dog shot, an airliner crew flying near Abilene, Texas reported that a "bright green object" had raced past their plane at their same altitude and on a parallel course, leaving a trail and then exploding into red fire balls ahead of them.

As the Buster-Jangle series continued through November, additional explosions were followed by fireballs flaming across Arizona, New Mexico, west Texas and northern Mexico. *The New York Times* reported some seven fireball sightings in eleven days and described the burst of observations as unprecedented.[42] The atomic tests continued and as clouds of radiation spread across the country, areas from Iowa to New York and New England produced sightings following the passage of the fallout. Interviewed in Albuquerque, Dr. La Paz referred to the surge in new fireball reports as being five times greater than any number of bolide class meteors previously recorded during a similar period of time.

During the spring of 1952, the Buster-Jangle series of atomic tests was followed by a new round of both air drops and tower shots, all aimed at rapidly advancing the construction of smaller and more efficient atomic weapons. Operation Tumbler-Snapper was conducted during April-June and the Army remained involved, with some 750 soldiers participating in Desert Rock IV, which involved tactical exercises and training during several of the explosions. During the April and May test shots, more substantive observations of physical objects began to appear - with actual formations of disc shaped objects being sighted over both the Nevada test site and from Nellis Air Force Base outside Las Vegas.

The sightings of May 1, the day of the Snapper Dog test shot, seem particularly significant - involving a number of military bases and atomic weapons sites. The Albuquerque paper carried reports of four unidentified objects appearing to "play tag" with a flight of Air Force bombers as the aircraft passed over the city. A newspaper employee observed the disc/cylinder shaped objects flying at the same altitude of the bombers, moving away from the aircraft then back towards them. He described the objects as having a diameter a third the size of the bombers and appearing to "tumble" in flight. That same day four personnel at the Sandia Base independently observed and reported three well defined, cylindrical objects "tumbling" while passing over the strategic atomic facility.[43]

That same day, over Davis-Monthan Air Force base outside Tucson, Arizona, a B-36 bomber was approached by unknown objects (disc shaped) which first overtook the bomber, then positioned themselves near the plane. One of the discs moved in exceptionally close, to be observed by several crew members from one of the aircraft's gun blisters. Both the air crew and witnesses on the ground described the discs, estimated to be 20-25 feet in diameter. After pacing the bomber, the discs moved off at extremely high speed, at an extreme angle of flight close to 90 degrees. After departing at speed, they then were seen to come to an abrupt stop and hover. This B-36 encounter was exceptionally detailed, although for unknown reasons virtually none of what appears to have been an extremely important sighting by the air crew - and some seven or more individuals on the ground - remained in Air Force files.[44]

Other reports from May 1 include multiple observations of a 5 disc formation over George Air Force Base in California, with the discs making 90 degree turns while flying in formation. The unidentified objects were apparently tracked by radar and interceptors were scrambled. The sighting was reported approximately one hour after personnel at the base had seen a mushroom shaped cloud in the direction of Las Vegas; that cloud was from the Snapper Dog test.

The Davis-Monthan disc formation was so structured and well controlled that the incident would later gain special attention in a study of controlled maneuvers by formations of unidentified objects. That analysis concluded that the objects were under intelligent control and that the nature of the observed maneuvers indicated technology far beyond contemporary capabilities.[45] Finally, on the afternoon of that same day several civilian AEC employees observed a slow moving silver object passing at some 5,000 feet above the Hanford nuclear complex.

The radiation cloud from the Snapper Dog test moved relatively slowly, during May 4/5 fallout was affecting New Mexico and on May 7 a bright green fireball was reported apparently descending into the Sandia mountains east of Albuquerque. On May 7, the next atomic shot, Snapper Easy, was triggered at the Nevada proving grounds. By May 9 the fallout cloud from that explosion reached the southeastern United States, particularly Georgia and South Carolina. As the fallout arrived over the new Savannah River atomic materials production plant in South Carolina, four DuPoint engineering employees working at the plant observed eight disc shaped objects flying over the facility.[46]

Wilson found that as the Tumble-Snapper atomic test series continued the correlation of fall out and unidentified flying objects remained, regardless of the direction taken by the windblown radiation. If the radiation moved east, sightings occurred in New Mexico; if the fallout continued north east, fireball reports were found following its path as far as Wisconsin. Of course at the time, many of the sightings were never officially reported to the Air Force - those which were (and involved fireballs) received short shrift given the official "preliminary" identification of non-meteoritic fireballs as anomalous atmospheric phenomena. The others were simply filed as individual unknown object reports, with no effort at pattern analysis.

From 1948-1951 there simply was no higher level intelligence study of the possible connection between unidentified aerial object reports and the nation's atomic warfare complex. That scenario simply did not receive any focused or special attention, from either AMC or Project GRUDGE. The geographic concentration of sightings in New Mexico did "stick" and would be noted during a reinvigorated Air Force study in 1952, but any larger, strategic issue related to the nation's overall atomic weapons infrastructure received only the most general mention.

The fact that the nation was in full scale warfare in Korea explains that lack of higher command attention to some extent – Korea and the Soviet threat were the overriding priorities for the Air Force during that period. Warfare in Korea, Chinese intervention, covert Soviet support for the North Koreans and the possibility of full scale Soviet military involvement all combined to maintain the tension of those early Cold War years – and concerns over continental air defense. But even given all that, and despite the Air Force's best efforts at explanation and reassurance, as far as the public and the media were concerned questions about flying saucers and unknown aerial objects simply refused to quietly fade away.

Chapter Nine Endnotes:

1. The Air Force had also determined that the jet F-82 interceptors were so limited in weapons capability that it approved a last ditch tactic for the navigator to bail out and the pilot to ram enemy aircraft if matters came to actual combat with Soviet Tu-4 Bull Russian bombers.

2. *Searching the Skies; The Legacy of the United States Cold War Defense Radar Program*, United States Air Combat Command, 1997, 21

3. Kenneth Schaffel, *The Emerging Shield; The Air Force and the Evolution of Continental Air Defense 1945-1969*, Office of Air Force History, 1991, 100-105

4. *Searching the Skies; The Legacy of the United States Cold War Defense Radar Program*, 20

5. "Base Personnel Sight Strange Objects", Kirtland AFB, New Mexico, March 21, 1950, NICAP http://www.nicap.org/500321kirtland_dir.htm

6. "4925th Test Group Sees UFO", Kirtland AFB, New Mexico, March 22, 1950, NICAP http://www.nicap.org/docs/kirt1950/500322_4925rep.htm

7. Charles Loeber. *Building the Bombs, A History of the Nuclear Weapons Complex*, Sandia Laboratories, Albuquerque, 2005, 11

8. Hanford site history http://en.wikipedia.org/wiki/Hanford_Site

9. Francis Ridge, HANFORD AEC PLANT/F-82/RV CASE, Moses Lake AFB, Hanford, Washington May 21, 1949, NICAP / The Nuclear Connection http://www.nicap.org/ncp/ncp-hanford49.htm

10. In 1955, following the Korean War, SAC was given new responsibilities for control over atomic bombs designated for the Air Force and by the end of 1956 fifteen Q area sites were complete and five more had been designated.

11. By the end of 1950, the American atomic weapons stockpile had grown from dozens to almost 300 bombs. In addition, American war fighting capability had also dramatically improved. The Strategic Air Command had been largely ineffectual until General LeMay took command of it in late 1948; by June of 1950, a major domestic attack exercise would show it to have become an extremely capable and potent force. Following the North Korean invasion of the South in the summer of 1950, on several occasions SAC bombers would be seriously considered for atomic strikes in Korea.

12. Lawrence Fawcett and Barry Greenwood, *Clear Intent*, 1984, 171

13. Lt. Colonel Mildren, "Memorandum on Flying Discs", Confidential, August 4, 1950

14. Bruce Maccabee, "The Oak Ridge Sightings" including all the Project BLUE BOOK Unknowns and, Saucers reported over Oak Ridge", NCP -14 paper http://www.nicap.org/oakridge/oakridgesightings.htmhttp://www.nicap.org/ncp/ncp-brumac3.htm

15. "Unconventional Aircraft at Oak Ridge, Controlled Area; Spot Intelligence Report", October 20, 1950 http://www.nicap.org/docs/NARA-PBB90-635-641.pdf

16. Kenneth Schaffel, *The Emerging Shield; The Air Force and the Evolution of Continental Air Defense 1945-1969*, Office of Air Force History, 1991, 95

17. Ibid, 126. Even with dramatically improved technologies, low altitude tracking remains a problem, especially with low profile aircraft. In 2015 a gyrocopter was flown from Pennsylvania to Washington D.C., landing on the White House lawn without being tracked or intercepted. NORAD continues to make adjustments to handle similar low altitude challenges. Wilson Brissett, "Learning to Track Low Profile Aircraft", *Air Force Magazine*, February 3, 2017 http://www.airforcemag.com/DRArchive/Pages/2017/February%202017/February%2003%202017/Learning-to-Track-Low-Profile-Aircraft.aspx

18. "Unconventional Aircraft at Oak Ridge, Controlled Area"; Spot Intelligence Report, October 20, 1950 http://www.nicap.org/docs/NARA-PBB90-635-641.pdf

19. Daniel Wilson and Francis Ridge, "Oak Ridge Security Guard Reports SpinningObject", AEC Incident Reports Trooper Isabell; FBI Incident Report Security Guards Clarke and Briggs, October 16, 1950; National Investigations Committee on Aerial Phenomena

20. http://www.nicap.org/oakridge501016dir.htm20 Op cit

21. The Oak Ridge Sightings, Including all the *Project BLUE BOOK* unknowns and Bruce Maccabee, "Saucers Over Oak Ridge", NCP -14 paper

22. Ibid

23. FBI Field Office #8, 19 October, 1950 http://www.nicap.org/docs/501016knoxville_fbi..pdf

24. Jeffery Richelson, *Spying on the Bomb*, W.W. Norton Company, New York, 85, 95 and 114

25. "The Mystery of the Green Fireballs", William Moore, Memo from Col John Meade, AC of S, G2, October 25, 1950

26. "Objects Sighted over Oak Ridge Tennessee", The Oak Ridge Mini-Flap, NCP-06, Nuclear Connection Project, NICAP http://www.nicap.org/ncp/ncp-nuc171-175.htm

27. FBI Report, November 10, 1950, NICAP document collection http://www.nicap.org/docs_oakridge/fbi501023doc3.htm

28. FBI and OSI reports, NICAP http://www.nicap.org/oakridge501105dir.htm

29. Edward Ruppelt, *The Report on Unidentified Flying Objects*, Doubleday and Company, Inc, New York, 1956, Chapter, Chapter 15, "The Radiation Story".

30. Ruppelt trip to Los Alamos and personal radiation investigations http://www.bluebookarchive.org/page.aspx?PageCode=MAXW-PBB7-936

31. Naval Research Inquiry into radiation detection incidents at Mount Polomar test facility http://www.bluebookarchive.org/page.aspx?PageCode=MAXW-PBB7-908Brad Sparks analysis http://www.nicap.org/detection/radiation/papers/palo521223radmemo.htm

32. Clear Intent, Fawcett and Greenwood, 174

33. "The Oak Ridge Sightings", The Nuclear Connection Project, NICAP: http://www.nicap.org/reports/501129oakridge_report.htm

34. Op cit http://www.nicap.org/docs_oakridge/fbi_501205.htm

35. Daniel Wilson, "Technical Approaches to the Problems of UFOs." /Detection of Radiation", Dec 5, 1950, NICAP http://nicap.org/radiation/501205radmemo.htm

36. "Radar/Visual Near Oak Ridge Control Area", December 18, 1950, RADCAT Case Directory, National Investigations Committee on Aerial Phenomena http://www.nicap.org/501218oakridge_dir.htm

37. Richard Rhodes, *Dark Skies*, 448-449

38. Harry S. Truman, *Memoirs of Harry S. Truman: Years of Trial and Hope*, 1946-1952, Doubleday, Garden City, New York, , 405

39. Robert Hastings, *UFO's and Nukes*, Author House, Bloomington, Indiana, 2008, 65-73

40. Ibid, 66

41. "Operation Buster-Jangle Fact Sheet", Defense Threat Reduction Agency http://www.dtra.mil/documents/ntpr/factsheets/Buster_Jangle.pdf

42. Robert Hastings, *UFO's and Nukes*, 68

43. Ibid, 48-49, 75

44. Dr. J. Allen Hynek, *The Hynek UFO Report*, Barnes and Noble, New York, 1977, 100-103

45. Michael Swords, "Major Fournet's Motion Study", January 27, 1953, A NICAP Project Report, Monday, 23 March, 2009, updated 8 March 2011 http://www.nicap.org/reports/motionstudy_ufois.htm

46. Robert Hastings, *UFO's and Nukes*, 75

Chapter 10

I Want Answers

In this chapter

- The official Project GRUDGE report – issued in 1949 – concluded that the flying disc/saucer reports contained no evidence of either advanced foreign technology or a threat to national security.

- The report's summary stated that UFO reports were the result of misidentification of conventional objects, mass hysteria and war nerves, fabrications and hoaxes or the product of "psychopathological" personalities.

- The report internally noted but failed to elaborate on the fact that 23% of the sightings reviewed had not been identified and remained classified as "Unknown".

- The findings of the GRUDGE report were consistent with the personal viewpoint of the new commander at the Air Materials Command, Colonel Harold Watson; Watson had previously stated that "It's all a bunch of dammed nonsense…there's no such thing as a flying saucer".

- The approach at the AMC UFO desk was to evaluate all reports on the premise that truly anomalous UFOs did not exist.

- During 1950/51 UFO reports from military and scientific personnel began to increase – detailed observations were made by technical and scientific personnel working at Holloman AFB and the White Sands test range secret balloon and missile projects.

- A clash in attitudes between the Air Materials Command and Pentagon Air Force Intelligence resulted in significant personnel changes at AMC and the initiation of a reinvigorated UFO investigation, designated *Project BLUE BOOK* in 1952.

In reviewing the unidentified object sightings and incidents surrounding the American atomic warfare complex during 1949-1951 it appears that the security concerns – and the onus of actual investigative field work – were almost entirely local or at best regional. The personnel closest to the incidents and most persuaded about the seriousness of them, those directly involved in security meetings, and the individuals actually investigating sightings in detail were from a broad range of services and security agencies – Air Force OSI, Army CIC, AEC Security and even the FBI local offices. While higher level representatives did become involved from time to time, there is little appearance of any alarm or proactive national security response from the headquarters offices and commands. To a large extent that lack of interest and engagement appears to have been driven by the acceptance at the Pentagon and among government agencies of the Air Force's official position on flying/discs saucers – stated in the final report of Project GRUDGE.

Project GRUDGE issued its conclusions on flying saucers/discs in 1949. The report was over 600 pages in length and its summary position in regard to both UFO reports and observers could only be viewed as negative:[1]

    a. There is no evidence that objects reported upon are the result of an advanced scientific foreign development; and, therefore they constitute no direct threat to the national security. In view of this, it is recommended that the investigation and study of reports of unidentified flying objects be reduced in scope. Headquarters AMC [Air Material Command] will continue to investigate reports in which realistic technical applications are clearly indicated.

    NOTE: It is apparent that further study along present lines would only confirm the findings presented herein. It is further recommended that pertinent collection directives be revised to reflect the contemplated change in policy.

    b. All evidence and analyses indicate that reports of unidentified flying objects are the result of:

        1. Misinterpretation of various conventional objects.
        2. A mild form of mass-hysteria and war nerves.
        3. Individuals who fabricate such reports to perpetrate a hoax or to seek publicity.
        4. Psychopathological persons.

The report did consider the risk of unidentified flying objects being used as a tool in psychological warfare however that was the only significant concern in regard to UFO reports described in the GRUDGE study.²

Given the rather harsh language in the report, it's important to consider the point that the majority of the military personnel, pilots, and radar operators making ongoing UFO reports were the same people expected to provide the nation's front line air defense against an anticipated Soviet preemptive strike. Many of the pilots were World II combat veterans. The scientists and observers at various secure test facilities were expected to develop the next generations of the nation's weaponry. And observers at the nuclear weapons facilities were the individuals providing security for the facilities as well as the scientists and technicians responsibility for building its atomic weapons.

The Project GRUDGE report served to establish the official Air Force opinion and was referenced in communications with other services and government agencies. Given its length and extensive technical appendices it was not generally distributed to the press, although a copy was made available in the Air Force Press Room. The standard Air Force response to public inquiries would become that reports of unknown aerial objects were simply misidentifications; there was no threat involved other than that of public overreaction. No mention was made of the fact that, buried in the huge report, some 23% of all sightings remained not only unidentified but designated as "unknowns".³

That position was firmly established in a directive from the Air Force Chief of Staff to the commanding General at AMC, issued on January 4, 1950. From that point on unidentified object incident reports were to be handled in the same manner as intelligence on any other subject. Special collections efforts, including field collections work, were to cease. The GRUDGE project file at AMC was to be retained as the official record of the flying saucer investigation.⁴ An emphasis was also placed on the use of the term UFO (short for Unidentified Flying Object/UFOB), stressing the point that such reports involved a lack of identification. UFO reports were to be treated simply as observations, being reported as standard air defense practice.

In an April, 1950 press appearance a Pentagon spokesman, Major DeWitt Searles, assured reporters that his standard response to the subject was that "As far as Air Force goes, there's no such thing as a flying saucer. Further there are no such things as flying chromium hub caps, flying dimes, and flying teardrops, flying gas lights, flying ice cream cones or flying pie plates. Thank you and good bye."⁵

Given the definitive wording in the official Project GRUDGE report and the views strongly and publicly expressed by Searles and Watson, it is understandable that personnel at the Air Material Command appear to have increasingly turned to standard explanations for UFO observations, to referring truly anomalous incidents to scientific consultants and to simply filing reports. Ultimately, a single officer, a lieutenant, was assigned to handle incoming UFO reports; within the technical intelligence group reports were increasingly subject to simple ridicule.

While AMC and its technical intelligence staff were still officially charged with taking the lead in evaluating and resolving ongoing reports of unidentified object reports, the personnel assigned to the "UFO desk" at Wright Patterson AFB appear to have become fundamentally bureaucratic in their approach to the job. Routine, conventional explanations became standard practice, reports were classified and then filed – "unknowns" simply filed along with the rest.

In order to more fully appreciate the impact of such an attitude, we have to step back a bit and probe more deeply into what was actually going on organizationally during the years 1949-1951, in the field, at AMC and in a broader sense with the Air Force itself.

Individuals closely connected to the Air Force's handling of unidentified object reports have commented that with the end of Project SIGN and the initiation of Project GRUDGE, a change in attitude had begun to set in at AMC. Based in their comments it appears that the basic perception had shifted to one of skepticism, As Captain Edward Ruppelt later put it: ..."everything was being evaluated on the premise UFOs couldn't exist. No matter what you hear or see, don't believe it."[6]

It became routine for technical intelligence personnel to quickly produce standard explanations in terms of misidentification or atmospheric/astronomical anomalies. Ruppelt observed that approach when he was assigned to AMC in 1951, located close enough to the people handling UFO reports to hear their discussions and comments on the reports they were reviewing. That impression was confirmed when he himself was assigned to the UFO desk and began to study and compare the files and reports from SIGN and GRUDGE. Dr. Allen Hynek, long time scientific consultant to the Air Force on UFO sightings, observed the same shift in the handling of reports.

It appears that the AMC personnel tasked with the subject may have fallen into something of a rut, simply matching up standard explanations to field reports and filing them. Beyond that the well-known attitude of the new chief at AMC technical intelligence, Colonel Harald Watson, may have been a factor. As previously noted, Watson's public statements about UFOs and those who reported them had made his attitude towards the subject quite clear – "It's all a bunch of dammed nonsense…there's no such thing as a flying saucer". People who saw them were "publicity hounds" or in the case of airline pilots, most likely "just fatigued", seeing windshield reflections as spaceships."[7]

The exact nature of the attitude which developed at Wright Patterson during 1949/1950 seems accurately illustrated in one of Ruppelt's exchanges with an "old hand" in AMC technical intelligence. Ruppelt asked why certain apparently credible reports had received such a minimal response. The reply he received says it all – "One of these days all of these crazy pilots will kill themselves, the crazy people on the ground will be locked up and there won't be any more flying saucer reports."[8]

Perhaps unexpectedly the more conservative Air Force approach did little to actually slow down the pace of UFO reporting. During 1950 UFO reports from within the military and from scientific personnel assigned to military projects actually increased in number. A comparison of consolidated UFO reports indicates that overall sightings at least doubled from those of the preceding year.[9] Individual sightings and reports also continued to come from the Hanford and Oak Ridge as well as from various locations in New Mexico.

Kirtland Air Force Base and the adjacent nuclear weapons complex at Sandia Base reported daylight observations of well-defined physical objects overflying those facilities. Flight activities at Kirtland, southeast of Albuquerque, New Mexico, had picked up with aircraft and personnel arriving to support the upcoming atomic tests at the new Nevada test site. On two successive days in March, UFO observations were officially documented in Air Force Spot Intelligence reports which were sent directly to Special Investigations office headquarters in Washington, D.C.

On March 21, 1950 three independent reports involving four observers were generated by Kirtland and Sandia Base personnel. They described silver/white objects flying in the vicinity of each other and engaging in dramatic maneuvers well beyond the capability of conventional aircraft. The observations extended over periods lasting from five to thirty minutes.[10] The following day, March 22, eleven members of the 4925th (Atomic) Test Group reported another daylight observation. That UFO was described as having the general shape of a "flying wing", flying at a height of 25,000 to 30,000 feet and passing over at extremely high speed, observed for less than ten seconds.[11] A Lashup air surveillance radar was operational on the West Mesa site near Albuquerque, however the spot reports make no mention of it being queried in regard to the visual observations from Kirtland and Sandia base.[12]

An increasingly busy schedule of missile and stratospheric balloon tests at the White Sands test range also produced ongoing daylight sightings of unidentified objects in transit flight over the area – as well as "loitering" around high level balloons and in the area of missile and rocket test launches. On several days in April, different sets of observers reported objects crossing the test area, demonstrating exceptional speed and in one instance flying at extreme altitude. The observations were made by multiple crews using sophisticated optical tracking equipment.

On April 27, members of a crew preparing to record the test of a Bell Aircraft air to ground missile (MX 776A) observed and optically tracked four unidentified objects flying very close together. The objects were recorded on film (a cinetheodolite instrument was being used for tracking the missile) at one of the tracking sites. The use of azimuth and elevation data from that site, as well as the azimuth reading from a separate site showed that the objects were approximately 30 feet in size and flying at very high altitude, on the order of 150,000 feet. The objects were not in view long enough to allow an exact speed estimate, other than that they were moving at a very high rate, well beyond that of conventional aircraft.[13] On May 4, during another weapons test, several Air Force crew members observed some eight unidentified objects and then tracked two objects in independent sightings, simultaneously observing and filming each separately with cinetheodolite instruments.

On two successive days in August similar unidentified objects were again observed in the area of the White Sands range and over Holloman Air Force Base. On the first day, a B-50 aircraft, operated by the 2754th Experimental Wing, was airborne, monitoring another Shrike MX 776A missile test. Ground observers reported that two circular/elliptical shaped unidentified objects moved into the vicinity of the B-50 and remained with it for some thirty minutes. During that period the aircraft made separate "runs" in preparation for the actual test launch.

Nine observers were involved in the sighting and the objects were described as exhibiting very high speed during "sprints" (at some ten times the B-50 speed) over short distances, displaying exceptional maneuverability. While doing so they maintained a consistent position with each other – at other times the objects appeared to remain stationary. The UFOs appeared to be emitting their own light, not simply reflecting the sun. Such reports demonstrate that in 1950 observers continued to provide descriptions which were entirely consistent with the physical profiles and flight characteristics described in the Air Intelligence collections profile initially developed in 1947.[14]

The following day, August 31, instruments were in place and a series of photos were taken of unidentified objects which were sighted at different times over some four hours. The objects crossed over the Holloman base at very high rates of speed and the base requested interceptors. Four F-86 jets from Kirtland AFB responded but were unable to sight or engage the objects during the hour in which they were able to actually remain over the area. The report from the incidents noted that the objects had a definite shape although their edges were not totally distinct; they were clearly three dimensional and seemed to rock or oscillate as they moved – at very high rates of speed. The objects were filmed but their rate of travel was so great that their movements could not be correlated well enough to obtain a concrete speed estimate.

Given how seriously the AMC technical intelligence and Project SIGN personnel had pursued concrete observational data during 1947 and 1948, it seems surprising to find how easily that ongoing, instrumented UFO observations of Dr. LaPaz (1949), from trained observers at Killeen Base (1949) and the White Sands Test Range (1949/1950) were simply routed into the AMC files, receiving no analysis beyond that individual incident classification. It seems clear that by 1950 the UFO desk at AMC had clearly moved into "filing mode".

The same could not be said about the national media. In March, 1950, an article written by Navy Commander Robert McLaughlin appeared in TRUE magazine. McLaughlin was an engineering graduate of the U.S. Naval Academy who had been in charge of Navy tests at White Sands – where he had become familiar with the wide variety of UFO sightings made during both missile tests and high altitude balloon launches. The Commander was convinced that UFOs were real and that they were extraterrestrial. He stated his views clearly and firmly and his article was cleared for release by the Navy. The article made a serious impression on the public and press – causing much dismay within the Air Force, especially among its public relations officers.[15]

In response the Air Force simply restated its official position, based on the 600 page Project GRUDGE report. That included an assertive stance with the other military services – illustrated in its responses to Fourth Army CIC in the southwest and to Army CIC at Oak Ridge discussed previously. The same stance is also evident in responses to other government agencies, including the FBI.

Given the number of atomic facility security memos the FBI had been copied on, it is no surprise that in 1950 Director J. Edger Hoover directed FBI personnel to make inquiries with the Air Force. Along with Army field commands, local FBI offices had taken the incidents at the atomic facilities seriously, even assisting with witness background checks at Oak Ridge. With ongoing warfare in Korea and a declared state of national emergency, certainly Hoover had reason to be curious about whether or not the Air Force was more concerned than was evident in its public statements.

In the spring of 1950, two FBI liaison agents were sent to pursue the matter with the analysis division of Air Intelligence.[16] The FBI agents were immediately advised that the whole matter of anomalous aerial object reports had been resolved; the Air Force Flying Saucer project had been completed and investigation of UFO reports was strictly a matter for local, base level investigation. The agents were also told that any apparent concerns over UFO sightings were unwarranted and totally a result of inflammatory magazine articles. In conclusion the agents were reminded that the FBI had chosen to drop out of flying saucer investigations back in 1947 – a not too subtle hint that they had been no help in the past and could leave the entire matter to the Air Force.

Of course, in the context of the larger national security priorities of those years, the Air Force and its intelligence groups certainly had more pressing strategic concerns. And it was true that the UFOs had demonstrated no obvious signs of hostility. In contrast, during April, 1950, Air Force intelligence offered its initial overall estimate of the Soviet atomic threat, following the detection of the first Russian nuclear detonation in August of the previous year.

Air intelligence chief Cabell projected a Soviet long range bomber force of some 1,200 planes by 1952. The Air Force commander, General George Kenney, felt that to be a low estimate and Secretary of Defense Hoyt Vandenberg also felt Cabell's estimate to be on the low side, Vandenberg himself felt that some 300 nuclear bombs would be available to the Russians by 1952. Kenney took the position, generally supported at the Pentagon, that when the Soviets felt they had sufficient nuclear striking force they would launch a preemptive attack on the United States. He believed that Russia was already essentially at war with the West and that the public and Congress needed to be educated to the fact that a virtual state of war already existed.[17]

The view of an imminent Soviet threat was further endorsed in the first ever United States National Intelligence Estimate of Soviet capabilities and before the end of 1950 the Central Intelligence Agency weighed in with its own opinion that the Soviet Union could be expected to provoke a general war at whatever time they felt their strength to be at its maximum – that point was again anticipated as potentially occurring within some two years, by 1952.[18]

In context of the known threats facing the nation, it's understandable that at the Pentagon level Air Force attention was not focused on the issue of UFOs – other than in terms of annoyance at the extent to which the press insisted on writing about them and the possibility of their interplanetary origins. As the FBI liaison agents had been told, the topic of flying saucers/UFOs had moved from "special" project status to routine handling through normal reporting. As necessary it was being handled though spot intelligence reports from local bases and with local inquiries by OSI special investigations personnel. Reports which were forwarded to AMC for further study most often produced a restatement of the standard assessment that virtually all sightings could be explained as misidentification of airplanes, balloons, birds or even "small detached clouds".[19]

Of course, from an operational standpoint, unidentified objects which could actually represent foreign reconnaissance, pre-attack probes or even an attack in progress remained an ongoing, everyday concern of all the military services. And by summer 1950, unidentified flying objects were once again becoming an immediate operational concern. As early as June 1, 1950, General Earle Partridge – Fifth Air Force commander headquartered in Japan – requested that a number of airspace violations by unidentified flying objects (including combined radar/visual observations) be investigated. That request was quickly forwarded to Air Intelligence Chief Cabell. With the North Korean invasion of the south later that same month, and with the commitment of extensive American forces to what became a full scale war on the Korean peninsula, unidentified aerial objects once again became a matter of both tactical and threat intelligence.[20]

At the time of the invasion of South Korea, the common opinion in Washington was that the North Koreans were acting directly under the influence of the Soviets. The attack was seen as a test of the Western powers' will to go to war over contested border challenges. In many quarters it was also perceived as a diversion from the more fundamental and increasingly imminent Russian threat to Europe or even the United States.

General Curtis LeMay, commander of the Strategic Air Command, adamantly opposed deploying SAC for a conventional bombing campaign against North Korea. He felt that it would only squander strategic aircraft and crews which should remain focused on their preparations for atomic warfare with Russia.

Both the State Department and Department of Defense advised President Harry Truman that Korea was simply an indication that the Soviet Union was the true threat to the United States. President Truman confirmed that view with a request to Congress for major increase in military spending; his request stated that the need was far greater than simply to deal with the Korean conflict.[21]

Strategically, the existential threat was perceived to be the Soviet Union and the primary targets of concern were inside the continental United States. Reporting, tracking and attempting to identify potential enemy air or maritime craft had always been a priority during times of war and combat. With the advent of the Cold War, atomic weapons, and the threat of devastating preemptive strikes, identification and tracking of aircraft approaching strategic areas and population centers became a peace time concern. Researcher Jan Aldrich points out that when a joint Army-Navy-Air unidentified object reporting regulation (JANAP 146) was issued in 1948, it was simply an extension of a reporting system used during the recent war.[22]

However a new version of the joint Army-Navy-Air regulation was issued in September 25, 1950. It added UFOs to the list of the types of sightings which should be reported.[23] That addition seems reasonable enough in light of the fact that many of the ongoing reports of unknowns sighted near military bases and national security reservations described shapes and maneuvers which did not match any known aircraft. The regulation provided instructions to all services and to both commercial and military pilots for the reporting of "vital intelligence sightings". The instructions including a list of sighting categories for UFOs and all reports were to be made according to the Communications Instructions for Reporting Vital Intelligence Sightings (CIRVIS).[24]

An examination of the regulation makes it clear that it was designed for the reporting of both aerial and maritime objects that might represent an imminent threat to national security.[25] Examples included in the regulation refer to unidentified formations of aircraft and the key information to be reported included speeds, direction of flight and other related data useful in tracking and intercepting the objects. Reports were to be made only if, in the opinion of the observer, the situation required "prompt defensive and/or investigative action by the US and/or Canadian Armed Forces." CIRVIS (aerial object) reports were essentially tactical threat advisories and were not intended to be exceptionally detailed – timeliness and communication were the priorities. Similar reports of waterborne objects were designated as MARINT reports.

The tactical/threat nature of JANAP intelligence reports is also evident in the directions for communication of such reports. CIRVIS and MARINT advisories were to be addressed to the nearest Air Defense command, Headquarters Continental Air Defense, Commanders of either the Eastern or Western Sea Frontier and to Chief of Staff, United States Air Force. Neither AMC nor the technical intelligence group at Wright Patterson were on the required distribution although certain reports of anomalous sightings did make their way to them.

Professor Alan Hynek, who served as an astronomical consultant to the Air Force, speculated that reports from highly classified military units or secret missions very likely would also not have been forwarded on to AMC at Wright Patterson. He cites conversations with air crew members who flew highly secret reconnaissance missions; the crew members stated that the circulation of any observations from their flights would have been highly compartmentalized at headquarters level – strictly limited by "need to know" restrictions about their activities.[26] Hynek noted that the UFO reports he reviewed were almost all designated at the lowest levels of either "Confidential" or "Restricted" classification, few carried even a "Secret" classification. In his analysis of the JANAP regulation, Francis Ridge also notes that most CIRVIS reports found in the Air Force files were brief, with few details, thus proving relatively useless for serious UFO investigations.[27]

As of fall 1950, unidentified aerial object reports constituted an increasingly serious issue of daily operational concern, both in the Korean theater and over the nation's military and strategic assets. From a threat standpoint, the possibility that the Soviets would enter into the Korean conflict, or even move to some sort of preemptive action should the U.S. use atomic weapons in Korea, was a very real concern. Reports of unknown aerial objects which could represent new Soviet technology, Soviet reconnaissance activity or psychological warfare were very much a responsibility of Air Intelligence and General Cabell – regardless of any prevailing attitudes at the Air Material Command.

Cabell's Air Force Intelligence (AFOIN) mission responsibilities gave him the authority to request that AMC and its technical intelligence division seriously evaluate UFO reports and keep his Pentagon intelligence groups well informed on the issue. Given that the nation was in a national state of emergency and in an undeclared war, technical collection on UFOs was a serious and time sensitive matter – but it also needed to be done quietly in order not to raise public fears or negatively affect the general morale of the nation.

Cabell's position on those points can be seen in the fact that as of July, 1950, Colonel Watson at Air Material Command was advised by Air Intelligence that UFOs were indeed an intelligence priority and should be treated accordingly. At that point in time Cabell had no direct chain of command authority over either the Air Material Command, or more specifically Colonel Watson's technical intelligence group within AMC. Nevertheless AMC was providing a support function to AFOIN and as a customer (with the rank of Major General) at the Pentagon, Cabell's views were something to be taken quite seriously.

Colonel Barber, an aide to General Cabell, provided Watson with some very specific guidance – AMC technical intelligence was expected to support AFOIN with a dedicated, ongoing analysis of UFO reports and there was to be no interruption of that effort. Watson was referred to the headquarters letter of January 12, 1950 – Reporting of Information on Unconventional Aircraft – which specified that any incidents determined to have intelligence value would be referred to headquarters intelligence for information; headquarters was to take care of any press response to the incidents.[28] Incidents which involved anomalous shapes, technologies, performance, maneuvers and capabilities were most definitely of interest to Cabell and Air Intelligence.

In a letter to Watson, Barber stressed that such intelligence collections were to be conducted in a very low profile manner, with no traveling teams, no field interviews and no publicity over the continuing investigations.[29] The only allowed response to any press inquiries would be that unidentified flying objects were simply a routine part of the overall Air Force intelligence effort. The letter made it quite clear that Cabell was serious about the subject but was also set on the collections and analysis work being done quietly, with absolutely minimal press visibility.

The letter from Barber to Watson was quite detailed and it began with the remark that it was being personally communicated "to save the bother of an officially coordinated directive". It concluded on the same note, suggesting that if Watson was unclear or had questions, he should call Barber for further discussion and advice.[30] In short, Watson's personnel were expected to be seriously searching for real intelligence that might be gained from UFO reports, but they were to conduct their work in a manner so as not to gain press attention and certainly not in a fashion which would raise public concern.

It appears that Colonel Watson was either not satisfied with the unofficial direction he was being given or determined that he did indeed want something in writing as far as an official policy guidance relating to statements to the press. An Air Force headquarters letter of October 12, makes mention of a call from Watson, requesting permission to release full details on unidentified object reports to the press. The memorandum describes this as a "problem", to be corrected by officially advising Colonel Watson as to the proper procedure for handling unidentified object reports. That official direction was contained in a headquarters letter to the AMC Commander, of October 15, 1950. That communication provided a "canned" format, giving Watson the only acceptable response to the press:

"We have investigated and evaluated _____ incident and found nothing of value and nothing which would change our previous estimates of this subject."

The actual results and evaluation of any incidents which were felt to have intelligence value were to be forwarded to Air Intelligence (AFOIN) for review and decisions related to the press.[31]

As 1950 passed into 1951, Air Force investigation of suspicious and truly anomalous UFO incidents remained fragmented. Observations were made and reported in field organization Spot Intelligence reports or to the responsible Office of Special Investigations. If OSI could not provide a reasonable explanation locally, a report might be referred to technical intelligence at Wright Patterson. Then it would most likely receive an innocuous explanation – or simply filed as an "Unknown".

Yet, General Cabell carried the intelligence responsibility of ensuring that reports involving potential new technology or some sort of Soviet activity be objectively and thoroughly evaluated. To do so he had to rely on the judgement of the personnel at AMC and as well as a variety of reports coming though other sources. Cabell's staff did monitor certain of the more suggestive reports, such as those from Oak Ridge, but carried out no intensive or extensive field inquiries. As far as can be determined, in terms of priorities Pentagon intelligence staff were primarily concerned with real time combat intelligence and the Soviet threat.

It seems fair to say that General Cabell continued to hold the issue of unidentified flying objects as a serious concern of Air Intelligence. And his concerns over undue media attention to the subject proved well justified. An Associated Press wire story in February, 1951 carried the title "Scientist Fears Flying Saucers Portend a 'Worse Pearl Harbor'".[32] The story quoted Dr. Anthony O. Mirachi, a chemist in the Air Force geophysical laboratory, who had independently conducted an in depth study of the fireballs reported over New Mexico. Mirachi had been the Cambridge Research Laboratories scientific consultant to Project Twinkle, the abortive attempt to resolve the green fireball phenomena with specially equipped cameras.

Mirachi stated that he had personally studied extensive files covering hundreds of reports from the areas of New Mexico which housed strategic atomic installations. He also shared information from the files including the detection of copper in a dust collection experiment by Dr. La Paz and speculated that the anomalous fireballs had ceased because foreign agents had learned of the TWINKLE camera project. He concluded that several of the fireball observations could only be consistent with "a missile programmed in advance." He felt that the objects' paths also suggested man-made guidance and did not correspond to natural phenomena such as meteors or drifting balloons. In short, he described foreign agents at work, enemy devices and a dereliction of duty on the part of the Air Force. Without a doubt Mirachi's article represented Cabell's worst fears about public concerns which might develop from further media attention to the subject of UFOs.

The Air Force reply to the article was brief and consistent – "In over 500 investigations we have made so far we have yet to find one concrete bit of evidence to back up these reports of flying saucers." However it did note that the Air Force was still involved in studying rumors of flying saucers, that task was being carried out by the Air Material Command center, under the direction of Colonel. Harold E. Watson.

Officially that response was entirely correct. But the view from inside, from someone close to the efforts going on at AMC and technical intelligence under Colonel Watson, might have expressed a less positive view of contemporary UFO investigations. Fortunately we have just that sort of inside view, provided by an AMC technical analyst, Captain Edward Ruppelt.

In January, 1951 the ongoing warfare in Korea had resulted in the Air Force calling Edward Ruppelt back to active service. He was assigned to intelligence work at AMC, specifically to a technical evaluation of the new Soviet MiG-15 fighter. According to Ruppelt, literally within hours of his arrival, he begin to hear talk of flying saucers. Ruppelt himself had over 2,000 hours of flying time and a number of combat service awards from World War II. He had seen a number of initially strange objects during his time in the air, but had figured out what they really were in seconds. His view was that if experienced pilots and air crews were seeing something unknown to them, something unidentifiable, it was something real and not a hallucination.[33] He quickly realized the officer handling the flying saucer reports sat only three desks away from him, but he was surprised to see that the officer and the others who joined him seemed to be doing nothing more than laughing as they discussed a sighting report from a commercial airline crew.

Ruppelt got a look at the report, found it detailed and especially credible given that a military intelligence colonel had been on the plane, observed the object and corroborated the pilot and co-pilot. He was quite surprised to see that the AMC personnel responded to the report with what he described as "a great big, deep belly laugh".[34] If Ruppelt was surprised, we can imagine General Cabell's reaction if he had witnessed the same incident.

With ongoing press interest, in particular the national attention to Dr. Miriachi's views about a potential new Pearl Harbor, a *LIFE* magazine editor was allowed access to the staff at AMC and given permission to actually check some of their files. The *LIFE* editor had lots of specific questions and the staff spent a good deal of time running around looking for files, not finding them and falling back on a response of "I'm sorry, that's classified". According to Ruppelt it was a trying visit and the *LIFE* representative was far from impressed with the standard responses about misidentifications, hallucinations and hoaxes.

Shortly afterwards changes began to occur. First a new Air and Missiles Branch Chief (Lt. Col. N. R. Rosengarten) was assigned to oversee the flying saucer inquiries and a new UFO desk officer (Lt. Jerry Cummings) was given the job of handling incoming reports. Cummings had been recalled to active duty as Ruppelt had been; he was new to the subject and as surprised as Ruppelt about the negative attitudes towards seemingly credible reports.

More importantly, within a few weeks (May 1951) the technical intelligence group at AMC was re-designated as the Air Technical Intelligence Center/ (ATIC) and officially became a field activity of Air Intelligence (AFOIN) at the Pentagon. Official designation as a field activity for AFOIN provided General Cabell and AFOIN with more formal control over ATIC and specifically its UFO investigative activities. In addition, the head of technical intelligence at AMC/Wright Patterson, Colonel Watson, was scheduled for reassignment. Watson would be replaced by Colonel Frank Dunn; the transition in command began later in that year and Watson was frequently away from AMC in the late summer of 1951.

In September, 1951 an anomalous Air Defense Command radar tracking incident – a very high speed track – gained considerable press attention. The radar track appeared to have been confirmed with a visual observation by two officers on an Air Force training flight. The incident was reported by ADC to both AMC and Air Intelligence at the Pentagon. The exact sequence of events which followed is unclear – reportedly some of Watson's "old guard" officers at AMC produced yet another traditionally dismissive explanation for the report without even bringing the report to the attention to the UFO desk at ATIC.[35] What exactly happened at that point remains a matter of debate but it appears that Cabell's office determined that ATIC should be involved and that a more substantive investigation of the incident was in order. Within hours two ATIC officers, Lt. Colonel Rosengarten and the UFO desk officer, Lieutenant Cummings, were off in a plane with operational orders directing them to investigate and personally brief General Cabell at the Pentagon.

The radar tracking incident appears to have triggered a high level discussion on the handling of UFO reports and Air Force credibility on the subject. Following their investigations, when the two ATIC officers arrived at the Pentagon to brief General Cabell, they found that others were present, including another general who had brought along a representative from Republic Aviation. That individual had already expressed the concerns of a number of top industrialists and scientists who were not at all satisfied by the type of response they and their people had been receiving from the Air Force in regard to UFO reports from the engineering and technical community.

The full two hour meeting with the two generals, along with several headquarters colonels who were apparently invited into the session, was recorded and at some point during the meeting Lieutenant Cummings was asked for a review of the UFO work being performed at AMC. Cummings was relatively new in the job and according to his friend Edward Ruppelt he was quite frustrated about the way the subject was treated AMC. At the time of the meeting he was also dealing with a serious lack of sleep from two days of travel and investigation and was scheduled to return to civilian status in the near future.

The result was that the lieutenant proceeded to give the very senior Pentagon officers in the room a full description of the highly negative and dismissive attitudes he had seen in play back at Wright Patterson – including the extent to which his own efforts to treat reports seriously had been rejected. Cumming's remarks appear to have confirmed Cabell's own concerns about the matter and the meeting ended with a round of extremely strong language, some purple faces, and an absolute demand from Cabell for some real answers.

Cabell was outspoken, "Who the hell is giving me these reports that every decent flying saucer incident is being investigated…I want an open mind… In fact I order an open mind…anyone who doesn't have an open mind can get out now!"[36] Afterwards Cummings and Rosengarten were sent on their way, with a directive to establish a serious UFO project and report back directly to General Cabell.[37] The reinvigorated UFO project, which Ruppelt later described as the "new" Project GRUDGE, was effectively underway as of October 25, 1951. Cummings initially headed the work – which was largely a two man task at that point – but he was soon released from active duty and returned to a government research project at Cal Tech.

In turn ATIC analyst Captain Edward Ruppelt was asked to step in and organize UFO incident collections and analysis so as to ensure that a serious inquiry continued. He was assured that once he got that done he could return to his work on Russian aircraft. Ruppelt brought a new level of energy and organization to the UFO project and he personally spent considerable time actively chasing down the most anomalous and credible reports. He also revisited all the SIGN and GRUDGE files, reevaluating a number of key reports which had received explanations, explanations which he often found to be superficial or questionable. He wrote about many of the earlier incidents and his follow on investigations in his 1956 book *The Report on Unidentified Flying Objects*.

Major General Cabell moved on from his position as Director of Intelligence at AFOIN by the end of the 1951, replaced by Major General John Samford. The new ATIC technical intelligence head, Colonel Dunn, and Ruppelt were called in to brief Samford and Brigadier General W. M. Garland on the UFO study project. Samford assigned Garland, as head of intelligence production, to oversee the ATIC effort. Ruppelt wrote that as part of the Pentagon briefing he had noted that unidentified aerial objects had been reported "more frequently around areas vital to the defense of the United States. The Los Alamos-Albuquerque area, Oak Ridge and White Sands Proving Ground rated high. Strategic Air Command bases and port areas ranked next.[38]

Ruppelt's recognition of a correlation between UFO reports and strategic facilities – and his highlighting it for the senior officers – is highly significant. It reflects the fact that even a cursory review of the UFO files quickly revealed a specific pattern in the sightings, a pattern which in turn suggested that the unidentified objects in question might well have a strategic/military focus. Even in his first command briefing, Ruppelt was aware of that possibility and he advised the senior AFOIN officers about it. It is also noteworthy that Brigadier General Garland had himself observed an unidentifiable aerial object. According to Ruppelt, Garland proceeded to made it clear that the Air Force and specifically ATIC, headed by Colonel Dunn, would be solely responsible for investigating and evaluating UFO reports from that point forward.

Changes in command, in organizational structure, and in attitude had all come into place for UFO inquiries by the end of 1951. With Ruppelt running the UFO desk, supported by Samford's interest and authority, investigations and studies were both moving to a much higher level of energy and intensity. They were being conducted with the nation effectively at war – even if undeclared – and with the Soviets still perceived as a very real enemy. The Soviets had surprised the Air Force with their new and impressive MiG-15 jet fighter. The MiGs, ostensibly flown by North Koreans but also covertly by experienced Soviet pilots, represented a serious threat to American bombers and fighters. Beginning in April 1951 and through January 1952 Russian MiG pilots shot down or damaged 148 United Nations aircraft, averaging a two to one kill ratio and bringing down the most advanced U.S. and British fighter jets engaged in Korean combat. The MiG was also a threat to the bombing campaign against North Korea, downing a number of SAC's B-29 bombers. Over 30 of the MiG pilots unofficially became Soviet "Aces" during that period.[39]

As for Russian offensive capability, in early 1952 American intelligence sources determined that Premier Joseph Stalin had ordered the construction of one hundred new tactical bombing squadrons. Worse yet, radiation sampling and materials analysis revealed that on October, 1951 a Russian nuclear test had involved an actual bomb, dropped by a long range Tu-4 strategic bomber. And in the spring of 1952 signals intelligence tracked the deployment of Tu-4 squadrons into new Soviet airfields in Siberia; there was an increasing fear that Russia would involve its forces directly in that conflict.

In addition, radar and radar/visual observations of extremely high speed UFOs passing over American military installations and Navy ships continued to come out of the Korean theater. In one incident a senior Air Force officer verified that radars were working correctly when an object was determined to have accelerated at a rate of over 650 feet per second, far beyond anything the human body could withstand.[40] Given the surprise represented by the appearance of the MiG-15 jets, there were very real concerns about possible new Soviet missiles or even more advanced rocket aircraft. In addition, with increased surveillance radar deployment inside the United States, an increasing number of anomalous, very high speed radar tracks began to be reported by continental Air Defense Command units.

In that military context, it is understandable that the revitalized UFO investigation at AMC received substantial headquarters support. In the spring of 1952 the effort was re-initiated as *Project BLUE BOOK*, officially replacing the earlier GRUDGE project. *BLUE BOOK* was to be conducted within ATIC by personnel in the Aerial Phenomena Group. During 1952 ATIC itself came under the direct command of Air Intelligence (AFOIR). Ruppelt remained with the Aerial Phenomena Group and *Project BLUE BOOK* until his release from active duty – other ATIC analysts would get the job of evaluating recovered samples of Soviet MiG-15, Il-10 and Yak-9 aircraft.

As early as his initial briefing with General Samford, Ruppelt had essentially returned the UFO investigation to the same "hard data" approach taken in the earlier SIGN project. He proposed a program of technical collections which might potentially resolve the entire issue by providing scientific proof that the anomalous objects were indeed craft, only craft operating with a type of totally unknown technology.

BLUE BOOK began as a return to the basics, with the goal of obtaining accurate measurements of the unidentified object's speeds, altitude and size. The difference would be that by 1952 the effort was to have access to resources far beyond those available to SIGN – surveillance radars were in place around many strategic facilities, all-weather and nighttime jet interceptors with onboard gun radar were being deployed, and the new Ground Observer Corps was operational. One of Ruppelt's early *BLUE BOOK* meetings was with the head of the Air Defense Command. He wanted observations from ADC and hopefully hard data from their radars and interceptors – particularly photos off the gun cameras in ADC fighters. Ruppelt himself personally pursued a number of UFO intercept reports, interviewing pilots, radar operators and base intelligence officers.

In addition to ADC, Ruppelt was active in meeting with a wide variety of Air Force personnel, Air Force science advisors and credentialed scientists. With authorization from General Samford, $100,000 was directed towards a statistical analysis of UFO reports by an Air Force consulting groups. Ruppelt did not name that organization in his book but we now know it to be the Battelle Memorial Institute. Battelle (focused on technology and statistical analysis), along with Cambridge Labs (Radar/Air Defense) and RAND Corporation (aircraft/missile studies) was one of the major scientific resources used by the Air Force during the 1950s. Battelle was already under contract (Project Stork) to evaluate the Soviet Union as a military threat and the UFO study (Project PPS-160) was simply added to their work under that contract.[41]

Ruppelt's search for good UFO reports ranged from ADC to the crews launching stratospheric balloons, on to news clippings, and even to private saucer research groups. In a review of flying saucer groups of the early 1950s, Jan Aldrich describes Civilian Saucer Investigations of Los Angeles (CSI-LA) as perhaps the most professional, and the most respected.[42] It had been formed in late 1951 and had strong participation by scientists and aeronautical engineers working with major aircraft companies in southern California. A number of the members worked at North American Aviation and it may well have been a representative of that UFO group who was brought into General Cabell's explosive briefing by Lt. Cummings. The group also included members who worked at Douglas Aircraft and Republic Aviation, and most likely members from Northrup and Lockheed as well.

Ruppelt and Colonel S. H. Kirkland of the ATIC analytical section met with CSI-LA members in April of 1952, the meeting reviewed investigative procedures and methodology. Ruppelt was impressed with their enthusiasm but felt that their plans were far too ambitious. Aldridge notes that the meeting is described not only in Ruppelt's book but also in a *Project BLUE BOOK* status report. Researchers have obtained a complete copy of the meeting transcript.[43] It is not only fascinating reading but provides considerable insight into Ruppelt, Kirkland and the ATIC mindset and views as of 1952. It also serves as a valuable illustration of the attitude change that had occurred in less than a year. In was a change which Ruppelt was serious about maintaining. He later wrote that objectivity was his watch word and that during his time on the project he transferred out three staff members who had become too pro or too con in regard to classifying reports as "unknowns".[44]

Captain Ruppelt was an engineer by training, holding a degree in aeronautics, and a technical analyst by Air Force career field. His approach to resolving the UFO question was fully in line with the accepted practice in technical analysis at ATIC – analysis driven by science and by hard data. Profile the intelligence target, track it, measure it, use hard data to characterize it, identify it and estimate its potential as a weapon/threat. Cabell had been adamant in restarting the analysis at AMC – "I want the answer to the saucers and I want a good answer!"[45] The question would be whether or not an aggressive program of technical intelligence collection and analysis, conducted by a staff with open minds, could provide that answer.

Chapter 10 Endnotes

3. PROJECT GRUDGE, August, 1949 http://www.bluebookarchive.org/page.aspx?PageCode=NARA-PBB85-75http://www.nicap.org/grudge/grudge_dir.htm

4. PROJECT GRUDGE, August, 1949 http://www.bluebookarchive.org/page.aspx?PageCode=NARA-PBB85-75http://www.nicap.org/grudge/grudge_dir.htm

5. Dr. J. Allen Hynek, *The Hynek UFO Report*, Barnes and Noble Inc. 1997, 9

6. "Chief of Staff Command directive to Air Materials Command", Wright Patterson Air Force Base, January 4, 1950 http://www.secretsdeclassified.af.mil/shared/media/document/AFD-110719-005.pdf

7. Douglas Larson, "The Air Force Has Flying Disc Debunker", NEA news release, dateline: Washington, DC, 4 April, 1950

8. Edward Ruppelt, *The Report on Unidentified Flying Objects*, Double Day and Company, Garden City, New York, 1956, 60

9. Ibid, 82

10. Ibid, 86

11. The UFO Chronologies, NICAP. Observations on trends by number and type of report have been taken from the information available online in the UFO Chronologies made available by NICAP. The consolidated yearly chronologies contain sightings from the Air Force *Project BLUE BOOK* files, integrated with other researched and credible sources. All observations are sourced and a large number are linked to source documents. This extensive resource is available through the work of Francis Ridge, Rebecca Wise (*Project BLUE BOOK* Archive), Dan Wilson, Brad Sparks (*Project BLUE BOOK* Unknowns), Loren Gross, Larry Hatch, Jean Waskiewicz, Richard Hall and others noted by Francis Ridge in the introductions to the chronologies. http://www.nicap.org/chrono.htm

12. Francis Ridge, "4925th Test Group Sees UFO", Kirtland AFB, New Mexico, March 21, 1950 http://www.nicap.org/docs/kirt1950/500321_4925rep.htm

13. Francis Ridge, "Atomic Test Group Witnesses UFO In Broad Daylight", Kirtland AFB, March 22, 1950 http://www.nicap.org/500322kirtland_dir.htm

14. David F. Winkler, "Searching the Skies; The Legacy of the United States Cold War Defense Radar Program", Headquarters Air Combat Command, June 1997, 140

15. Wilber L. Mitchell, Data Reduction Unit, "Objects observed following MX776 test of April 27, 1950 http://www.nicap.org/nmexico/miscl/whitesands2.htm

16. *Project BLUE BOOK* archive http://www.bluebookarchive.org/page.aspx?PageCode=NARA-PBB85-495

17. Michal Swords and Robert Powell, *UFO's and Government; A Historical Inquiry*, 90-102

18. Ibid, 95

19. General Richard Kenney to General Hoyt Vandenberg, April 29, 1950 http://www2.gwu.edu/-nsarchiv/nukevault/special/doc03d.pdf

20. Raymond Garthoff, "Estimating Soviet Military Indentions and Capabilities", Center for the Study of Intelligence, Central Intelligence Agency

21. *Project BLUE BOOK* archive http://www.bluebookarchive.org/page.aspx?PageCode=NARA-PBB85-500

22. Michal Swords and Robert Powell, *UFO's and Government; A Historical Inquiry*, 101

23. Larry Hancock, *Surprise Attack; From Pearl Harbor and 9/11 to Benghazi*, Counterpoint Publishing, Berkeley, California, 2015, 115-116

24. Jan Aldrich, "JANAP – 50 Years", *UFO Updates* http://www.ufoupdateslist.com/2003/may/m18-003.shtml

25. JNAP 146 document http://docslide.us/documents/janap-146.html

26. New versions of CIRVIS communications and reporting directives would continue to be issued from 1950 on, proscribing confidentiality for all such reports and placing increasingly strict limitations on both military and commercial pilot reports. Researchers have had to go through a number of Freedom of Information Requests to gain samples of the various CIRVIS documents such as Air Force Regulation 55-88 (CIRVIS) Under JANAP 146: Reporting of Vital Intelligence UFO Encounters. http://www.ufoevidence.org/documents/doc1483.htm

27. JANAP "146 General Description and Purpose of Communications Instructions for Reporting Vital Intelligence Sightings" http://docslide.us/documents/janap-146.html

28. Dr. J. Allen Hynek, *The Hynek UFO Report*, Barnes and Noble Inc. 1997, 50-51

29. Jan Aldrich, "JANAP – 50 Years", *UFO Updates* http://www.ufoupdateslist.com/2003/may/m18-003.shtml

30. Michal Swords and Robert Powell, *UFO's and Government : A Historical Inquiry*, 500

31. Larry Hancock, *Surprise Attack; From Pearl Harbor and 9/11 to Benghazi,* 102-103

32. Colonel Barber, AFOIC, "Memorandum for Colonel Watson", AMC, July 7, 1950

33. "Chief of Staff Command directive to Air Materials Command", Wright Patterson Air Force Base, October 18, 1950 http://www.secretsdeclassified.af.mil/shared/media/document/AFD-110719-005.pdf

34. "Scientist Fears Flying Saucers Portend a Worse ' Pearl Harbor'", *Daily Oklahoman,* February 26, 1951, 1, 2 and 20, AP Wire Service, Fran Ridge Commentary, NICAP http://www.nicap.org/articles/MirarchiArticle.htm

35. Edward Ruppelt, *The Report on Unidentified Flying Objects*, 83-84

36. Ibid, 84-85

37. Michael Swords and Robert Powell, *UFO's and Government: A Historical Inquiry*, 239-241

38. Ibid, 240

39. Edward Ruppelt, *The Report on Unidentified Flying Objects*, 92-94

40. Ibid, 116

41. Diego Zampini, "Russian Aces over Korea / Mikoyan-Gurevich Mig-15 Fagot pilots", November 2004, updated January 27, 2012

42. For a detailed coverage of this and similar reports, readers are referred to Richard Haines work on Korean Theater UFO's, Richard F Haines, *Advanced Aerial Devices Reported During the Korean War*, Lightening Design Associates, 1990

43. Edward Ruppelt, "Seven Status Reports for Project Stork", National Archives, The Computer UFO Network http://www.cufon.org/cufon/stork1-7.htm

44. Jan Aldritch, "Civilian Saucer Investigation (Los Angeles)", SIGN Historical Group, Project 1947 http://www.project1947.com/shg/csi/csiintro.html

45. MINUTES OF MEETING OF CIVILIAN SAUCER INVESTIGATIONS HELD WEDNESDAY, APRIL 2, 1952, 8:00 PM, IN THE MAYFAIR HOTEL, LOS ANGELES, CALIFORNIA, SIGN Historical Group, Project 1947 http://www.project1947.com/shg/csi/csi_minutes.html

46. Edward Ruppelt, *The Report on Unidentified Flying Objects*, 114

47. Michael Swords and Robert Powell, *UFO's and Government: A Historical Inquiry*, 127

Chapter 11

Defense of the Capital

In this chapter

- A new Air Force UFO project (*BLUE BOOK*) is directed to deal with UFOs as a priority air defense issue.

- Air Intelligence proposes the creation of special ATIC/Air Defense teams to obtain coordinated interceptor gun camera/radar tracking data on UFO appearances over three strategic areas – Albuquerque, Seattle and the New York/Philadelphia corridor.

- The Air Defense Command sees alert fighter scrambles increase dramatically – especially over the vital northeastern corridor.

- All the records for number of UFO reports are broken; senior officers become highly concerned over the "alarming increase" in reports and the new trend to East Coast sightings.

- Air defense and SAC exercises increase, including the first hemispheric Air Defense Command test (Sign Post) however none of them generate waves of UFO reports or press coverage.

- During the summer months a wave of East Coast air defense alerts sends interceptors against both day time and nighttime UFOs – intercepts are repeatedly made only to have the targets display evasive action and maneuvers capable of breaking radar gun locks and moving out of contact.

- President Harry Truman calls a special meeting with senior Air Force officers in regard to the "Defense of the Capital".

With the launch of *Project BLUE BOOK* it appeared as if Air Intelligence and the technical intelligence group at Wright Patterson AFB were taking a more open approach to the problem of UFOs – at a minimum treating them as a very real issue of air defense. The new Air Intelligence Chief, Major General John Samford, had placed Brigadier General W.M. Garland in overall charge of the renewed UFO inquiry and in January, 1952 Garland emphasized the need for "positive action" in a memorandum to Samford. The letter noted persistent reports of "unusual flying objects" over both coasts and particularly in the vicinity of atomic energy production and testing facilities. It also resurfaced the concern that the Soviets might have pushed ahead with German technology, developing advanced weapon carriers in anticipation of their own atomic weapons.

Garland pointed out German development of mid-air refueling as an enabler for possible Soviet incursions over the continental United States, as well as in support of a potentially decisive air campaign against the West. In a proactive vein, Garland also proposed the creation of ATIC/Air Defense teams to engage in an attempt to obtained coordinated interceptor gun camera/radar tracking data on UFO appearances over the Albuquerque area, the Seattle area and the New York/Philadelphia corridor. His letter to Major General Samford also makes it clear that at as of early 1952 the Soviets were still suspects in regard to certain ongoing UFO reports and that UFO identification was definitely an air defense issue.[1]

Garland's concerns about advanced weapons carriers were very much in line with defense issues being raised within a small "Special Studies Group" which reported to Samford. The Special Studies Group was led by Stefan Possony, at the time with the Institute for Advanced Study at Princeton and also serving with the Office of Naval Warfare's psychological warfare staff. His specialties were air power and psychological warfare and he had authored an acclaimed and widely read book, Air Power, in 1949.[2] In early 1952, Possony remained especially concerned that the Soviets had used German technology to field some type of very advanced weapons carrier; he was sent on a mission to Germany that spring to further explore that possibility. It appears his concerns about the possibility of an advanced Soviet weapons delivery system may have been an influence on both Samford and Garland. Possony also visited Ruppelt and consulted with the *BLUE BOOK* staff at ATIC.

In general terms the *BLUE BOOK* mission operated much like the original Project SIGN. Although Ruppelt himself held a relatively low rank, he was energetic, traveled extensively, involved himself in considerable field work and established a broad network of contacts. He appears to have been involved with not only Air Force units such as the Air Defense Command but to have networked with virtually anyone willing to discuss the subject– from paid scientific consultants, to engineers and professionals and even private UFO study groups.

However a major difference between SIGN in 1948 and *BLUE BOOK* in 1952 was that the *BLUE BOOK* staff were working in the military context of a virtual state of war. Although Korean armistice talks had begun in July, 1951, they had proved fruitless. United Nations forces were engaged in what was described as an "active defense", holding their positions, establishing strong points for patrol and observation and in facing counter attacks by Chinese forces in battalion and regimental strength.

Air Force, Navy and Marine aircraft remained constantly engaged, carrying out extensive attacks against North Korea's hydroelectric dams and other sites along the Yalu River, the border between Communist China and North Korea. One series of bombing raids shut down the entire North Korean power grid for some two weeks. In turn, Communist Chinese units began regimental sized human wave attacks against the UN lines, in their own effort to pressure a favorable settlement at the armistice talks. It was the year of intense, bitter and bloody battles for Old Baldy, Heartbreak Ridge and other nameless positions that made newspaper headlines and entered into American combat history. Ground combat in Korea remained pervasive, and so did heavy American casualties; the air campaign continued, increasingly targeting ammunition and fueling depots near Communist front line positions.

Suspense over possible expansion of Soviet involvement remained high. Clearly its logistics support was ongoing, but would the Soviets choose to actually intervene – or to preempt? Intelligence had determined that the Soviets did have atomic capable, long range Tu-4 bombers. A Tu-4 had dropped an atomic bomb in a fall 1951 test. SAC reconnaissance flights located a string of upgraded airfields across Siberia, capable of supporting the Tu-4 bombers.[3] The threat of a surgical, one way strike across the Arctic was still taken to be very real. Continental air defense was of immediate concern, the question was whether or not the United States could obtain sufficient advance warning of an incoming attack - and effectively defend against it.[4]

Some progress had been made in that regard, Air Defense Identification Zones had been established along the Canadian border, the east and west coast and around key strategic facilities. The zones mandated flight plan reporting for both commercial and military aircraft.[5] The Skywatch network of ground observers was largely in place by July, 1952. Some three hundred thousand volunteers shared shifts at sixteen thousand observation posts along the west coast, the northern tier borders and the populous northeastern states.[6]

However exercises had raised serious questions about the ability to spot low level penetrations as well as to the responsiveness of the command and control network. And the Korean War had laid heavy claims on combat aircraft and crews. As of spring 1952 no more than 300 to 400 combat aircraft were available to respond to an actual attack on the continental United States.[7] The situation was especially concerning since the new all-weather jet interceptors (equipped with batteries of unguided rockets for attacking bomber formations) were strictly limited in range. The F-86 Sabrejet had an operational range of only 330 miles and the F-94 Starfire no more than around 800. In order to maintain full alert at the interceptor bases, pilots spent more than a hundred hours a week on base.

Although the new jet interceptors had onboard gun radar, in many instances nighttime interceptions proved difficult, especially without experienced ground control intercept (GCI) guidance, supported by height finder radars. Given that it had little to no experience with Soviet air doctrine, Air Defense Command assumed it would face a combination of both high and low altitude attacks, very possibly under challenging weather conditions. The reality was that any concerted attack was likely to succeed.

In one SAC exercise a flight of fifteen B-36 bombers departed their base in Arizona. Instead of returning to land as per their flight plan, the bombers approached their field, dropped down to five hundred feet and flew south some three hundred miles over Mexico before heading out over the Pacific. The "bomber stream" flew north at low altitude – no more than one thousand feet – for a full day, to a point near Vancouver Island. At that point they moved up to forty thousand feet and headed southeast towards targets across the Pacific Northwest.

Although they should have been detected by radar, at least for some portion of their approach, all fifteen bombers proceeded to their targets and conducted successful attacks with bomb drops which would have been devastating even with conventional weapons. They avoided all Air Defense Command efforts to track or intercept them.[8]

And in April, 1952 the worst fears of Soviet preemption appeared to be coming true. On April 16, Air Force Intelligence warned Air Defense Command that classified sources were suggesting "ominous" Soviet activities. While those sources remain classified to this day, additional information suggests that the warning was produced by signals intelligence intercepts tracking the movement of Soviet Tu-4 "Bull" bombers into the newly identified Siberian forward air bases.

The full story of what happened on April 16, 1952 remains undisclosed and somewhat mysterious. Only in recent years have researchers become able to describe certain of the events of that day – which totally escaped any press coverage at the time. Joel Carpenter and Francis Ridge provide us with the most comprehensive story of the April air defense readiness alert and the following is based on their work and their 2002 monograph.[9]

The first actual warning came from a remote observation post in the Bering Sea. What appeared to be vapor trails from four aircraft were sighted moving east-southeast towards the continental United States. That sighting was reported to a control center at Elmendorf Air Force Base near Anchorage, Alaska. From Elmendorf the report was routed to McChord AFB base south of Tacoma, Washington and then on to Hamilton AFB in California. By the time the report made its way to Air Defense Command headquarters at Ent AFB in Colorado it was midnight local time. ADC staff immediately notified the Royal Canadian Air Force and its own sub-commands, raising an alert for its perimeter surveillance radar sites.

While that alerting was in progress, ADC command at Ent attempted to directly contact Elmendorf AFB in Alaska – only to have the line go dead, producing frustration and more concerns. At approximately 3:30 Ent Combat Operations Center woke the ADC vice commander and informed him that a "hot" situation was in progress. With only limited information, he hesitated to call a full alert for ADC interceptors and Army anti-aircraft gunnery units. As he continued to evaluate the situation with his staff, another urgent report arrived. An Eastern perimeter radar site at Presque Isle, Maine, reported five unidentified objects being tracked incoming towards the northeastern states.

It appeared to be exactly the sort of coordinated Soviet strike which had been anticipated – coming in over the same polar routes that SAC itself was charting for strikes against the Soviet Union. Two apparent formations of unidentified objects, condensation trails and radar tracks but no visual identification. The vice commander at ADC had no real choice and a nationwide Air Defense Readiness alert was ordered.

Both the Pentagon and SAC were informed. SAC moved to launch its alert bombers and all alert interceptors were manned; backup aircraft were moved to alert status. The Tactical Air Command and Air Reserve units were directed to hand off their aircraft to Air Defense Command control. Within half an hour Army anti-craft sites were manned and interceptors were in the air towards the radar tracks coming into the East Coast.

Later, and only with successful aerial interceptions, visual identification and radio contact, it was determined that the unidentified tracks were being made by commercial airliners, all far off course and off schedule. They had reported their flight plan deviations to Canadian air traffic control centers but those changes had not been passed on to the Air Defense Control centers. For the Air Force as a whole, the events of April 16, 1952 emphasized that its ability to identify friend from foe in real time remained limited, there were clearly issues in air defense communications and air space control and even a handful of unidentified objects could present a challenge. The incident itself had occurred under the most favorable conditions – daytime sightings and surveillance radar tracks at considerable distance from actual targets. The Soviets were unlikely to be that considerate in their choice of tactics for any actual preemptive attack.

The ongoing concerns related to the problem of unidentified flying objects are illustrated by the April 29 issuance of a new Air Force directive. With Air Force Letter 200-5, all commands were directed to forward sightings to ATIC by wire, with a copy going to the Pentagon. The letter also authorized *BLUE BOOK* to contact any Air Force unit in the United States without going through chains of command. Such an order was virtually unprecedented and Ruppelt himself noted that it gave the project an immense reach – and a considerable amount of prestige.[10]

In retrospect it is easy to see that *BLUE BOOK* was not authorized as just a routine intelligence collections task, the reinvigorated UFO project was an integral element of a broad initiative to address weaknesses in the nation's air defense. Dealing with unidentified flying objects was a critical part of the air defense effort. As early as 1948, George Valley of MIT had become involved with the SIGN inquiry, obtaining copies of its files and beginning a study of what it was going to take to differentiate hostile unidentified flying objects as actual targets for an air defense system – a system which would have to deal with the threats of the coming decade, including high speed jet bombers and guided missiles. By 1950, Valley was serving as Chairman of the Air Defense Systems Engineering Sub-Committee, working under the Air Force's Scientific Advisory Board.

Under his watch an early computerized air traffic control project was taken over by the Air Force for the air defense mission. Work on computerized radar tracking began immediately, with oversight by the Air Materials Command. Actual development work was largely done under Air Force agreements with Watson Laboratories and by Cambridge Research Laboratories – primary technology contractors to the Air Force.[11] By early 1952 contracts for the development of a new and innovative air defense system were in place. Ultimately the effort would carry the same priority as the World War II Manhattan atomic project – and cost far more.

As the events of April, 1952 demonstrated, a World War II type air defense, even with improved radar and jet interceptors, was immensely challenging when a surprise attack could come at any time and from across any border. Major improvements were going to be necessary for all aspects of tracking and interception as well as communications and overall command. But it would years before the new system – eventually designated as SAGE – became operational, beginning only in 1958.

In the meantime, it was critical that improvements be developed around known threats, and it was increasingly important to differentiate between "bogies and bandits". Project SIGN needed to quickly and finally determine the true nature of the high speed, highly maneuverable UFOs which were increasingly being tracked on ADC radars and engaged by alert interceptors. The frequency of alert fighter "scrambles" increased dramatically as spring turned to summer in 1952. By July, Major General Roger Ramey, Deputy Chief of Staff for Air Force operations was being quoted by the press as saying that it was standard procedure to scramble interceptors upon reports of unidentified flying objects and that interceptors had already taken to the air hundreds of times.

Ruppelt elaborated on that practice by stating that UFOs, as unidentified objects, were by definition unknowns and required no special order for interceptors to be scrambled. However air defense ground control held the decision to scramble on unidentified radar tracks and faced a real quandary with tracks that appeared to indicate objects moving either too fast or too slow to be conventional air traffic.[12] In his book Ruppelt also discussed, at considerable length, a problem which Ramey had avoided in his public remarks. The fact was that in a significant number of incidents the UFO intercept attempts had either failed or been frustrated by apparent engagements with targets which could easily out maneuver the jets – or simply leave them behind at will in high speed departures.

The intensity of the air defense intercept effort – with many attempts taking place at night or in bad weather – was going to take a toll on both aircraft and crews. A survey of New York Times articles reveals that during the early 1950's (between 1951 and 1956) some 185 interceptors of all services were lost over the United States and adjacent coastal waters. Accidents and crashes cost the lives of more than 200 Air Force, Navy and Marine personnel.

BLUE BOOK had resources, it had Pentagon level attention, it had a unique, high priority access directly to the field commands dealing with UFO incidents and it could bypass normal chains of command. As it turned out, the one thing it did not have was time. Ruppelt was going to great lengths establishing a broad and well organized collections effort, he was also bringing scientific consultants on board and making arrangements for a statistical analysis of a comprehensive catalog of reports. From his writings, it appears that Ruppelt would have preferred to focus on hard core and highly credible reports from military personnel, especially from pilots and ADC radar operators. There was certainly amble opportunity for that, no doubt stimulated by Air Force Letter 200- 5. He relates that as of April, 1952 sighting reports were at an all-time high and that they were all from military installations.

Credible sightings represented an opportunity but the surge of reports also meant that increasingly Ruppelt and *BLUE BOOK* were being called upon simply to provide responses to inquiries from the Pentagon, briefings for senior staff and responses for public relations use. A civilian (Al Chop) on the Air Press desk at the Pentagon also was assigned to deal with the increasing volume of media inquiries and an Air Force officer (Major Dewey Fournet) was designated as the UFO liaison at the Pentagon.

In a repetition of events during Project GRUDGE, from an Air Force public relations perspective *BLUE BOOK* was being sucked back into the task of public reassurance and by summer that role would become an increasing drain on its resources – and on Captain Ruppelt's own time. As Ruppelt himself put it, "In early June, 1952, *Project BLUE BOOK* was operating according to the operational plan that had been set up in January 1952" – then it happened – "all the records for the number of UFO reports were not just broken, they were disintegrated…the summer of 1952 was just one big swirl of UFO reports, hurried trips, midnight telephone calls, reports to the Pentagon, press interviews and very little sleep".[13]

What was becoming clear in the *BLUE BOOK* office was that there was an increasing geographic trend to the total number of sightings. By June the office situation map was showing an increase of reports from the East Coast. *BLUE BOOK* was not the only intelligence group monitoring the surge in reports or the trend to the East Coast. In mid-June Ruppelt was called to the Pentagon to brief his boss at ATIC, General Samford (Chief of Air Force Intelligence), members of Samford's staff, two Navy Captains from the office of Naval Intelligence and certain other individuals he could not name in his book. Upon arrival Ruppelt was advised by Major Fournet that senior officers were concerned about the "alarming increase" in UFO reports. And by the end of June, the earlier trend in sightings towards the East Coast was being confirmed by a series of jet interceptor scrambles from bases in Massachusetts, New Jersey and Maryland. F-94s were sent aloft, directed toward unknowns, locked on to targets with onboard gun radar and then had the radar locks broken by apparent high speed and violent maneuvers.[14]

That was just the beginning, life at *BLUE BOOK* was going to become even more frantic during July and August. In his book, Ruppelt discusses a number of seemingly credible late spring/early summer reports from across the nation, ending up with the dramatic series of July and August incidents over the nation's capital. Those incidents involved a mix of nighttime radar tracks, a number of visual observations of mysterious lights and a total failure of ADC interceptors to respond in a timely fashion or to effectively engage objects even when they obtained gun radar locks or visual sightings. Interestingly, a wave of East Coast UFO reports had indeed been anticipated, although the predictions did not match what would actually occur.

Captain Ruppelt mentioned in his book that an unnamed source had advised him that there might well be a burst of sightings in the northeast that summer. Thanks to the work of Richard Hall and research by Brad Sparks we now know that Ruppelt had been visited by AFOIN Special Projects Group leader Stefan Possony and it appears likely that Possony had been Ruppelt's source.[15] Possony was apparently aware of the first ever hemispheric wide air defense test - scheduled for July – and cautioned Ruppelt that it could well generate a wave of UFO reports, especially over the densely populated northeast.

The exercise, designated Sign Post, involved simulated raids against major American and Canadian cities, with a focus on both seacoasts. American and Canadian bombers made actual attack runs and thousands of ground observers supported ADC radar units and interceptor units in an effort to deal with a broad, simulated Soviet attack. The same hemispheric defense exercise, designated Tail Wind, was also conducted the following summer, in July, 1953.[16] Apparently Possony, with his psychological warfare background, was quite interested in the effect the July, 1952 exercise might have on the general public, and the extent to which it would generate UFO reports.

Joel Carpenter's research provides us with the details of other summer 1952 penetration exercises conducted by SAC. Those included a July 1 flight by nine B-36's out of Carswell AFB in Texas to a staging area off Newfoundland, Canada - returning to conduct a high altitude, formation radar bombing strike on New York City. Again, on August 6, a wing of 19 B-36's flew to a point over Maine, where they were engaged by Air Defense Command jet fighters. The interception proved to be largely unsuccessful and the bombers flew on to a simulated strike against Philadelphia. Both SAC missions were considered successful (from SAC's perspective, not that of the Air Defense Command), once again demonstrating the relative weakness of even an improved American air defense.[17]

With information now available, it appears that even before the SAC simulated attacks, before the Sign Post exercise and well before what was going to occur over the nation's capital in late July and August, something very much like a focused, strategic reconnaissance of America's northeastern corridor and the Washington D.C. security region was being conducted. During late May and June, Army defense radar units northeast of the Capital District repeatedly tracked unknown objects at altitudes around 18,000 feet, objects capable of tremendous bursts of speed. One of the Army personnel involved described the fact that his unit was ordered to load their 90 mm anti-aircraft guns and actually fire on the intruding objects if possible.[18] UFO incidents extended up the coast to the New York area. On multiple occasions interceptors were scrambled from McGuire Air Force Base in New Jersey, but the objects always departed before they could arrive.

By the beginning of July reports of unidentified objects over the northeast were beginning to coincide with the some of the first SAC exercises of the summer – but it was not the Air Force bombers which were being misidentified as UFOs. Two such incidents, considered significant by Captain Ruppelt, have been explored in considerable depth by Francis Ridge, Dan Wilson and Brad Sparks.

As noted previously, on July 1, one of the first SAC training missions of the summer was in progress, with 9 B-36's departing from Texas to a staging area off Newfoundland. Their mission would take them from the staging point southwest, proceeding over Massachusetts and Connecticut in a simulated radar bombing mission against New York City on July 2.[19][20]

On that same morning two F-94 jet interceptors scrambled to intercept a UFO which had been visually reported by the Ground Observer Corps; the object was traveling southwest across Boston. The object was not tracked on Air Defense radar and the interceptors failed to locate anything based on the GOC directions. However a two civilians located northeast of Boston did observe the vapor trails from the interceptors and in scanning the sky observed two silver, cigar shaped objects traveling southwest across Boston – at a speed just a bit faster than the apparent speed of the jets.

The objects looked to be at a higher altitude than the jets, which were apparently searching back and forth for something at or below their own altitude. The couple's sighting was confirmed by the report of an Air Force captain leaving his home northwest of Boston; he saw the two jets and noted a silvery cigar shaped object traveling south. The sighting itself could have had nothing to do with the SAC exercise, however it appears that two unidentified objects were in the air over Boston that morning.

Some two hours later, the flight of nine SAC B-36 bombers which had originated in Texas was over New Jersey, on its way to Newfoundland. At that point in time the nine aircraft were being tracked by students in a radar training class at Fort Monmouth, New Jersey. While monitoring the bombers' flight, the students and three instructors observed two unidentified objects appear on the display. The unknowns came from the northeast, moving at a slower speed than the bombers. They then appeared to slow further, loitering or "hovering" over Fort Monmouth at high altitude (50,000 feet) for some five minutes before taking off to the southwest in a "terrific burst of speed".

Ruppelt describes the fact that when the unknowns appeared, an instructor and some of the trainees went outside, observing two shiny objects in the same location as indicated by their radar. They visually monitored the objects stopping, staying in place and then rushing off to the southwest at the same time as the targets moved off the radar display in the same direction. At the same time, the SAC flight had proceeded on to the northeast.

A plot of the UFOs from Boston and New Jersey suggests that the two unknowns had indeed come down across Boston, moved southwest, crossed Long Island and then crossed paths with the SAC flight. After hovering over Fort Monmouth for a few minutes, the UFOs had moved on towards Washington – BLUE BOOK located a George Washington University physics professor who had observed a dull gray object appearing to hover northwest of downtown D.C. for some eight minutes. The professor noted that several hundred people had observed the same object, and a brief newspaper report confirmed that hundreds of calls had come in to the paper.[21]

A large number of military aircraft were indeed in the air over the northeast during July and August, 1952, however in contrast to Possony's concerns, the UFOs that would be reported were not misidentifications of bombers or interceptors. Instead, highly credible observers would provide detailed descriptions of truly anomalous objects, at times flying in formation and displaying performance characteristics totally at variance with those of conventional aircraft.

One striking example of such a highly anomolous sighting comes from the observations, made at twilight, by the pilot and co-pilot of a Pan American DC-4 airliner on a flight to Miami. At the time their aircraft was over the Chesapeake Bay, Maryland, and approaching Norfolk, Virginia. The encounter would come to be referred to as the "Nash-Fortenberry" incident, named after the pilots themselves. The sighting itself involved six extremely "fiery" disc shaped objects moving in a very tight, stacked, echelon shaped formation and maneuvering at high speed. The formation was then joined by two more identical discs; all the objects then formed into a line and quickly departed from the area if the DC-4.

The incident is significant not only for the quality of the observation, but for its resemblance to a handful of virtually identical stacked disc formation reports. Major Fournet included it in his detailed analysis of UFO formations and formation maneuvers. From an Air Defense perspective, the encounter is only one more example of observers, including Skywatch teams, sighting UFOs which ADC apparently neither tracked nor attempted to engage.

In itself, the "Nash-Fortenberry" observation suggests that there were multiple disc-shaped objects operating over the Maryland/Virginia corridor as of early July, 1952. That view is further supported by an observation made the following day, at the same time and also in the vicinity of Hampton Roads (which includes Norfolk, Hampton, Virginia Beach and Chesapeake).

For military context, Hampton Roads represented the largest concentration of Air Force, Navy, Marine Corps and Coast Guard facilities on the East Coast. In 1952 the Norfolk Naval Operating Base alone would have been classified as a strategic national target. It housed the Atlantic Fleet Command as well as a major Naval Air Station – which was growing into the largest air base on the East Coast. The Norfolk facility was a major source for Navy aircraft parts as well as a rework facility, its industrial component employed thousands of civilians, with a 1950s era payroll of nearly $45 million dollars.

On July 17, Paul Hill was employed as a scientist at the National Advisory Committee for Aeronautics at the Langley Research Center in Hampton, Virginia. After reading local newspaper headlines describing the previous day's UFO sighting by the Pan American pilots, he decided to go down to the water at twilight and take a look at what might be happening in the general area of the earlier observation. Along with another person, he parked by the Hampton Roads waterfront and shortly both individuals saw two amber colored spheres come inshore towards them, at an altitude later triangulated to be 15,000- 18,000 feet and an estimated 500 miles per hour. Flying side by side, the objects made a left turn, came to a virtual stop and began a "jittering" motion. The two remained in formation and performed a series of maneuvers which Hill knew from professional experience were far beyond any contemporary aircraft.[22]

Within a few minutes, a third object came in from the Atlantic, over Chesapeake Bay. Then a fourth object came up the James River, to join the formation. Intrigued by the sighting, Hill investigated and obtained confirmations from multiple Skywatch ground observers who had sighted the objects. The head spotter told Hill that he had previously been advised by their Richmond GOC filter center to report only aircraft and since they knew the UFOs in question were not conventional aircraft they had made no report. The observers did provide Hill with the necessary data for triangulation and a height estimate.[23] An Air Force fighter pilot who observed the objects while off duty also confirmed the sighting, including Hill's speed estimate. Hill reported the incident to his NACA supervisor as well as to the local base air intelligence office. The net result was simply the filing of a written, local report.

Hill's subjective impression was that the group of unknown objects had joined together in the process of what appeared to be a general reconnaissance of the area, including the various local military facilities and very possibly extending on to installations further up the east coast. A broader review of sightings over the east coast, particular down the length of the strategic Boston to northern Virginia corridor appears to support that perception.

In retrospect none of the air exercises of 1952, neither the very large scale hemispheric Sign Post air defense test nor the SAC training missions, appear to have produced any particular UFO reports – or even much in the way of media coverage other than some local press descriptions of the defense test. In contrast, sightings such as those over the Chesapeake Bay did produce local newspaper coverage. However, it was only a matter of days before a broader level of press attention was drawn to UFO sightings on the East Coast.

During the evenings of July 19-20, and July 26-27, incidents over the nation's capital garnered the sorts of headlines the Air Force most definitely did not need or want:

> "Flying Saucers Reported in Air Force's Backyard", *The Boston Globe*, July 22, 1952
>
> "Jets Can't Find Them – Air Force after D.C. Saucers", *The Washington Daily News*, July 23, 1952

"CAA Officials Own Story - *How Radar Spotted Whatzits the Air Force Couldn't Find*", The Washington Daily News, July 29, 1952

Hidden within the newspaper stories, but no doubt of considerable interest to foreign intelligence services, was a second story. It was reported that no official air defense alert had been generated within the Air Defense Command. When Civil Aeronautics Aviation at the Washington National Airport Air Traffic Control Center had called the ADC they had been told only that their report would be forwarded up the chain of command. The result had been that when interceptors (either one or two, there were conflicting reports) eventually did appear over the Capital the first night it was some three hours after the first unknown radar tracks had been observed at Washington National. Subsequent newspaper stories related that the jets normally stationed at Andrews Air Force Base to defend the Capital had been temporarily moved to a base in Delaware due to runway work at Andrews.

Objectively, the first night's experience was a mixture of unidentified radar tracks and unidentified lights. Three radar sites were involved - long range approach control radar (ARTC) at Washington National and tower approach control radars at both Washington National and Andrews Air Force Base. There were also a number of observers in the air (commercial airliners) and on the ground.[24]

Given that all the radars were used solely for air traffic control, they provided compass bearing, location and distance but none of them had height finder capability to determine the altitude of the targets. The unidentified radar targets were tracked over restricted areas, including the White House, but only on one instance did all three radars pick up the same apparent target, which then disappeared off their radars at the same time.

Perhaps more significantly, as the interceptors finally neared Washington, the unknown targets disappeared, only to show up again some five minutes after the fighters departed Capital air space. Unfortunately, even as of this date, research has provided no documents which would indicate that the Air Force queried the ADC radar site providing coverage for the Capital area. Officially there appears to have been no Air Defense Command alert; Air Force statements were that neither Air Defense Command radar nor Skywatch ground observers had reported any UFOs. Why the Air Force would not have pursued and brought forth negative ADC tracking in support of its public statement that the reports were all a matter of misinterpretation of false radar returns created by temperature inversions is unclear – unless the Air Defense Command radars had actually confirmed unknown object tracks.

What is clear is that ADC was becoming increasingly involved with a series of unidentified radar tracks and visual observations over the East Coast, beginning the evening after the first Capital incidents.[25] During the evening of July 22 and well into the early morning of July 23, several F-94 interceptors were scrambled out of Dover Air Force Base in Delaware. GOC volunteers had reported a number of unidentified colored lights moving in arcs and then blinking out suddenly. In one instance an F-94 crew obtained a gun lock on a UFO some 9,000 feet ahead of it, at an altitude of 30,000 feet. The return suggested an aircraft sized object but almost immediately the UFO successfully evaded the jet by making a right turn, dropping in height and disappearing from the radar display. During the incident ground radar made one tracking confirmation and the pilots of the interceptors reported visual confirmations of unidentified objects thirteen times.

Other interceptor alerts and attempted intercepts followed. At 7:30 am on July 23, the Navy initially tracked a UFO over Montauk Point, the eastern tip of Long Island. ADC radar picked up the object - F-94 interceptors were scrambled out of Otis Air Force Base and F-86 jets out of Westover Air Force Base, both in Massachusetts. Westover AFB generated four different Spot intelligence reports related to observations over Massachusetts. In addition the base generated a report to NORAD describing a scramble of interceptors against a UFO over Rhode Island.

That same morning three F-94 jets were scrambled to engage UFOs reported over Pennsylvania. An unsuccessful attempt to engage an object over Pottstown, Pennsylvania lasted for some 4 minutes around 9:30 in the morning. The three interceptor crews (pilot and radar operator) reported visual observation of a large pear shaped silver object flying at a relatively slow speed of one hundred to two hundred mph with a smaller, delta shaped object circling below it at extremely high speed (*BLUE BOOK* filed the incident as "unidentified").

Later that day two F-94 interceptors observed 3 cylindrical objects in a "stacked formation" at very high altitude; the fighters climbed to 46,000 feet and as they did so the formation appeared to move upwards, to an estimated 80,000 feet. As the day proceeded, the Air Force continued to scramble interceptors to deal with UFO reports over Massachusetts. Another "stacked formation" of UFOs had been reported and around mid-morning on the 23rd, an F-94 patrolling south of Boston observed a large spinning object emitting a blue light fly past it at a distance of approximately a mile. The pilot circled, put the jet on afterburner and the interceptor moved to within a mile of the UFO, in hot pursuit. In response the object made a ninety degree turn and flew directly at and over the jet. The pilot again reversed course and attempted pursuit, only to see the object pull up and out of sight.

That evening, ADC radar picked up another unidentified track and an F-94 was scrambled to intercept. The pilot made visual sighting of a bluish green light and then obtained a gun radar lock – only to have the UFO accelerate away and out of contact. That same evening the flight crews of three interceptors flying out of Otis AFB near Cape Cod, Massachusetts, observed rapidly moving lights maneuvering above them. One jet moved up to their altitude and obtained a radar gun lock. Flying on afterburner the interceptor closed to within a thousand yards – at which time the UFO evaded the jet with a hard break down and to the right, moving off the interceptor's gun radar. The radar return had suggested an aircraft sized physical object.

While the initial Washington National radar tracks had gained some negative attention for the Air Force, the real East Coast story appears to have been in the days that followed, when Air Defense Radars and Interceptor pilots engaged in a number of very real defensive actions against physical objects under both daylight and nighttime conditions. Interceptors were scrambled and maintained on patrol; they repeatedly did intercept UFOs – only to observe controlled evasive action with maneuvering and speeds which quickly broke onboard gun radar locks even during successful interceptions.

In retrospect this series of incidents appears to have been a true national security event, one that both NORAD and ADC should have actively investigated; if they did so no records of such an inquiry have been discovered to date. On the other hand, given the failure of the defense network, it's possible that any documents related to such investigation were placed under a high level of classification.

Regardless of that speculation, there is simply no doubt it was a very busy week for the Air Defense Command and its personnel stationed along the strategic northeastern corridor. And on the evening of July 26 matters became even more frustrating for interceptor crews and more embarrassing for the Air Force as a service.[26] The media coverage and newspaper headlines also became even more dramatic.

Shortly after 9 pm on the evening of July 26, ARTC radar at Washington National observed the appearance of a "line abreast formation of four "saucers", as well as a number of lone UFO returns. A call to the Andrews AFB tower confirmed that their radar was also showing the unknowns. Radars at both sites appeared to be tracking a particular return, located over an approach range station and a National Airlines flight was advised – the airliner made a visual observation which confirmed unknown lights at that location. At that point the UFOs began to move around the area at high speeds. Events proceeded in a similar manner to the previous Washington National incident and once again it was over two hours before the first Air Force interceptors arrived over the Capital. It is clear that multiple flights of F-94s were sent over the course of the evening, there were at least two separate flights and there may have been more.

Once again, civilian ARTC controllers were given the task of guiding the interceptions – with no height finding radar available. Many of the lights being reported were at quite low altitudes, radar plots were coming from different locations and in general the evening proved once again to be an exercise in total frustration for the interceptor crews. In one case frustration moved to actual fear among all involved when a pilot visually observed a group of glowing objects approach his interceptor. Ground radar confirmed the objects actually encircling the aircraft – fortunately after a few tense moments both pilot and ground tracking observed the objects simply depart the area of the interceptor.

Once again, evidence of Air Defense Command involvement in the incident seems to be missing. No commentary or documents reflect ADC radar tracking of any of the objects or for that matter monitoring of the interceptor flights. ADC radar and crews with height finder radar and ground control intercept experience should have been directing the jets, instead the record shows the pilots were receiving their guidance only from the civilian radar operators, with limited information available from their approach control radar equipment. It seems almost impossible that ADC was not involved in the second, all night, U.S. Capital UFO incident. Yet no subsequent statements from the Air Force indicated otherwise. And once again the headlines were brutally embarrassing – and national.

"Air Force Explains Two Hour Delay in Chasing Objects Over the Capital", *New York Times*, July 29, 1952

"Saucer Outran Jet, Pilot Reveals", *The Washington Post*, July 28, 1952

"Saucers Outrun Jets at Washington", *Kansas Daily Tribune*, July 28, 1952

"Saucers Swarm Over Capital", Cedar Rapids Gazette, July 27 1952

Captain Ruppelt later wrote that he had received a call from President Truman's air aide at ten pm the evening of the 27th, Truman had personally requested an update on what was going on in the skies above the Capital – but Ruppelt could offer no real answers for him. In the days that followed, the Air Force offered nothing more than speculative remarks on temperature inversions – either to the press or the President. At that point in time the Air Force had been officially investigating "flying saucers" for some five years, they had been and still were unable to positively identify their nature or their origins.

The apparent lack of any meaningful Air Force response was not the sort of thing to satisfy a man like Harry Truman. Combat in Korea remained very real – Truman had replaced General Mathew Ridgway with Mark Clark in May, the Air Force was still actively engaged in its interdiction bombing campaign (Operation Strangle) and by summer enemy probing and patrolling actions had become much more aggressive. Artillery duels were ongoing and UN efforts to establish new patrol bases was met with a furious Chinese counter offensive. The American 45th Division suffered over one thousand casualties in June alone. There was no sign of any resolution to the negotiations, effectively the U.S. was still in a state of national emergency and open warfare.[27]

Based on what researchers have discovered, it appears that President Truman responded to the Washington National UFO events in two ways – both of them personal. With no adequate answer from the Air Force he turned to the Director of Central Intelligence, Walter Bedell Smith. Exactly when and how that contact occurred is still debated but there is little doubt that it did and that Smith was asked to assess the UFO reports in terms of national security.

And on September 3, President Truman held a special "off the record" meeting on "Defense of the Capital". The meeting was attended by his Air Force aides, Brigadier General Garland, several staff officers from the Directorate of Intelligence, and representatives from RAND Corporation and the National Security Resources Board.[28] Later in September Garland was moved into a position as new chief of Air Technical Intelligence Center at Wright Patterson.[29]

No details of the meeting are available, whether any classified details of Air Force investigations of the Capital events were discussed is purely speculative. What is almost certain is that the President would have expressed his own concerns over the recent UFO incidents, the Air Force's performance and the apparent problems with the air defense of the nation's Capital. If a tape recording or transcript of the meeting were available it would no doubt prove educational.

During the fall of 1952, the Air Force continued its new technical and scientific efforts effort to characterize and identify anomalous flying objects (flying saucers) once and for all – were they true "unknowns" or was it all just a matter of misidentification and unfamiliar atmospheric phenomena. Air Defense Command was left with the operational task of dealing with real time unidentified object reports including CIRVIS alerts, unknown radar tracks and the scrambling of fighters for interception attempts.

In a few instances interceptors were able to close with the UFOs, only to be consistently outmaneuvered and outdistanced. And in the background, the CIA's Office of Scientific Investigation had begun its own inquiry into the subject. Captain Ruppelt was well aware of the CIA initiative on UFOs. He referenced it in a December, 1952 letter to Air Defense Command in which he had to cancel a scheduled briefing due to the heavy work of preparing for a planned CIA scientific panel review. He noted that the CIA was concerned about UFO reports being used as a tool of psychological warfare - or as a diversion during an actual attack (such concerns had been mentioned in Air Force studies as early as 1947).

Ruppelt also expressed his hope that a CIA scientific panel would address the establishment of "a system for rapidly sorting out false reports or reports of known objects and phenomena".[30] In reality, the CIA's interest in the subject, expressed in recommendations from its Office of Scientific Investigation as of that December, were a good bit more ambitious.

Chapter 11 Endnotes

1. Brigidier General W. M. Garland, "Memorandum for General Samford" (SECRET), January 3, 1952 http://www.project1947.com/fig/1952a.htm

2. Michael Swords and Robert Powell, *UFOs and Government: A Historical Inquiry*, Anomalist Press, San Antonio, TX, 2012, 150 – 151

3. Curtis Peebles, *Shadow Flights: America's Secret Air War Against the Soviet Union*, Presidio Press, Novato, California, 2002, 29

4. The first Soviet B-29 copied aircraft had been completed in the spring of 1947 and flew on May 19, 1947. Flight tests continued through 1949, and full-scale production of the aircraft, under the designation Tu-4, began in 1947 at two separate aircraft plants; a third plant was added in 1948. According to Russian sources, when production of the Tu-4 finally finished in 1952, a total of 847 bombers had been produced. Western estimates of the Tu-4 build were much higher, assuming up to 1,300 would be deployed by 1954.

Immediately after serial production of the Tu-4 was initiated, work began to adapt the bomber to strike at American territory. Some airplanes were outfitted to carry nuclear bombs and were designated "Tu-4A." During re-equipment, the bomber was equipped with a thermostatically controlled heated bomb bay, a suspension unit for the bomb was developed and biological protection devices for the crew were supplied. Some Tu-4 bombers were equipped with aerial refueling devices, and avery few were outfitted with additional fuel tanks located under the wings. They were deployed in 1952, though the majority of the Tu-4's were not re-equipped with air refueling. In 1948, work on the "Comet" missile project was initiated to equip a modified Tu-4 with two KS-1 air-to-surface missiles and a special guidance system. The first Tu-4K prototype was finished in 1951, with production testing in 1951 and 1952. Between July 1952 and January 1953 the bomber was tested and subsequently deployed with naval aviation.

5. "Searching the Skies: The Legacy of the United States Cold War Defense Radar Program", United States Air Combat Command, June 1977, 20–25.

6. Kenneth Schaffel, *The Emerging Shield: The Evolution of Continental Air Defense*, Office of Air Force History, Washington, DC, 1991, 158.

7. Ibid, 160-165

8. James V. Edmundson, "Six Churning and Four Burning Part III," 92nd USAAF-USAF Memorial Association http://92ndma.org/92bw/sixchurningpt3.pdf.

9. Joel Carpenter and Francis Ridge, "UFOs and Alert Scare, April 1952," June 2002, www.nicap.org/ncp/nn-020628.htm.

10. Edward Ruppelt, *The Report on Unidentified Flying Objects*, 132-133

11. Kent Redmond and Donald Smith, *From Whirlwind to MITRE; The R&D Story of the SAGE Air Defense Computer*, The MIT Press, Cambridge, Massachusetts, 2000, 78

12. Edward Ruppelt, *The Report on Unidentified Flying Objects*, 129

13. Ibid, 139-141

14. Ibid, 147-150

15. Richard Hall, "The 1952 Sighting Wave", *National Investigative Committee on Aerial Phenomena*, May 31, 2016 http://www.nicap.org/waves/1952fullrep.htm

16. The Hemispheric Air Defense Test, *TIME Magazine*, Monday, July 20,1953 http://content.time.com/time/magazine/article/0,9171,889809,00.html

17. Richard Hall, "The 1952 Sighting Wave", National Investigative Committee on Aerial Phenomena, May 31, 2016 http://www.nicap.org/waves/1952fullrep.htm

18. Audiotape interview of Jay Nogel by Roy Craig, Craig files at Cushing Archival Library, Texas A&M University, Swords and Robert Powell, *UFOsand Government: A Historical Inquiry*, 153

19. Daniel Wilson, "UFOs and B-36 bombers, July 1, 1952", communication to Francis Ridge, National Investigations Committee on Aerial Phenomena, April, 2005 http://www.nicap.org/reports/mon_520701wilson.htm

20. Brad Sparks, "Radar Case At Fort Monmouth & Flight of B-36's", National Investigations Committee on Aerial Phenomena, April, 2005 http://www.nicap.org/reports/520701fortmonmouth_sparks.htm

21. Edward Ruppelt, *The Report on Unidentified Flying Objects*, 77

22. Paul Hill, *Unconventional Flying Objects, A Scientific Analysis*, Hampton Roads Publishing, Inc. Hampton Roads Virginia, 1995, 44-46

23. Ibid, 46

24. Edward Ruppelt, Chapter 12; The Washington Merry Go Round, "The Report on Unidentified Flying Objects", 156-191; Kevin Randle, *Invasion Washington; UFO's Over the Capital*, Harper Torch, New York, 2001, 32-42; "The Washington National Sightings", Brad Sparks, Barry Greenwood and Francis Ridge, RADCAT Case Directory, NICAP http://www.nicap.org/520719wns_dir.htm

25. Kevin Randle, *Invasion Washington; UFO's Over the Capital*. 61-67; Fran Ridge and Richard Hall, *BLUE BOOK* Unidentified Cases #152, 1554, 1556, and 1567; Fran Ridge and Richard Hall, "The 1952 Sighting Wave; Radar-Visual Sightings Establish UFO's as a Serious Mystery"NICAP http://www.nicap.org/waves/1952fullrep.htm

26. Edward Ruppelt, *The Report on Unidentified Flying Objects*, 163-166 and Kevin Randle, Invasion Washington; UFO's Over the Capital, 68-76 also Dan Wilson, Brad Sparks and Francis Ridge, "The Washington National Sightings", July 26-27, NICAP http://www.nicap.org/520726wnsdir.htm

27. US Army Campaigns, Korean War, US Army Center of Military History http://www.history.army.mil/html/reference/army_flag/kw.html

28. The President's Day, September 3, 1952, Truman Library http://www.trumanlibrary.org/calendar/main.php?currYear=1952&currMonth=9&currDay=3

29. Brigadier General William M. Garland, U.S. Air Force biographieshttp://www.af.mil/AboutUs/Biographies/Display/tabid/225/Article/107003/brigadier-general-william-m-garland.aspx

30. Brad Steiger, "Edward Ruppelt memorandum to Air Defense Command", December, 1952 *Project BLUE BOOK*, Ballantine Books, New York, 1976, 406

Chapter 12

Unidentified - Or Unknown

In this chapter

- A series of UFO interceptions during 1952/53 raised the question of whether the Air Force's next generation fighters and its massively expensive SAGE automated air defense network would be able to deal with the speed, acceleration and maneuvering capabilities being reported.

- The Air Defense Command recorded ongoing incidents of long distance radar tracks, involving highly maneuverable UFOs with speeds up to 2,000 miles per hour and beyond.

- Identification of targets and discrimination of actual threats in time to interdict them were the keys to Air Force plans for the systems being developed to carry the nation into the 1960s – the anomalous UFO incidents raised the air defense question of whether or not that was even possible.

- *BLUE BOOK* investigated close range, visual observations by pilots and found them to be credible but insufficient for absolute confirmation – new incidents involving airborne radar, ground radar, pilot observations and even gun camera photos proved no more definitive.

- A covert survey of astronomers revealed the almost universal scientific concern that any personal association with the subject of UFOs would be academically catastrophic for the careers of professional scientists.

- Investigation of a series of UFO/radiation measurements suggested truly anomalous aerial devices (the data were real; the radiation spikes were real) but a review panel found the data simply "not conclusive".

- Detailed motion studies of UFO formations suggested highly advanced technology with the capability for dynamic and synchronized high speed maneuvers.

By 1952, reports of anomalous flying objects had been a subject of intelligence concern for years – beginning with the nightmare devices and foo fighters of the war years, through the appearance of flyer X's, ghost rockets and X tracks immediately following the war and onwards following the flying disc/saucer reports of 1947. From the beginning, the basic question was whether or not such reports could actually be associated with a new enemy device – first German, then Russian. If the reports did relate to a real foreign device, was some unconventional technology being deployed in an actual weapon or was it strictly a matter of psychological warfare. A secondary interest was whether or not any novel technology could be identified and exploited.

The military intelligence problem was that of identification, threat assessment and possible exploitation. But some seven years later there had been no definite identification of either origins or anomalous technology, certainly no exploitation and no concrete evidence of an actual threat. In the interim a very real threat, a nuclear equipped Soviet super power with atomic weapons and long range bombers, had emerged. That threat was unquestioned, and there were calls for a dramatically improved air defense network to deal with the Soviet threat. Work had already begun to transition early development efforts on an automated approach control radar system into what would be a groundbreaking, computerized air defense network.

By the end of 1952 engineers from MIT and IBM were already informally working on an air defense computer, even before contracts were finalized.[1] The following year the Air Force became involved in testing and the integrated system which ultimately came to be designated SAGE, the Semi-Automatic Ground Environment. The name was complex and far too innocuous to describe its true mission. It was to be a system which allowed networked computers to process and coordinate data from multiple radar sites – directing radar controlled Skysweeper anti-aircraft guns, jet interceptors and new ground to air missiles in attacks on incoming Soviet bombers.

SAGE was being developed to detect, communicate with and control entirely new weapons specifically designed to defeat surprise air attacks. A whole generation of new and advanced jet fighters, the Century series, was in development, to be armed with Falcon and Genie air to air missiles including versions carrying atomic warheads. Several types of ground to air anti-aircraft missiles were being developed – NIKE Ajax, NIKE Hercules, BOMARC – carrying first conventional explosives and later atomic warheads. The anti-aircraft missiles were to be placed around major American cities and SAC air bases; there were also plans for extended radar defenses across Canada and into the Arctic as well as offshore in the Atlantic and Pacific oceans.

There is no doubt that air defense was a priority for the nation and that dealing with unidentified flying objects was a big part of the air defense challenge. Scientists from Lincoln Laboratories, associated with the Massachusetts Institute of Technology, would be working with the Air Force in developing the automated air defense system.

As previously noted, MIT physicists and consultants including George Valley had already been involved in reviewing UFO incident files.[2] Their interest was understandable, being able to differentiate real and potentially hostile aircraft from anomalous atmospheric or electromagnetic phenomena was a serious concern for a system which was going to be based largely in radar tracking of threats. An associated concern, which seems largely absent from Air Force memoranda, was the increasing number of Air Defense Command radar track reports suggesting "unknowns" which would easily defeat any of the new weapons under development. If such unknown radar tracks did represent real objects, SAGE might be able to plot them but actually engaging them would be problematic.

In January, 1952 over Nenana, Alaska, air defense ground radars as well as airborne radars in F-94 interceptors tracked an inbound target at an apparent speed of well over 1,000 miles an hour, very possibly even beyond 2,000. Intercepts were attempted but the target reversed course heading outbound at a speed estimated at 1,500 mph. During the next two hours the interceptors remained on patrol, with additional targets detected for short periods of time at low altitudes, but with no successful visual contacts. Ruppelt examined the incident, and found that those involved, including some very experienced radar professionals, were quite convinced that a real object was involved, one which had reacted to being tracked and engaged. The case was officially written off as weather related simply because no other conventional explanation was supportable.[3]

Similar, very high speed radar tracks[4] continued to be reported throughout the year. In April the 147th AC&W Squadron site in Duncanville, Texas tracked a UFO for almost 200 miles at a speed estimated to be above 2,000 mph. The target was at high altitude, above their height finder's 42,000 foot beam range. That same month, a site in Moriarty, New Mexico tracked a target over some 70 miles, with an apparent speed of over 4,000 mph.

In June, a clear, sharp return appeared on radar at Kirksville, Missouri. The track was plotted for over a hundred miles until it disappeared off the scope; the estimated speed was 4,000 mph. By July, similar very high speed tracks were becoming almost common. Williams Bay, Wisconsin reported an incident with tracks by three different ADC radars, all indicating multiple objects moving westwards at some 3,000 mph. Osceola, Wisconsin reported eleven objects with a truly amazing apparent speed above 12,000 mph and Belleville, Illinois reported three tracks moving at an estimated speed of around 3,000 mph. August and December saw a similar reports from Congaree, South Carolina - in August ADC radar reported a 4,000 mph track and then in December an object which traveled at an apparent speed of 6,000 mph, stopped for one minute and reversed its path.

ADC radar sites were not alone in making such alarming reports. As early as September, 1950 members of an MIT radar research group had been involved in tracking two F-84 trainers flying a straight, level course at approximately 400 mph. While tracking the fighters, with no apparent problems with its radar equipment, the MIT team detected a UFO on a path intersecting the jets and flying at a similar speed.[5] The pilots were advised but there was heavy haze and no visual sighting was made. The unknown object passed directly in front of the jets, with the returns from it and the fighters nearly merging. The UFO then made a sharp right turn and accelerated at a speed estimated to be around 1,500 mph – the maneuver was calculated to have imposed an acceleration effect of some 15 g's, far beyond any technology of the time.

Those sorts of radar reports created a fundamental problem for the Air Force. If they were real the service was facing actual unknowns with capabilities totally beyond its ability to counter. If they were weather related, astronomical, unknown electromagnetic phenomena, or even operator errors, some solution for identifying them was critical to the overall air defense mission – and to the idea that an automated, computerized, radar driven system could be trusted with the nation's defense. Identification of targets and discrimination of actual threats in time to interdict them were the keys to all the plans – and the new weapons systems - but was that even possible?

Successful unidentified aerial object interception and engagement were key to air defense, and initially a major hope of Ruppelt and *BLUE BOOK* as well. Captain Ruppelt investigated and later wrote about a number of attempted UFO intercepts. Intercepts were particularly important to him because it had long been hoped that good aerial photographs would provide definitive proof the flying saucers were real, resolving the question of simple misidentification. Years earlier Project SIGN had generated a request for interceptors for assignment to such a task – that request was rejected because of a lack of available aircraft. In January, 1952 General Garland, at AFOIN had proposed setting up three ATIC/ADC teams to obtain radar and visual photographs. He proposed locations known to routinely generate quality UFO reports – Seattle, Albuquerque and New York/Philadelphia.

That proposal appears to have gone nowhere, but with a focus on continental air defense and more interceptors being deployed it seemed that normal air security operations might well provide the close up visual observations and gun camera photos that would finally lead to UFO identification. Interception and identification of unidentified objects was a core mission for ADC and it was routinely tracking and intercepting both military and civilian aircraft that had failed to file flight plans and pilots who were flying off course or over security areas.

In his personal inquiries, Ruppelt investigated a number of attempted UFO intercepts. After leaving the service, he began his own book with an incident involving pilots flying F-86's, assigned to the 34th Air Defense Division (unnamed in Ruppelt's book but identified in his later writings[6]) in Albuquerque.[7] In that incident a radar near the group's base had picked up an unknown track at about ten in the morning – it appears not to have been an ADC radar as it had no height finding ability – at 700 mph, slowing to only 100 mph near a close by airfield. Two jets were scrambled, but as they neared the target began to fade. The radar operators concluded the object had either quickly dropped below their beam, or moved above it. After a search at 40,000 feet one jet was sent to 20,000 and one much lower, around 5,000 feet at the lower limit of the radar.

At that point the lowest jet's pilot saw a saucer shaped object moving at a high speed, "down on the deck". He managed to close to within 1,000 feet of the UFO and after a couple of minutes even closer, to some 500 feet. There was no doubt about the shape and unknown nature of what was certainly a very real craft. At that point the UFO began to pull away and the pilot did the only thing he could to stop it, he opened fire with his machine guns. Seemingly oblivious, the saucer simply pulled up and in seconds it was gone.

Ruppelt detailed the incident, and explained why an official report was never filed. It wasn't that the pilot's experience was not believed, later the group's commanding officer proposed that he be allowed to set up a special squadron of "stripped down" jets to chase UFOs. Ruppelt wrote that the request made it to Air Defense Command headquarters, only to be rejected due to the lack of available aircraft.

The New Mexico incident illustrates the extent to which identification of true "unknowns" via intercept and engagement was going to remain extremely challenging, even in the case of daylight sightings and close range visual observation. As Ruppelt noted, it wasn't that the pilot's observation was not accepted as factual – but even at close range, visual observation by pilots simply was not enough for conclusive identification. Throughout 1952 similar incidents, even those involving ground observers and radar tracking proved no more definitive. That can be seen in two extended attempts to intercept, track and engage UFO's penetrating the northern tier radar screen which covered the Canadian border.[8]

In late July, 1952, an ADC radar site in Michigan registered a radar track coming south across Lake Huron at approximately 625 mph; a check of flight plans showed no aircraft registered for a cross border flight on that path. Three F-94 interceptors were already on patrol and one was directed towards an intercept at 20,000 feet. As the fighter was vectored onto the UFO both the pilot and onboard radar operator visually acquired a large bluish white light "many times larger than a star". The light began to take on a reddish aspect and diminish in size as if it were moving away, at that moment the Ground Control Intercept (GCI) operator radioed that the UFO had made a one hundred eighty degree turn back north and was indeed moving away from the interceptor.

The pilot kicked in his afterburner and began pursuit, at the same time his onboard radar operator gained a solid lock on the target, with the display registering an image indicating that the object was the apparent size of a B-36 bomber. The jet closed, approaching within some four miles of the target with both it and the UFO being tracked by the ADC radar. At that point the light brightened and the object pulled ahead of the jet, breaking the onboard radar lock. Ground control advised the pilot that the target had doubled its distance from the jet in a single sweep of the radar beam.

Ground radar continued to track both the jet and the target, which alternatively slowed down and sped up – whenever the interceptor was moving into onboard gun radar range. The target's bursts of speeds were incredible, several times it appeared to travel four miles in a single ten second sweep of the antenna, translating to something like 1,400 miles per hour. Every indication was that the target was responding to the interceptor, and that its changes in speed were related to the relative distance of the jet.

Flying on afterburner, the jet began to reach the limit of its effective range and had to break off and return to its base. The UFO appeared to slow down at that point, and proceeded beyond ground radar range. The incident had involved both ground based and airborne radar, visual observation by two aircrew members, as well as several indications of intelligent maneuvering on the part of the UFO – including its 180 degree turn upon approach of the interceptor.

Those directly involved with the incident definitely felt that the Air Defense Command had detected an unknown entering American airspace across the Canadian border, an unknown which was able to closely monitor the F-94 interceptor and consistently outmaneuver and outperform it, at speeds over twice that of any contemporary jet fighter. However in practical terms, the object remained unidentified, the incident was labeled an unknown and it was simply one more case for the files.

It was exactly the sort of incident that would continue to frustrate both the Air Defense Command and *Project BLUE BOOK*. It's hard to imagine that any of the proposals for aircraft to be designated to intercept and obtain data on UFOs could have produced any more solid data than that the Central Michigan incident - or another that occurred only a year later, on August 12, 1953.

That intercept began with a Ground Observer Corps sighting in South Dakota.[9] A GOC volunteer reported an unidentified light hovering to her east and called the sighting in to her filter center. The report was relayed to an ADC radar site where two operators quickly went outside, observed the light and watched it begin to move at the same time the volunteer advised that the target was beginning to move over Rapid City. The radar operators then located the target on their radar, at the location described by the ground observer.

A patrol interceptor, an F-84 Thunderjet, was in the air and was immediately given directions to the UFO. Once given the proper vectors, the pilot immediately identified the target and accelerated to intercept it. Ground based radar tracks were obtained for both the jet and the UFO, which flew away from the jet - seemingly putting on added speed whenever the jet closed distance. The F-84 chased the UFO for some 120 miles, tracked by the ground radar. At that point it reached the limits of its fuel range and turned to head back to base; as the jet turned the target reversed its course as well, following the jet.

As the first interceptor landed, a second was scrambled and vectored towards the UFO, at an altitude of 20,000 feet. The second jet visually acquired the target and at that point the UFO turned to the north and moved off with the jet in pursuit. Once again both the F-84 and the UFO were concurrently tracked on ground radar, each showing plainly as solid objects. The pilot of the second jet then performed a series of tests to ensure that what he was chasing was indeed real, turning off his instrument lights and swinging the nose of the aircraft to ensure he was not simply seeing a reflections of something inside his cockpit – he wasn't. To prove it, at that point he began to close on the target, switched on his radar gun sight and the weapons radar lock display came on. There was no doubt in the pilot's mind that he was chasing a real target, and that the target was able to outfly him for the next 160 miles. At that point the second jet was also forced to abandon pursuit due to low fuel; the UFO continued north, observed by more observers at another GOC filter center, who had been alerted to the chase.

Similar incidents continued throughout 1952/53 and beyond, across the continent from Alaska to Texas. In July, 1952 a patrol F-94 (Starfire) flying out of Elmendorf Air Force Base made radar contact with an unknown at a range of some 14,000 yards. The unknown's speed was slightly greater than the jet at the time and the pilot accelerated in a climb to intercept. In response the target also increased speed, pulling away from the jet. The UFO leveled off at around 18,000 feet altitude and then departed, simply leaving the interceptor behind.

That incident was actually quite representative of the ongoing failures to intercept UFOs capable of truly anomalous speeds, acceleration and maneuvering – most commonly by the time interceptors arrived, scrambled in response to GOC reports or radar tracking, the unknowns had simply left the area. In some instances pilots caught glimpses of them leaving but aircraft camera photos were rare and when enlarged simply showed blurred images of oval or circular objects, contributing nothing to actual identification.[10] Reports from 1952 and following years document combinations of simultaneous ground and air radar tracking, ground and air observer visual confirmation, and responsive UFO maneuvers including both evasion and what appeared to be intelligent interactions with the interceptors.

It certainly seemed as if certain unknowns were capable of detecting Air Force interceptors, responding to them and outdistancing them at will – but only enough to demonstrate that they literally could not be caught or engaged. Yet, as with the encounter over Albuquerque, the northern border penetration of Michigan in 1952 and the North Dakota intrusion of 1953, none of the interceptions produced any concrete identification. As Ruppelt had said of the Albuquerque incident, visual descriptions of such objects might be generally consistent but they did not offer the opportunity to "gain any definite facts.... the pilot did see something…but no matter how thoroughly you investigate the incident that something can never be positively identified."[11] Even the highest quality intercepts were producing no absolute identifications; they were simply generating more unknowns for the files.

There were also pilot and crew reports of communications interference, temporary failure of controls and electrical system problems during UFO encounters. Readers are referred to Jerome Clark's comprehensive study of such reports in his book Strange Skies; Pilot Encounters with UFO's.[12] Clark provides a comprehensive examination of such incidents, for military, commercial and private aircraft – covering not just reports from the United States but globally as well.

In reviewing Air Force reports related to incidents such as those above there is little to no official mention of another rather obvious element in the encounters. The pilots and ground personnel certainly were aware that in such encounters the best jet fighters the Air Force could field, guided by the new ADC radars and ground controllers, were able to locate and move within a relatively close distance of the suspect targets. Yet they were totally ineffective at engaging them in a military sense. In fact the fighters appeared to have been totally at the mercy of the UFOs they were sent to intercept and potentially engage. Still, even though the unknowns could outperform the interceptors, even though they could outrun them and reverse course almost instantaneously to follow the jets – in none of the incidents did they overtly take any action against the interceptors and their crews other than in appearing to "tease" them.

The anomalous objects remained unidentified, however they demonstrated no obvious signs of being hostile. Air Force pilots and crews did report encounters in which the UFOs appeared to be engaging in "dog fight" maneuvers with them, demonstrating incredible turning ability and speeds in proceeding to a position behind the fighters, pacing them and then accelerating past them. When pursued, the objects would speed out of reach, only to return and either fly at high speed past the interceptor or simply trail the plane for a distance until the aircraft ran low on fuel and had to return to base.

Military aircraft were lost during attempted UFO interceptions – especially during bad weather conditions or over water. But while certain incidents produced speculation and gossip about UFO hostility, in no instance was there any hard evidence that the objects being chased had intentionally caused any damage to the aircraft involved. In a number of incidents, such as the chases described above and the striking example of a group of unknowns essentially encircling an interceptor over Washington, D.C., the UFOs involved did nothing more than demonstrate an obvious ability to frustrate any attempt to actually engage them. As with the foo fighters of World War II, no actual attacks were observed and no aircraft could be specifically tied to hostile action.

Despite the disappointing efforts to identify the unknowns via radar tracking and interceptions, Ruppelt and *BLUE BOOK* still had access to more resources and more scientific contacts than the earlier Air Force inquiries. The Battelle institute was formally contracted to perform a statistical analysis of the *BLUE BOOK* report collection. Dr. Alan Hynek, who had previously served as an astronomical consultant on the UFO projects, was asked to unofficially - and somewhat covertly - survey the professional astronomical community on their opinions of UFOs. And during the fall of 1952 Ruppelt collected a considerable body of information on another aspect of the UFO phenomena – a body of incidents referred to as the "radiation story".

That story involved numbers of scientists and technicians at different locations, a variety of instruments and a number of documents related to actual records of UFO/radiation incidents and related instrument recordings.[13] Ruppelt pursued the story at some length because he was beginning to sense that no matter how many credible observations and radar tracking reports were collected, without hard scientific data the fundamental questions relating to UFOs were simply not going to be resolved. He needed to find recorded data which would demonstrate that anomalous technology was associated with the sightings. In the fall of 1952 it appeared that what he was hearing from a number of scientific contacts might just give the project something "to get our teeth into", data that would be technically convincing and persuasive in a scientific review.[14]

Ruppelt's "radiation story" quest is fascinating, although ultimately frustrating. In retrospect, as early as August, 1952, Ruppelt had been warned of the difficulties that would be encountered in getting scientists to go on record in regard to the subject of UFOs. That month Dr. Hynek had submitted the results of his unofficial, personal survey of astronomers, noting that due to the sensitivity of the subject, he would not even be able to actually name the great majority of the 45 individuals interviewed.[15] Hynek described an almost universal concern that any personal association with the subject would be academically harmful to the astronomer's professional careers.

At least one individual told him that even if he saw a UFO he would say nothing about it; the general response was that any involvement in the subject would have to be done under complete anonymity. The majority were neither hostile nor overly opinionated, it was simply not a professional interest for them. In contrast five of the forty five had seen what they considered UFOs and were personally, if not "professionally", interested. There was also an overwhelming fear of publicity. It was felt that a single newspaper mention of their name in regard to a UFO sighting would be sufficient to brand them as "questionable among their colleagues".

Hynek's paper was a clear warning that Ruppelt might find a great deal of interest among certain scientific and technical individuals but that he would also find little enthusiasm in associating their names with data which they might have collected. That reality was reinforced in Ruppelt's discussion of his own radiation investigation. In writing about that effort he gave no names at all and obscured both the locations and affiliations of the individuals that he interviewed over several months' time. Fortunately, his writing has been supplemented by the release of a series of BLUE BOOK documents relating to his radiation investigation and those records are available online at the Project BLUE BOOK Archive, a document collection established by Tom DeMary and supported by a number of UFO historical research groups.[16]

The radiation story had originally begun back in 1949, with a number of scientists and technical volunteers at the Los Alamos facility – all of whom were unimpressed with the official inquiry into the UFOs which many Los Alamos personnel had been observing. The group and its organization are mentioned in an AEC internal November 3, 1949 memo on the subject of Aerial Phenomena. The memo identifies ten volunteers as having been cleared for access under provisions of the Atomic Energy Act; they were to pursue their research outside their regular assigned tasks.

The volunteers were to use personal equipment as well as certain laboratory equipment made available to them. They were all trained and experienced in scientific observations; the memo states that several were former military and that it was hoped their efforts would obtain more satisfactory answers than were emanating from the National Military Establishment. In time the group adopted a name for themselves - the "Los Alamos Birdwatchers Association", based on their initial efforts to observe and obtain good photographs of UFOs in the Los Alamos area. Electromagnetic detection/recording devices were deployed in order to corroborate visual sightings with instrument readings. The group included high caliber scientists including a future director of the Las Alamos labs, Harold Agnew.[17] Several of the individuals later formed a second group, specifically focused on measuring and recording radiation during overflights of UFOs.

Ruppelt began his own narrative of the radiation story[18] with the description of certain details of incidents which occurred at an "unnamed lab" in the fall of 1949; he was almost certainly referring to the personnel at Los Alamos who remained convinced that something truly anomalous was occurring in and around their facility. While the Los Alamos Birdwatchers were pursuing visual tracking and recording, two scientists working in the laboratory of Dr. William Carter noted a sudden, temporary spike in radiation. Spikes in radiation at atomic facilities were taken seriously in terms of personnel safety, however a check of the equipment revealed it to be in good working order and no explanation for the short lived, anomalous levels of radiation was forthcoming.

While the first two scientists were still pondering the matter, another staff member came back from a trip to a nearby town; he related that while approaching the facility on his return he had observed three silvery objects in a V formation moving over the lab. The timing of their passage was estimated to have coincided with the radiation spike. Later Ruppelt had the opportunity to speak with two AEC physicists and they were able to offer further details. They informed him that the laboratory personnel were so intrigued by the incident that they decided if it occurred again they would quickly go outside and look for the passage of a UFO – three weeks later another spike occurred and a dark object was observed passing over the facility.

All in all, four different incidents occurred in which spikes in radiation were found to correlate with the passing of UFOs.[19] This generated sufficient interest for Los Alamos staff to arrange for various aircraft to be flown over the facility to determine if airborne equipment might somehow affect the radiation detector. It didn't, but since there was no positive confirmation of UFO causality, the incidents were filed as equipment malfunctions, regardless of positive equipment inspections and tests.

According to Ruppelt's source, he and two of the scientists involved in the initial incidents remained so intrigued that about a year after the initial incidents they set up their own test site, on an isolated mountain top, using specially designed detection equipment. This particular group referred to themselves as the "mineral club", at least partially to explain their trips as "rock hounds" into the mountains surrounding Los Alamos. The equipment was operational by late 1950 and operated for three months with no noticeable variations in radiation. However on Dec 10, 1950, a substantial spike in radiation accompanied the passage of a silvery, circular shaped UFO. Similar radiation spikes correlated with UFO passages occurred three times over the next two months, with the passing of one UFO confirmed by radar. The scientists involved in the project were well networked within the research community and over time they shared the details of their detection set up, their recordings and other data with peers and interested parties, none of whom could find a flaw in the experiment or offer an atmospheric or astronomical explanation (even sunspot patterns were checked).

It is possible that some of the "mineral club" members may have become aware that as early as the fall of 1949 another scientific facility had also experienced abnormal radiation spikes which were visually correlated to the passage of UFOs.[20] Those incidents were observed in the course of cosmic ray monitoring for the Naval Electronic Laboratory at the Mount Palomar observatory in California. Personnel at the Palomar facility operated detection equipment which carried out continuous radiation monitoring. Several individuals were involved with the incidents but a key visual observation came from a weather bureau scientist assigned to the observatory.

On October 8, 1949 Harley Marshall was on his way to the observatory powerhouse to take certain weather readings and check on the Geiger counters used in the Navy experiments. During that trip he observed a group of nine bright, circular objects, organized in an obvious geometric formation – actually one V within a larger V. Upon arriving at the powerhouse, Marshall noted that there had been a radiation spike, evident on the pen recorders attached to the detectors, a spike which trailed off over a period of time. He called Navy technicians assigned to the project who checked the equipment, found no malfunctions and reported the incident up their chain of command. Apparently the Navy kept the incident largely to themselves at the time.

Further, unexplained spikes in radiation were registered, along with UFO visual observations. News of the Palomar events ultimately did make its way back to Los Alamos as well as to a number of aircraft/technology engineers in the Los Angeles area - part of the social network that Ruppelt would later contact in pursuit of rumors about UFOs and radiation.

Documents now available suggest that the Office of Naval Research did eventually communicate certain basics of the Palomar incident to the Air Force at Wright Patterson during 1950 but that the AMC staff simply wrote the incident as an equipment issue - based on a subsequent Navy opinion that the spike was the result of a "circuit problem". No details of the original ONR communications were retained.[21] Ruppelt's inquiry determined that a series of Geiger counters had been involved in the Palomar incident, all spiking at the same time. The local scientists and technicians had been highly critical of the high level Navy conclusion of circuit failure and noted that several individual detectors had simultaneously recorded the anomalous radiation spike.[22]

As context to the overall radiation story it is important to note that with the availability of actual documents pertaining to the Palomar radiation incidents, the official Navy finding comes into serious question. UFO case researcher Brad Sparks, well known for his ground breaking document collection work as well as for his technical analysis of UFO incidents, evaluated a letter written in 1952. The letter was apparently a response to inquiries to the Navy about the radiation incident at the Navy Electronics Lab at Palomar. The Navy letter is brief and specifically identifies the Palomar radiation spikes as relating to a single faulty fuse holder.[23] Fortunately, the documents accompanying the letter provide a much more detailed view into the equipment's actual testing by the Navy and Sparks' analysis of the overall body of information is devastating to the official Navy conclusion. Readers are referred to Sparks' comments, which incorporate interviews with Palomar personnel by Dr. James McDonald.[24] That commentary includes the following points:

The official Navy report states that following the anomalous radiation recordings of October, 1949 no other radiation spikes occurred – yet the report immediately contradicts itself by noting "further reports" in January, 1950, some three months after the initial incidents. Follow on research by Dr. James McDonald also revealed a January visual sighting by Palomar Observatory engineer Bruce Rule. Sparks points out that Rule became Chief Engineer at Palomar and Mount Wilson Observatories and had been a synchrotron radiation equipment engineer since 1949.

The Navy report states that only in January, following an additional anomalous radiation detection, was the equipment sent to the Naval Electronics Lab for a detailed check. Yet interviews conducted by Dr. McDonald with Palomar personnel revealed that the return and checkout by the lab was done in October, after the first serious of anomalous radiation spikes – which occurred over some ten days, ceasing with no obvious explanation.[25] The electronics lab inspection followed an extended series of tests involving different types of aircraft flying over the detection equipment. The Navy flew aircraft over Mount Palomar on October 21 and November 2; the aircraft were equipped with different types of radio equipment, radio altimeters and radars. The flights were intended to see of any of the equipment would produce an effect on the Geiger counters, none did.

The date of the initial Navy Electronics Lab equipment testing is confirmed by a statement that as of November 23, 1949 the Navy Electronics Lab at Point Loma had examined the equipment and was able to offer no equipment related explanation for the anomalous readings – Dr. Albert B. Focke, writing for the NEL, specifically commented "We are completely at a loss to find any reasonable explanation for the equipment behavior."

The next radiation incident, in January, 1950 apparently resulted in the unit being sent back to the NEL. At that point, while physically handling the equipment, technicians noted – only once – that jarring the fuse clip could produce an alarm and a "slight jump" by the recording pen. The report of that effect contains no reference to an "off scale" pen response as was observed during the actual incidents at Mount Palomar. More importantly the original October spikes were recorded with the equipment mounted in place, and stationary during operation. Personnel associated with the equipment at Mount Palomar flatly denied that a "circuit interruption failure" (the official terminology give to the fuse clip short) would have produced the repetitive, full deflection spikes recorded on the instrument.

Sparks points out that it may well have been the dismantling, transport (between Mount Palomar and Point Loma) and reassembly on two separate occasions that actually loosened the fuse clip, resulting in the single short observed during its second trip to the electronics lab.

Later, on site attempts to produce a malfunction extended to physically shaking the power circuit at both the device and at the wall electrical outlet connection. Only once during a number of attempts did that have any effect at all on the unit, further attempts produced no effect at all. All in all, the Navy may have officially satisfied itself with a brief and simplified explanation – but it was not one which was actually replicated in testing – and only occurred after multiple instances of the equipment being disassembled, transported, reassembled and physically shaken.

Ruppelt continued to be interested in the possibility of collecting hard data in the form of radiation detection readings correlated to UFOs. He had the opportunity to discuss the subject with an Air Force Colonel, unnamed in his book, but actually Colonel Hood – chief of the Nuclear Powered Aircraft Project located at Oak Ridge Tennessee.[26] During July, 1950 Hood and a physicist from Vanderbilt University had conducted research into the correlation of UFO overflights at Oak Ridge with a series of unexplained radiation spikes. A large number of radiation detectors were in place throughout the Oak Ridge complex and the Colonel was able to gain access to Air Defense Command records showing unidentified radar tracks over the security area. In several instances the UFO tracks coincided with spikes from radiation detectors.[27]

Following that study, an exceptional incident occurred in which two scientists from the Colonel's nuclear aircraft project sighted a circular object moving over the complex. Upon investigation it was determined that at the same time ADC radar had tracked a UFO, an interceptor was scrambled only to get a brief glimpse of the object as it moved off the ADC radar. Detection equipment over the area of the complex where the object had been reported did show increased radiation at the time of the incident.

Colonel Hood was convinced that the radiation spikes at Oak Ridge were truly anomalous, he and the physicist had developed an extensive plan for placement of other types of detectors and the deployment of magnetometer equipped aircraft. He felt that with sufficient measurements the radiation spikes could be positively correlated to the passage of UFOs and verified by magnetic field changes through the use of the magnetometers – that would have provided considerable information about the propulsion system in use on the craft. The Colonel's proposal was never implemented. As with the earlier waves of sightings in New Mexico and Texas, just as a serious detection system was being discussed, the wave of sightings at Oak Ridge faded away at the end of 1950.

Ruppelt's 1952 conversations with Colonel Hood included the discussion of various types of radiation detection instrumentation that might be used with UFO intercepts. The Colonel did confirm for Ruppelt that his project's nuclear aircraft work had made it clear that the passage of even a shielded atomic powered aircraft would be detectable by ground based radiation monitors. With specially designed magnetometers it might well be possible to detect atomic powered craft at ranges of up to 70,000 feet. Radiation detected by ground based instruments would not be dangerous and would drop off quickly, however it would definitely be measurable.

That conversation supports an observation made by Brad Sparks in his study of the incidents at Mount Palomar. Geiger-Mueller tube type detectors do not measure the energy of the radiation, they are counting devices, calibrated in regard to rate of tube ionization. A spike in radiation count does not mean that there is an intense amount of radiation present, not necessarily even a dangerous level other than in regard to prolonged exposure. Radiation spikes as reported in Ruppelt's "radiation story" indicate a temporary presence of an abnormal level of radiation – an anomaly. The various incidents Ruppelt investigated appear to be consistent with the Colonel's remark that the passage of an atomic powered aircraft would be detectable by a temporary spike ("excursion") in the detector.

Ruppelt wrote of examining a number of *BLUE BOOK* file reports which recorded anomalous radiation spikes concurrent with UFO sightings; unfortunately he gives no details of that review work and no surviving records have been located which document it. At the end of his narrative, he described presenting the body of research to a group of Air Force scientific consultants (unnamed) who found it suggestive but who were unwilling to put their names on paper in regard to it or any use of it in a new investigation – the bursts of radiation were real and unexplained, however any positive correlation to UFOs was simply "not conclusive". None of the scientists were willing to risk their reputations without something much more fully documented. In the end Ruppelt's idea for a new, structured radiation study went the same way as the earlier proposal for a new, instrumented UFO monitoring program- nowhere.

Towards the end of 1952 *BLUE BOOK* faced a quandary, despite the energy being expended and regardless of high level support, no progress was being made on actually identifying the unknowns, much less resolving the question of origins. The radiation inquiry had seemed to hold the possibility of proving in the existence of unconventional technology but even with multiple sets of data from instrument readings it had not proved to be scientifically conclusive. The scientists who were presented with the radiation story data simply refused to take a position, describing the data as too limited. They also declined Ruppelt's appeal to back a push towards an extensive radiation observation project.

While Ruppelt had personally pursed the radiation story, Air Force headquarters officers, including Major Dewey Fournet, were intrigued with another aspect of the UFO observations, one that seemed to suggest that the unknowns were both intelligently controlled and capable of in-flight maneuvers totally beyond conventional technology. The observed performance of the unknowns involved in a number of tracking and intercept incidents strongly suggested "reactive behavior", something noted in the very first Air Force comments of 1947.

A substantive number of the best reports from military and commercial pilots, as well as the Air Defense Command, describe "evasive" behavior of the unknowns approaching aircraft. Contacts with fighters attempting to engage and closely approach unknowns increasingly seemed to generate reactions beyond simply evasion. In a purely military context, such behavior was quite recognizable, the unknowns responded not by fleeing but by simply out-flying or outmaneuvering, demonstrating their own superiority

The speed and maneuverability as well as the proactive response of the unknowns suggested unconventional capabilities and seemed to indicate intelligent control of some sort. Beyond that, numerous sightings of multiple objects, from pairs to larger "formations" extended the argument for intelligent control – and given the maneuvers of some of the larger groupings also suggested dramatically advanced technology.

During 1952, Fournet became the UFO/*BLUE BOOK* program monitor at Air Force Headquarters; his regular assignments were within the Technical Capabilities branch and the Current Intelligence branch of Air Intelligence. With his own background both as a pilot and as an engineer, and with a deep involvement in the high profile UFO reports of 1952, Fournet determined to perform his own analysis of a series of observations which he came to feel demonstrated intelligent control and advanced technology.

That analysis became referred to as the Fournet "motions study". At the end of 1952, the study was sent up the Air Intelligence chain of command, approved and signed off on all the way up to the desk of AFOIR chief of intelligence Major General Samford. Ruppelt later commented on Fournet's view that the motion study proved that certain of the unknowns were indeed under intelligent control, and noted that Fournet had sent the study up the Air Intelligence chain of command.

Since the work was done outside of ATIC it seems that no copy of the analysis was actually retained by *BLUE BOOK*. For years it seemed that all traces of Fournet's work had gone missing. Anecdotal remarks suggested that the Fornet study had been made available to a CIA inquiry into UFOs but no traces of it could be found. Ultimately, UFO historian Francis Ridge's patient document digging turned up a single page, a page apparently prepared for a presentation of some sort. The page immediately before the handout contained the notation "Basis for Maj. Fournet's presentation to the OSI [CIA Office of Scientific Intelligence] Advisory Group.[28]

Ridge shared his find with researcher Michael Swords, retired professor of Natural Science and editor of the The Journal of UFO Studies, who evaluated the handout, and the formations it illustrated on a case by case basis. Based on his own knowledge of UFO cases, the time period in which Fournet was involved with UFOs and the likelihood that the cases were in date order, Swords felt that he could identify certain of the actual UFO reports relating to several of the formations illustrated on the handout, allowing him to offer commentary on how Fournet might have become focused on those particular incidents.

Among the observations shown on the Fournet "motions" chart are several incidents of structured formations, including not just simple V shaped geometries as might be seen in bird flights but diamond formations and a very unusual vertical stack (a formation we have previously noted multiple times including in the Nash-Fortenberry observation).

In addition to those structured formations, highly anomalous maneuvers included an observation of five white discs first seen in flight with three in front and two behind. That incident had involved two objects passing overhead and darting around in zig zag motions – only to suddenly move into a tight V-formation. At that point the entire formation made an almost 90 degree turn, speeding out of sight. In another instance a random grouping of objects shifted into a perfect V structure, only to reform into two rows with the objects spaced at perfect intervals. Yet another sighting involved a V formation switching in flight to an echelon which then moved as a unit, with a rolling motion along its long axis.

Knowing the sorts of sightings which had so impressed Fournet, and apparently his superiors at Air Intelligence, is interesting in itself. But more importantly, Swords concluded that the handout revealed a key insight of Fournet's – an insight which appears to have escaped Ruppelt himself.[29] Swords succinctly pointed out that Fournet was looking at the reports both as a pilot and an engineer, seeing not just formations but the fact that the dynamics of aircraft in formation flight are unique, not at all similar to the loose groupings adopted by birds and certainly nothing like a group of attached balloons. Swords describes it as "hard geometry", implying both constant adjustment and in regard to changes in attitude or direction, some sort of communication.

Swords also points out the corollary, given the dramatic changes in formation and the speeds involved absolutely no aircraft of the time - even the most advanced, - contained the technology to accomplish such complex in flight maneuvering. Fournet's conclusion was that the motion studies revealed both intelligence and a truly unknown source for the objects – they were real, intelligently controlled and their origin was truly unknown.

While it is true that the technology required for such elaborate, "hard geometry" maneuvers was unknown in 1952 that is no longer the case. With the advent of miniaturized, high speed computers and advanced wireless communications technology there is ample evidence that as of 2016 advanced unmanned aircraft were becoming quite capable of the sorts of complex maneuvering described in the UFO formation reports.

Small, even tiny unmanned drone craft are capable of integrated operation, flying in "drone swarms". The drones are capable of collective decision making, adaptive formation flight and can even restore their formations in a "self-healing" behavior if individual drones fail or are destroyed. The same technologies have already been applied to larger aircraft (although in smaller formations). In one 2016 test three Navy aircraft released a swarm of some 100 small drones, which quite successfully engaged in fully integrated, autonomous maneuvers. Those small craft were themselves individually capable of speeds above 400 miles per hour.[30]

By the end of 1952 a number of factors appeared to support the idea that some UFOs were not simply just unidentified flying objects but truly anomalous "unknowns". Yet the intelligence mission was to positively identify the unidentified objects, determine their actual origin and offer an opinion on whether or not they presented a real and present threat. On those three points Ruppelt could offer only one factual assessment, that there was no evidence that UFOs represented a military threat, specifically not a threat to the national security of the United States.

Ruppelt stressed that point in all his briefings, including those conducted for the Air Defense Command.[31] Perhaps a bit frustrated himself, it appears that as the year was ending Ruppelt had begun to move on from his initial focus on anomalous technology to the more pragmatic air defense challenge of "rapidly sorting out false reports or reports of known objects and phenomena."[32] With available information, it seems impossible to judge whether or not Ruppelt was personally changing his focus or whether the system was changing it for him. As we will see, the events of early 1953 were going to dictate that – regardless of anyone's personal views – the official Air Force approach to UFOs was about to reset itself once again.

Chapter 12 Endnotes

1. Kent Redmond and Thomas Smith, *From Whirlwind to MITRE; The R&D Story of the SAGE Air Defense Computer,* The MIT Press, Cambridge, Massachusetts, 2000, 183

2. Michael Swords and Robert Powell, *UFOs and Government: A Historical Inquiry*, 174-176

3. Alaskan Radar Case, Nenana, Alaska, January 22, 1952, RADCAT Case Directory, NICAP http://www.nicap.org/520122nenana_dir.htm

4. "The 1952 Sighting Wave, Radar-Visual Sightings Establish UFO's as a Serious Mystery, NICAP consolidated reports chronology - 1952, National Investigations Committee on Aerial Phenomena. http://www.nicap.org/waves/1952fullrep.htm

5. Daniel Wilson, "The Provincetown Documents", NICAP Chronology, 1950 http://www.nicap.org/reports/500921provincetown_report.htm

6. Colonel Methaney (later Brigadier General) was the commander of the 34th Air Division at Kirtland Air Force Base, Albuquerque Pilots from the 34th were involved in the UFO interception and firing incident described in Ruppelt's book. http://www.af.mil/AboutUs/Biographies/Display/tabid/225/Article/106287/brigadier-general-william-a-matheny.aspx7

7. Edward Ruppelt, T*he Report on Unidentified Flying Objects*, 4-5

8. Ibid, 171-172 also "Key Radar Visual" Central Michigan, July 29,1952, NICAP http://www.nicap.org/reports/520729rep.htmhttp://www.nicap.org/reports/520729doc7.htm

9. Captain Edward Ruppelt, "What The Air Force Found Out About UFOs", *TRUE Magazine,* http://www.nicap.org/true-rup1.htmAlso Brad Sparks, Francis Ridge, Joel Carpenter, "The Rapid City / Ellsworth AFB Incident (Radar/Visual), August 5, 1953 http://www.nicap.org/530805ellsworth_dir.htm

10. Michael Swords and Robert Powell, *UFOs and Government: A Historical Inquiry*, 216

11. Captain Edward Ruppelt, "What The Air Force Found Out About UFO's, *TRUE Magazine,* http://www.nicap.org/true-rup1.htm

12. Jerome Clark, *Strange Skies; Pilot Encounters with UFOs,* Citadel Press, Kensington Publishing Corp, 2003

13. Index of Detection/Radiation documents, NICAP http://www.nicap.org/detection/radiation/papers/

14. Edward Ruppelt, *The Report on Unidentified Flying Objects*, 201

15. Brad Steiger, *Project BLUE BOOK*, Ballentine, New York, 1976, 268-284 Dr. Alan Hynek, "Special Report on Conferences with Astronomers on Unidentified Aerial Objects to the Air Technical Intelligence Center at Wright Patterson Air Force Base, August 6, 1952

16. "Preparation for the trip to Los Alamos and the West Coast", December 28, 1952 also a series of some thirty documents related to Ruppelt's radiation inquiry which follow his memo in the *BLUE BOOK* archive files. *Project BLUE BOOK* Archives. http://www.bluebookarchive.org/page.aspx?PageCode=MAXW-PBB7-922

17. Michael Swords and Robert Powell, *UFOs and Government: A Historical Inquiry*, 85-86

18. Edward Ruppelt, *The Report on Unidentified Flying Objects*, 201-209

19. Michael Swords and Robert Powell, *UFOs and Government: A Historical Inquiry*, 105

20. Ibid, 85-87

21. Telephone conversation record "Reports on Palomar", Fournet call to Ruppelt, November 4, 1952 http://www.bluebookarchive.org/page.aspx?PageCode=MAXW-PBB7-929

22. "Trip to Los Alamos on October 25, 1952, meeting notes. November 3, 1952 http://www.bluebookarchive.org/page.aspx?PageCode=MAXW-PBB7-936

23. Letter, Director of Naval Research, Pasadena Branch, to Chief of Naval Research, December 23, 1952 http://www.bluebookarchive.org/page.aspx?PageCode=MAXW-PBB7-908

24. Brad Sparks, March 2, 2016, NICAP http://www.nicap.org/detection/radiation/papers/palo521223radmemo.htm

25. Index of Detection/Radiation/Papers, NICAP http://www.nicap.org/detection/radiation/papers/530227radmemo.htm

26. "Visit by Colonel Hood to WADC". November 4, 1952 http://www.bluebookarchive.org/page.aspx?PageCode=MAXW-PBB7-930

27. Edward Ruppelt, *The Report on Unidentified Flying Objects*, 160-161

28. Michael Swords, "Major Fournet's Motion Study, Intelligence Study", NICAP Project Report, March, 2011 http://www.nicap.org/reports/motionstudy_ufois.htm

29. Michael Swords, "Fournet's Motions Study, Intelligent Motions", International UFO Reporter (IUR), Vol 33 No 1, 8-15 http://www.nicap.org/articles/iur33-1_intelligent_motions_swords_article.htm

30. Dave Majumdar, "Pentagon Tests Drone Swarm Super Weapon", War Is Boring, January 12, 2016 https://warisboring.com/pentagon-tests-drone-swarm-super-weapon-2029e0d8fb1b#.k8mk1rkvx

31. Brad Steiger, *Project BLUE BOOK*, Ballantine Books, New York, 1976 Edward Ruppelt, "Excerpts from *BLUE BOOK* briefing for Air Defense Command, , Appendix E, 397

32. Ibid, 406

Chapter 13

Ownership

In this chapter

- The Air Force owned the UFO problem, it accepted reports from other services and government agencies but in a clearing house role; following the brief involvement of the Navy in endorsing the Project Grudge report the Air Force had shown no interest in inviting the FBI, the Army, or the CIA into its investigative efforts.

- Even with the 1952 surge in UFO reports, numerous unsuccessful aerial intercepts and a clear pattern of sightings over the strategic northeastern corridor and the nation's capital, the Air Force took no specific initiative to extend the problem to the broader national intelligence community or to elevate it to the level of the National Security Council.

- Following the July, 1952 incidents over Washington D.C., President Harry Truman sought answers regarding the possibility that UFOs were an urgent national security matter.

- Within the CIA the Office of Scientific Intelligence (OSI) was assigned to evaluate the UFO problem from an intelligence perspective, including the Air Force's approach and work on the subject.

- In September, 1952 the OSI rendered an opinion that UFOs were a true national security problem, that the Air Force approach was deemed to be too limited and that a major technical and scientific inquiry should be launched under CIA direction.

- After further study and consultation, in December, 1952 the OSI advised the Director of Central Intelligence that immediate action should be taken to elevate the UFO problem to the level of the National Security Council based on the concern that "sightings of unidentified objects at great altitudes and traveling at high speeds in the vicinity of major U.S. defense installations are of such nature that they are not attributable to either natural phenomena or known types of aerial vehicles."

- The DCI moved to take the subject to the NSC by way of its Intelligence Advisory Council. In turn the IAC (which included General Samford, chief of Air Intelligence) took the position that in order to authorize such a move the council would require formal scientific endorsement - leading the CIA/OSI to organize a high profile Scientific Advisory Panel on Unidentified Flying Objects.

During 1952 *Project BLUE BOOK* and Air Intelligence were struggling with their mission of UFO identification and origin. At the same time, the Air Force as a service was dealing with the increasingly challenging public and press relations aspect of unidentified aerial objects – surfaced once again by their repeated appearances over the nation's capital, and the apparent inability of the Air Force to do anything about them. President Truman was not the only person concerned about the defense of the nation's capital but he was pursuing the issue behind closed doors – the press continued to bring such concerns into national headlines.

By that point in time the nation as a whole had been talking about and asking for answers on the subject of flying discs/flying saucers/ UFOs for some six years. And despite a huge amount of media coverage, ongoing regional and national newspaper headlines and a series of relatively sensational articles in national magazines, it was the Air Force which remained singled out as the "owner" of the intelligence problem of UFOs. When the media wanted answers, it went to the Air Force. When UFOs appeared to swarm over the nation's capital during the summer of that year it was the Air Force that held a press conference. When the President was concerned, his first thought was to call his Air Force aide and ask him to find out what was going on.

In contemporary terms that ownership was not nearly as surprising as it may seem to us today. Up to and through World War II, intelligence work - whether it be collections, analysis or even counter intelligence - primarily rested with the military services. Each service had its intelligence units, and its own priorities. Army Intelligence and Navy Intelligence pursued their own activities and the extent to which information was shared was largely a matter of communications between senior military staff at the War (Army) and Navy Departments in Washington D.C. Few military historians would disagree that intelligence was highly "territorial" in pre-war years - or that inter-service and inter-agency rivalry continued as a major issue following the war, as the nation moved into a new era of Cold War with the Soviet Union.

It was the Cold War and ongoing fears not only of Russian expansionism but of what was seen as a global Communist movement that drove the explosive post-war expansion of the nation's intelligence structure, to a scale which would previously have been simply inconceivable. When the flying saucers began to make headlines in the summer of 1947 the American intelligence community largely consisted of Army Intelligence, Navy Intelligence and a limited amount of foreign collections performed by overseas employees of the Department of State. The first post-war effort to move towards consolidating intelligence had been with the establishment of the Central Intelligence Group but there had been very limited progress in terms of actual integration of intelligence or any overall coordination of collections or analysis.

When unknown aerial objects appeared over the nation in the summer of 1947, the obvious intelligence problem was that of potential Russian reconnaissance or pre-strike familiarization flights. The flying discs/saucer reports were taken to be an issue of continental air defense and the Army Air Force (AAF) naturally took both the initiative and responsibility for responding. There was no presidential directive to that effect, no executive order, and at that point in time none of the national security groups (Joint Chiefs of Staff; National Security Council; Central Intelligence Agency) were in existence; they would be authorized and established by the new National Security Act of September, 1947.[1] The flying discs/saucers fell under the AAF's mission of air defense and airspace security and that was that. With the passage of the National Security act that fall, the Air Force also became an independent service, taking the problem with it and continuing to treat it as an issue of air defense, almost certainly related to the emerging Soviet threat.

When the Navy was invited to at least peripherally join in the problem and when an official report was issued by Project GRUDGE in 1949, signed off on and supported by the Navy, that report effectively represented the position of the intelligence community. The Central Intelligence Agency was a relative newcomer to that community, coming into existence only in the late fall of 1947. It had not been invited to join in the flying saucer study, in fact certain aspects of the CIA's role were already being questioned both by the individual military services and the new office of the Secretary of Defense.

The CIA was felt to represent a challenge to the traditional intelligence prerogatives of the services as well as a competitor for resources.[2] In turn the CIA felt that its mission was being obstructed even as it was attempting to organize and staff its new functions. During the first years of the CIA's activities there was active criticism of its work, in particular that of its Directorate of Science and Technology and the Office of Scientific Intelligence.[3] Certain of the new agency's assessments and findings were contested by the military services and in October, 1948 Secretary of Defense James Forrestal received an internal Department of Defense report characterizing the CIA's intelligence work in science and technology as being highly inefficient.[4]

Following that, a report from the new National Security Council described the CIA as not yet being able to carry out its role of coordinating a scientific intelligence effort; that opinion went directly to the President's office. By January, 1949 the CIA was removed from its primary position of being the scientific intelligence advisor to the President's office, the national Research and Development Board and the Atomic Energy Commission. That left the military services with primary roles in scientific intelligence, with the Office of Naval Intelligence dealing with the aspects of Earth Sciences (applicable not only to undersea warfare but to missile and rocket development) and the Air Force involved with weather data and operational activities in support of the Atomic Energy Commission.[5]

Intelligence historian Jeffrey Richelson writes that the military continually pushed back against the CIA, specifically attempting to "roll back" the authority of the Directorate of Science and Technology for several years, certainly well into the 1950s. That push-back was certainly still quite active in 1952/1953 and Richelson notes that it had a very negative impact on morale at the CIA.[6] Still, the Directorate carried on and its scientific and technical intelligence staff continued to provide input to the CIA's National Intelligence Estimates, including those related to the Soviet Union.

Contention between the services and the CIA continued through the second half of the 1950s and there were strong differences of opinion between Air Force Intelligence and the CIA in regard to first the "bomber gap" and later the "missile gap" with the Soviet Union. It would only be with the CIA's U-2 aerial reconnaissance program, its impressive move into satellite surveillance photography, and the work of the National Photographic Interpretation Center that the Agency would successfully assert its technical capabilities in military intelligence collection and analysis.

But that would be years later and in 1952 the Air Force quite clearly held the intelligence problem of UFOs. On occasion Army intelligence and even the FBI had been rebuffed in efforts to join into the Air Force's technical intelligence investigations. The Air Force was accepting reports from the other services and government agencies but in a clearing house role; it was owner of the problem and the mission. Of course by that time, the whole issue of flying saucers/UFOs had moved into the public domain, becoming a matter of ongoing media interest and public relations management – both anathema to intelligence services. An attitude seems to have developed among other services and agencies that the Air Force had claimed the problem - and they could be left to bear the consequences.

Of course by 1952, the new national intelligence and security infrastructure was continuing to expand and evolve. The effects of the National Security Act of September, 1947 had been far ranging. In addition to separating the Air Force as an independent service, it had also established a higher level of national military authority, headed by the Secretary of Defense. The act resulted in the consolidation of the pre-existing War Department and Navy Departments in 1948 and the new National Military Authority was renamed the Department of Defense in 1949.

The 1947 legislation also established the National Security Council (NSC), whose members serve as primary policy advisors the President - with a focus on foreign policy and national security issues.[7] In addition to providing the President a forum for discussion and consideration of national security related policy matters, the NSC was designated to serve as the central point for tasking and communicating with the nation's military and intelligence groups. The Secretary of Defense served as a member of the NSC, while the military services provided advice and intelligence through the Chairman of the Joint Chiefs of Staff or designated JCS representatives. The Joint Chiefs of Staff had been established with its own multi-service Joint Staff and a Joint Intelligence Committee. Their Joint Intelligence Committee was tasked with providing information to the Chiefs and also served as the channel for communicating JCS directives on intelligence priorities and tasking to the individual military services.

By law the Central Intelligence Agency, through its Director, was charged with advising the NSC on matters relating to intelligence and national security; the Director was also authorized to make recommendations for the coordination of activities by the various groups and agencies involved in intelligence activities.[8] The NSC was directly supported by its own Intelligence Advisory Committee (IAC; later renamed the U.S Intelligence Board in 1958), composed of the heads of the various intelligence agencies. The IAC was itself chaired by the Director of Central Intelligence (DCI), the head of the Central Intelligence Agency. The IAC not only provided the NSC with national and specific intelligence estimates but served as the NSC's channel to communicate with the national intelligence community.

That arrangement was not always a happy one, with ongoing contention between the members of the IAC and the Director of Central Intelligence. In the early 1950's the view of the IAC members was that the DCI should simply be representing them and taking their direction. DCI Walter Bedell Smith's position was that the IAC should simply function as an advisory body - rather than holding with any direct control over tasking for the CIA.[9]

Despite such bureaucratic issues of control and territory, the reality of the situation was that national intelligence priorities and direction come from the NSC in the form of National Security Council Intelligence Directives (NSCIDs), either at the original direction of the President or with his concurrence. The official National Security Council Intelligence Directives represent the formal operational guidance and tasking of the national intelligence community. They also "state in general terms, the responsibilities of the DCI (CIA) and other components of the intelligence community."[10]

To be perfectly clear, the CIA officially functioned under the direction of the President and the NSC, its intelligence priorities and tasking were those of the President and the NSC. Its Director was authorized to offer recommendations on intelligence activities which might involve the military services and other agencies but acceptance of those recommendations occurred only with a decision by the NSC and the approval of the President. Obviously the President could also take a national security matter directly to the CIA Director, just as in a Commander in Chief role, the President could take military and security issues to the Secretary of Defense, the head of the Joint Chiefs of Staff or the commanders of the individual services.

This background may seem complex and a bit overwhelming, but it is important in understanding why the issue of UFOs never specifically became a matter of national security tasking for the broader intelligence community. On occasion the Air Force did communicate upwards in regard to the UFO problem, earlier we discussed General Cabell's 1948 briefing of the JCS Joint Intelligence Committee and his submission of an Air Force report to that group. Beyond that, certain UFO incidents were discussed at the level of the NSC's Intelligence Advisory Committee – although those appear to have been on an incident by incident basis.[11]

Any broader national intelligence community involvement would have had to come either through a Presidential initiative or by direction of the NSC, with the issuance of a specific NSCID. We have no absolute way of knowing that such a thing never occurred but based on extensive work by UFO historians we do know of one instance where the possibility of taking the subject of UFOs to the IAC, and with its concurrence, to the NSC, was at least raised.

As discussed in the preceding chapter, in early 1952 *Project BLUE BOOK*, with approval from Air Intelligence chief General Samford, had been initiated with a mission of resolving the outstanding questions about UFOs – were they real craft of some sort, did they utilize advanced technology and what were their origins. As with Project SIGN in 1948, by spring 1952 the Air Force UFO project was looking at the fundamental questions related to the unidentified aerial objects, reaching out to scientists and to formal academic studies. There were also proposals on the table for a significant Air Force expansion of technical collection, including the establishment of extended, scientifically instrumented collections networks.

Ruppelt's description of the UFO inquiry circa 1952 suggests that senior officers within Air Intelligence were open to the possibility that there were true "unknowns" involved in certain incidents. And in that context "unknown" meant truly alien, not of terrestrial origin. Ruppelt wrote that there was serous talk of that possibility but that "no one at ATIC, in the Air Force or in the whole military establishment was qualified to give a final yes or no" on that assessment.[12] As in 1948, such an official finding would have required major technical confirmation and scientific agreement. Getting that sort of buy-in and endorsement continued to be as great a challenge in 1952 as it had been in 1948.

Dr. Alan Hynek had initially served as an astronomical consultant to Project SIGN. As he later described his role, the Air Force project needed someone to "weed out the obvious cases of astronomical phenomena - meteors, planets, twinkly stars".[13] As Director of Ohio State's McMillian Observatory, he was the closest professional astronomer to Wright Patterson AFB and relatively available to review UFO reports. Hynek played a very limited role with Project GRUDGE but returned as an Air Force astronomical consultant following the formation of *Project BLUE BOOK*, once again focused on astronomical solutions but involved with the review of a large number of reports.

As part of his work for *BLUE BOOK*, Dr. Hynek was asked to conduct an informal survey of astronomers on the subject of UFOs. His findings – formally reported to the project – made it clear that as a scientific community, astronomers remained unwilling to even engage with the subject. Years later he would write that the overwhelming scientific response to the question of

UFOs had been "militantly negative" – so much so that it appeared to him to be totally out of proportion. Hynek's experiences also led him to the observation that "a scientist will confess in private to interest in a subject which is controversial or not scientifically acceptable but will generally not stand up and be counted in committee".[14] There is no record of Ruppelt and Hynek discussing this particular issue but Hynek's report to BLUE BOOK on his survey of astronomers certainly should have provided a caution.

In 1948 SIGN had worked frantically on both the identification and origins problems; in 1952 Ruppelt and BLUE BOOK were following the same course, and coming up with the same lack of immediate success. Ruppelt had been unable to provide concrete answers when the UFO issue made national news in the Washington D.C. incidents of July, 1952. President Truman had requested a military aide query the Air Force about what was going on over the nation's capital. The Air Force response to the press had been less than satisfactory – apparently the same could be said for responses to the President.

Given Truman's character, it appears that he acted proactively - if the Air Force had no answer then perhaps the CIA could come up with one. If there was a national security threat in play, the CIA Director would reasonably be expected to provide the President with an opinion. There is no official historical record of how that request was registered – given that the two men were well acquainted it seems reasonable that it could have been as simple as a telephone call.

The CIA's involvement with UFOs during the following few months is complex, convoluted and remains a matter of considerable debate among UFO researchers. Matters are complicated by several issues including the fact that much of the dialog at the DCI level appears have been verbal and undocumented. There was obviously an evolution of opinions inside the CIA, and as the months passed, elements of territorial conflict appear to have come into play – especially when the CIA's Office of Scientific Investigation became sufficiently engaged with the question to propose that a major technical and scientific inquiry be launched under CIA direction.

During the first weeks of the CIA's new involvement with the UFO problem, the internal dialog from its first working group appears to have carried much the same dismissive attitude that had been apparent in its 1948 comments on the subject. A preliminary internal opinion paper, of July 29, commented that a large percentage of the Air Force reports appeared "phony", asserting that there were less than one hundred "reasonably credible" reports in the Air Force files. It also suggested that in all probability all the reports could be explained as misidentification – or worse - if sufficient information were available.[15] That appears to have been something of a "knee jerk" assessment, issued before any real review of what had been going on with the Air Force more recently, including the work of *BLUE BOOK* under Ruppelt and General Samford.

By September 11, DCI Smith received a report and proposal from the Assistant Director of the Office of Scientific Intelligence, H. Marshall Chadwell. That report is especially useful in that it begins with a statement of the full nature and scope of the UFO intelligence "problem" as it was being addressed by the OSI. That problem is described in three parts: a) Determine whether there are national security implications in regard to UFOs, b) Determine if the study and research currently being conducted is adequate and c) determine what further investigation should be initiated, by whom and under whose direction.[16]

The report accurately pointed out that the Air Force was the only organization investigating UFOs and that Air Intelligence had handed off that activity to ATIC at Wright Patterson. Chadwell then noted that the core group at ATIC consisted of only one reserve Captain, two Lieutenants and two secretaries. That group relied on other Air Force personnel and consultants for collections and scientific study. His commentary also singled out that fact that the Air Force approach was strictly on a case by case basis, "designed solely to attempt a satisfactory explanation of each individual sighting as it occurs."[17]

Somewhat surprisingly, especially given the negative and dismissive initial CIA study group assessment of some five weeks earlier, Chadwell characterized the Air Force work to date as valid - but only to the extent that it dealt with individual reports. From a scientific perspective the Air Force approach did not address fundamental questions related to the causes of the reports nor any solutions which would allow more immediate identification and classification. He stated that after conversations with ATIC personnel, review of reports, and discussions with CIA consultants, that his conclusion was that the Air Force approach was insufficient. The CIA's own scientific consultants had advised that the actual solutions would only be obtained through an extensive study of atmospheric, ionospheric and extraterrestrial phenomena, with the opinion that explanations lay at the fringes or just beyond current scientific knowledge.

As of September, Chadwell and OSI's view of the UFO matter was quite different than what had been expressed within the CIA only a few weeks earlier, at the end of July. His assessment concluded that the UFO reports did in fact constitute a national security issue – both in terms of potential psychological effects and the creation of an air vulnerability situation based in the identification and discrimination issue.

Chadwell highlighted the implicit psychological threats, recommending that the DCI pursue that particular issue with the National Security Council and proposing that programs be implemented to minimize the potential of public panic associated with foreign nations using UFOs for psychological warfare purposes. Of course the psychological issues of the UFO problem were nothing all that new, they appear as concerns in the very first Air Force assessments of 1947 and 1948. What Chadwell's air defense comments did not identify nor elaborate on were the increasing number of failed, radar directed intercepts evident in the newest UFO reports of 1952.

While the Air Force had consistently raised the issue of psychological impact over several years, they had never actually attempted to elevate the UFO problem to a level of national security based on psychological or air defense issues. In September 1952, Chadwell proposed that after consideration of all the related issues the matter was serious enough for the DCI to take the topic of UFOs to the National Security Council - along with the opinion that the Air Force's approach would never resolve the fundamental problem. Beyond that Chadwell recommended a new, broad scientific inquiry to address and resolve the fundamental identification problem. His report includes language stating that an action to take the matter to the NSC would be within the statutory authority and obligation of the DCI.

So, after only five weeks, not only had Chadwell and the OSI become positive that there were fundamental national security threats associated with UFO reports, the DCI was being encouraged to take the matter directly to the National Security Council. Based on comments in Chadwell's report in regard to potential consulting work with MIT and Lincoln Labs, OSI had also set the stage for the CIA being the driver in a broad based scientific study of the UFO phenomena – almost certainly involving the same institutions and scientific consultants that were already working on the air defense problem for the Air Force, in the early stages of prototyping what would become the SAGE system.

To what extent Chadwell's enthusiastic approach to the problem was supported or encouraged by DCI Smith is largely unknown; no evidence has yet emerged that Smith immediately considered taking Chadwell's proposal to the NSC or for that matter to President Truman. There is also no indication that he considered taking it to the Intelligence Advisory Committee at that point in time.

What is clear is that Chadwell and OSI continued to pursue the subject, with further ATIC contacts and the involvement of their own consultants. In addition Chadwell continued to promote the subject with the DCI. On October 2, a second report was sent to DCI Smith, restating much of what was in the September document.[18] In this second memorandum, Chadwell went so far as to list three recommended actions, including appropriate draft letters for the Director's use in moving forward with them.

First the DCI was urged to immediately advise the NSC that there were national security issues involved with the UFO problem and to propose action on the matter. A letter (Tab A in the report) was attached for that action. Chadwell also recommended that Smith take the matter directly to the national Psychological Strategy Board (PSB) and included a letter for that as well (Tab B). The DCI was urged to form a CIA working group involving the Psychological Strategy Board and other parties to move forward with a program of public information to minimize concerns and reduce the risk of panic.

Chadwell's focus on the psychological warfare issue and the PSB, as well as the proposal for the CIA to lead in what would essentially be a domestic propaganda effort – targeting the American public – was very much in tune with the general mindset of the time. Psychological warfare had been taken very seriously during World War II, the British Political Warfare Executive and the American Office of Strategic Services (OSS) had established a joint psychological warfare division which had been very active in targeting German forces in occupied Europe. In its earliest days a number of the CIA's senior officers had seen service in the OSS and were very much attuned to the subject of psychological warfare.

In 1946 the new Central Intelligence Group had officially advised President Truman on its assessment that the Russians were covertly using rockets and missiles as part of a psychological warfare program targeting the Scandinavian nations. Concerns of foreign psychological warfare targeting the western bloc remained ongoing and in 1951 President Truman had established the Psychological Strategy Board as an adjunct of the National Security Council. The Board included the deputy secretaries of State and Defense as well as the Director of the CIA. A representative of the Joint Chiefs of Staff was to sit on the board as its military advisor.[19]

Concerns over flying saucers and UFOs as possible psychological warfare devices had been expressed in all of the Air Force intelligence studies, from the very first estimates of 1947 though Project GRUDGE. The American military itself had become very involved with psychological warfare in the Korean conflict, it had become a fixture in military activities there during 1951.[20] The CIA was also increasingly focused on embedding propaganda in foreign media as news, using special interest groups (student groups, unions, etc.) as channels for placing information which would ultimately reach foreign news sources. Rumor campaigns had been one of the most effective tools for the OSS during the war and would continue to be a focus for the CIA – giving its personnel a keen appreciation for the potential impact of well-conceived gossip and rumors.[21]

In addition to overseas campaigns, as early as 1952 the CIA had begun a program of domestic media and news influence. A Congressional inquiry in 1976 collected information from the Agency demonstrating that the CIA had collaborated with dozens of American journalists. Connections had also been established with many of the leading newspaper publishers and news services.[22] In that context, it is not surprising to see Chadwell advancing the psychological elements of the perceived national security issue, or proposing a CIA led project related to desensitizing and reassuring the American public. What is surprising is to see Chadwell - as the Assistant Director in OSI - being so assertive as to provide the CIA's Director with actual letters for his use with the NSC and PSB – especially if he had not received some level of direction or at least encouragement. Yet to this point no documentation has been found relating to any specific approvals or encouragement being given to OSI and Chadwell on the subject.

Regardless of the lack of such a paper trail, it certainly seems that in the fall of 1952 the CIA, having assigned the UFO problem to the OSI, was working towards a proposal for the creation of a major scientific investigative effort directed towards that problem. Such an effort would have left the Air Force to deal with individual incidents and would have moved the entire issue upwards within the national intelligence community. Chadwell clearly intended that it become a matter of NSC tasking – something which would have involved IAC concurrence and the issuance by the NSC of a formal NSCID.

It is at that point in which the matter becomes even more convoluted - and to some extent questionable as to who was pursuing what agenda. Officially the next CIA action involved Chadwell providing a personal briefing to DCI Smith at the beginning of December. According to the CIA's own history of the events it was at that point at which Chadwell was ordered to draft memoranda in regard to elevating UFOs to a national intelligence priority though issuance of an NSCID; that proposal would be used by the DCI.

The official CIA history also says that it was only then, in December, that DCI Smith ordered further internal work on the subject, including additional work with scientific advisors and with the Air Force. The problem is that the documents now available show that the CIA history account is totally out of chronological order - Chadwell had proposed elevation to the NSC in early September and provided letters to Smith in early October!

The CIA history goes on to relate that in his early December meeting with Smith, Chadwell recommended priority action to Smith based on "sightings of unidentified objects at great altitudes and traveling at high speeds in the vicinity of major U.S. defense installations are of such nature that they are not attributable to either natural phenomena or known types of aerial vehicles."[23]

Now that we can view the actual documents which contain the reports/recommendations from Chadwell to DCI Smith in both September and October, 1952 we see that the context for Chadwell's original proposals for NSC elevation and a CIA organized scientific study was something far different than what he was supposedly advocating in early December. His initial proposal was based in advice from CIA scientific consultants - to the effect that resolution of the fundamental problem of UFOs lay in a scientific study of phenomena at the fringes or just beyond known science.

Yet in early December, the CIA history tells us that Chadwell was asking for immediate action based on UFOs being a "priority" national security issue - due to the fact that they appeared not only to be actual unknown aerial vehicles (not unknown natural phenomena) with totally unconventional capabilities but because there was a strong suggestion that they might be making controlled flights focused on major U.S. defense installations.

To put it mildly, that is a major shift in focus from September and October. Suddenly it was not just that UFO reports contributed to an air vulnerability issue or were a matter of psychological concern, but UFOs were a "priority" national security issue because they were "not attributable to either natural phenomena or known types of aerial vehicles" - certainly something that would demand immediate attention from the entire intelligence and defense research and development community as well as separate study by top level scientists.

If DCI Smith had accepted that view, he would have been justified in personally taking such an urgent matter directly to the President. Of course one of the problems would be that Chadwell had to have based his assessment on the Air Force case files and the Air Force was itself quite aware of the association between highly anomalous object reports and ongoing flights over strategic facilities. An obvious question would have been why the CIA felt UFOs were such an urgent matter if the Air Force itself had not already elevated such sightings to the level of a national security issue or proposed them as a priority for the IAC or NSC.

Smith appears to have concurred with Chadwell, but only to a limited extent. There were ongoing communications, both written and verbal, between the two men and at some point a fuller understanding of the exchanges of November and early December may still emerge. What we do know as fact is that DCI Smith did move the topic on to the IAC, placing UFOs and the possibility of an NSCID on the agenda for the IAC meeting held on December 4, 1952.[24] As the IAC Chair, DCI Smith's office scheduled regular IAC meetings and handled the agendas for them. The action items listed for the December 4 meeting included the discussion of two specific tasks related to UFOs.

The first was an IAC action to authorize the DCI/CIA to enlist the services of selected scientists to review the available evidence in light of current scientific theories. The second was to authorize the DCI/CIA to draft and circulate a proposed NSCID which would express the committees' concern and authorize coordination with appropriate non-IAC departments and agencies. If after review of the draft, the IAC moved to support it then the matter would be taken to the National Security Council for presentation and discussion.

Those agenda items indicate that while DCI Smith was bringing UFOs to the national security table, it was certainly in a much more restrained fashion than Chadwell had proposed - and nothing at all consistent with the urgency or in the strategic context which the CIA history relates that Chadwell had expressed to him in their most recent meeting. In fact it appears that Smith had seriously "adjusted" both Chadwell's message and his proposal.

We know that only because researchers have obtained access to a draft memorandum, prepared by Chadwell in support of an NSCID, most likely to be circulated in the event that the IAC had responded positively to the CIA presentation in the December 4 meeting and asked for a draft for review. That memorandum reads very differently than anything Chadwell had written that fall and far differently than his reported conversation with Smith in early December - although it did support taking the intelligence issue of UFOs to the NSC and the Secretary of Defense.[25]

That letter, written as coming from DCI Smith, did raise the issue of national security but strictly in the context of air defense vulnerability, from the perspective that UFOs were some type of scientific phenomena that might potentially be generated and put under control by foreign powers. The draft proposal called for the Department of Defense to lead a scientific investigation of the phenomena, with assistance of the agencies of the IAC. Chadwell's cover letter makes it clear that the intent of this memorandum would be to get the NSC to institute a major scientific inquiry.

He also suggested that the IAC's "watch committee", which operated under CIA direction, be tasked with monitoring indications of Russian activity in regard to UFOs or UFO reports. That would have been a very interesting proposition, in line with what we will be exploring in later chapters of this work – but it also seems to imply that the watch committee, and its indications analysis group, may not have been routinely tracking UFO report activity as part of their Soviet warnings intelligence work up to that point.

There is little doubt that we lack the full story of what was going on internally at the CIA in regard to the UFO intelligence problem during the late fall and winter of 1952. From a distance it is hard not to conclude that the OSI was pushing the matter with more intensity and with a broader scope than the DCI was prepared to personally support. In addition, something seems to have seriously affected Chadwell's own views at some point in November. His reported remarks to DCI Smith at the beginning of December point not to unknown natural phenomena, but most specifically to unknown aerial devices with totally unconventional flying capability – devices apparently targeting strategic American defense facilities. That characterization had not come up previously, and seems to have faded away within days, not becoming a part of either the IAC presentation or the draft NSCID proposal.

We do know that there were Air Force files highlighting those same concerns, we also know that Ruppelt had even presented the strategic facility correlation during his first briefing of Generals Samford and Garland and that both officers had concurred with the seriousness of the matter. Yet the Air Force had never expressed those concerns with the same urgency and national security implications that the CIA historian tells us Chadwell did in the first days of December. We also have no record that ATIC or General Samford were actually preparing a national security level proposal, even though Ruppelt writes of his hopes that the matter would be taken to higher levels, possibly even the President.[26]

There has been considerable analysis and speculation about what might have been driving Chadwell to take such a strong position with the DCI, but whatever it was does not appear to have translated forward (and upwards) with the same fervor or urgency from DCI Smith. Of course there is one alternative explanation. We know that Smith himself was in something of a power struggle with the IAC at that point in time. The IAC members wanted him simply to be their representative, with the IAC tasking the CIA through him. But DCI Walter "Beetle" Smith had a completely different view of who should be tasking whom.

Perhaps the UFO issue ended up becoming a matter of interagency politics - no doubt other members of the IAC, in particular the military intelligence services, would have pushed back against any effort to essentially take UFOs away from the Air Force while opening up a major new scientific investigation project under the CIA's aegis. Chadwell was even proposing that such a project use scientific resource from MIT and Lincoln Labs – institutions and personnel that the Air Force was already directly involved with on its new air defense initiative.

Did the OSI end up putting the CIA Director in a position of not just asking for elevation of UFOs to a higher level of national security consideration, but doing so in a manner so as to capture a huge new project for the OSI (a department with its own history of rejection by the military and other agencies)?[27] Was DCI Smith's IAC meeting agenda an effort to take the matter to the IAC while not actually "claiming" it for the CIA? Is that why DCI Smith himself did not chair the meeting? Was Chadwell directed to write a draft NSCID proposal which was essentially an out for Smith, shifting the scientific study to Department of Defense if the IAC decided to take the matter to the NSC? In short, did the events of December, 1952 reflect bureaucratic maneuvering or did DCI Smith simply decide that it was best to move much more cautiously and not risk questions being asked as to why the CIA was treating Air Force data more seriously and with more urgency than the Air Force itself?

There certainly are suggestions of internal and external political maneuvers being in play throughout the CIA's 1952/53 involvement with the UFO problem. Given the OSI's repeated proposals for a major new scientific investigation, such turf battles are be no major surprise. What is also no surprise is the IAC's response to Chadwell's presentation. Before considering the proposal of an NSCID, the members wanted a formal scientific endorsement that such a study was viable and that the data being held by the Air Force was of the type and nature to justify a commitment of top American scientific assets – assets already in demand for a vast range of Cold War projects. If top scientists would sign on to the problem, the proposal could go forward to the NSC, but scientific endorsement had to happen first.

In short, the IAC meeting left the CIA with the task of assembling a panel of leading scientists to evaluate the Air Force data and endorse the CIA's proposal. As with most such matters, it was a compromise solution, providing a justification for the IAC were it to move forward and once again effectively deferring the matter to the scientific/academic community. And in the end the scientific panel which was convened for that task was composed almost entirely of physical scientists. It goes without saying that such a group would need very "hard" data to put its reputations on the line endorsing a new national security initiative related to UFOs.

A considerable amount of research and commentary exists in regard to the CIA review panel which was convened to offer an opinion to the IAC. Ruppelt even discussed it tangentially in his UFO book, commenting that the Air Force did not have the "pull" to bring absolute top level scientists together for a week or two in order to conduct a detailed and through scientific review of the UFO question.[28] Ruppelt described the Air Force as "working through other government agencies" to organize a "high court" (Ruppelt's term) for a scientific review.

From his perspective the committee was to deliver one of three verdicts – all UFO reports were explainable as known objects or natural phenomena, existing reports simply did not contain sufficient data for a conclusion, or interplanetary spacecraft were actually involved in certain UFO reports. If the conclusion was "interplanetary" the committee's findings would go first to the National Security Council and then to President Truman. What Ruppelt did not reveal was that in the fall of 1952 it was actually a CIA initiative which was driving the elevation of UFOs upwards within the national intelligence community.

Officially the scientific "high court" which Ruppelt had anticipated was designated the Scientific Advisory Panel on Unidentified Flying Objects – organized and convened under the direction of the CIA and the Office of Scientific Intelligence but with the data being presented to the panel selected and prepared by the Air Force/ATIC. The panel's final report came to be known as the Robertson Report, in recognition of the panel's chairman, Howard Robertson. As detailed earlier, during World War II Robertson had been a senior technical advisor to the War Department as well as to Supreme Headquarters Allied Expeditionary Force (SHAEF) in Europe. Robertson was personally involved with the intelligence effort to identify and evaluate the foo fighters and mystery lights which had begun to have a noticeable impact on Allied aircrew morale during the final year of the war.

Robertson and the other scientists assigned to the wartime mystery light inquiry had been unable to positively determine the nature of the "foo fighters" and their general conclusion appears to have been that those reports were a matter of misidentification, escalated by aircrew nerves, further driven by media attention. Documents from the period suggest that the intelligence groups involved with those inquiries considered the whole matter to be largely a diversion and waste of resources.

In terms of background, the members of the Scientific Advisory Panel convened by the CIA were all physicists and certainly carried star class academic credentials. Robertson himself was a mathematical physicist who devoted a good deal of his time to cosmology; Luis Alvarez (radiation physicist, University of California) would later win a Nobel Prize in physics; Samuel Goudsmit (atomic physicist, Brookhaven National Labs); and Thornton Page (University of Chicago, involved in both astrophysics and operations research) participated in all four days of panel meetings. Lloyd Berkner, an atmospheric physicist from the Carnegie Institution, only joined on the final day - after all the Air Force presentations and panel discussion had taken place. Frederick Durant III, a CIA missile expert, functioned as an associate member but his role was primarily that of secretary, taking minutes and notes.

J. Allen Hynek, astronomer and Air Force consultant from Ohio State, was listed as an associate member but only joined the panel for certain parts of the meeting. According to Hynek he was personally treated as part of the Air Force presentation, not as a panel participant. Two members of the panel Dr. Alvarez and Dr. Thronton had not previously served as CIA consultants and were brought on as Ad Hoc consultants for the panel's work. Interestingly the memorandum covering their employment notes that they had been cleared only to a security level of SECRET, raising the question of what security limitations had been placed on the material being provided to the overall panel.[29]

CIA/OSI personnel including Chadwell, Fred Durant and Phillip Strong participated in the panel, with Chadwell offering opening remarks on the IAC and the role of the panel. He positioned that role as assessing threats to national security posed by the UFO phenomena. Chadwell was followed by Strong, who enumerated the security issues as viewed by the CIA including the psychological warfare elements. The introduction of the psychological element seems strange given the physical sciences orientation of the members and apparently that also puzzled the panel. Robertson himself questioned whether or not a specialist in mass psychology should have been included and Goudsmit stated that that the UFO problem itself looked "psychological" to him.

Air Force presentation of individual UFO reports and discussion of certain materials such as films occupied the panel for some two and a half days.

During the third day the panel held a general discussion and began to address their conclusions (Berkner only joined the panel on the afternoon of the third day). Panel Chair Robertson volunteered to draft a report for the panel and did so over that evening; the fourth day the panel reviewed and finalized that report. What little we know from primary sources as to the panel's actual approach to the subject and the attitude of the participants comes from a combination of their final report and remarks from both Hynek (Air Force consultant and panel advisor) and Page (panel participant), both men offering their comments well after the fact and relatively privately.

Hynek commented that the panel reviewed a relatively small number of individual cases, dismissing most of them without any lengthy discussion. Hynek described himself as "stunned" by their constant recourse to scientific "authority" rather than actual analysis in passing judgement. However he also pointed out that the data being introduced in presentations was "not convincing in the sense that a physicist wants something to be convincing."

Page related that the panel members were told by Robertson – in closed session of only the members – that their job was to reduce public concern and show that UFO reports could be explained by conventional reasoning.[30] Unfortunately we do not have a list of what specific incidents were reviewed in the sessions but based on Hynek's comments, it appears that certain of the cases we discussed in previous chapters – specifically those with detailed measurements and triangulation data such as the material from Killen Base/Fort Hood – were either not introduced or not discussed in any detail. The best insight we do have comes from a listing of the types of material which was made available to the panel:[31]

SCIENTIFIC ADVISORY PANEL ON

UNIFIED FLYING OBJECTS

14 - 17 January 1953

EVIDENCE PRESENTED

1. Seventy-five case histories of sightings 1951-1952 (selected by ATIC as those best documented).

2. ATIC Status and Progress Reports of Project GRUDGE and Project *BLUE BOOK* (code names for ATIC study of subject).

3. Progress Reports of Project STORK (code name for Battelle Memorial Institute contract work supporting ATIC).

4. Summary Report of Sightings at Holloman Air Force Base, New Mexico.

5. Report of USAF Research Center, Cambridge, Mass., Investigation of "Green Fireball" Phenomena (Project TWINKLE).

6. Outline of Investigation of U.F.O.'s Proposed by Kirtland Air Force Base (Project POUNCE).

7. Motion Picture Films of sightings at Tremonton, Utah, 2 July 1952 and Great Falls, Montana, August 1950.

8. Summary Report of 89 selected cases of sightings of various categories (Formations, Blinking Lights, Hovering, etc.).

9. Draft of manual: "How to Make a FLYOBRPT," prepared at ATIC.

10. Chart Showing Plot of Geographic Location of Unexplained Sightings in the United States during 1952.

11. Chart Showing Balloon Launching Sites in the United States.

12. Charts Showing Selected Actual Balloon Flight Paths and Relation to Reported Sightings.

13. Charts Showing Frequency of Reports of Sightings, 1948 - 1952.

14. Charts Showing Categories of Explanations of Sightings.

15. Kodachrome Transparencies of Polyethylene Film Balloons in Bright Sunlight Showing High Reflectivity.

16. Motion picture of seagulls in bright sunlight showing high reflectivity.

17. Intelligence Reports Relating to U.S.S.R. Interest in U.S. Sightings.

18. Samples of Official USAF Reporting Forms and Copies of Pertinent Air Force, Army and Navy Orders Relating to Subject.

19. Sample Polyethylene "Pillow" Balloon (54 inches square).

20. "Variations in Radar Coverage," JANP 101 (Manual illustrating unusual operating characteristics of Service radar).

21. Miscellaneous official letters and foreign intelligence reports dealing with subject.

22. Copies of popular published works dealing with subject (articles in periodicals, newspaper clippings and books).

The panel does not appear to have reviewed the patterns of UFO sightings from Los Alamos, Oak Ridge, Hanford, Sandia Labs or White Sands (data that would have supported Chadwell's earlier concerns about strategic installation overflights). Reportedly they dismissed any detailed discussion of broader patterns brought forward in the presentations, reviewing and commenting only in regard to individual reports. In the end, the panel concurred on the conclusion that the evidence presented to them showed no indication that the UFO phenomena constituted a "physical threat" to national security. In short, their finding was that the reports of anomalous objects did not relate to unknown physical devices which constituted any type of threat (no overtly hostile actions had been presented in any of the Air Force reports).

The panel's official report also repeated the same air vulnerability and psychological warfare comments called out in Chadwell's September letter to DCI Smith, stressing issues of false alarms and clogged channels of communications. The creation of false reports could also be used as hostile propaganda, to generate distrust in authority and induce hysterical public behavior. Based on that assessment, their recommendation was that the threat implicit in UFO reports be minimized through a program of training and public education, while preparing those agencies responsible for security to quickly and effectively recognize actual hostile actions.

Based on the full Robertson panel report (only available to the public after several decades through the persistence of document researchers such as Dale Goudie) it becomes clear that that the panel dismissed the possibility of the unknowns as representing any type of extraterrestrial device and once again equated "unknowns" with unidentified conventional objects or incompletely understood natural phenomena. Their finding was that there were no true "unknowns" at the core of the sightings – any unknown element would have/could have been resolved if sufficient and accurate data been collected and available.

In that sense, the panel's physicists proved little different from the majority of establishment scientific opinion that had been expressed from the earliest days of the 1947 sightings. With his years of experience, Alan Hynek described that scientific view most succinctly - "For any UFO report, when regarded by itself and without reference to similar or related reports, there can always be found a possible commonsense explanation, even though the probability may be small."[32]

As a follow up, the Robertson panel paper was submitted to the IAC. The report and certain remarks by panel members were incorporated by into a CIA/IAC report (the Durant report). That document also included the commentary that "most" UFO sightings could be readily identified with conventional aircraft, balloons, astronomical, or natural phenomena – any other unknowns could be explainable with further data collection and study. The IAC circulated the Durant report to its various agencies, and with the lack of scientific endorsement for a broader inquiry the possibility of an IAC proposal to the NSC simply faded away.

The Air Force actually requested that it be allowed to make public the panel's conclusions (the panel's report had been classified as SECRET) and to name its participants. The CIA's position on that request was that in no case should the CIA's involvement with the advisory panel be revealed, nor should certain of its conclusions and recommendations. The identities of the advisory panel's members were also not to be disclosed.[33]

Much has been written about the Robertson panel and its report, there remains considerable debate over possible hidden CIA and Air Force agendas. Perhaps the greatest mystery is exactly what Chadwell and Smith discussed early in December – specifically what it was that prompted Chadwell to so strongly assert the urgency of the matter, including the implication that strategic installations were being overflown and the suggestion that it was being done by real objects demonstrating technologies which were so unconventional they might well be extraterrestrial.

We know from Ruppelt that he, Samford and Garland had all discussed that same possibility. What we do not know is exactly what appears to have persuaded Chadwell of the same thing and why that sense of urgency and those specific concerns appear to have disappeared only days later, in the agenda that Smith prepared for the December 4, IAC meeting.

We will leave that mystery to the dedicated UFO historical researchers, for the purposes of this work the CIA involvement of 1952/53 appears to have ended the chances that the intelligence problem of UFOs might be officially tasked as a broader mission for the overall national intelligence community. The subject did not move on through the IAC to the NSC, no NSCID was issued and for that matter the issue of UFOs appears not to have been officially tasked to the Watch Committee, or that committee's indications intelligence analysts. In short, the Air Force had taken the intelligence problem of UFOs in the beginning, and it would continue to hold it over some three decades.

Ruppelt and senior officers such as Generals Samford and Garland had endorsed and pursued an expanded Air Force technical/scientific study during 1952 - Ruppelt describes that in some detail. To a large extent the Robertson Panel's scientific assessment must have undercut that effort as much as did the OSI's move for a new scientific initiative. In the end, irrespective of any turf battles that might have come into play, the panel's assessment undercut all proposals for any broad scientific investigation. Before long even those who had been open to real unknowns - perhaps even involving extraterrestrials - began to become more circumspect in their remarks and positons.

In March, 1953 Ruppelt was interviewed on the subject of UFOs and treated the entire subject rather humorously in his comments, stating that in all his travels he had never seen a report that "couldn't be explained by natural phenomena."[34] It is hard to believe that he and other Air Force presenters such as Fournet and Hynek had gone into the Robertson panel hearings with that attitude. Yet by March Ruppelt even remarked that he had no idea why he had carried a Geiger counter on his trips – while we know from his own writing and from *BLUE BOOK* reports that he had taken the "radiation story" story quite seriously, only to be frustrated by the lack of scientific endorsement based on the data he went to so much effort to collect.

In retrospect such shifts in remarks simply lead to head shaking. Ruppelt clearly spent an extended amount of time reviewing UFO case files but apparently placed none of the Killeen/Fort Hood technical material in front of the Robertson Panel. Researchers later located that information in the *BLUE BOOK* files – not just reports but copies of the actual Army plots, maps and triangulation measurements. Ruppelt wrote that UFOs were "habitually reported from "technically interesting places" but then separately stated that "a study of reports from military bases and atomic weapons storage sites produced fewer reports than would be expected from any given area in the United States".[35] With the information now available we know that to simply be untrue, waves of sightings at sites composing the atomic warfare complex clearly stand out.

Regardless of such apparent contradictions, by the spring of 1953 the issue of UFOs had returned to being primarily an operational problem for the nation's air defense command and a public reassurance challenge for the military. In response both the Joint Chiefs of Staff and the Air Force moved to establish new practices to deal with those tasks. Those directives and practices addressed UFO reports both from an air defense perspective (in terms of the only true "physical threat" being that of a preemptive Soviet attack) and in regard to the potential psychological threat posed by UFO reports themselves (in terms of both public trust issues and their manipulation by the Soviets as an element of psychological warfare). Over time the new directives and regulations (of 1953 and 1954) would have a significant effect on the quantity and quality of UFO reports being collected and reported by *Project BLUE BOOK.*

Chapter 13 Endnotes

1. The infrastructure for a significantly expanded new national intelligence community was established by the National Security Act of September, 1947 https://history.state.gov/milestones/1945-1952/national-security-act

2. Jeffrey T. Richelson, T*he Wizards of Langley; The CIA's Office of Science and Technology,* Perseous Books Group, 2002, 1

3. The Office of Scientific Intelligence was officially created on December 31, 1948 but operationally integrated and organized only during 1949. CIA Historical Series, The Directorate of Science and Technology, The Office of Scientific Intelligence, 1949-1968 https://www.cia.gov/library/readingroom/docs/osi_1949_68_volume_1.pdf

4. Jeffrey T. Richelson, *The Wizards of Langley; The CIA's Office of Science and Technology*, 3

5. Ibid, 4

6. Ibid, 6-8

7. National Security Council, "White House Briefing Room" also Jeffrey Richelson, *The U.S. Intelligence Community*, Perseus Books Group, Fourth Edition, 1999, 17 https://www.whitehouse.gov/administration/eop/nsc

8. Jeffrey Richelson, *The U.S. Intelligence Community*, Perseous Books Group, Fourth Edition, 1999, 17

9. Ibid, 439

10. Ibid, 374-379

11. Michael Swords and Robert Powell, *UFOsand Government: A Historical Inquiry*, 266

12. Edward Ruppelt, *The Report on Unidentified Flying Objects*, 199-200

13. J. Allen Hynek, *The UFO Experience*, Henry Regnery Company, Chicago, Illinois, 1972, 1

14. J. Allen Hynek, *The Hynek UFO Report,* Barnes and Noble Books, 1997, 14

15. Michael Swords and Robert Powell, *UFOsand Government: A Historical Inquiry*, 172

16. Ibid, 503-507 also http://www.unacknowledged.info/1952-chadwell-smith-cia-memo/chadwell-smith-memo-dec-1952/

17. Op cit

18. Chadwell (OSI) to Smith (DCI) memorandum, October 2, 1952 https://www.cia.gov/library/readingroom/docs/DOC_0000015339.pdf

19. Harry S. Truman, President of the United Sates, Executive Order #128, Directive Establishing the Psychological Strategy Board, June 20, 1951 http://www.presidency.ucsb.edu/ws/?pid=13808

20. Major Albert C. Brauer, "Psychological Warfare in Korea, Public Opinion and Propaganda" paper, Georgetown University, 1953 https://library.ndsu.edu/ndsuarchives/sites/default/files/digital/files/2010/04/KoreanWarPSYCHOLOGICAL-WARFARE-KOREA19513.pdf

21. The Office of Strategic Services: Morale Operations Branch, CIA Historical Document, April 30, 2010 https://www.cia.gov/news-information/featured-story-archive/2010-featured-story-archive/oss-morale-operations.html

22. Hugh Wilford, *The Mighty Wurlitzer; How the CIA Played America*, Harvard University Press, Cambridge, Massachusetts, 2008, 225-229

23. Gerald K. Haines, "CIA Role in the Study of UFO's, 1947-1990, CIA Library https://www.cia.gov/library/center-for-the-study-of-intelligence/csi-publications/csi-studies/studies/97unclass/ufo.html#ft25

24. Intelligence Advisory Committee Minutes, Directors Conference Room, CIA Building, December 4, 1952 https://www.cia.gov/library/readingroom/docs/DOC_0005516074.pdf

25. Michael Swords and Robert Powell, *UFOs and Government: A Historical Inquiry*, "Unidentified Flying Objects (Flying Saucers)", Marshall Chadwell to Secretary of Defense, undated, 186-187 and 202

26. Edward Ruppelt, *The Report on Unidentified Flying Objects*, 200

27. Perhaps the most dramatic example of DCI directors being politically "trapped" in their own department's initiatives can be found in the Cuba Project under DCI Allen Dulles; in the later phases of that project – which ended in disaster at the Bay of Pigs –Dulles increasingly distanced himself from his own personnel and removed himself from direct involvement in the actual operation.

28. Edward Ruppelt, *The Report on Unidentified Flying Objects*, 200

29. Panel members not already serving as CIA consultants were brought on as "Ad Hoc" CIA contract employees and paid for their participation. Their fee was a nominal $50 per day. "Consultants for Advisory Panel on Unidentified Flying Objects", Memorandum from Assistant Director Scientific Intelligence to Director, Central Intelligence, January 9, 1953

30. Michael Swords and Robert Powell, *UFOs and Government: A Historical Inquiry* 186-187 also Page's notes to a talk to the Society for Scientific Exploration, 30 May, 1987 and Thornton Page to James L. Klotz, 3 October, 1992

31. Dale Goudie, correspondence related to FOIA requests with the Central Intelligence Agency, Computer UFO Network (CUFON) http://www.cufon.org/cufon/robert.htm

32. Allen Hynek, *The Hynek UFO Report*, 24.

33. Phillip G. Strong, Deputy Assistant Director, Subject: UFO Report (Secret) in letter to Dr. Lloyd V. Berkner, President, Associated Universities Incorporated.

34. Michael Swords and Robert Powell, *UFOs and Government: A Historical Inquiry*, 210 also Peter Wyndon, Saint Louis March 9, 1953 ,

35. Edward Ruppelt, *The Report on Unidentified Flying Objects*, 212

Chapter 14

Reduction and Reassurance

In this chapter

- During 1953/54 *BLUE BOOK* began a return to attitudes and practices which had been common during the GRUDGE era. New Department of Defense (Joint Chiefs of Staff) guidelines for reporting UFOs in relation to potential security threats imposed security controls and legal penalties for military and government employees – and even civilians under certain circumstances.

- Investigation of UFO reports increasingly moved to field level, first within the Air Defense Command – new Air Force regulations directed that UFO investigations "must reduce the percentage of unidentified to the minimum."

- Military airspace control expanded dramatically – pilots not complying with regulations faced not only interceptor scrambles but legal action and fines.

- Unidentified aerial object reports were significantly reduced during the air defense challenge and identification process, however scrambles were conducted against thousands of unidentified radar tracks a year.

- CIA historical claims that new, highly secret reconnaissance aircraft "accounted for more than one half of all UFO reports during the 1950s and 1960s" are extremely questionable.

In the preceding chapter we discussed what did not happen in 1953, the fact that the intelligence problem of UFOs was not elevated beyond the Air Force, not assigned to a broader national intelligence community with specialized analysts and not referred to a new, in depth scientific study. Instead, any question of ownership was settled – the Air Force owned the problem, and it was going to continue on its case by case approach. It was an approach which the CIA had rightly assessed as being appropriate but definitely limited in terms of resolving the highly anomalous reports which had no readily apparent, conventional explanation.

For much of 1953 the routine at ATIC/*BLUE BOOK* remained the same, however as transfers and discharges occurred positions at the UFO desk were not filled. Ruppelt himself went on a temporary two month duty assignment and when he returned found that the *BLUE BOOK* military staff consisted of one Lieutenant and an Airman first class. The ambitious proposal for setting up a network of instrumented tracking stations was been turned down at Air Force headquarters and in terms of investigative resources ATIC's UFO work was returning to the state it had been in at the time of Ruppelt's arrival during the post-GRUDGE period.

Ruppelt was keenly aware of the limits of *BLUE BOOK*'s investigative resources and remarked on it during his travels, in particular during his contacts with the Air Defense Command (ADC). During his briefings for the ADC, there was discussion of supplementing ATIC resources with an ADC field intelligence unit – the unit was new, only established in February of 1953. General Garland, newly in command at ATIC, approved of the idea and the Air Defense Command's 4602nd field intelligence unit (later designated as the Air Intelligence Service Squadron) was directed to provide support for field investigation of UFO reports.

During combat, field intelligence is tasked with identification, recovery and initial processing of enemy aircraft as well as the interrogation of enemy pilots and crew. Field intelligence units had been very busy in Korea, especially in regard to the new Soviet jet aircraft first encountered there. In 1953 the new 4602nd unit was headquartered in Colorado, along with the Air Defense Command. The intelligence unit was a relatively small, with only 34 officers and 97 airman. However its personnel were located within commands across the country and were authorized to call on those commands for the use of aircraft and resources as required. It seemed a good fit for UFO identification, one that would keep the ADC unit's personnel involved in field work and help establish communications channels with other commands.[1] The 4602nd was reorganized in October, 1953, with support for ATIC in UFO investigations being formally added to its mission.[2]

At first the availability of new field resources appeared to be a real boon to the UFO desk at ATIC, with *BLUE BOOK* driving the process of investigations. However, beginning in 1954 new directives and regulations began to affect a number of practices related to UFO inquiries, ultimately moving a good deal of the work out from under the centralized control of ATIC/*BLUE BOOK*. Those changes were driven by a series of Joint Chiefs' directives and new versions of Air Force regulations. The new rules imposed much tighter controls on information related to all unknown object reporting – specifically including the types of reporting covered under the CIRVIS (CIRVIS / Communications Instructions for Reporting Vital Intelligence Sightings) regulations. The first step towards tighter control of the public release of information on unidentified object sightings was incorporated in a new version of the Joint Chiefs' communications instructions for reporting sightings of possible airborne and waterborne threats.

Sightings involving "potential and imminent national security threats" had already been designated and defined as requiring CIRVIS reports. A new directive – JANAP 146(C) – covering such reports was issued by the Joint Chiefs of Staff on March 10, 1954.[3] The operational instructions for the reports remained basically the same; the directive described what types of observations were and were not suitable for CIRVIS reporting as well as the preparation and transmission of reports.

What was new were the additional security constraints governing such reports. CIRVIS reports were now prohibited from being transmitted outside the defined reporting structure, the contents were not to be made available to the press or public or revealed in any manner. The security related legal codes cited with the directive effectively placed all military personnel and government employees under a security seal relating to their reports. Disclosure was a punishable crime, with penalties up to a ten thousand dollar fine and ten year prison sentence. It placed not only the reports but the communication of them under security control. Given that it was to apply to "all persons" involved in CIRVIS reports, it could be used to restrict any sort of comment or disclosure from civilians if they had reported their sighting and it had become the subject of a CIRVIS report.

The Air Force followed the Joint Chiefs' JANAP directive with its own new operating policy for conducting UFO investigations inside the Air Force. The Air Defense Command was tasked with the initial investigations of anomalous/unknown object reports. That new approach was formalized in August, 1954 by Air Force regulation AFR200-2. That regulation defined all phases of how the Air Force would be handling the reporting of Unidentified Flying Objects (FLYOBRPT).[4] The regulation acknowledged that as of August, 1954, Unidentified Flying Objects (UFOBs) reported up to that date had posed no actual threat (in terms of hostile action). However it stressed that new types of foreign aircraft, aerial devices and missiles might well be observed and reported as UFOB's. That possibility demanded that sightings be reported to the Air Force immediately and the regulation established the protocol for dealing with such reports.

Commanders of all Air Force activities were tasked with internally communicating and providing information and evidence pertaining to unidentified aerial objects – including reports from other services and from civilians. The Air Defense Command was directed to conduct all field investigation of reports originating from inside the continental United States. ADC was also given the job of field identification. If ADC personnel could not provide an identification the incident was to be forwarded to ATIC for further inquiry. All Air Force commands were directed to cooperate with ADC in its field investigations, up to and including providing air and ground transportation.

ADC personnel were provided with guidance for field investigations and directed to contact local aircraft control and warning units, pilots and crews in the area of the report, or any other sources who might have factual data and corroborating evidence. They were advised to consult with civilian weather personnel, local astronomers, military and civilian airport tower operators and operations staff as well as other potentially useful sources. The regulation noted that the 4602nd Air Intelligence Service Squadron (AISS) was to be treated as a resource in such field investigations – the unit had assets deployed throughout the country and was highly mobile. ADC officers investigating UFO reports were encouraged to contact the AISS via the Air Defense Command, direct communications between field units and the 4602nd was authorized.

Information relating to UFO reports was to be reported promptly, either by teletype or in writing depending on its apparent intelligence value. Priority was given to electronic reports which were to be directed to ADC headquarters, the nearest ADC unit, ATIC and the Director of Intelligence at Air Force Headquarters.

In summary, the newest version of AFR 200-2 delegated UFO investigations to the Air Defense Command, specifically to ADC field units, with support as requested from 4602nd personnel. In practical terms, the regulation moved the initial filtering of UFO reports away from Wright Patterson ATIC personnel and out to the field – with a strong endorsement for local identification – quick local identification. To encourage that the regulation specifically directed that Air Force activities "must reduce the percentage of unidentified to the minimum."

In addition, the new guidelines informed Air Force commands that it was only permissible to release information on UFO reports if there had been a positive, conventional identification. If there was no easy explanation the only allowable response was that the report that been referred to ATIC for evaluation. It would be ATIC's decision on whether or not any data were "worthy of release". The Air Force was moving forward with a focus on two elements of the intelligence problem – rapid identification and public reassurance.

When Ruppelt returned to civilian life in late 1953 a noncommissioned officer was given temporary charge of the UFO desk; later Captain Charles Hardin took over as the head of the project. As had happened when GRUDGE succeeded SIGN, the post-Ruppelt personnel at *BLUE BOOK* were reportedly less than enthusiastic about UFOs. Ruppelt described Hardin as not only not believing in them but thinking that anyone who did was crazy.[5] It certainly appears that Hardin did comply with the newly stated mission of reducing the percentage of unidentified reports to a minimum.

The Air Force drive to reduce the percentage of reports ultimately classified as "unidentified" was in play at ATIC but clearly extended to the ADC's 4602nd field intelligence unit as well. In his research on that unit, Kevin Randle located several unit history documents and investigative summaries. The notes from a Commander's briefing on June, 1954 stressed that UFO/UFOB investigations were very important because while the Air Force had satisfactorily resolved the vast bulk of sightings reports, it was up to the unit to "solve the small percentage of unsolved sightings."[6] A 4602nd Unit History from September, 1955 confirmed the units' fundamental UFO mission – it emphasized that the goal of UFO identification had been and would remain "to allay hysteria by systematically squelching rumors and illusions".[7]

The 4602nd did actively assist with UFO investigations. Unit records show that during the period from August 1954 to July 1955 they received 306 preliminary reports. Of those 198 were resolved by work at unit headquarters, 40 through field investigation and 60 were forwarded to ATIC for resolution – 37 for lack of sufficient data and 23 as "unknowns".[8]

Procedural changes at ATIC/*BLUE BOOK* were also in the works. In line with the overall Air Force direction of minimizing the number of reports listed as unsolved/unidentified it was decided that in future reporting the category of "identified" would be broadened to include assessments of both "probable" and "possible". That option offered more opportunity for field investigators to close out reports locally and in its own reporting *BLUE BOOK* began to combine those two subcategories into its classification of "identified".[9] Not surprisingly, the percentage of identified cases showing up in *BLUE BOOK* status reports began to show a marked shift upwards.

Over time the changes in Air Force investigating and reporting practices did produce a significant "improvement" in identifications. In previous years unidentified cases had routinely run at a level of twenty percent, and up to thirty percent on occasion. Under the new Air Force guidelines, by the end of 1956 *BLUE BOOK* was able to report "unidentified" incidents as being less than one percent; it would manage to hold those percentages in the three to five percent range for years.[10] That trend was destined to continue throughout the remainder of the decade, in 1958 a new version of Air Force regulation 200-2 reaffirmed that the percentage of unidentified must be reduced to a minimum – an obvious air defense goal but also one that would reassure the press and public as the nation faced new fears over Russian satellites and intercontinental ballistic missiles.

The effort to resolve UFO investigations in the field was further reinforced with the issuance of a new version of JANAP 2002-2 in 1957. In accordance with that directive local unit intelligence personnel were tasked with the preliminary identification and classification of UFOs, reports involving unidentifiable/anomalous objects were still to be referred to ATIC.

During 1956, the 4602nd had been disbanded, succeeded by a much reduced field intelligence group, the 1006th Air Intelligence Service Squadron. In 1957 the 1006th was moved from the Air Defense Command and placed under the command of Air Intelligence, with its headquarters at Fort Belvoir, Maryland. Under the new JANAP 1957 regulation, ATIC was authorized to call on the 1006th in support of UFO investigations as necessary; it seems not to have done so very often. Following its 1957/58 transition the unit was reorganized under Air Intelligence and the newly designated 7602nd Field Activities Group appears to have been assigned some very interesting missions relating to the recovery (Project Moon Dust) and transport (Project Blue Fly) of satellite and space debris.

By the late 1950s UFO investigation had become truly a field responsibility, with preliminary investigations performed by unit level officers, passing incidents to ATIC only as necessary, and with *BLUE BOOK* largely devoted to reconciling them against conventional explanations if at all possible and doing little more than filing the truly anomalous ones into its archives. The net result of the Air Force's new focus and approach was a definite increase in identifications, during the period of 1954-1957 the number of UFO reports classified as "unknowns" was also significantly reduced.

It must also be noted that the new JANAP reporting regulations – including the imposition of security controls and penalties – had a noticeable impact on the reporting from certain categories of military and even civilian observers. That appears to be true for military and especially civilian pilots. During the earliest years of UFO observations, commercial pilots had been the source of some of the most detailed UFO observations. However anecdotal reports and actual surveys of pilots suggest that professional concerns as well as negative airline attitudes led a common pilot attitude that officially reporting UFO encounters was something to avoid unless absolutely necessary.[11]

Press contact practices related to UFO reports also went through their own changes. The JANAP directive of 1954 required that all reports made to the military, including those from pilots and aircrews, would become security controlled. Information was to be released to the press and public only by the local investigating unit. Air Force statements and press responses on UFOs became increasingly void of detail, especially details relating to radar tracking or similar technical corroboration. That public relations approach had been tested as early as 1948, when Air Intelligence was wrestling with how to respond to a surge in ongoing media inquiries. It was to become standard Air Force operating practice throughout following years.

Local bases were to reassure the public with identifications, if questions were raised they could respond that ATIC was working the report. If the press pushed the issue to the Pentagon, Air Force press contacts could call on ATIC for authoritative responses. The process worked well from one perspective, slowing down communications and adding a delay loop to minimize public and press attention. Aside from that, from 1954 through much of the 1960's the Pentagon and *BLUE BOOK* would fare just as poorly at actually satisfying the press and public as GRUDGE had done during its much briefer tenure.

Certainly there were some understandable explanations for these Air Force actions. The most obvious was simply an effort to deal with the growing numbers of sightings and reports which began in 1952. In that year the sheer number of UFO reports had literally overwhelmed ATIC and *BLUE BOOK*. Ruppelt described the fact that there was very little time for actual investigations since everyone was rushing around simply trying to respond to both higher command and the press about new reports coming in daily and sometimes hourly. And while the number of reports ending up at *BLUE BOOK* did drop following 1952, during the following years even the annual totals remained two to three times what they had been previously – ranging from relatively slow years of 450 reports through peaks of over 1,000 in other years.[12] The ATIC/*BLUE BOOK* staffing and structure of 1952 (and later years) could never have dealt with those sorts of numbers in any meaningful fashion.

Of course as far as military reports were concerned, the surge in numbers is perfectly understandable – the more you look, the more you see. We have already discussed the increase in unidentified radar tracks resulting from even the limited number of defense radar installations that began to come into play in the early 1950s, especially those covering the restricted air spaces in New Mexico and around the Hanford and Oak Ridge atomic plants. And while the high cost of a permanent, continental air defense network had remained a matter of debate and political jousting for some four years at the beginning of the Cold War, the emergence of the Soviet Union as an atomic warfighting competitor ultimately overcame all those objections. An urgent move towards a true continental air surveillance network was triggered by the knowledge that the Russians had atomic weapons capability. Subsequently the Soviet explosion of a hydrogen bomb in August, 1953 provided the stimulus for the development, funding and full scale deployment of the automated SAGE air defense system in the early 1960s.

From 1951 onward, the quickly and dramatically expanding air defense network produced an unprecedented number of unknown aircraft reports – a great many coming from radar tracking. Radar detection was vital to air defense, World War II had proved that. However false tracks could be produced by equipment issues, atmospheric/weather phenomena and even flights of birds and insects. Experienced radar operators learned to discriminate many of the false returns but with the rapid growth of the network, it took time for many of the military trainees to develop that level of expertise. With both Skywatch and the new radar facilities going operational during 1951/1952 the number of suspect sightings and tracks rose dramatically, building into hundreds per month.

The surge in reports was also stimulated by the addition of new Air Defense Identification Zones in 1952. Flight plan reporting was added to cover northern tier states and Alaska. Seacoast zones on the east and west coasts were already in place (Atlantic and Pacific ADIZs) as well as the Bangor, Maine ADIZ and Seattle, Washington ADIZs – controlling incoming air routes to the Northeast and Pacific Northwest.[13] Special ADIZs were also in place for Albuquerque and Knoxville (Oak Ridge) – as well as special prohibited flight areas in New Mexico, and Tennessee.

Federal regulations required flight plans for all aircraft intending to cross the Canadian border and those operating above 4,000 feet altitude. All flights based on the use of instrumented piloting (IFR) also required filed flight plans, although pilots operating under visual flight rules (VFR) at lower altitudes did not. Under the new "Defense Visual Flight Rules", flights above 4,000 feet were required to file flight plans including estimated time of arrival (ETA) and transit altitude. Changes of ETA over 5 minutes and deviation from flight plan of over 20 miles required notification – pilots were allowed to descend without notification only within 20 miles of their destination. No planes without radio communications or filed flight plans were allowed to cross the Canadian border, doing so carried the risk of serious penalties from the Civil Air Administration.

Military airspace control was an immense challenge. Commercial air carrier traffic grew rapidly, there were an estimated 4,000 crop duster type aircraft in operation and over 59,000 other aircraft were estimated to be using continental airspace annually.[14] Obviously with that many aircraft in use, violations of the rules were not uncommon, especially in the early years of the ADIZs (1952 into 1955).

To communicate the seriousness of the matter, pilots were advised that Air Force interceptors would be scrambled for violations. Pilots failing to file flight plans, not complying with the regulations for notification of changes or entering prohibited areas could face an interceptor "scramble" as well as legal action and fines. They were warned that the Air Force could not fail to respond to each incident, given the clear and present Soviet threat any unidentified flight could represent a potential "disaster". With American forces stretched so thin around the world the threat of war with Russia was felt to be imminent. Flying magazines of the day even featured detailed discussions of flight procedures to be followed in the event of a surprise atomic attack or flying under wartime conditions.

Local approach radar operators at commercial and military airports were also sources for unknown aircraft reports. But beyond airport approach corridors the majority of the nation's airspace was uncontrolled and dependent on pilot observations to prevent mid-air collisions. In the post war years there was no nationwide network of Civil Aviation Authority (CAA) radars to track and control commercial airline traffic. It was only following a terrible airliner collusion over the Grand Canyon in 1956 that work began on a separate network of air traffic control radars.[15] Reaction to the 1956 midair collision also resulted in legislation to establish a new, independent air safety agency, the Federal Aviation Administration. That legislation directed the establishment of a common military/civil air navigation and traffic control system.

Bringing that about took time, it was only in 1959 that the first civil radar system begin a feed into the air defense network and it took some time to integrate all the civil aviation radars into the air defense system. Ultimately some 23 radar sites were placed to monitor air routes at altitudes above 15,000 feet – but that civilian system was not actually completed until 1960. The military airspace control effort demanded that if identification could not be made through any other means it was necessary to scramble interceptors to contact and positively identify suspect aircraft. Interceptors were scrambled based on reports from the new Ground Observer network as well as either military or civilian ground based radar tracking.

Given the identification challenge, a new level of interceptor command and control was going to be necessary and in 1952 a major initiative was launched to develop a unified system of controlled interceptions (GCI; ground control interception). Ground observer corps filter centers, radar sites and a variety of other sources including Navy installations and ships were to transmit information on suspect targets to common GCI Centers.

At the GCI control centers, operations personnel plotted both known flights and unidentified tracks on large Plexiglas boards. Based on that information interceptors could be launched and guided by ground controllers. Some radar sites still lacked height finding capability but at a minimum aircraft could be vectored to the vicinity of the target. Through 1953 and 1954 there were still a relatively limited number of fighters available and in many instances they had to fly a considerable distance to perform intercepts – with fuel limitations often restricting their search and loiter time in the vicinity of the target. In 1952 some 600 aircraft were deployed for combat operations in continental defense, that number dramatically increased only by 1955, with available interceptors increasing to more than 1,200 aircraft.[16]

The rapid growth in available interceptors and the deployment of fighter squadrons to a series of air bases throughout the nation was accompanied by the replacement of anti-aircraft gun batteries by new anti-aircraft missile batteries. Nike Ajax batteries began to become operational in 1954, the first located in Maryland. The Nike Ajax had a range of 30 miles and was designed to defend against Soviet bomber formations. It was succeeded by the Nike Hercules with more than twice that range, able to hit jet bombers up to 70,000 feet in altitude with first high explosive and then atomic warheads.

By 1962 over 260 Nike sites would be established and operated by the Army, mounting over 4,000 missiles. Major cities were surrounded by entire rings of missile sites, Chicago with 22 batteries, Los Angles with 16 and New York with 19; Nike batteries were also positioned in Alaska and in Greenland to protect the huge radar and air bases there.

The number of U.S. interceptor squadrons also substantially increased, going from 21 in 1951 to 54 by 1953; units were deployed to air bases whenever possible but some operated out of commercial air fields.[17] Nike batteries were placed on local military reservations and Army facilities whenever possible but in many instances land had to be purchased or leased. Local communities were sometimes not happy with the sudden appearance of missile batteries and Army troops manning them; the batteries required a considerable number of personnel. Popular books and movies such as Rally Round the Flag Boys highlighted conflicts between communities and the Army over the new missile installations.[18] But while the new missiles might have raised local concerns, it was the deployment and ongoing flight operations of the jet interceptor squadrons which provoked the most attention and in many cases vocal citizen complaints and opposition.

Interceptor activities were ongoing, ranging from GCI training and practice missions – including exercises against SAC bombers – to airborne patrols over protected and strategic defense zones. In addition there were the actual "scrambles" to intercept unidentified aircraft / "unidentified airborne objects" triggered by visual reports from Skywatch volunteers and military personnel, by deviations from flight plans or by unidentified radar tracks.

It's hard to appreciate the actual level of air defense activity at this distance in time, but during the 1950s the nation truly came to operate in anticipation of imminent nuclear attack. Magazine articles and best seller fiction captured the public fears but one particular story, by well-known Saturday Evening Post writer Frank Harvey, captured the issues related specifically to air defense deployment of the new interceptor groups.

The story featured a newspaper man in a small town, well away from any strategic targets and distressed by the impact that the deployment of Air Force fighters to a local civil aviation airport was having on the community. The Chamber of Commerce was irate, concerned that the deployment was going to undermine their efforts to bring in commercial air service and that it was tearing up the field itself. The majority of the citizens were more focused on the sudden twenty four hour a day disturbance of their lives (and sleep) by interceptors blasting out under full after burner at all times of the day and night.

The story followed the newspaper man's experience in a firsthand look at "scrambles" and interceptions – riding in the back seat of an F-94 Starfighter on a night time exercise against SAC B-36 bombers and coming to understand that the local field was functioning as part of a shield protecting a key SAC base some hundred miles distant. In the end he underwent a major change in attitude…"in his mind he imagined that the bomber that had just sneaked in under the radar screen from the south was not a B-36, but a strange make, instead of the star and bar of the USAF, the emblem on its flank was bloody red."[19]

Fears of a surprise Soviet attack were all too real throughout the 1950s and early 1960s, with ongoing international confrontations and covert military activities between American and Soviet surrogates a constant in Latin America, South East Asia and even Africa. It was not just SAC that considered itself to be operating in a state of undeclared war, the Air Defense Command operated as if combat were imminent. Its interceptor squadrons responded to unidentified aerial objects not just as bogeys but as potential bandits. In previous chapters we covered the point that standard mission of the ADC meant responding to "anything unidentified that flies in the air". Standing orders were to intercept, identify, obtain radio contact and divert – or force the suspect craft down using whatever means were necessary.

We previously cited Major General Roger Ramey's remark that "interceptor airplanes have raced aloft several hundred times as the result of sightings of unidentified objects." That statement might have seemed stunning to the press in 1952, but there are indications it was far below the actual levels of air defense activity. There has been much discussion of the number of American aircraft lost during the 1950s, especially the early years of that decade. And it's true that fighters were lost chasing unidentified objects, some of which were never identified. However those losses actually speak to the challenge of air defense, not to the subject of true "unknowns".

An online search on Air Force interceptor activity reveals some very important research, in the form of commentary by respected researcher Brad Sparks. Sparks remarked on a British television special in which author Timothy Good discussed the numbers of USAF pilots killed in response to unidentified object reports. Spark's information is extremely important in understanding the actual level of interception and identification activity.[20]

Sparks pointed out that his own research into Air Defense Command histories revealed that the ADC operated under the same "virtual" wartime footing as the Strategic Air Command. The operational rules for ADC interceptor squadrons assumed that that any given alert jet scramble might end up with a fighter engaging a Soviet bomber.

Given the huge increase in post war commercial and civil air traffic – as well as military air training and transport flights in conjunction with the Korean War – it is not at all surprising to find a surge in the number of unidentified aircraft reports during the early 1950s, especially given that the Air Defense Identification Zones were new and not part of established pilot routines. Sparks stated that he had found the number one cause of the "unidentified tracks" was the failure of military pilots to file flight plans with the Air Defense Command. Civilian aircraft violations were actually fewer than those generated by Air Force and Navy pilots.

Spark's studies of the ADC records revealed that some 32,000 unidentified radar tracks were generated in 1951 – increasing to 35,000 in 1952. Such numbers were an immense challenge, reducing them via challenge and real time investigation was critical. In practice the initial numbers of unidentified aerial object reports were significantly reduced during the challenge and identification process. Sparks found that approximately half of the unidentified radar tracks had been readily identified. However interceptor scrambles were indeed conducted against some third of the tracks, meaning some 11,000 actual interception efforts per year. Given that level of activity no wonder there were public complaints from the vicinity of fighter bases, and loss of aircraft during night time and foul weather scrambles.

In one sense the air defense challenge of dealing with a constantly escalating number of unknown radar tracks, a growing number of unidentified visual sightings from the Ground Observer Corps and literally thousands of aerial intercept incidents offers an explanation for the Air Forces' moves to push UFO identification as far into the field as possible. Producing identifications as quickly as possible was a very basic air defense requirement. Reducing the number of incidents referred as "unknowns" helped the system – both the ADC and ATIC – from being overwhelmed. In theory it also helped in the mission of reassuring the public that the Air Force had the UFO situation well in hand.

Yet there were negative effects of the decision to press for identification and to manage the files and numbers to reassure the press and public. The pressure for identification and efforts to reduce "UFO noise" may have been successful in regard to the overall Air Force mission but the approach did little to address the fundamental intelligence problem of truly anomalous UFOs – as the Office of Scientific Investigation had noted in its assessment of *BLUE BOOK*.

This brings us to a second aspect of the Air Forces' regulation changes which increased security and control of communications related to UFO reports.

Those changes clearly were intended to support the overall Air Force goal of reducing press coverage and limiting public discussion of UFO sightings. However, by the mid-1950s there was a less obvious but pragmatic justification for efforts to restrict the amount of information reaching the public in regard to certain types of incidents.

At that point in time the relationship between security, public reassurance and press communications was becoming increasingly complex – exacerbated by the flight testing of a number of new and highly secret aircraft, rockets and even specialized high altitude balloons. Security concerns for such projects were taken extremely seriously within the military, both internally in regard to personnel observing the new devices and at the locations where development and initial testing were being conducted. Press commentary on the details of what was in fact a new aircraft, missile, weapons system, or reconnaissance device would simply have been a gift to Soviet intelligence.

In more recent years the extent to which new generations of aircraft might have produced UFO reports has been widely discussed. It also appears that in later years the Air Force and even the CIA seized on classified aircraft and balloon projects as a generic explanation for a great number of the reports which had officially been classified as "unknown". In reality the degree to which such devices actually produced the type of UFO reports which could be considered as truly anomalous "unknowns" is quite questionable.

One frequently cited example of secret devices dramatically stimulating UFO reports relates to the very high altitude U-2 reconnaissance aircraft, capable of operating at altitudes far above conventional airplanes, up to 70,000 feet. Unpainted test aircraft flying at altitude and with large, highly reflective wings were claimed to have produced a great number of UFO reports, especially from pilots who could appreciate that the objects were at altitudes unreachable by conventional aircraft.

Eventually a CIA historical study asserted the claim that the secret, very high altitude reconnaissance craft were largely to blame for the surge of UFO reports which began in the 1950s. The study maintained that Air Force personnel routinely were secretly supplied with information on U-2 flights, allowing them to identify the reports – but requiring that they still treat them as unidentified as far as the public was concerned. Somewhat surprisingly the CIA report also claimed that very high altitude CIA photo reconnaissance aircraft – first the relatively slow U-2 (Dragon Lady) and then the very high speed SR-71 (Blackbird) – "accounted for more than one half of all UFO reports during the 1950s and 1960s".[21] That claim seems unlikely for a number of reasons, one being that the most dramatic surge in UFO reporting began during 1951/1952, some three years before the prototype U-2s began to fly in 1955.

While there is little doubt that a few unidentified object reports could have been generated by such aircraft, there are several points which bring the claims of the CIA historical study into question. First, the U-2 was a very high altitude but relatively low speed aircraft. Certainly the U-2, with a cruising speed of some 475 miles per hour, was not producing the mysterious two to four thousand mile per hour tracks which air defense radars began to report beginning in 1952. Nor was it routinely outrunning and out maneuvering Air Force interceptors.

The U-2 was capable of an impressive ascent – climbing at an angle close to 45 degrees – although its design resulted in a much slower rate of descent.[22] But nothing about its speed or maneuverability would have made it especially notable to a ground level observer or even to pilots, even given its high rate of climb it took the U-2 considerable time to ascend to its operational altitude. Once at altitude the aircraft left no condensation trail and any observer close enough to it for a physical description would have viewed it as a conventional aircraft, looking more like a glider than anything else. At maximum altitude and at its most "mysterious", it would have been reported as simply a relatively slow moving, "glinting" object traveling at exceptionally high altitude.

In contrast the A-12 (the initial aircraft developed by the CIA and first flown in 1962) as well as its Air Force successor, the SR-71, would most definitely have appeared as an anomalous radar track in terms of both speed and altitude, breaking records at Mach 3.3 (2,531 miles per hour) and reaching heights of 85,000 feet. Yet at high speeds it was certainly not highly maneuverable in terms of lateral turning ability.

The one A-12 maneuver that has been compared to UFO sightings, an apparent ability to hover and then accelerate upwards at high speed, was described as the "dipsy doodle" in a Popular Mechanics article.[23] The "dipsy doodle "maneuver began at 30,000 feet and involved the aircraft descending at an angle of 30 degrees for some ten to twenty seconds, then immediately accelerating upwards at Mach 2. The maneuver is described as beginning at a distance of over five miles high and the reversal in direction would have occupied only seconds. With that in mind even a brief review of UFO "hovering/acceleration" reports argues against the A-12/SR-71 "dipsey doodle" as a source. Many of the descriptions of "hovering" UFOs involved sightings of objects at relatively low altitudes, and with structural details of objects clearly not matching the

A-12. Even more importantly a good many of those reports were made before the A-12 ever began flying.

In contrast to the CIA report claims, early experience with sightings of the A-12/SR-71 (in reality a very large and very noisy aircraft) tend to confirm that both military personnel and commercial airline crews can be trusted to provide accurate descriptions of unknown flying objects – even during unexpected encounters. In his book *Dark Eagles*, Chester Peoples describes several sightings made during the period in time in which the aircraft was still extremely secret and being flown out of a classified facility in Nevada.[24]

As he describes it, the aircraft was "large, loud and distinctive looking", and some of its flights "ranged across the southwestern United States". The first problem was to reconfigure its departure routes so that its sonic boom was not routinely heard during takeoff. But aerial encounters were not so easily controlled. One Air Force pilot flying towards a gunnery range in the same areas as the A-12s were operating encountered one of the new planes. Being close enough to distinguish its shape, he immediately recognized that it was an experimental aircraft. In another incident a formation of Air Force jets encountered and reported the A-12; they were simply told not to talk about their sighting; undoubtedly no further reports were filed on the incident.

Commercial pilots also observed the A-12 in flight, one pilot saw it at least twice, once in the company of chase planes during a flight test – apparently the pilot had no doubts about what he was seeing, radioing only that he had sighted a "goose and two goslings". Peoples' estimated that perhaps twenty to thirty pilot sightings were made of the A-12. Word quickly circulated within the air and space community that something very new and very "hot" was being tested over the desert southwest.

There is good reason to doubt that either the U-2 or the SR-71 made any sort of major contribution to UFO reports over the United States. And when observers were positioned to observe and describe their shapes and flight characteristics, they quickly realized that they were aircraft – just as they had the very high speed X-15 rocket plane during the years in which it was carried out of Edwards Air Force Base and launched on flights across California and western Nevada.

Irrespective of any secret aircraft sightings which the Air Force might have known of but not have been able to acknowledge, there is simply no historical evidence to show that the overall increase in unknown aerial object reports was actually driven by new spy plane flights. There were specific surges ("waves") in *BLUE BOOK* unidentified sightings in given years, including 1952, 1954 and 1957 but the level of day to day unidentified sightings and tracks – the "noise" level – was driven by the dramatic expansion of the continental air defense network and the overall increase in both military and commercial air traffic over the United States.

There are several important points to be taken away from this discussion. First, "unidentified" meant exactly that – for the ADC that designation did not automatically imply any anomalous appearance or even unconventional flight characteristics. Unlike the first years of flying saucer/disc reports, beginning in 1952 and on to contemporary times a great many unidentified flying object/suspect aircraft reports involved no visual sighting at all. Large numbers of reports came from radar tracking of aircraft failing to file flight plans or diverting from plans that were filed.

Second, the increasingly larger numbers of unidentified aerial objects showing up in military activities were being driven by a substantially enhanced air defense system. Radar tracks that appeared to violate ADIZ regulations demanded identification – as did tracks of aircraft whose type, purpose, origin and destination were undetermined. In and of themselves the growing number of preliminary observations/radar tracks simply represented increased "noise" in the system.

Third, some level of serious identification work was required for an unidentified object observation/track to become designated as truly "unknown". Even with preliminary checks and queries, some reports remained unidentified due to failed intercepts and the lack of any visual inspection – or in many instances simply the loss of radar tracking during the identification process. "Unknown" in operational air defense terms meant a suspect aircraft – or later a missile or satellite track – which simply could not be identified or otherwise resolved with a conventional explanation.[25]

Local units/commands were encouraged to resolve UFO reports with identifications whenever possible, even if the identifications could only designated as probable – those explanations could be shared with the public and media. Unknown airborne objects with truly unconventional speeds, maneuvering, acceleration or apparent propulsion characteristics not in conformance with known types of aircraft and missiles were referred to ATIC/*BLUE BOOK* for further investigation – with ATIC bearing the burden of any media follow up that might be deemed suitable.[26]

Over twenty plus years the total Air Force experience with unidentified aerial objects involved tens of thousands of incidents, including unidentified visual sightings and radar tracks. The vast majority of such incidents were resolved and identifications were made. A small percentage were treated as anomalous enough to be forwarded on to ATIC. Those reports received further evaluation – with the degree of actual investigation depending somewhat on the era and personnel involved. The great majority were identified (at least as "probable") and filed, along with those that ultimately could only be designated as "unknown".

For reference, as early as 1955, the *BLUE BOOK* files contained some 3,200 reports – as compared to the tens of thousands of incidents initially reported as "unidentified" in an air defense context. Following final classification, the reports were archived and showed up in *BLUE BOOK* statistical reports, with "unknowns" diminishing to the point of routinely being less than 3% annually from 1955 through the remaining lifetime of the project.

And that – essentially – was that. For the Air Force it was an operational problem of air defense identification and a public relations program of reassurance – and with only two exceptions there was literally no advanced analysis of the full body of archived reports. The first exception related to a project that was originally initiated in 1952, as part of the new, short lived drive to bring scientific methodology into the Air Force UFO study.

The original Air Force contract with the Battelle Memorial Institute had called for a statistical analysis of the full collection of BLUE BOOK reports as of 1952. Initially the study was to be completed that year but in fact it went on much longer, finally finished well after Ruppelt himself had left the Air Force and General Samford had been transferred to a new assignment.

According to Ruppelt, Battelle was actually asked to make two studies. One focused on the sources making such reports – intended to determine how much any individual could truly observe and remember. The intent of that analysis was to improve the interrogation and report forms being used by the Air Force. The second study was intended to statistically examine the observations in order to "profile" a typical "flying saucer", a step towards creating a filtering system for field reports.

The Battelle statistical study becomes visible to us in conjunction with BLUE BOOK special report #14 of May, 1955. It was also cited in an October, 1955 Air Force press release which stated that a "private scientific group under the direction of the ATIC at Dayton Ohio" had completed studies which proved that there were no such things as UFOs. Apparently the Air Force decided to assert that position based on the premise that the Battelle statistical analysis had found no proof that UFOs (unknowns) were unique in terms of the reports analyzed.

Yet, a review of one of the main statistical techniques used (chi squared) within the Battelle report demonstrates that there was virtually no possibility that the "knowns" studied were the same as the "unknowns" – suggesting that the "unknowns" being reported were indeed anomalous. Dr. Hynek confirmed that particular point and later commented that the Air Force seemed to have totally disregarded the actual results of the Battelle chi-squared tests in its press statements. As to whether or not the "unknowns" in the Battelle study sample were or were not flying saucers/extraterrestrial craft (the type of UFOs implied in the Air Force press release), that certainly was not something that the study had been constructed to address, or could have addressed through statistical analysis.

Early students of the Battelle study such as Leon Davidson, an engineer who worked on the atomic bomb project at Oak Ridge and Los Alamos and later as an engineering design supervisor for the AEC, noted several additional problems with the work, including its highly questionable failure to develop a useful profile/characterization of a typical unknown. The Battelle study maintained that there was insufficient "uniformity" in witness descriptions to develop a profile or model of a typical UFO.

Yet readers will recall that after only three months of studying the early 1947 reports, the very first Air intelligence assessment clearly "profiled" a specific set of physical shapes and described commonalities in speeds, maneuvers, acceleration and other basic characteristic. That profile enabled them to write a very specific intelligence collections memorandum. Even the GRUDGE report stated that a predominate number of daylight reports described "metallic disc like objects" and noted the fact that modeling (profiling) them was actually not at all difficult.

Despite similarities in certain of the actual Battelle incident drawings, it must be noted that Special Report #14 presented illustrations for a number of UFO cases which appear to have been selected to picture a maximum diversity in shapes and sizes (shape and size being only two attributes of any full profile).

In addition, Special Report #14 itself acknowledged that as the Battelle study proceeded, it was determined that one of the most significant factors in evaluating "unidentifieds" as true "unknowns" was the characteristic of motion. Battelle even stated that there was an obvious need to address "maneuvering" as a part of the study – yet a small footnote was used to point out that the importance of motion and maneuvering had become evident too late to revisit that factor and reevaluate the case data – so no factor for maneuvering was included.

Of course, as Dewey Fournet had demonstrated in late 1952, maneuvers (in particular formation maneuvers of multiple UFOs) were particularly important in evaluating intelligent control as a factor in the reports. Fournet was convinced that aspect alone suggested that certain sightings of unknowns involved actual craft. However it appears that Battelle had not been given guidance in regard to reviewing motion and maneuvering (nor speed, acceleration and other attributes) in its profiling effort, in consequence it simply took a pass on using "maneuvers" as factor in evaluating the cases it studied – even after realizing their importance. Along with the chi-squared issue, Battelle's questionable failure to derive a common UFO profile raises questions about the public version of its report.

Another issue that stands out with *BLUE BOOK* Special Report #14 is that the portion of the Battelle study assessing the frequency of UFO reports as referenced to geography has no obvious strategic or military orientation. The information is presented in the context of twelve regional areas, which are referred to as "Strategic Areas", and which each include several states. The study notes that strategic areas were defined by "concentration of sightings". Yet although the southwest and northwest show up as strategic areas, each with relatively high numbers of sightings compared to the other regional areas, there is absolutely no finer level of correlation to military bases, the atomic warfare complex facilities or any criteria which would have revealed statistical relationships between report concentrations and national security.

Even the earliest Air Force intelligence studies noted the importance of sightings associated with strategic facilities such as the well-known atomic manufacturing complexes at Hanford, Los Alamos and Oak Ridge. Ruppelt had readily noted the apparent relationship between UFO reports and key atomic facilities. He had covered that in his first briefing for General Samford in December. 1951. Given that awareness, it seems striking that Battelle would not to have been directed to develop a geographical mapping framework which would have allowed it to statistically evaluate UFO reports against a complete picture of the nation's most strategic facilities.

Certainly the released version of the Battelle report gives us no useful information pertaining to observations at the key national weapons storage sites established between 1946 and 1952, including Manzano Base outside Albuquerque, Clarksville Base near Fort Campbell (Tennessee/Kentucky), Medina Base outside San Antonio, and Killeen Base between Waco and Austin Texas. Two additional national stockpile sites were established in the 1950's, including Bossier base adjacent to Barksdale AFB in Louisiana. During that same period SAC atomic bomb dispersal storage sites were also established at Loring AFB in Maine, Ellsworth Base in South Dakota, Fairchild AFB outside Seattle, Traffic (Fairfield Suisan Field) outside San Francisco and Westover AFB in Massachusetts. Any meaningful statistical study of UFO reports over "strategic areas" would have certainly have needed to consider those locations.

There is a figure in the Battelle study which shows the frequency of sightings at a more discrete level, but it is based in geographic subdivisions of one degree of latitude, a purely arbitrary scale and with no annotations to reference actual strategic locations. A closer examination of that particular figure also raises serious questions as to whether the tabulated reports represent the full picture of observations around all strategic facilities – the numbers presented do not appear to capture several of the concentrations of reports which we have previously reviewed.

This particular issue has led to speculation that more focused strategic studies were done but only provided in a classified version of the report – obscured for security reasons in the material provided in the more widely distributed, public version. It seems we are left with two choices – either the tasking for Battelle was not sufficient to produce a useful study (drastically undermining the military intelligence value of the study) or a truly targeted study was conducted, with the actual results withheld for security reasons – obfuscated by the relatively meaningless material in the study made publicly available.

Given the Air Force position taken with the issuance of Special Report #14 (an obvious attempt at public reassurance) it is not surprising that we find no further analytical studies – internal or external – of the Air Force UFO files until one final scientific contract project more than a decade later. Yet in the face of its continuing negative position on the subject of UFOs, the Air Force remained the official national collection point for UFO reports, both from government agencies in general and from the public. Given that the Air Force had also been left to serve as the front line in terms of mitigating public concern and fears over UFOs, its spokespeople continued to carry on the role of reassuring the public throughout the 1950's and well into the 1960s.

Local base spokespersons were allowed to and did talk about reports that were identified, but not those that were not. Pentagon public relations officers were faced with issuing reassurance even in those instances in which no positive identification was available – or in some instances where the official identification was less than intuitively credible. Explaining each and every UFO sighting remained a challenge and life sometimes became especially difficult for Air Force spokespersons.

In August, 1965 wire stories and newspaper headlines featured a wide spread wave of evening UFO reports from the mid-west extending southwards to Oklahoma and Texas. Over the following day those same wire services carried an early Air Force response (obviously hurried) stating that the sightings had simply been bright stars in constellation Orion. Unfortunately for Air Force credibility, the same wire services quickly carried rebuttals from several planetariums pointing out that Orion is a winter constellation, not visible from the central United States during early summer evenings. The stars named by the Air Force were simply not in view at the time of the reports. Such Air Force explanations proved unsatisfactory – although entertaining – to the press, which also found *BLUE BOOK* scientific consultants such as Dr. Hynek to be targets of opportunity.

Less than a year after the Orion constellation embarrassment, in April, 1966, the Air Force came under intense public and media pressure over UFO reports in Michigan. In response the Air Force rushed Dr. Hynek into the field to evaluate a number of the sightings. While interviewing a individuals at Hillsdale College, Hynek was forced into early press interviews and made the remark that given the location of the Hillsdale sighting, it was possible that it had been produced by glowing swamp gasses. Hynek was later adamant that his remark covered only one particular set of reports, in which "faint lights" over swampy areas had been observed – however the national press had a field day with UFO/Swamp Gas headlines.

The affair ended in calls for a Congressional investigation of UFOs by two congressmen from Michigan, one being Gerald Ford, who would go on to become President. Hynek was not amused, the Air Force was not amused and Hynek himself later speculated that the incident had led the Air Force to once again refer the issue of UFOs to an external scientific study. That study, performed by the University of Colorado, remains particularly questionable but it ultimately did allow the Air Force to extract itself from serving as the official national voice on UFOs.[31]

The issues with the University of Colorado study and in particular with the report it published in 1967 – widely known as the Condon Report – have been written about extensively. Readers are referred to the Condon Report itself (available in print) and to a critique by one of its original project staff members, David Saunders – *UFO Yes! Where the Condon Committee Went Wrong*.[32]

Regardless of objections and challenges, the Air Force acceptance of the negative conclusions contained in the Condon report (many of which were in direct conflict with actual research within the report itself) provided a scientific opinion sufficient to allow the Air Force to disband *Project BLUE BOOK*. As of December, 1969 the Air Force formally announced the end of its role in serving as the national collection point for UFO reports and any vestige of official intelligence filtering of further UFO reports ceased.

The Air Force and the military in general certainly continued to deal with unidentified aerial objects in terms air defense and operational reporting of potential security threats. Yet the fundamental intelligence problem remained. The Air Force investigations – much as the CIA had assessed them during the fall of 1952 – had been strictly incident and identifications oriented. Lacking any deeper studies of multiple incidents over an extended period of time the fundamental questions related to truly anomalous, unconventional and unknown aerial objects remained not just unanswered but basically unaddressed.

Chapter 14 Endnotes

1. Secret History of the 4602d Air Intelligence Service Squadron", Sampler of documents from Unit History, January 29, 1996, Center for UFO Studies (CUFON) http://www.cufon.org/cufon/4602smpl1.htm

2. Kevin Randle, *Project Moondust,* Avon Books, New York, 1998, 81-82

3. JANAP 146(C) Communications Instructions for Reporting Vital Intelligence Sightings From Airborne or Waterborne sources, Letter of Promulgation The Joint Chiefs of Staff, Joint Communications-Electronics Committee, Washington D.C. March 10, 1954, Computer UFO Network http://www.cufon.org/cufon/janp146c.htm

4. Air Force Regulation No. 200-2, Unidentified Flying Objects Reporting, Intelligence, Department of the Air Force, August 12, 1954 http://fas.org/spp/military/docops/usaf/afr200-2.htm

5. Jerome Clark, *The UFO Book*, Visual Ink, Detroit, Michigan, 1998, 468

6. Kevin Randle, *Project Moondust*, 88

7. Ibid, 86

8. Ibid, 87

9. Dr. J. Allen Hynek, *The Hynek UFO Report*, Barnes and Noble Books, New York, 1997, 243-249

10. Jerome Clark, *The UFO Book*, 468

11. Ted Roe, "Aviation Safety in America; Unidentified Aerial Phenomena and the Under Reporting Bias", May 29, 2002 http://www.narcap.org/files/narcap_TR-8_2002.pdf

12. Dr. J. Allen Hynek, T*he Hynek UFO Report*, 245

13. Vera Foster, "ADIZ", *Flying Magazine*, 1952, 34, 48 https://books.google.com/books?id=15HnYySUWm4C&pg=PA48&lpg=PA48&dq=flight+plan+filing+violations+1952&source=bl&ots=LoO5f8rxYf&sig=Ssode86MHMDgZrejJrvEjhf1I1c&hl=en&sa=X&ved=0ahUKEwjkgcOS9ozOAhVK4oMKHZ_qBoUQ6AEINTAF#v=onepage&q=flight%20plan%20filing%20violations%201952&f=false

14. Ibid, 48

15. 1956 "Grand Canyon Airplane Cash a Gamer Changer," CBS News, July 8, 2014 http://www.cbsnews.com/news/1956-grand-canyon-airplane-crash-a-game-changer/

16. Kenneth Schaffel, "The Emerging Shield; The Air Force and the Evolution of Continental Defense, 1991, Table 3 Air Defense Aircraft

17. Ibid, Table 2, Interceptor squadrons assigned ADC, by type

18. Bob Crowther, Screen: "Suburban Farce; 'Rally Round the Flag, Boys!' at the Palace", *The New York Times*, December 25, 1958

19. Frank Harvey, *Scramble Nighthawk, Jet,* Ballantine Books, New York, 1955, 122-138

20. Joe McGonagle, Commentary by Brad Sparks on ITV Central Extra Time UFO programme "1,000 pilots Killed in UFO Interaction" with Timothy Good, broadcast June 3, 2008, UFO Updates, June 8, 2008 http://www.ufoupdateslist.com/2008/jun/m09-002.shtml

21. Gregory Pedlow and Donald Walzenbach, "The CIA and the U-2 Program, 1954 to 1974", History Staff, Center for the Study of Intelligence, Central Intelligence Agency, 1998 https://www.cia.gov/library/center-for-the-study-of-intelligence/csi-publications/books-and-monographs/the-cia-and-the-u-2-program-1954-1974/u2.pdf

22. Curtis Peebles, *Dark Eagles, A History of Top Secret Aircraft*, Ballantine Books, New York, 1995, 33

23. Joe Wilson, "The CIA's Secret UFO Files (Skeptical)", *Popular Mechanics*, UFO Evidence http://www.ufoevidence.org/documents/doc2027.htm

24. Curtis Peebles, *Dark Eagles, A History of Top Secret Aircraft*, 63-64

25. Air Force Regulation 200-2, Department of the Air Force, February 5, 1958 http://www.nicap.org/directives/afr200-2_020558.pdf

26. Air Force Regulation, 200-2, Department of the Air Force, August 12, 1954 http://www.cufon.org/cufon/afr200-2.htm

27. Study No. 102-EL-55-2.79, "Analysis of Reports of Unidentified Aerial Objects", Project No. 100-73, May 5, 1955, The *BLUE BOOK* Archive, NICAP http://www.nicap.org/docs/pbbsr/BBA-PBSR14.pdf

28. Jerome Clark, *The UFO Book; Encyclopedia of the Extraterrestrial*, Visual Ink, Detroit, Michigan, 1998, 483-484

29. Leon Davidson, *Flying Saucers: An analysis of the Air Force Project BLUE BOOK Special Report No. 14*, Ramsey Wallace Corp, 1966. For additional detail on the Air Force handling of the Battelle report in conjunction with *Special Report #14*, readers are referred to commentary from researchers Michael Swords, Fran Ridge, Brad Sparks and Bruce Maccabee provided on the NICAP website. http://www.nicap.org/reports/sr14_ufois.htm

30. Special Report #14, Project *BLUE BOOK*, May 5, 1955, Figures 31 and 32

31. J. Allen Hynek, *The UFO Experience, A Scientific Inquiry*, Henry Regnery Company, Chicago, 1972, 195-196

32. David R. Saunders, *UFO's Yes, Where the Condon Committee Went Wrong*, World Publishing, 1969

Chapter 15

Beyond BLUE BOOK

In this chapter

- Huge collections of official documents, incident technical studies, press reports, and oral histories are now available, including the full *BLUE BOOK* incident archives.

- *BLUE BOOK* ultimately classified some 700 incidents out of 15,000 as "unknown" however upon detailed examination that figure is questionable.

- An online listing of some 1,500 true "unknowns" out of the *BLUE BOOK* archives is available online courtesy of NICAP.

- Reports contained in the *BLUE BOOK* archives all received at least some level of field investigation and follow up inquiry by military officers – succeeding years have produced lists of tens of thousands of UFO reports, however those lists vary considerably in regard to the extent to which reports are screened, filtered and categorized.

- The availability of the original *BLUE BOOK* archives does allow for new studies using strategic intelligence techniques never applied to that body of information – techniques associated with indications and intentions analysis.

- The practices of warnings/indications analysis – in particular its longer term, chronological examination of patterns, trends and activity anomalies – provide insights into the fundamental problem of UFO "unknowns" which individual incident technical studies did not produce.

The Air Force termination of Project *BLUE BOOK*, announced in December, 1969, meant that it was leaving the fundamental questions of UFOs behind it, no doubt with some relief.[1] As it had repeatedly pointed out, there had been no overt evidence of hostility in the reports, no sign of an active threat and despite the earliest concerns nobody really suspected the Russians any longer. What was left unsaid was that standard practices of technical intelligence simply had proved ineffective in resolving the problem of the true unknowns – the most highly anomalous observations. There is little doubt that the Air Force was quite content to leave that mystery behind it. As a military service its primary concerns were still the very real challenge of the Soviet Union – which after a decade had finally moved into a position of strategic nuclear parity with the United States – as well as the very real and expanding combat going on across Southeast Asia.

Yet despite the negative report of the contract University of Colorado UFO study and the Air Force exit, popular interest in UFOs remained high. In particular, the theme of UFOs as potential alien visitations to planet Earth continued and UFOs as alien craft became a standard topic in the entertainment and publishing industries. The subject has become so culturally embedded and its images so significant that entire books have been devoted to its print, television and movie imaging.[2] As of this writing in 2017 thousands of contemporary UFO sightings and reports continually appear on a host of Internet websites and blogs dedicated to anomalous phenomena.[3] UFOs also remain a constant topic on numerous television shows, Internet radio and pod casts.

The perception of UFOs as alien craft has become so culturally pervasive that one author, aerospace historian Curtis Peebles, was moved to write a 1994 book devoted to chronicling the entire history of the "flying saucer myth".[4] While psychologist C.G. Jung had written of the matter as a psychological phenomenon as early as the 1960s, Peeples moved the subject into the arena of cultural anthropology and the generation of myth cycles. A cover endorsement for People's book and its conclusions refers to his "enjoyable" account of "gullibility's, psychodramas, and mysteries both solved and unsolvable". Perhaps not surprisingly, that endorsement is from Frederick C. Durant III, acting secretary of the Robertson Panel (the CIA Special Advisory Panel on UFOs), and author of the final CIA/Durant report to the IAC in 1953.

In contrast, the subject of UFO sightings and reports, as well as the intelligence communities' handling of them, has become a matter for dedicated and intense historical research – research devoted to obtaining, publishing and analyzing primary documents. Such documents include the original *BLUE BOOK* archives as well as extensive materials from the early military investigations and a far ranging sampling of other materials relating to the operational reporting of unidentified flying objects.

Researchers have assembled huge collections of official documents as well as technical studies, press reports, articles, and oral histories; they have also made a significant amount of that research available on the Internet. The amount of primary and secondary material now available is truly daunting, but even more so are the listings of UFO sightings and reports. The starting point for such listings is undoubtedly the extensive *BLUE BOOK* archive research done by Don Berliner and Brad Sparks. That research is available in a listing (available at NICAP) of some 1,500 true "unknowns", excerpted and reassessed from an estimated 15,000 *BLUE BOOK* UFO reports archived during the lifespan of the project.[5][6]

Beyond the official, *BLUE BOOK* files (which all received some basic level of investigation and vetting by military officers) there are separate lists of tens of thousands of UFO sightings extending into current years. Those lists vary considerably in regard to the extent to which reports are screened, filtered and categorized. The Mutual UFO Network has over 400 volunteer field investigators in the United States and Canada who screen and evaluate the majority of sightings which are submitted to the organization, classifying reports as information only, insufficient information, identified, UFO or hoax. Between the years 2000 and 2016 MUFON investigators screened 95% of over 81,000 reports submitted to it, classifying 31 percent as "unknown".[7]

In 1974, following the Air Force's decision to close down its role as a UFO collection point, the National UFO Reporting Center (NUFORC) was established.[8] NUFORC has become a referral point for UFO reports from virtually all government agencies as well as military facilities and even 911 dispatch centers. It operates a telephone hot line for reports and has taken tens of thousands of calls since becoming operational. NUFORC registers large numbers of reports, some 5,000 a year, many of which are electronically filed into a master list by way of an online data entry form.[9] Its website provides online access to the data, indexing the master list of reports by year, state and shape of object – the NUFORC annual index also provides totals for each year's reports from 1945 to the current year (and even for earlier historical sightings).[10]

In addition to such compiled historical listings, there is also a good deal of interest in current trends and there are a number of websites devoted to statistical and trend analysis. UFO Stalker currently indexes over 74,000 reports which it obtains from MUFON. Stalker graphically maps the sightings, showing trends by city and geography – both by month and year.[11] However Stalker simply takes the full MUFON list of sightings, with no differentiation of MUFON screening classifications. That means that all categories of sightings, including those evaluated by MUFON as both "identified" and "hoaxes", show up on Stalker maps.[12]

Additionally, Max Galka, a data modeling and visualization specialist, has applied mapping and trending tools to produce a graphic representation of some 90,000 of the NUFORC reports, comparing the locations of sightings and the related numbers of reports.[13] Concentrations are mapped, and tallied, both for states and locations (including cities and airports).

Perhaps the most daunting contemporary UFO report listing is that of the UFOCAT database maintained by the Center for UFO Studies (CUFOS). Its collection, based in some thirty years of work by a number of scientific investigators including David Saunders and Jacques Vallee, contains some 109,000 UFO reports and is available on CD.

It should also be noted that the exit of the Air Force and the refusal of any government agency – including the Federal Aviation Administration – to collect and evaluate UFO reports has evoked serious professional concern that the failure to report and study potentially dangerous aerial encounters actually constitutes a flight safety issue. A contemporary study of pilots' failures to report UFO sightings and aerial encounters makes it clear that the most common reason for not reporting has become a combination of concern over the internal/safety paperwork involved and the issue of ridicule in regard to such reports.[14] The frequency of unreported incidents, in an increasingly complex environment of advanced aircraft, drones, UAVs and a host of new aerial devices, led to the formation of a professional organization devoted to the reporting and study of aerial safety incidents related to anomalous aerial objects – the National Aviation Reporting Center on Anomalous Phenomena (NARCAP).[15] Readers will find technical studies of contemporary aerial encounters as well as pilot surveys and interviews in the technical report collection available from NARCAP.[16]

Respected scientists have also developed their own "filtered" UFO report databases and incorporated them into specialized collections for professional statistical analysis of both cycles and trends – including how many reports are generated by year, month and even day of the week. Jacques and Janine Vallee performed some of the earliest statistical studies of UFO reports. Vallee, a mathematician, astronomer and NASA consultant, and his wife, a professional data analyst, described their work in *Challenge to Science; The UFO Enigma*. Using a specially prepared catalog of some 3,000 sightings, their computer based statistical study examined various elements of "periodicity". Their studies included a search for patterns including "waves" in sightings, the correlation of population density with sightings, concentrations by time of day and durations of certain types of sightings.[17]

As Vallee himself noted, a major challenge in such work proved to be relating any obvious patterns to specific causality. Among other possibilities he mapped patterns related to solar activity, thermonuclear explosions and even the closest orbital approaches of Mars to Earth (something discussed in certain of the early Air Force reports). In addition Vallee examined possible geospatial linkages in the paths of widely reported UFOs (the "straight line" phenomena; a concept originated by Aime Michel in his studies of UFO reports in France) and looked for patterns in certain classes of sightings as well as in witness descriptions of object size based on the distance of the observer.

One of the couple's particularly interesting findings was that observers relatively close to unidentified objects described them has having a generally consistent size/diameter, while observers who felt the objects to be more distant perceived the objects to be notably larger. Vallee related that to a well-known psychological/perceptual effect, known as the "moon illusion". The effect has generally been thought to be the result of a perceptual comparison of an object to distant reference points, in the instance of the rising moon relating its size to the horizon.[18] While the exact mechanism of the interaction between the optical and neural elements involved in the perceptual effect is still being debated there is no doubt that it is an observational fact and that it occurs with physical objects.

Vallee points out that in the UFO context, such a correlation between observational distance and size estimating suggests that real physical objects are involved in the reports which show the distance/size differential – since the perceptual effect would have no relevance to observations which were illusions, hoaxes, lies, or simply delusions of some sort.[19] This sort of detailed statistical analysis delves into more detailed aspects of UFO observations and allows a certain amount of profiling of the observers making reports. But as Vallee found, while it may help confirm the actual existence of certain UFOs as real physical objects, it provides us no information about origins and little insight into intentions.

Using Air Force *BLUE BOOK* reports as data, Dr. Alan Hynek dealt with both statistical analysis and some aspects of probability in his book *The UFO Experience, A Scientific Inquiry*. One of his key points in introducing the work was to point out that the only truly significant UFO reports are those with high degrees of strangeness, the sorts of truly anomalous observations that characterize a true "unknown".[20] Sightings reach that status only after they have been seriously and competently investigated. Hynek notes that even with the many thousands of UFO reports generated during the *BLUE BOOK* era, only some 700 "unknowns" were listed in their files. It should be noted that a detailed reassessment of the *BLUE BOOK* archives suggests that a considerable number of the ATIC staff classifications could reasonably be challenged; more objective estimates place the number of true "unknowns" in their files at more than double their official count. The work in Hynek's book focuses on his methodology for describing various classes of reports in terms of both "strangeness" and "probability". His approach to "strangeness" is particularly interesting in that he uses it to magnify the amount of data available from the observation – in addition to standard estimates of speed, distance and size.

Hynek examined several categories of observations including "Nocturnal Lights, Daylight Discs, Radar-Visual and Close Encounters" in terms of both the type of witness making the observations and the geographic distribution of such reports. While highlighting key incidents in each category and offering personal observations, one of the main thrusts of the work is an examination of the difficulties that the subject presents to the established, professional scientific community – the "Invisible College" as Hynek describes it – and his observation that in the end the scientific approach may not be able to provide an agreed upon solution.[21]

Physical science has historically relied on experimental practices and repeatable observations. It operates most efficiently when an observation can be predicted and even replicated. Hynek commented that not only have UFOs remained totally beyond any sort of experimental control but their appearances remain almost entirely transient and unscheduled.[22] Surprise appearances pose a particular problem for the scientific observer, limiting how much information can be collected during any given incident. Only a truly extensive network of instrumented, technical data collection sites could address such an issue – while such networks were proposed during the Air Force inquiries, none were ever actually implemented.

Surprisingly, based on actual incidents previously reviewed in this work, it seems that Hynek might have been overstating his case in regard to the complete unpredictability of sightings as well as the lack of early instrumented data available for scientific study. He makes no mention of the timed and triangulated observations made at Killeen Base (which did reach the *BLUE BOOK* files) or of the numerous "radiation story" incidents which provided records and measurements. And Hynek himself related several instances of instrument assisted, long duration UFO observations by high altitude balloon launch teams, as well as a variety of radar-visual incidents – some involving objects traveling extended distances and with observations from multiple locations.

There is also the possibility that the basic scientific stumbling block may well be less a matter of hard technical data than a general, professional unwillingness to pursue it. Hynek certainly felt that the institutional scientific community was extremely resistant to the entire subject of UFOs. The frustrating and ultimately tragic personal experiences of respected atmospheric physicist Dr. James McDonald support the perception of professional scientific career risks associated with the subject. Dr. McDonald's commitment – and struggles – with scientific approach to UFO research illustrate the extent to which the establishment reaction can destroy a career and ultimately a life. That statement may sound overly sensational, those unfamiliar with Dr. McDonald's story can evaluate that for themselves with the material now available on his efforts and researches. Readers are referred to the full story of McDonald's experience, described in the book *Firestorm, Dr. James E. McDonald's Fight for UFO Science* by Anne Druffel.[23] A reading of the FBI's investigation and comments on Dr. McDonald – obtained and made available online by the Center for UFO studies – further illustrates the negative official attention such efforts at actual scientific study can draw.[24]

Dr. Hynek specifically commented on the possibility that from a purely academic viewpoint, by its own internal logic "the scientific framework excludes certain classes of phenomena of which UFOs may be one."[25] Following his work as a consultant for the Air Force, Hynek went on to found the Center for UFO Studies (CUFOS), dedicated to a scientific investigation of the UFO question.[26] In pursuit of that goal he sought out and hired a full time staff member, astronomer Allan Hendry, to serve as the center's primary investigator. Hendry's wife, Dr. Elaine Hendry (a physicist) assisted in his investigations. During the 1970s Allan Hendry personally examined and researched over a thousand UFO reports, finding most to be explainable – but also isolating a core of reports were totally inexplicable.

Hendry was taken to task by both skeptics and believers, praised for his rigorous work and dammed for his refusal to accept more than a small percentage of cases as true anomalies. Ultimately CUFOS' financial problems led to the elimination of Hendry's position, but reportedly at about that same time he had come to the conclusion that scientific methods were simply not going to produce any conclusive results. Apparently frustrated by his experience he totally departed the field of UFO studies – his personal experience appears to reinforce Hynek's concerns in regard to the challenge of a classic physical sciences approach to the problem.

In summary, following the collection of tens of thousands of sightings, investigation and vetting of a core of truly anomalous unknown object reports, extensive statistical analysis, and physical science analysis we are left with the simple likelihood that in a number of instances experienced and credible observers have indeed observed something very real. Real aerial devices which demonstrate capabilities (especially in the areas of propulsion, acceleration and maneuvering) that are totally behind existing technology. Fifty years of inquiry have simply confirmed the original assessment in the first Air Force report on the subject produced in the fall of 1947.

But – there remains a road not taken and a category of intelligence practices which were never applied to the UFO problem. Over some three decades the military intelligence approach to UFOs was consistently one of individual incident investigation. From its earliest dealings with the problem of unidentified aerial objects – "nightmare devices", "mystery lights" or "foo fighters" – through the Flyer X's and Ghost Rockets and on to the flying discs, saucers and UFOB incidents, the intelligence approach was conventional and consistent.

If the objects were real, if they were being operated by an enemy and possessed the capabilities being reported, they would become a true national security issue – if and when some evidence of actual hostile/threatening activity emerged. When that didn't happen and when the sightings could not be explicitly tied to the Germans or Japanese – or later the Russians – public morale and public relations concerns always became predominate and the official responses turned to reassurance and explanations involving misidentification, natural phenomena, and hoaxes.

The CIA/OSI assessment of 1952 pointed out the fundamental limitations of the Air Force approach, and while the OSI proposed an expanded scientific study, there was also a mention of referring the subject to a level of strategic intelligence by assigning UFO report tracking to the Soviet analysis activities of the Watch Committee. Yet none of the OSI's proposals came to fruition and the failure to elevate UFOs to a higher level of national security tasking meant that the subject received no long term, strategic intelligence study.

The fact that UFOs were not elevated to a higher level of intelligence tasking also meant that there would be no group with the authority – and the appropriate security classifications and need to know – to pull together the increasingly fragmented reports of special interest. Observations and data related to highly anomalous objects both in the atmosphere and in space would increasingly register with sensitive and compartmentalized sources – including data registering with technical assets under control of the CIA, the NSA, NORAD and even newer agencies that came into being as space and satellite collections literally exploded in following decades.

Each of those organizations maintained its own separate reporting systems, controlled access to information deemed intelligence sensitive, and administered its own practices for controlling sensitive and compartmented information. Even with Top Secret clearances, individuals within an organization are required to undergo special security vetting for programs/information designated as sensitive and compartmented. A common example of that type of information (known as "code-word" information) is associated with Special Access programs, for which special TS/SCI (Top Secret/Special Compartmented information) clearance is required.[27]

Personnel clearances and even "need to know" within one service or agency have no automatic inter agency transfers and each service/agency can accept, require additional checks or reject clearances from the others. Individuals with Air Force Top Secret clearance are not automatically granted Navy or CIA Top Secret access and none of them would have been granted automatic AEC Q Clearance. Normally even when clearance access is granted it is only granted for a specific purpose or even a specific meeting, as with the Robertson Panel. It's a system designed for protecting national security, certainly not as an enabler for any truly broad based scientific study or even intelligence analysis.

Only on a few occasions did the subject of truly anomalous UFO reports rise to even the level of discussion by the Intelligence Advisory Committee. One such incident occurred on September 20, 1957 when Air Defense Command reported that multiple radar units had tracked an object proceeding in what appeared to be a straight line from the area of Long Island to Buffalo, New York and on westward towards Chicago. The object made its westward transit at an altitude of 50,000 feet and a speed of 2,000 miles per hour.[28] An IAC meeting reviewed the report, the CIA weighed in with the observation that the Soviets had no known technology that could accomplish such a flight and no obvious motive. In the end it appears once again a truly inexplicable incident was written off as an "atmospheric phenomena". Interestingly, some two weeks earlier, the Soviets had launched the first artificial earth satellite – with an orbital speed of approximately 18,000 miles per hour.

The amounts of data flowing into the nation's technical monitoring assets, including its space surveillance systems (both radar and astronomical) grew almost beyond belief during the 1960s and in the decades that followed. Specific agencies were interested in certain types of anomalous objects and phenomena (in space, the atmosphere and underwater) but to a large extent the most interesting military system observations of "unknowns" continued to be short term and unpredictable. NORAD would generate a flash report, the National Military Command Center would be notified. But the end result was that that such incidents remained time critical and if no imminent or actual threat was confirmed those observations (and their related technical data) simply passed into various highly secure data storage systems.[29] With no high level UFO national security "problem" tasking, and no official authority for classified, multi-source collection, data compartmentalization was the natural result.[30]

There is no doubt such anomalous observational data exists, much of it very likely applicable to the fundamental UFO technical intelligence problem. However its true extent remains unknown and at this point classification and security issues make it highly unlikely that it will ever be assembled into an integrated collection. Earlier we discussed the point that both operational and technical collections (sources and methods) security issues blocked certain incidents and data from reaching ATIC/*BLUE BOOK*. After that project's closure, there was no place and no authority to further accumulate or archive even routine UFO sightings – and no requirement outside of CIRVIS threat notifications that military personnel or commercial pilots report UFO sightings.[31]

The bad news is that the type of data that *BLUE BOOK* might have collected in ensuing years is lost to us. The good news is that, thanks to the dedicated work of UFO historical researchers, we do have the archived reports which *BLUE BOOK* did collect. That data, and in many instances further investigation and analysis of the original reports, is archived and a good amount of it has even been placed onto Internet sites.

In addition, we have available the practices and techniques of strategic intelligence analysis, techniques never applied to the entire body of *BLUE BOOK* data. Those practices – warnings/indications/intentions analysis – were specifically developed to work with collections of data in which each individual observation could not be absolutely verified.

Strategic intelligence analysis, as compared to tactical/combat oriented intelligence practices, gained considerable attention during the earliest years of the Cold War.[32] The influential American Joint Intelligence Committee (JIC) – with its origins in the war time British/American Allied JIC – was empowered to produce strategic intelligence assessments not only for the Joint Chiefs but also for "higher authorities", both during and immediately after the end of the war. Given the climate of the time, by 1946 the JIC began to focus its work on the emerging Soviet Bloc, evaluating not only the military capabilities of the Soviet Union but its economic and political environment.

A great amount of its work was involved in assessment of Soviet motivations and capabilities; the mission was that of estimating the likelihood and potential timing of preemptive warfare against the West. The JIC's work predated the Central Intelligence Group and was quite competitive with it. Its first post-war studies estimated that the Soviets would be unable to engage in global warfare for an extended period of time. Given post-war Soviet activities in Eastern Europe and Stalin's own aggressive remarks, that attitude quickly changed and the JIC turned to a much more alarming view of an imminent Soviet attack; in March 1946 they began working under the assumption that hostilities could commence on or about January, 1948.[33]

Warning and indications intelligence – as differentiated from technical intelligence, scientific intelligence and military/tactical intelligence – began to receive increased attention immediately following World War II. Many of the techniques and practices which it incorporated came from the extensive collections and analysis work conducted during the war, work dedicated to anticipating enemies' broader military plans and intentions. Following the war those practices evolved into a distinct function, characterized as "warnings" intelligence, devoted almost entirely to the anticipation of military action by Communist bloc countries against the United States and its allies, or against other nations nominally part of the Western bloc.[34]

Cynthia Grabo, one of the earliest post-war practitioners of the specialty, described a possibly apocryphal story from within the intelligence community; it relates to the specific origins of warnings intelligence under the Truman Administration. President Truman was reportedly an avid reader of intelligence reports and after immersing himself in quantities of conflicting opinions and rumors about possible Soviet action against Berlin the President pointedly asked who it was that was keeping track of all those indications he was receiving.[35] He apparently wanted someone to reconcile them all and give him a single, intelligence assessment. When told there was no mechanism to provide a unified opinion he became adamant that would change – and change quickly.

Apocryphal or not, it is true that the origin of the first interagency working group to deal with indications analysis occurred during the first post-war Berlin crisis. A committee – appropriately designated the Ad Hoc Committee – was organized to develop a combined estimate of Soviet intentions towards Berlin. Officially the request for that assessment had come from the Office of

Naval Intelligence, and the Director of the CIA responded by putting the Ad Hoc Committee together, with its first meeting in March, 1948. The meeting was chaired by an analyst from the CIA's Office of Reports and Estimates.[36]

Given the challenge of inter-agency agreement, it took several days – and apparently continued pressure from President Truman – for the committee to reach an estimate they could all accept. The ensuing Soviet blockade of Berlin kept the new committee at work updating their estimate for the remainder of 1948. In 1949 British Intelligence requested that the Central Intelligence Agency review the British indications checklist of actions which would suggest that the Soviets were preparing to occupy West Berlin.[37] The request was forwarded to the Ad Hoc warning committee.

The Ad-Hoc committee continued to meet under CIA auspices, at the same time an Army Intelligence group was also producing comparable analyses and reports. Ultimately the work of the Ad Hoc committee was praised in a review by the National Security Council and in 1950 by the CIA Director. The North Korean attack of June, 1950 prompted more frequent meetings and a move towards forming a more formal warnings intelligence group. In her historical synopsis of the origins of warnings intelligence Grabo notes that up to that point in time there was virtually no collaboration on research between agencies and no coordination of reports.[38]

Combat in Korea spurred a dramatic change in sharing information and by January, 1951 all services as well as CIA, State, FBI and AEC were participating in what had become referred to as the Joint Intelligence Indications Committee (JIIC). At that point, the group was re-designated as the Watch Committee, and tasked with reporting to the Intelligence Advisory Council, which in turn served the National Security Council and through it the President.

The actual practice of what became known inside the national intelligence community as Warnings/Indications/Intentions intelligence carried both real time and longer term elements. Indications of potential threats and actual impending attacks had to be evaluated on an ongoing basis, with weekly and sometimes daily analysis. More in depth analysis relied on chronological tracking of patterns and trends over months and even years. Monitoring of specific activities against indicators might at any time suggest impending actions including military initiatives by what had become known as the Sino-Soviet bloc (China and North Korea had joined Russia as mortal enemies of the West). The "intentions" of the Sino-Soviet bloc were assumed at all times to be hostile, meaning that the focus was specifically on threat indicators. Post war indications analysis became a function practiced specifically to provide assessments of when and where the Cold War might go hot.

The Watch Committee was intended to function as an interagency effort, however the State Department offered little support and in addition to CIA staff, Cynthia Grabo from Army Intelligence and Tom Beldon from Navy Intelligence played seminal roles in the ongoing development of warnings and indications intelligence.[39] The practice of national intelligence warnings has continued from those earliest days until contemporary times. While documents are limited for the earliest period, more contemporary material is available and demonstrates that indications intelligence and national warning has remained a vital part of U.S. intelligence up to the present day.[40]

Warnings "watchlist" reports were provided daily to the Intelligence Advisory Council and its successor in 1958, the Foreign Intelligence Board. Advisory studies were also sent to both the CIA Director and the IAC. Monthly studies were sent to senior military service leadership. Few actual documents are available on either the early work done by the Watch Center personnel or later by the National Indications Center staff. One early document found in the Watch Center files is a copy of the Army intelligence indications list for the Far East, under the topic of potential Chinese military action in Korea. That list was prepared during the summer of 1950 and contained some serious cautions of impending Chinese military intervention – based in intelligence that no Chinese contract shipments through Hong King were scheduled beyond the end of September.

Sudden changes in logistics activities – including shipping and transportation practices – are always seen as important indicators; the anomalous and unexplained move to cancel all Chinese contract shipping out of Hong Kong by the end of September proved to be exceptionally "predictive". The first movements of Chinese troops towards Korean combat began on October 5, 1950, actual contact and combat began on October 26, 1950. More than a month passed before the first massive Chinese attacks began, the exact reasons for the delay remain unknown but indications had continued to accumulate – including a warning of intervention given to the Indian ambassador in Beijing on October 3. Additional indicators had registered for some weeks before actual Chinese troop movements were observed.[41]

Intelligence analysts using indications methodology had actually warned of the North Korean attack on South Korea as well as Chinese intervention in Korea. The problem was that for a host of political and organizational reasons – including General Douglas MacArthur's personal and staff opinions – the warnings were not accepted by military or national leadership. Despite the failure with having its warnings actually accepted, the Watch Committee continued its work with a CIA officer assigned as its permanent chair.[42] It continued to function under the IAC and later the Foreign Intelligence Board.

What had begun as a multi-agency threat assessment activity focused on the initial Berlin crisis – the Ad Hoc Committee – evolved into the Watch Committee, tasked with ongoing warnings analyses. As the initial Russian threat in Europe expanded to a global confrontation between eastern and western blocs of nations, the effort grew into a broad based national intelligence estimating function, directed against the entire Sino-Soviet bloc.

By 1954 a National Indications staff group was formed and in 1955 the National Indications Center was officially designated to support the mission of strategic/warnings intelligence. The National Indications Center (NIC) operates on a 24-hour staffing schedule, organized on the watch center model established by the Strategic Air Command. Early in the Cold War SAC set the standards for what came to be accepted as real time warnings and alert coordination. Its own Command and Communications center at the Pentagon evolved into the National Military Command Center.

The practices of strategic indications analysis are relevant to the intelligence problem of UFOs for two separate reasons. First, in 1952 even the CIA/OSI proposal on the UFO problem noted that the subject of UFOs could well have been raised to higher level of strategic intelligence study – a draft OSI proposal suggested that monitoring of UFO incidents related to possible Soviet action be added to Watch Committee action lists. Second, and more important is the possibility that the techniques of warnings/indications analysis – in particular its longer term, chronological monitoring of patterns, trends and activity anomalies – might provide insights into the fundamental problem of the "unknowns" which technical intelligence practices had failed to successfully address. Indications analysis cannot resolve issues of absolute identification and origin, on the other hand it can offer suggestions in regard to "intentions".

Certainly some of the reports and incidents associated with UFOs could have been relevant to the work of indications analysts, either within the Air Force itself or at the level of national indications studies. The Watch Committee and later the National Indications staff focused almost entirely on the Soviet Union and the Warsaw Pact as their target, reviewing warnings indicators and providing both a daily warnings watch list and special studies. Their mission focused on providing strategic/advance warning of a possible attack on the United States by the Soviet bloc, including China (the Sino-Soviet Bloc).

Although a certain amount of intelligence can be obtained from technical sources (signals and electronic intelligence being primary examples), indications analysis depends heavily on inference, based on specific sets of activities (indicators) which suggest that a threat is coming into being.[43]

The action list developed for monitoring the Sino-Soviet bloc contained some one hundred and twenty three separate indicators of potential offensive action – activities monitored for changes over time, with trends or sudden changes suggesting possible steps being taken towards hostilities. Two of those key indicators were "Active reconnaissance by aircraft, submarines or surface vessels" and "Increased intelligence collection efforts against key targets".[44] It would appear that observations relating to both of those indicators should have included Air Force intelligence data on observations of unidentified flying objects penetrating American continental airspace – especially if those intrusions appeared to target American military forces, bases and key strategic targets.

In would be very interesting to determine whether or not the Air Force, possibly at the level of the Soviet air threat staff at Air Intelligence, were forwarding selected UFO reports to the CIA, and in particular to the Watch Center – or later the National Indications staff. It is possible that such a high level linkage did occur, perhaps undisclosed to either UFO desk at ATIC or CIA staff within OSI. What we do know, based on a single document from May, 1952, is that the Watch Committee was indeed monitoring reports of new and novel aircraft, most likely as part of their Soviet indications tasking. That information comes from a June 9, 1952 memorandum from Wright Patterson/ATIC to the Directorate of Intelligence Office at Air Force Headquarters.[45]

The memorandum states that Watch Committee Report #95, from May 28, 1952 referred to a second photograph of a new type of aircraft – and ATIC wanted copies of the photos. The photos were mentioned in the Indications Analysis section of the Watch Committee report. The available information doesn't tell us whether the photos are of actual Soviet aircraft or simply of an unidentified aerial object. What is clear is that ATIC was aware of the Watch Lists reports and seeking information from the Watch Center in at least this one instance. The memo is also interesting in light of Marshall Chadwell's later (December, 1952) CIA proposal to formally include the Watch Committee in an expanded UFO study.

Outside of this single document, we have no further information on the day to day operations of the Watch Committee and what sort of UFO reports it might have evaluated. Cynthia Grabo writes that aside from the actual Watch

Reports and certain policy documents the day to day records of what specific information was being accessed and evaluated were not archived.[46] And despite researchers' best efforts, the Watch Reports themselves have not been located and appear to have been destroyed. This leaves us with no records providing any detail on their sources of information, or the processing of it, including queries back to source groups – and specifically no information on whether or not (or from what source) unidentified object reports might have been fed into indications analysis.

The Air Force memorandum noted above suggests that Watch List reports did go to the Air Force, both to ATIC and to Air Intelligence as well as to CIA/OSI. What they might have revealed about incidents pointing towards Soviet reconnaissance, penetrations or even preparations for sabotage remains unknown. The sourcing side of any possible information exchange also remains unknown. While the Watch Committee reports were going to the Air Force, it is unclear what the Air Force was sending into the national warnings intelligence system. Given that indications analysis is not tactical it seems reasonable that CIRVIS reports would not have been routinely sent to the National Indications Center – such reports were intended to represent an immediate threat already in progress.

It is possible that during some periods Air Intelligence provided specific unidentified object reports suggestive of covert Soviet reconnaissance or aerial collection against key military or atomic warfare complex targets – although Chadwell's proposal suggests that was not happening in 1952. Of course such information would have been highly classified and closely held. It may also have been routinely destroyed under sensitive document control procedures – it certainly appears that the bulk of the NIC records were themselves destroyed.

Further research on the Air Intelligence side of any exchange seems worthwhile but extremely challenging. As of this writing, the primary historical document, History of the Headquarters, USAF, 1949-1950 (Chapter II Strategic Plans and Programs) discusses Air Intelligence activities as primarily focused on offensive planning and Soviet vulnerabilities. It does mention study of U.S. vulnerabilities but makes no specific mention of providing Air Force intelligence collections to either the CIA or the National Indications staff. It appears that Air Force intelligence was distributed primarily through the Air Intelligence Digest and the National Intelligence Survey, as articles and studies rather than as discrete, real time incident data.[47]

Unfortunately the reality of classified documents processing and control, as well as the distance of some six decades, suggests that we have little chance of gaining access to the actual historical data or any direct insights as to how indications intelligence specialists might have incorporated and assessed UFO reports. Still, UFO historical researchers have come up with challenging and unexpected finds on many occasions, perhaps something unexpected in regard to an Air Intelligence – National Indications Center connection will emerge in time.

Fortunately the application of indications/intentions analysis to the entire body of *BLUE BOOK* archived data is something that can still be done, perhaps even more effectively given that the archived reports span some 22 years over three decades. The caution is that such an effort will not provide the concrete, definitive answers on identification and origins that the Air Force sought. In addition, it could never claim to provide the totality of proof which technical intelligence is required to generate. Before actually venturing into any indications analysis, it's important to fully appreciate what it can and cannot do as compared to technical intelligence.

A classic example contrasting the difference between indications analysis and technical intelligence can be found in the Cuban missile crisis.[48] A number of warnings indicators began to be triggered by observations made during the summer of 1962, including changes in patterns/quantities of Soviet merchant vessel traffic, Eastern bloc merchant ship loading and routing, Cuban dock security, the standard sizes of shipping containers coming into Cuban ports and types and numbers of Soviet "visitors" arriving in Cuba. Even more significantly all the changes/anomalies began to occur during the same relatively short period of time, suggesting the possibility of some single Soviet intention as a driving factor. The trends were sufficient for the CIA's DCI to go out on a limb and begin floating the scenario that the Russians might very well be preparing to install intermediate range ballistic missiles (IRBMs) in Cuba.

The DCI's view was largely rejected both within the CIA and by the broader intelligence community, as well as within the Kennedy Administration. It was felt to be far too radical an assessment; surely the Soviets would not be telegraphing their intentions – what possible motive could they have for such a risky move? The indications were there, but indications analysis can only suggest, not confirm. At best the practice tests a given scenario, it cannot prove it. It was left to technical intelligence collections in the form of aerial photographic overflights and signals intercepts to provide the actual confirmation that the DCI had been right – months earlier. Indications analysis had simply provided a suggestion with trends and patterns characterizing possible intentions; technical intelligence had proven the scenario to be a reality.

Another example comparing indications and technical intelligence during the Cold War involves the well-known dialog over bomber and missile "gaps" with the Soviets. Throughout the 1950s Air Force intelligence consistently produced indications based warnings that the Soviets were deploying strategic weapons which put the United States at risk of preemptive attack. First it was the construction and deployment of long range, strategic jet bombers and later the deployment of intercontinental ballistic missiles. There was no doubt that the Soviets had the ability to build each weapon and there were indications of both development and construction. But the fundamental question was the whether they or not bombers and missiles were actually being built in sufficient quantities and deployed in a fashion to support a preemptive strike.

The Air Force maintained that threatening levels of construction and deployment were occurring and those assessments were accepted by the Eisenhower Administration – the response was an immense expansion of American military spending. It remained for technical intelligence, in the form of CIA high altitude reconnaissance flights – and ultimately satellite photography – to provide the data that proved the Air Force scenarios were actually unfounded.

Indications/Intentions analysis offers no final conclusions, no concrete solutions. It functions more in the nature of a hypothesis in science – serving as a process for testing a supposition or proposed explanation of observations. It begins with the statement of a scenario; in strategic/warnings intelligence that scenario normally involves a specifically stated threat. The next step involves the identification and itemization of activities/observations which would suggest that such a threat is coming into being – or may already exist – resulting in a warning being issued.

In terms of the process, an indicator can literally be anything. Grabo writes that it can be a fact, a possible fact, an observation – anything that provides some insight into whether a given scenario is real, or if already accepted, is in the process of changing.[49] An individual piece of data can even be ambiguous, only a possibility – the patterns, trends and anomalies in the entire body of observations are what matters in terms of overall support for the hypothesis, the "scenario". All of which means that in practice indications/intentions analysis is a long term process, requiring extended chronological listings of observations. The longer the chronology, the larger the baseline, the more likely it is that analysis can characterize recognizable patterns and trends – and differentiate anomalies.

In more contemporary times the flexibility and value of indications/intentions analysis has become widely recognized in areas far outside the national intelligence community. Its practices have been adopted for strategic business planning, competitive positioning and financial analysis. It has also become a standard practice in numerous venues where uncertainty is a consistent issue.[50] The downside is that, at best, indications analysis is basically a process of reasoning and deduction. As practiced by true professionals an element of mathematical probability can be added, but in the end it is still fundamentally the testing of a hypothesis and cannot in itself provide anything like absolute confirmation.

Strategic intelligence and specifically indications/intentions analysis is a technique which appears never to have been applied to the UFO intelligence "problem". In a very limited effort to remedy that, and to go beyond *BLUE BOOK* (while staying within the bounds of military issues and known intelligence practices) we will now proceed down the indications analysis line of inquiry, examining a series of increasingly broad scenarios related to possible UFO intentions.

As a first step, we will examine a limited baseline scenario, one first expressed in the initial Air Force assessment of fall of 1947. This first scenario deals with the possibility that the Soviet Union was preparing for a surprise preemptive strike on the United States, an attack which would cripple its ability to conduct atomic war fighting and prevent its intervention against Communist military action in Europe and Asia. The indicators we will consider actually appeared on the Sino-Soviet bloc tracking list used by the National Indications Center staff.

This baseline exercise will deal with the nation's strategic targets as they existed during the period of the Ad Hoc Committee and into the first years of Watch Center activities, 1947-1952. Primary strategic targets include the atomic materials production centers at Hanford and Oak Ridge, the weapons design, assembly and atomic storage facilities at Los Alamos and Sandia Base outside Albuquerque and the initial Q sites developed for atomic weapons storage and dispersal to Strategic Air Command bombers.

Secondary targets include the key aircraft plants outside Seattle, Washington and Los Angeles, California as well as major transit airfields and Navy logistics ports on the East and West coasts – attacks on those targets would have slowed any conventional military response to Soviet expansion across Europe or in Asia.[51]

This first exercise will also give us a baseline for the larger question of whether or not certain relevant and credible UFO observations provide positive indications of reconnaissance flights over the strategic target list, and if so, whether or not the Russians were the ones conducting them.

Chapter 15 Endnotes

1. The order to terminate the project was announced by Air Force Secretary Robert Seamans Jr. on December 17, 1969. ATIC ceased taking new reports and began actually closing down the UFO desk and archiving its files in 1970

2. Eric Nesheim and Leif Nesheim, *Saucer Attack; Pop Culture in the Golden Age of Flying Saucers*, General Publishing Group Inc., Los Angeles, 1997

3. Both MUFON and NUFORC continue to receive close to 5,000 UFO reports annually and MUFON electronically filed 82,000 sighting reports during the period of 2000-2016

4. Curtis Peebles, *Watch the Skies; A Chronicle of the Flying Saucer Myth*, Smithsonian Institution Press, Washington and London, 1994.

5. Brad Sparks and Don Berliner, "The *BLUE BOOK* Unknowns", NICAP http://www.nicap.org/bluebook/unknowns.htm

6. For Background on the compilation of the *BLUE BOOK Unknown* list, see Brad Sparks detailed overview on sources and methods. http://www.cohenufo.org/BlueBook-UFOUnknowns-OnNIDSSite.htm

7. Personal communications with Robert Powell, head of MUFON's Science Review Board and MUFON Director of Research since 2007, January, 20, 2017. Powell is a member of the UFODATA project and the Society for Scientific Exploration.

8. The National UFO Reporting Center http://www.nuforc.org/

9. The National UFO Reporting Center, Information and Polices as well as UFO Sighting Report Form http://www.nuforc.org/General.htmlhttp://www.ufocenter.com/reportform.html

10. Ibid http://www.nuforc.org/webreports/ndxevent.html

11. UFO Stalker http://www.ufostalker.com/ufostalker/statistics

12. Personal communications with Robert Powell, head of MUFON's Science Review Board and MUFON Director of Research since 2007, January, 20, 2017

13. Max Galka, *Map of UFO Sightings*, Metrocosm http://metrocosm.com/map-of-ufo-sightings/

14. Richard F. Haines, "Listing of Unreported Cases with Claimed Reasons Why", Table 6, *Aviation Safety in America – A Previously Neglected Factor,* National Aviation Reporting Center

on Anomalous Phenomena, October 15, 2000 http://www.narcap.org/reports/narcap.TR1.AvSafety.pdf

15. "Origins and Mission, National Aviation Reporting Center on Anomalous Phenomena", NARCAP http://www.narcap.org/About/About_NARCAP.html

16. Technical Reports, National Aviation Reporting Center on Anomalous Phenomena http://www.narcap.org/Research/Technical_Reports.html

17. Jacques and Janine Vallee, "Cycles of Activity", *Challenge to Science, The UFO Enigma*, Henry Regnery Company, Chicago, 1966, Chapter 8

18. Bob King, "Moon Illusion is all in your Head", *Sky and Telescope Magazine*, November 24, 2015 http://www.skyandtelescope.com/observing/moon-illusion-confusion11252015/

19. Jacques and Janine Vallee; "Cycles of Activity", *Challenge to Science, The UFO Enigma*, Chapter 8, 165

20. J. Allen Hynek, *The UFO Experience, A Scientific Inquiry*, Henry Regenery Company, Chicago, Illinois, 1972, 24

21. Ibid, Chapter 12, *Science Is Not Always What Scientists Do*, 192-213

22. Ibid, 231

23. Anne Druffel, Firestorm, *Dr. James E. McDonald's Fight for UFO Science*, Voyagers, 2003 https://www.amazon.com/Firestorm-James-McDonalds-Science-Voyagers/dp/0926524585/ref=sr_1_1?s=books&ie=UTF8&qid=1475068751&sr=1-1&keywords=dr+james+mcdonald+ufo

24. FBI File Collection, Dr. James E. McDonald, Center for UFO Study http://www.cufon.org/cufon/fbimcdon.htm

25. Allen Hynek, *The UFO Experience, A Scientific Inquiry*, Ibid, 232

26. Center for UFO Studies http://www.cufos.org/org.html

27. Sensitive compartmented information (SCI) is information developed from extremely valuable and sometimes unique intelligence sources, collections methods, analytical practices and tools –sometimes described more simply as "sources and methods". Although sometimes referred to as "above Top Secret", this sort of information/data does not necessarily hold a special classification in and of itself. The data itself may sometimes be de-compartmented or even declassified eventually – both the data and the details of its collection that are protected by

the SCI access control. Some information originally treated as code word, SCI controlled access concerning the sources, technology and methods of the early U.S. spy satellite programs of the 1960s is now being released, some four decades after the fact. At the time that same information was among the nations most guarded secrets. See also: Department of Defense Manual, Sensitive Compartmented Information (SCI) Administrative Security Manual: Administration of Information and Information Systems Security http://www.dtic.mil/whs/directives/corres/pdf/510521m_vol1.pdf

28. Michael Swords and Robert Powell, *UFO's and Government, A Historical Inquiry*, Anomalist Books, San Antonio, 2012, 266 and 279

29. Howard Blum, *Out There*, Simon and Schuster, New York, 1990, SPADATS Incident, Chapter 1, 25-32

30. John B. Alexander, *UFO's, Myths, Conspiracies*, Realities, St. Martin's Press, New York, 2011, 26 – 28

31. Ibid, 96-97

32. Larry Valero, "The American Joint Intelligence Committee and Estimates of the Soviet Union, 1945-1947", Central Intelligence Agency Library, 2-3 https://www.cia.gov/library/center-for-the-study-of-intelligence/csi-publications/csi-studies/studies/summer00/art06.html

33. Ibid, 8-9

34. Cynthia Grabo with Jan Goldman, *Handbook of Warning Intelligence*; Complete and Declassified Version, Rowman and Littlefield, New York, 2015, 2-3

35. Ibid, 4

36. "Learning to Estimate, 1948", CIA Historical Document, updated April 30, 2013 https://www.cia.gov/news-information/featured-story-archive/2008-featured-story-archive/learning-to-estimate-1948.html

37. "A Brief History of Indicators Analysis", Public Intelligence Blog, Nightwatch Archives http://phibetaiota.net/2012/10/nightwatch-a-brief-history-of-indicators-analysis/

38. Cynthia Grabo with Jan Goldman, Handbook of Warning Intelligence; Complete and Declassified Version, 4

39. "Cold War Years", Nightwatch, October 11, 2012, Kforce Government Solutions, Inc. (KGS) https://www.kforcegov.com/services/IS/NightWatch/NightWatch_12000193.aspx

40. DIRECTOR OF CENTRAL INTELLIGENCE DIRECTIVE NO. 1/5, NATIONAL INTELLIGENCE WARNING, (Effective 23 May 1979), supersedes DCID 1/5 effective 18 May 1976. http://fas.org/irp/offdocs/dcid1-5.html

41. Cynthia M. Grabo, Anticipating Surprise; Analysis for Strategic Warning, University Press of America, New York, 2004, 112-113

42. Gerald K. Haines and Robert E. Legett, Watching the Bear: Essays on CIA's Analysis of the Soviet Union, Government Printing Office, 11-12

43. Diane M. Ramsey and Mark S. Boerner, "A STUDY IN INDICATIONS METHODOLOGY", CIA publications library, updated August 4, 2011 https://www.cia.gov/library/center-for-the-study-of-intelligence/kent-csi/vol7no3/html/v07i3a08p_0001.htm

44. Ibid

45. Memorandum, Wright Patterson ATIC to D/I Headquarters USAF, for AFOIN, June 9. 1952 http://www.bluebookarchive.org/page.aspx?PageCode=NARA-PBB90-237

46. Cynthia M. Grabo, "The Watch Committee and the National Indications Center: The Evolution of U.S. Strategic Warning, 1950-1975 as referenced by Lock K. Johnson, "Strategic Intelligence an American Perspective", International Journal of Intelligence and Counter Intelligence, Jan 9, 2008 http://www.tandfonline.com/doi/abs/10.1080/08850608908435109

47. Dr. Alfred Goldberg and Dr. Robert Little, History of Headquarters USAF, 1 July, 1949 to 30 June, 1950 and History of Headquarters USAF, 1 July 1950 to 30 June, 1951, Air University Air Historical Liaison Office, Department of the Air Force, 195455, Chapter II Strategic Plans and Programs

48. Larry Hancock, Surprise Attack From Pearl Harbor and 9/11 to Benghazi, Counterpoint Press Limited, Berkeley California, 20122015, 180-181

49. Cynthia M. Grabo, Anticipating Surprise; Analysis for Strategic Warning, 3

50. C. Fleisher and B. Bensoussan, Indications and Warning, Business and Competitive Analysis, FT Press, 2007, , Chapter 24

51. National atomic weapons stockpile sites went into construction as early as 1946 and all were operational by 1952. They included Manzano Base outside Albuquerque, Clarksville Base near Fort Campbell (Tennessee/Kentucky, Medina Base outside San Antonio. Killeen Base between Waco and Austin Texas circa 1950. Two additional national stockpile sites were established in the 1950's, including Bossier base adjacent to Barksdale AFB in Louisiana.

Secondary dispersal sites at SAC base included Loring AFB in Maine, Ellsworth Base in South Dakota, Fairchild AFB outside Seattle, Traffic (Fairfield Suisan Field) outside San Francisco and Westover AFB in Massachusetts.

Chapter 16

Indications / 1947-1952

In this chapter

- The UFO intelligence collections profile first constructed by the Air Force in the fall of 1947 proved accurate as a description of the unidentified objects reported by military, scientific and security observers through 1952 – and beyond.

- A baseline UFO incident survey focused on indications of reconnaissance, ferreting and attack familiarization flights over key American strategic targets.

- A series of same day UFO reports, in June of 1947, which might well have been the first indication of foreign reconnaissance of strategic American targets.

- Preliminary Air Intelligence concerns that unidentified flying objects were being "operated for photo reconnaissance purposes" or to "ferret out our defense capabilities", targeting strategic military and national security facilities.

- Focused intrusions during 1949 and 1950 indicating prolonged low altitude technical collections targeting American atomic production and weapons storage facilities.

- An evolving pattern of UFO interceptions indicating proactive testing of the air defenses over high security atomic weapons facilities and air defense bases.

- A major change in pattern during 1952, indicative of broad strategic reconnaissance of the nation's population centers in the northeastern corridor as well as and major military installations on both coasts and northern tier Air Force bases.

The scenario being examined in this baseline indications survey is that of Soviet reconnaissance in advance of a pre-emptive strike against the United States – a strike which would eliminate or severely disable American atomic warfighting capability and prevent the nation from sustaining any major military involvement overseas. The period under study is 1947-1952. In a broader sense any unknown party could be substituted for "Russians" although if this exercise had been conducted during the time frame addressed, undoubtedly it would have been directed towards the Soviet Union. In terms of data, the standard methodology for any observation to be used in an indications study begins with a serious effort to "separate the wheat from the chaff" to the greatest extent possible, focusing on the most reliable and experienced sources and data.[1]

Given the subject at hand, arguments against any particular piece of data – in this instance any specific incident/observation – will always be found. While the practice itself does not demand that any particular piece of data be totally validated, we will turn to the most concrete observations possible. Preference will be given to daylight visual observations at close to moderate range, where some shape of the object being observed can be defined. In a very few instances we will include twilight or night sightings where a physical object was observed, including incidents with radar confirmation. The reader will notice that this approach leads us to very much the same core UFO profile as was outlined in the first Air Force intelligence work of 1947 and 1948 – highly reflective, apparently metallic discs/ovals/cylinders displaying high speeds, exceptional maneuverability, formation flight and at times evasive action.

When possible, preference will be given to multiple witness observations and visual sightings supported either by instrumentation or by technical means such as radar or other electronic intelligence. The bulk of the incidents evaluated and discussed will be taken from the list of some 1,700 BLUE BOOK archived reports compiled by Brad Sparks (updated as of 2016)[2] and the NICAP composite chronological UFO report listing of some 1,500 incidents.[3]

In terms of the witness detail offered, in this first exercise and in those to follow, we focus on observations from military personnel, commercial pilots, and to a much lesser extent security and law enforcement officers. Whenever possible we also rely on and cite official reports.

The reader should be aware that issues with eyewitness testimony have been thoroughly studied and need to be acknowledged; we have tried to observe the cautions from such studies in assessing all observer reports. The following special cautions are derived from the work and writing of Elizabeth Loftus[4] and Peter B. Ainsworth[5] specialists in the field of eyewitness testimony.

In general, the longer the observation the more detail is acquired, however studies have shown that extraordinary, novel and unusual events do enhance the retained detail and tend to fix memories, enhancing retention – at least during the short term. Somewhat surprisingly strong emotions during an observation have been found to increase witness focus, producing more detail. Fear has the opposite effect, except in observers with combat experience or individuals routinely exposed to danger. Prior experience in dangerous environments (producing a level of desensitization) tends to inhibit anxiety and reduce the impairment of observations.

In terms of retention, forgetting occurs extremely rapidly – first day reports are the most accurate, after a week there is a noted effect on accuracy and information from other sources can quickly contaminate memory. The risk is that original memories can be "overwritten" with new detail from other sources. And over time old and new information tends to fuse, suggesting that oral histories done more than a year after an event have to be approached with great caution.

With those points in mind, a good deal of selectivity has been applied in terms of the witness details presented in the relatively brief data points given for the incidents included in this survey. In particular, details taken from oral histories done at a considerable distance in time from the observations are presented with qualification and only if there appears to be sufficient corroboration from other sources – as well as consistency in observations.

Given that the scenario being studied is quite tightly focused on reconnaissance and attack familiarization flights, we also need to establish a context for recognizing those sorts of activities. In that regard we have a definite advantage in that we can examine in detail the real world aerial reconnaissance practices of the period – in terms of the actual Soviet bloc reconnaissance which the United States itself conduced, beginning in the immediate post-war years.

Those activities give us an inside view into different types of aerial collections missions as well as the actual tactics employed, including the types of flight paths and maneuvers involved. At the risk of overgeneralization it is important to note that that reconnaissance practices varied greatly depending on different missions – ferreting (Electrical and Signals intelligence), capabilities assessment (broad based Photographic and Signals collections) and pre-attack intelligence (tightly focused photographic, radar and infrared mapping).

Of all the missions "ferreting" is perhaps the highest risk; aircraft on such flights are specifically directed against areas known or suspected to have an active air defense. The purpose of the mission is to trigger that defense into activating search radars, fire control radars and air defense communications networks. The ferret aircraft has to appear to become a threat, even simulating an actual attack – prompting a "battle of wits" between the air defense radar operators and the electronic warfare crew of the ferret or on a companion aircraft operating along with it.[6] Beginning in the final months of World War II and increasingly during the Cold War, Air Force and Navy ferret aircraft routinely flew missions around the Soviet bloc borders – as of this writing in 2017 the United States still flies similar missions around the Russian Federation, North Korea and China.

The reason for repetitive ferret missions is simple, the targets know they are being tested and in turn consistently change the technical characteristics of their own equipment as well as their communications practices. If the goal is to have an accurate, up to date picture of those defenses, ferreting must be ongoing. By 1948 standing orders were issued for Air Force electronic reconnaissance flights to be made as often as possible, using all available equipment and personnel to build a picture of Soviet air defenses around their Siberian facilities. Frequent repetition of the search missions was considered to be mandatory.[7] At one point there were as many as three ferret flights a week against flown against Vladivostok – Russia's major Siberian port and the center of its Asian military efforts?[8]

If ferret missions were high risk, photo reconnaissance was only marginally less so given that it also involved flights directly into denied and defended territory – flights in daylight, with little chance of being totally undetected. Many of the earliest American, and British post-World War II photo flights over Soviet and Chinese territory were conducted by special camera equipped fighter aircraft, making what were effectively high speed dashes over coastal targets, penetrating only a limited distance inland and relying on surprise and speed to get in and out. In 1949, two of the Air Force's first combat jets, the F-80, were modified as photo reconnaissance aircraft and flown on missions over the Soviet occupied Kurile Islands northwest of Japan. Early in 1950 the jets were flown on missions over the Soviet mainland and in particular over military targets around Vladivostok, the largest Russia city in Siberia – located near the borders of both China and North Korea.[9] Due to photography needs, the flights were made during daylight and were not at all covert – relying on speed and surprise.

Those flights were followed by the use of a more advanced, RF-84 Thunderflash aircraft, flown over Vladivostok at 39,000 feet in 1951. In 1951 the Royal Air Force flew two photoreconnaissance Spitfire MK- 19's (with a sprint speed of almost 450 mph) over targets on the Chinese mainland as well as important island port facilities. The Spitfires were equipped with camera equipment that could take oblique photographs so that the pilot did not have to fly directly over this targets but could operate the cameras from some distance away.[10]

The only alternative to very low penetrations and a reliance on surprise was to fly very high and fast. It is worth noting that even in the earliest missions the aircraft being used for aerial reconnaissance were the most advanced – and fastest – available. That would become a common practice for overflights during the Cold War. The aircraft used had to be either exceptionally fast or operate at exceptionally high altitude – the preference was for both.

The argument that a foreign nation would not use its most advanced technology on reconnaissance and overflight missions (exposing them to accidents and foreign recovery) is a common one found in early UFO study commentaries. However the reality of denied area reconnaissance actually demonstrates that the most advanced aircraft available were used – or even specially designed for aerial reconnaissance work. The SR-71, the most technologically sophisticated and fastest known manned aircraft ever developed, was repeatedly flown over broad stretches of Russia, China, Cuba and other "denied" territories.

As soon as possible, in 1952, the U.S. Air Force adapted its newest, most advanced, jet bomber (the B-47) to reconnaissance duties. The missions were not simply along Russia's borders but deep into Soviet territory, with flights over Moscow and the heart of Russia. In May, 1954 six RB-47s took off from England, refueled off the coast of Norway and flew towards Russia in two, three plane formations. Earlier that month a flight of RB-45 Tornados had flown a high risk mission over the Russian capital. The RB-47 mission was equally high risk, flying over and beyond the huge Russian Navy facilities at Murmansk.

The SAC missions were far ranging, including efforts to build a comprehensive picture of Soviet military capabilities; they took the reconnaissance aircraft across broad sweeps of territory, observed by Russian defenses at multiple sites. The Soviet threat was felt to be so existential that the risk that aircraft would be attacked and possibly shot down was accepted; diplomatic protests were simply assumed. SAC aircraft were indeed engaged by Soviet fighters on several missions, one flight even exchanged gunfire with Russian fighters, with the B-47's tail gun coming into action.[11]

In order to gain the most possible information from such high risk missions, multiple aircraft were commonly flown in concert. One reason for pairs and formations of aircraft was to combine extensive signals/electronic intelligence on one aircraft with a photo reconnaissance companion. The advantage being that the SIGINT/ELINT aircraft could monitor radio and radar transmissions, directing their companions to high interest targets including air defense installations. Multiple aircraft were also useful for "ferreting", the practice of essentially teasing air defense installations to go active for tracking and engaging so that the exact details of their transmissions and even command and control communications could be monitored. As early as 1952, combinations of P2V-3W Neptune SIGINT aircraft flown by the Navy and B-50 photoreconnaissances planes flown by the Air Force were used in monitoring Soviet radar and air fields along Soviet territory in Siberia.[12]

In regard to photo-reconnaissance, if the mission was worth the high risk of flying across long stretches of denied territory, multiple aircraft provided not only more photographic coverage, but redundancy as well. Beginning in the spring of 1956 and lasting for some three months, the Strategic Air Command treated the Soviets to what could only be considered a "wave" of daylight overflights involving first pairs of aircraft and then entire formations. Most flights penetrated only a short distance beyond the Soviet northern borders, probing for air defense installations and searching for suspected long range bomber airfields.

However a number of missions flew directly into Russia, as far as the Ural Mountains. How many of the missions were photo reconnaissance – as compared to radar mapping for attack planning – is open to question, but SAC's attack plans were based on radar mapping of ground terrain features for both navigation and bomb runs. Following some 156 missions during that period of time, the climax was the flight of six RB-47 SAC aircraft. The planes took off from Thule Greenland, headed north over the pole and penetrated deep into Russia, finally exiting over the Bering Straits to land in Alaska.[13]

As time passed, much of the direct overflight aerial photographic missions over denied and heavily defended targets would be increasingly be handed off to satellite imagery, however new developments in photographic technology and side looking camera and imaging systems meant that very special aircraft could acquire targets not just laterally but at great distances, without penetrating borders and certainly without flying directly over their targets. Specialized and heavily customized craft were developed specifically for such work. An Air Force program named Big Safari accomplished wonders in terms of building and fitting aircraft with folded optics systems camera systems – one unit had an effective focal length of 204 inches.

The oblique cameras could obtain high quality photographs of targets at angles five to fifteen degrees below the aircraft's horizon. Effective camera range extended as far as 75 miles to the side of the aircraft. Side looking camera and radar systems were developed and integrated into relatively small aircraft such as the B-57.[14] The capabilities of the RB-57 (reconnaissance version) came to include not only oblique photographic and radar imaging but infrared mapping as well.

Of course, none of this was widely known during the early years when Air Force intelligence staff and scientific consultants were offering commentary on UFO reports. Such practices were new and missions highly compartmentalized, they would be held secret for decades after the various missions (the losses of American pilots and air crews would be held secret as well).

With some understanding of aerial reconnaissance practices we can now move to our actual baseline study. Now, it's back to the summer of 1947 and a search for observations which would suggest aerial reconnaissance – specifically Soviet reconnaissance against strategic American targets.

1947 Incidents

A series of same day UFO reports, in June of 1947, might well have been the first incidents registering as reconnaissance/familiarization/preemptive strike indicators. Four observations were made in the same day, over a period of less than one hour. The first sighting was of three "flat" objects traveling faster than a fighter aircraft. The objects were seen near Richland, Washington and were reported traveling northwest. That flight path would have taken the objects along the western edge of the Hanford atomic reservation. Approximately half an hour later, three individual observers at different locations reported groups of objects flying near Mount Rainer and Mount Adams in the Cascade Range, some 200 miles northwest of Richland and southeast of Seattle, Washington. The observers all described multiple objects – flat or disc shaped – having a metallic appearance and flashing or glinting in the sun.

A possible flight path along the length of the restricted Hanford reservation is certainly suggestive. By that point in time the general locations of the American atomic facilities were publicly known, there had even been Soviet informants working and reporting from some of them. But the sites were situated in restricted security zones and caution would have been advised for any aerial reconnaissance – there would have been no general knowledge of how minimal American air defenses were in 1947 and even 1948. The lack of any apparent effort to track or intercept reconnaissance flights over vital American targets might have well been a surprise even to the Soviet military, which was itself already pressing forward at a level of wartime urgency on the construction of extensive surveillance radar networks both around its borders and its key facilities.

The sightings from central Washington were not the only data pointing towards possible reconnaissance of atomic warfare facilities during the summer of 1947. On July 5, a report from Albuquerque, New Mexico described five discs, first flying east over the city and with one circling back after passing. That afternoon five individuals observed a single sphere shaped object moving in and out of clouds over the city. Of course Albuquerque was one of the most strategic targets in the nation, housing not only the Sandia base atomic weapons facilities but the actual storage sites for the nation's first atomic bombs.

In terms of additional reconnaissance of military facilities, in mid-August, Rapid City air field (later Ellsworth AFB) produced a striking night time observation by an Air Force intelligence officer. The officer observed some twelve elliptical objects, each the size of a B-29 bomber, flying in a tight diamond formation and making a shallow descent to an altitude estimated to be five thousand feet over the base. The formation moved relatively slowly – three to four hundred miles per hour – made a turn and climbed away to the southwest while accelerating.

Rapid City/Ellsworth, with its strategic northern location, would later become the location of a SAC Q site atomic bomb dispersal facility, that facilities' exact construction start date appears undocumented. Most importantly Ellsworth became a highly strategic base for SAC. It served strike forces of B-29 and B-36 bombers as well as functioning as a key base for the SAC long range reconnaissance versions of each aircraft – aircraft used to survey the polar attack routes into Russia.

The summer UFO sightings included additional observations reported from very large, and very strategic military facilities. They included important West Coast installations as well as forward bases on both the northwest and northeast trans-polar corridors – routes which senior Air Force officers viewed as a likely Soviet paths for preemptive strikes on the continental United States.

The first, on July 6, 1947 was a report of a "highly reflective", flat /round object the size of a C-54 transport, moving very fast over the huge Fairfield-

Suisan field (later Travis AFB) near San Francisco, California. The object was reported by an Army Air Force captain and his wife who described it rolling from side to side as it passed. Fairfield-Suisan was the West Coast hub for logistics flights across the Pacific and would become a key SAC base for both strategic bombers and very long distance SAC reconnaissance missions. One of the SAC Q site atomic bomb dispersal facilities would also be established at the base.

A month later, on August 14, the key Air Defense base located just north of San Francisco (Hamilton field) and responsible for West Coast defense, produced a striking report. The assistant base operations officer and a B-29 pilot both observed two shiny, round objects fly at high speed across the base at an altitude of six to ten thousand feet. One object flew straight and level while the second moved from side to side around it, much like a fighter escort.

Further out on the polar access routes other air bases, in both Alaska and Newfoundland, were reporting UFO observations. On July 11, Elmendorf air field in Anchorage produced a report from members of an AACS (airborne air control squadron). Two officers, a major and a colonel, reported a relatively small metallic, spherical object traveling at great speed across the base at ten o'clock in the morning. The object was at the relatively low altitude of three to four thousand feet, flying underneath scattered clouds.

The day before, on July 10, three Pan American Airways ground crewman at Harmon Field, Newfoundland, Canada – a major transit base for both military and commercial flights across the Atlantic – had observed a silvery disc/wheel shaped object the size of a C-54 transport fly at a high rate of speed over the base at an altitude estimated to be no more than ten thousand feet. The object left a dark, bluish-black trail before moving upwards and cutting a path through the clouds as it accelerated away. The following month, on August 14, three AACS airman at Harmon observed two small, crescent-shaped objects zigzag at very low altitude (some 1,200 feet) over the base at a very high speed, disappearing into clouds to the west. A few seconds later a third, similar object came out of the clouds, following the path of the previous two objects towards the west.

These sightings were all high quality, at reasonably close range and with characterizations of well-defined physical objects. In several instances the object's actions are consistent with the types of formations and maneuvers we would expect in reconnaissance over either unfamiliar or defended targets – with one object flying cover for another during a low altitude pass, or low altitude overflights being made at exceptionally high speed with evasive action such as zigzagging. Those types of maneuvers are much the same as those carried out in later years by U.S. photo reconnaissance jets carrying out high risk, low altitude missions against denied/heavily defended targets in Cuba during the missile crisis of 1962 or facilities in North Viet Nam later in the 1960s.

It should also be noted that groups or pairs of objects were common in these 1947 sightings and that descriptions of them were relatively similar – explaining why a profile of shapes and motions is found in even the earliest intelligence reports. It is hardly surprising that at the end of August the Collections Branch of the Air Intelligence Requirements Division took the position that the flying disc/flying saucer reports included a core of real sightings of actual physical objects. That initial finding, titled "Flying Saucer Phenomena", was submitted to the Deputy Chief of Staff for Air Force Research and Development at the end of August, 1947.[15]

By the end of the year, in December, Air Intelligence prepared a summary report on "flying discs", the report commented on the commonality of "disc" shaped objects in the sightings and noted that both air and ground observations had been obtained from many competent observers including rated Air Force officers.[16] The Air Intelligence report also raised the concern that the flying objects were being "operated for photo reconnaissance purposes" or to "ferret out our defense capabilities", remarking that sightings had been made over strategic military and national security facilities – but not in any significant number.[17]

In regard to that qualifier, it should be pointed out that the locations of American strategic targets such as air bases and even atomic reservations were public knowledge. They showed up on maps, they were covered in the newspapers. Following the war the American atomic bomb program was openly and widely discussed. The only aspect of American atomic development which took years to be fully appreciated, even within the security system, was the extent to which it had been compromised by Soviet espionage. With that perspective, Soviet aerial reconnaissance of strategic American targets would not have needed to be as far ranging and extensive as that which SAC carried out in following years against the Soviet Union. Russia imposed intense security measures in concealing its own military capabilities, ensuring they did not appear on maps and using an extensive set of address, postal and other covers to make them as invisible as possible.

1948 Incidents

A scan of UFO reports from 1948 is striking in that the possible pattern of tentative, pre-strike reconnaissance that appeared during the summer of 1947 simply disappeared. There were no further reports from the same strategic facilities or from new ones after August, 1947. Only a single report from a strategic area is found in 1948, although that was from what would have to have been considered perhaps the most strategic target in the nation at that point in time.

On July 27, at eight thirty in the morning, a journalism professor from the University of New Mexico in Albuquerque observed a metallic disc remaining stationary over that city for some ten minutes. Other than that, no further daylight observations comparable to the reports from 1947 were noted. That report is interesting not only in terms of the ability of the object to remain stationary but in the length of its station-keeping over what would have been suspected to be a high security area. Yet there is no indication that it was tracked by the military nor was it engaged by fighters or air defenses. If it was a continuation of the previous year's visits, it would have been clear that air space over the nation's arguably most critical atomic facility and its sole store of atomic bombs was totally undefended.

What did begin in 1948, and only in December of that year, were the first sightings of what would come to be a veritable wave of mysterious green fireballs. And those reports came from the specific region in which the nation's two key facilities for atomic bomb design, manufacturing and storage were located – central New Mexico, from Los Alamos in the north to Albuquerque at in the center of the state.

Beginning in December, 1948 observers at Albuquerque and Los Alamos began to report a series of distinctive nighttime green fireballs. On December 6 an AEC security inspector reported a green fireball which passed directly over the Sandia Base nuclear weapons assembly site, on December 20 a green fireball was triangulated passing west of Los Alamos and on December 28 a security officer at Los Alamos reported a slowly falling white fireball which he watched for several seconds as it descended to a low altitude (estimated to be six thousand feet), exploding in a green flash which lit up a cloud above it.

The initial thoughts of the Air Force Office of Special Investigations officers responding to the green fireball reports were that they might very well be flares, especially given that some were seen at low altitudes.

1949

We explored some six months of anomalous green fireballs reports from New Mexico in great detail in earlier chapters; those bear no direct relationship to the types of sightings we are focusing on in this scenario but it is interesting that one of the first reactions to this new type of nighttime mystery light was that the green fireballs represented some sort of Soviet "ranging shots" targeting key atomic facilities.[18]

As we discussed earlier, there was actually some physical evidence (which apparently did not receive any substantive Air Force attention), which might have supported the speculation that some novel type of rocket or stratospheric artillery shell was being launched into the continental United States. Prominent physicists who reviewed scientific data on the fireballs (including triangulated altitude estimates) also speculated that the observations could by produced by specially developed artillery shells or very small, pencil sized, rocket projectiles.

Given the earlier conclusion that the Soviets had actually used rockets to conduct psychological warfare in Scandinavia, such concerns and speculations were not totally unfounded – and remain an interesting subject for further historical research. In respect to possible Soviet reconnaissance activities, it seems that the fireballs would have been either psychological warfare or a diversion, taking public and military attention away from other, more intrusive activities.

What we don't find in 1949 UFO reports is once again as important as what we do – which leads to a type of negative indication. As in 1948 there is a dearth of reports which would suggest any pattern of broad, comprehensive strategic reconnaissance. The multiple daytime disc and ball shaped objects formation flight reports from 1947 are gone. The low altitude, high speed passes over strategic air bases are not in evidence. Daylight, physical objects reports from strategic atomic facilities are still present, but limited to single objects and single observations. On March 8 two observers at the Los Alamos facility reported an aluminum colored object moving horizontally, first at high speed and then slowing to descend, passing over the restricted area. The object encountered no air defense measures.

In contrast, on May 21, at 1:20 pm in the afternoon, the Air Defense radar detachment assigned to the Hanford complex detected a stationary object over the reservation. The object then departed at a high rate of speed. An F-82 fighter from the nearby Moses Lake base was sent up and at 2:20 pm the pilot detected a bogie on his own radar – but the target faded as he began pursuit. Two days later, on May 23, three fighter pilots at Moses Lake reported the early morning sighting (8:45 a.m.) of a small but bright silver light traveling at very high speed in level flight at an altitude of between ten thousand and fifteen thousand feet.

Such "reconnaissance" relevant incidents from 1949 are well documented in the Air Force BLUE BOOK files but as an interrelated body of data they seem to have received no special discussion in Air Force studies of the period. The same can be said for several months of incidents which certainly could have been interpreted as indications of prolonged low altitude intelligence collection targeting American atomic warfare facilities.

Beginning in March, 1949, security personnel at Killeen Base in Texas began reporting a series of nighttime reports of mysterious lights, relatively small and with many at low to virtually ground level altitudes. During March at least a dozen Army security patrols reported unidentified lights traveling over restricted areas or dropping down towards them, disappearing in midair.

During the following month patrols reported more mystery lights, several of them at ground level. One incident included the description of a metallic cone being trailed behind a light only a few feet above the ground. In April the Killeen Base/Fort Hood security area also began to generate sightings of daylight objects passing over at low altitude. Shortly before noon on May 5, 1948 two Army officers observed a pair of oblong white discs pass over a firing range at some two to three hundred miles per hour. That same month a series of organized Army spotter posts performed multiple instrumented observations and triangulated the altitude and movement of a number of unidentified lights – all at low altitudes and relatively short distances. April also saw the first reports of severe radio interference during observation of the UFOs.

The mystery light observations continued through May, with more tracking by the network of spotters. A few well defined physical objects were observed during the Killeen base sightings, operating at very low altitudes and even ground level but the majority of reports involved mysterious nighttime lights. If reconnaissance was involved in those incidents, it was being conducted at very low altitude and accompanied by considerable diversionary activity.

Amazingly, during the three month period of observations there was apparently no ability or effort made to track the objects by radar and no interest in deploying an air defense response. What we see in the files are repeated, very low altitude intrusions over and within what was being constructed to be one of the nation's early atomic storage sites (AEC Site B) as well as the adjacent construction of a major SAC air base (Gray AFB) – occurring with no military response at all to them. The incidents continued to occur without interruption in the face of special Army security forces assigned to the construction areas and with the entire operation adjacent to Fort Hood, the nation's largest Army installation, which itself hosted major armored and artillery training centers.[19]

During the midst of the observations at Killeen Base, on April 27, General Cabell did brief the Joint Intelligence Committee on the unidentified flying object problem and subsequent to his briefing a Top Secret "Analysis of Flying Object Incidents in the United States" was distributed to a restricted list of offices.[20] Cabell's briefing of the JIC was general in nature – reviewing the official Air Force investigation up to that date – reference was made to green fireballs but nothing seems to have been mentioned about the ongoing Killeen base incidents which had been underway for some six weeks. Figures in the accompanying report did provide a profile of the objects being reported with over 70% described as discs, spherical/elliptical or cylindrical in shape.

The only remark in the report directly relevant to our scenario was that "It is unlikely that a foreign power would expose a superior aerial weapon by a prolonged ineffectual penetration of the United States". It appears that "ineffectual" was being related to the lack of any actual hostile actions; in that sense the entire SAC reconnaissance program over the Soviet Union would have been considered "ineffectual" – clearly it was not and in that sense the report's observation appears quite questionable. While it was true that no attacks had actually occurred, in retrospect it would be difficult to argue that – if penetrations were indeed involved – they were ineffectual or that they had not revealed that there was essentially no military defense in place for strategic American bases and facilities.

1950

To a large extent sightings in 1950 repeated the pattern that had developed during 1949. There were reports of UFOs over the installations in New Mexico – on February 25 a dozen AEC security personnel at Los Alamos reported a metallic silver cylinder over the facility, flying slowly and then speeding up. It flashed as it oscillated and changed course during its passage. The sighting was similar to previous ones in which cylinders had passed directly over atomic facilities.

Sandia Base and Kirtland AFB in Albuquerque reported further sightings – consistent with earlier years' reports. On March 21 between one and one thirty in the afternoon, several witnesses observed silver colored objects maneuvering over the restricted areas – the objects appeared to be extremely maneuverable, zigzagging and with the ability to make right angle turns and immediately reverse position. There was a general impression that they were engaging in a sort of exhibition, not unlike that seen in "dogfights" with aircraft engaging each other. During the sightings two small white objects were seen traveling directly over the weapons storage area. The following day elven members of the 4925th Test Group (Nuclear) at Kirtland reported seeing a daylight UFO and additional reports of objects appeared in the press.

One particular 1950 observation was of a type that would become increasingly common. With the deployment of surveillance and air defense radar, incidents involving "radar only" unidentified object reports appear in the BLUE BOOK archives. They often produced fighter scrambles but almost universally the fighters failed to intercept the UFO in question – or if they did it was only for a brief encounter with no visual sighting and no useful physical description.

However a report of March, 1950 is particularly interesting as it came from Selfridge AFB in Michigan. Selfridge was a major Air Defense Command base, hosting several interceptor squadrons. For over an hour, two separate radars – each operating at its own distinct frequency range – simultaneously tracked a UFO which alternated between seemingly random (evasive?) movements and station keeping in the exact position for minutes at a time. While the apparent position of the object remained the same on both radar displays, at one point in time the two radars did indicate differences in the object's altitude. Jet fighters were scrambled but were apparently unable to make contact or otherwise engage.

For some reason this incident and any further details are missing from the BLUE BOOK archives – but the personnel involved felt that the tracking was so solid, over such an extended period of time, that there was simply no doubt the radars were tracking the same object. In fact the event was viewed as being so credible that it led to a letter from a general at ADC headquarters personally advising the Director of Air Intelligence on the matter, declaring that there was simply no combination of atmospheric or electric phenomena that could account for it and noting that the frequency of credible radar tracking of unknowns was increasing.[21]

While it was a "radar only" incident, with no visual confirmation, the report from Selfridge AFB set the stage for an increasing number of similar reports that began to occur during 1950 and on into 1952. The reports were increasingly suggestive of intentional "ferreting", not just reconnaissance, with objects intentionally probing the military response around restricted areas and military bases – and appearing to actively engage with interceptors sent to identify them.

That trend in "ferreting" type reports is particularly noticeable at Oak Ridge, Tennessee. The 1950 series of incidents at Oak Ridge appears to be truly anomalous when compared to the broader pattern of UFO reports, as much so as the 1949 Killeen/Fort Hood incidents. Neither location had any extensive history of sightings, either during the national wave of reports in 1947 or before each experienced their own independent spike in incidents. And the spikes in reports at each lasted for only three to four months, including very low level incidents where objects were encountered at ground level by security personnel.

The most obvious difference in the reports from Killeen Base in 1949 and Oak Ridge in 1950 was that at Oak Ridge military radar was in place, interceptors were available and beginning in October both groups and individual UFOs were visually observed, tracked by radar and targeted for fighter scrambles. Incidents were reported on October 12, 15, 16, 20, 23, 24; November 3, 5, 29, 30 5; December 14, 18, 20, and finally January 21. The last incident involved a UFO sighted on radar by a patrolling F-82 fighter. The pilot was given approval to engage, his gun radar "locked on" and the intercept attempts over the highly restricted X-10 (plutonium production) plant complex failed – not once but three times.

It appears that each time the interceptor approached firing range, the radar target rapidly descended down into the restricted area of the plant and the pilot broke each firing run due to flight restrictions.[22] The Air Force evaluation of the incident – as with the majority of similar failed intercepts over the next three years – would be that the radar UFOs were actually false echoes based on temperature inversions or other atmospheric reflective phenomena.

Alternatively, numbers of pilots and radar operators were convinced that they were indeed attempting – and failing – to engage highly responsive targets which were readily able to outmaneuver the fighters or, alternatively, drop out of their radar beams to levels too low to be targeted. Air Defense Command's ongoing failures to engage simulated low level attacks by SAC bombers offer support for view that the contemporary air defenses were simply unable to cope with low altitude intruders.

1951

The pattern of UFO observations during 1950 was much like the years 1948 – 1951 and once again does not appear to support any pattern of broad, ongoing strategic reconnaissance. The daytime pair and formation flights of 1947 were still not routinely repeating themselves. Low altitude, high speed UFO passes over strategic air bases are not in evidence. Daylight, physical object reports from strategic atomic facilities are present in 1951, but still limited to single objects and single observations. Only at the end of the year, on December 7, 1951, at 8:15 in the morning is there a report from an AEC security guard at Oak Ridge, Tennessee – of a twenty foot square object, white-gray but not metallic. The object flew relatively slowly from above a nearby ridge into some clouds, then back to the ridge and returning into the clouds.

Certain observations of 1947 had given rise the concerns over pre-attack reconnaissance of strategic military targets or even attack familiarization flights. However those types of observations did not continue with any consistency during the following years of our baseline period. In contrast, what might be described as a pattern of "sampling" emerged following 1947 – focused on strategic atomic facilities. The one thing that did remain a constant through all the years from 1947 through 1951 was the general lack of any effective military deterrent to the appearance of the UFOs over and within the restricted areas associated with the strategic facilities, either by the Air Force or the Army.

That UFO focus on strategic atomic facilities did not stand out during 1947 but becomes clear during the following years. It stands out in any review of the BLUE BOOK report archives, and was quite apparent to Captain Edward Ruppelt when he took point at the Air Force UFO desk. He made a point of it in his first briefing to the new Director of Air Force Intelligence, Major General John Samford and his assistant for intelligence production, Brigadier General William Garland in early 1952. Which takes us to the year 1952 – and a level of UFO activity which tends to obscure virtually any patterns other than the sheer, dramatic increase in number of UFO sightings.

1952

Analysts searching for indications of possible pre-attack activity would certainly have found it in the UFO reports of 1952. In fact there would appear to be considerable cause for worry and as we have discussed, there certainly was in some quarters. Concerns over a UFO focus on the nation's atomic warfare complex would have been supported – but not in terms of just focused sampling as indicated in the patterns of earlier years. During 1952 all the most strategic facilities were generating reports.

It began at what was perhaps still the key atomic warfare nexus – the restricted area outside Albuquerque which included Kirtland AFB, the Sandia Base weapons design and assembly works and the Manzano bomb storage site. Incidents at the Albuquerque sites began in March and continued for months.

On March 15 an Air Force officer observed a dull aluminum colored object, shaped like a flattened oval, sitting stationary over the Sandia Mountain range to the east of Kirtland AFB; the object remained in the same position for a period of some fifteen minutes. At that time the object departed at a relatively slow speed estimated to be one hundred fifty to two hundred miles per hour.

Several additional sightings occurred, beginning in May. The first was in mid-afternoon (3 pm) on May 10. An Air Force colonel and his wife reported seeing two disc-shaped objects fly a straight, level course over the city at an altitude estimated at twenty thousand feet. In a pattern reminiscent of some of the early 1947 sightings, one object followed the other at higher altitude while the lower object "wavered" on its axis. The overflight was slow, taking some five to ten minutes – no radar track appears to have been obtained.

On May 23, beginning at 4 pm and for some 45 minutes, a silvery/aluminum colored disc was observed to the west of Albuquerque by several air defense personnel at the 135th AC&W (aircraft control and warning) site on Kirtland AFB. The object was seen at considerable distance, at a low altitude of one thousand to three thousand feet – observed through binoculars, a transit telescope and a theodolite. The object was bright, enough so to be noticed and observed visually. Detail was visible through the optical instruments, including a flat bottom and a rounded top – but no conventional identification could be made.

The object remained stationary before ultimately moving to the right and descending below the horizon. Efforts to track the object by radar and later to intercept with an F-86D fighter proved unsuccessful, possibly because of its very low altitude.[23] It should be noted that both the description and movement of this object appear to be very similar to the observation of March 15, with the March object stationary to the east and the May object stationary to the west. Another sighting followed on May 28 (two circular objects maneuvering at high speed over the city).

The sightings over Albuquerque were followed by reports from Oak Ridge with the first being an evening intercept and fighter engagement on June 21. In that incident a ground observer post spotted the UFO, it was confirmed by air defense radar and successfully intercepted by an F-47 fighter. Upon closing with the UFO, the target was visually observed as a small white blinking light – which proceeded to make what appeared to be a number of abortive ramming attacks against the fighter.

Other atomic facility reports include Oak Ridge on June 23 (bullet shaped object flying straight and level), another at Albuquerque on June 28 (two silver discs high in the sky suddenly climbing vertically), a sighting at the Hanford works on July 5 (a commercial pilot and crew saw a circular disc directly above the site), July 19 at the new Savannah River atomic plant in South Carolina (witnessed by a very large number of AEC personnel), a July 22 sighting at Los Alamos (eight large, round aluminum colored objects flying straight and level and then moving randomly over the facility for some twenty five minutes) and once again at Kirtland AFB in Albuquerque on July 26 (just after noon with eight to ten orange objects in triangular formation, very fast movement).

In a final daylight sighting from Los Alamos, on July 29 several observers witnessed a white object moving across the sky at 10 am in the morning, gyrating during its passage. Jet interceptors from Kirtland arrived about five minutes later (suggesting that the object had been tracked on radar) and their contrails were seen moving off in the direction in which the object had flown. In later months unidentified lights were reported over Sandia Base, Los Alamos and once again over the Killeen Q site. With that degree of activity, with daylight observations from multiple witnesses at each location, with the consistent failure to track and engage the UFOs an analyst would have had to assess that a positive strike indicator was appearing – with both reconnaissance and ferreting directed against the core of the nation's atomic warfare complex.

In addition to the atomic facilities, other reports raised the possibility of a much broader strategic reconnaissance. A wave of reports, radar tracking and failed UFO interceptions indicated a focus on the nation's population centers on the east coast, from Boston down to Washington D.C. – including the targeting of the largest Navy logistics base on the East Coast, Hampton Roads near Norfolk Virginia. These East Coast incidents were previously covered in considerable detail, beginning with the July 14 Nash-Fortenberry commercial airline pilot night time sighting of highly maneuverable "stacked" formations of red "coin shaped" objects in the vicinity of Newport News. Their sighting was confirmed by a second air crew and two evenings later a NACA (later NASA) engineer observed four objects approach and maneuver over the Hampton Roads area; Skywatch volunteers and others corroborated his observation.

Later, on July 26, ground observers reported unidentified lights near Langley Air Force Base (adjacent to Hampton and Newport News); interceptor crews and other ground personnel observed four round objects in V formation. The objects were reportedly tracked by both Navy radar at Norfolk and by airborne radars. It has to be stressed that Naval Station Norfolk was headquarters for the Atlantic Command, the largest Navy facility on the East Coast and operational headquarters for the fleet air command – it would also come to house the largest air base on the East Coast and was arguably the most strategic conventional military target in the Eastern United States.

In terms of potential pre-attack activity, other aspects of the 1952 UFO wave was perhaps even more suggestive. Sightings were coming in from a large number of air defense installations and interceptor bases, ranging from forward defense sites on the polar routes to major bases around the perimeter of the nation.

As early as January 22, observers at a ground radar post near Fairbanks, Alaska worked a UFO intercept with two F-94 jet fighters. A very high speed target had been tracked by the ground radar – the target was giving evidence of repeated and dramatic course reversals, incoming and outgoing. The incident began just after midnight and once the interceptors were in the target area they tracked two targets over the period of an hour. Both fighters obtained various radar locks during that period. On at least one occasion one had to take evasive action from an apparent head on pass, tracked on radar only.

No visual contact occured during the interception efforts but based on the radar tracking the incident had all the appearance of an aggressive ferreting encounter. Another Alaska incident occurred on July 24 near Elmendorf AFB. An F-94 interceptor made radar contact with a fighter sized object. At the time the target was traveling only slightly faster than the jet, with a radar lock the fighter climbed to engage only to find the target pulling away. As the target reached an altitude of some eighteen thousand feet it leveled off and increased speed, at that point the fighter broke off the chase. In contrast, military bases on the northeastern polar access route appear to have observed no UFOs during this period, but on August 29 a Navy patrol plane flying west of Thule, Greenland reported three white disc-shaped objects first hovering and then joining into a triangular formation and flying away.

During the summer months of 1952 air bases across the continental United States became heavily involved in what might have been taken to be targeted reconnaissance and increased ferreting. On July 9, Rapid City AFB (later Ellsworth AFB) reported – for the first time since 1947 – a group of unidentified objects moving directly over the air field. Four members of the SAC 717th Strategic Reconnaissance Wing observed three white discs pass over at very high speeds, each trailing the other by approximately one minute. Northern tier air defense also engaged in a series of night time engagements, including one west of Port Huron, Michigan on July 28-29 which involved ground radar tracking, a chase by F-94s with airborne radar locks and visual observation of a flashing light at the position of the radar target.

Another incident occurred on July 29, involving civilians and personnel at Great Falls AFB. A number of witnesses near Ennis, Montana observed three discs maneuvering in a clear daylight sky during the period of approximately one hour. Later that afternoon Air Force personnel at Great Falls observed two to five disc shaped objects, one hovered for several minutes while the others circled it. The Great Falls observation involved a large number of people over a period of close to an hour but apparently no radar tracking was obtained and no interceptors were scrambled.

August brought more air defense activity around the northern tier bases. On August 1 air defense radar in Ohio tracked a UFO during mid-morning. Two F-86s were scrambled, the pilots made visual contact and climbed to their ceilings of 48,000 feet, obtaining a weak airborne radar return. Working at their maximum altitude they obtained gun camera footage showing a medium sized silver colored sphere/disc estimated to be at sixty thousand feet. After tracking the object for some distance the fighters broke off the attempt to engage. Camera footage confirmed the UFO image and demonstrated that the object was indeed in motion.

Such local incidents, only on occasion reported in the press, were largely overshadowed in both the public attention and in Air Force public relations comments by the national news story of the repeated appearance of nighttime radar tracks and unidentified lights over Washington D.C. A number of military related incidents and reports were simply lost in that national story. Other incidents indicative of pre-attack reconnaissance never received any national attention. In particular there were a number of apparent intrusions over major air defense installations on the West Coast.

Two of the major West Coast air defense installations of the early Cold War years were Hamilton Field, just north of San Francisco and George Air Force

Base in southern California, east of Los Angeles. Several interceptor squadrons were stationed at both Hamilton field and at George AFB. Hamilton field recorded UFO observations in 1947 but nothing more matching our scenario of reconnaissance/ferreting occurred until 1952.

On August 3, 1952, in a daylight afternoon sighting, two pilots observed (using binoculars) two circular, silvery objects at an estimated altitude of twelve to eighteen thousand feet. The objects moved across the base at a jet speed, dropping in altitude and being joined by eight more objects, traveling in pairs. As in several of the other reports we have noted, the pilots commented that in their passage the initial objects were darting and maneuvering in what appeared to be a display of aerial dog fighting.

By that point in the summer, George AFB had already had its first UFO reports, a series of them, all in May. On May 1 four individuals, three at one location and another four miles away, reported the daylight sighting of five white discs flying very low and very fast over the base. Apparently radar did track the flight and fighters were scrambled but no further details relating to tracking or attempted intercepts are available in the reports.

A few days later, on the morning of May 9, two F-86 pilots as well as a ground observer sighted a round silver object in flight over the base and on May 13 an afternoon observation by both the pilot and observer aloft in a training aircraft reported a white/silver round object overhead of their aircraft. The object was at an estimated altitude of 45,000 feet and remained in the area for some thirty minutes before it disappeared, leaving at a terrific speed.

The year 1952 was simply overwhelming in terms of the total number of UFO incidents. So overwhelming that it was easy to miss the purely strategic and military element of the reports coming in from across the country. Certainly a threat analyst could have pulled out a number of incidents – far more than in 1947 – supporting an indication of pre-strike activities. And at least in the early months of the year, the Russian card seems to have remained on the table in regard to UFOs.

And in the broader strategic context, by the spring of 1952 it increasingly appeared that all the elements for a Russian surprise attack were coming into place – as had been predicted in numerous intelligence studies over the previous three years. American airborne radiation sampling had confirmed that Soviet nuclear tests had proceeded to the point of actual bomb development and testing – compared to earlier explosions which had been of "nuclear devices", not actual weapons. The most recent test had definitely been of an actual bomb.

Signals intelligence had also tracked flights of Soviet Tu-4 long range bombers into a series of forward air bases in the Soviet Far East; that was viewed as a positive indication of attack staging and the aircraft were felt to represent an imminent threat.[24]

The fear of some sort of preemptive air strike was so great that the Joint Chiefs ordered a new program of shallow daylight overflights of Soviet territory, extending some twenty to twenty five miles inland from the coast. Navy and Air Force aircraft flew on joint ferret missions, with a focus both on airfields and radar sites. A number of such intelligence collection missions were flown between April and June, 1952.[25] As of the end of July, 1952 a threat/warnings analyst focused on sightings over strategic American targets should been quite worried – there certainly appeared to be sufficient data to support indications of reconnaissance, ferreting and even attack familiarization flights.

Yet during the following three months of the year, the sheer number of credible sightings involving so many UFOs actually weighed against Soviet involvement. It was simply far more than would have been necessary, and far too much of an actual warning. Beyond that there was another obvious and negative indicator. Given that for months there had been ongoing and totally fruitless efforts to intercept UFOs over strategic targets it was obvious that if the Soviets had craft with the capabilities being observed they could move at will across the nation. With that sort of advantage why not just attack – at once?

Chapter 16 Endnotes

1. Cynthia M. Grabo, Anticipating Surprise; Analysis for Strategic Warning, 131

2. Comprehensive Catalog of 1,700 Project Blue Book UFO Unknowns: Database Catalog Not a Best Evidence List – NEW: List of Projects & Blue Book Chiefs Work in Progress (Version 1.26, Jan. 31, 2016). Compiled by Brad Sparks © 2001-2016 http://www.nicap.org/bb/BB_Unknowns.pdf

3. Richard Hall, Keith Chester, and Dick Hall, "The UFO Chronologies", National Investigations Committee on Aerial Phenomena http://www.nicap.org/520414lacrosse_dir.htm

4. Elizabeth F. Loftus, *Eyewitness Testimony*, Harvard University Press, Cambridge Massachusetts, 1996

5. Peter B. Ainsworth, *Psychology, Law and Eyewitness Testimony*, John Wiley and Sons, New York, 1998

6. William E. Burrows, *By Any Means Necessary; America's Secret Air War in the Cold War*, Farrar, Straus, and Giroux, New York, 2001, 8-9

7. Ibid, 101

8. Ibid, 10

9. Curtis Peebles, *Shadow Flights; America's Secret Air War Against the Soviet Union*, Presidio Press, Novato, California, 2002, 8-9

10. Ibid, 16-17

11. Ibid, 49-53

12. Ibid, 30-31

13. Ibid, 123-127

14. Bill Grimes, *The History of Big Safari*, Archway Publishing, 2014, 25, 32-33, 90-91,

15. Michael Swords and Robert Powell, *UFO's and Government / A Historical Inquiry*, Anomolist Books, San Antonio, Texas, 2012, 40

16. This collection initiative was ordered by General Schulgen of the Air Intelligence Requirements Directorate. Schulgen and the Directorate reported to General Cabell, head of the USAF Directorate of Intelligence.

17. "Analysis of Flying Saucer Reports", Memorandum for the Record, To Director of Intelligence, Director of Research and Development, December 18, 1947

18. "Unconventional Aircraft", Headquarters Fourth Army memorandum, January 13, 1949 http://www.nicap.org/docs/490113_poland.gif

19. "A brief history of Killeen Base; Now West Fort Hood", Fort Hood Texas, U.S. Army http://www.hood.army.mil/history/1950/a_brief_history_of_killeen_base.htm

20. Report by the Director of Intelligence, USAF, to the Joint Intelligence Committee on Unidentified Aerial Objects, Project 1947 http://www.project1947.com/fig/jic.htm

21. Dr. J Allen Hynek, *The Hynek UFO Report*, Barnes and Noble Books, 1997, 114-117

22. Daniel Wilson, January 21, 1951 UFO and F-82 fighter over Oak Ridge, Tenn. http://www.nicap.org/oakridge/oakridge510121docs.htm

23. Copy of original Air Force investigation available courtesy of NICAP http://www.nicap.org/docs/520523kirtland_docs.pdf

24. Larry Hancock, *Surprise Attack; From Pearl Harbor to 9/11 to Benghazi*, Counterpoint, Berkeley, California, 2015, 129

25. Curtis Peeples, *Shadow Flights; America's Secret Air War Against the Soviet Union*, Presideo, Novato, California, 2002, 30-31

Chapter 17

Not the Russians

In this chapter

- Concerns of focused reconnaissance targeting both strategic military bases and key atomic warfare facilities were consistently noted and commented on in Air Force intelligence studies and discussions from 1947 onwards.

- Indications of such activities extend beyond geography to the operational aspects of the UFO incidents reported by both military and security personnel.

- Operational indicators are evaluated by comparing incident reports against known reconnaissance practices and mission profiles – no such operational analysis or profiling is evident in the Air Force studies and reports.

- Air Force studies also lacked any specific/detailed analysis of UFO incidents as proactive testing of American air defenses – a standard pre-attack indicator.

- Operational analysis of the benchmark survey period reveals a number of negative indicators for the scenario of Russian involvement.

- A reconnaissance focused study of the benchmark period highlights a very curious mix of both standard and highly anomalous UFO behaviors/practices.

Our baseline review of the first six years of UFO reports from the continental United States does reveal a pattern of incidents/observations suggesting focused reconnaissance of both strategic military bases and key atomic warfare facilities. In itself that is certainly no new insight or discovery. The outlines of that pattern were quite visible to Air Force intelligence personnel and concerns about reconnaissance and testing of air defenses show up as remarks or notes in virtually every intelligence report or assessment made up to 1952 – even the most negative reports continued to note that certain sightings suggested foreign intrusions.

Air Intelligence documents of early 1952 confirm that concerns over Russian involvement were still in play as of that date, and *BLUE BOOK* head Captain Edward Ruppelt personally affirmed that he discussed patterns of observations over strategic facilities in his briefing to the head of Air Intelligence even before the formal initiation of the new *BLUE BOOK* UFO project. Exactly those concerns stimulated Generals Samford and Garland to push for a greatly expanded technical collections effort, setting up specific networks of instrumented observation stations.

By the fall of 1952 a new CIA/OSI UFO study proposal cited the pattern of observations over strategic facilities as a true national security issue, one of immediate concern. In retrospect it's actually interesting to ponder why something quite so obvious – and so suggestive – seemingly faded away over time. That is an issue we will pursue in a following chapter, when we move to summarize a much longer view of the fundamental unidentified object intelligence challenge.

But first, in the context of our baseline indications survey, there remains the issue of something that seems to be missing from the Air Force discussion and concerns of those first years, especially after the earliest assessments of 1947 and 1948. While there was considerable discussion of UFO sightings related to geography and possible targets, there was limited analysis of any changes in the operational characteristics of the unknown objects over time. With a closer look, and comparison to the actual American reconnaissance and ferreting practices of the period, there are indications of reconnaissance and defense probing that go far beyond geography. An analyst looking for indications of reconnaissance and technical collections would normally compare known techniques and actual mission practices to the suspect observations.

A number of the UFO reports describe low to medium high speed flights over strategic facilities and military bases – such "dashes" would be very consistent with standard practice for low altitude penetration of defended targets. So would the reports describing two objects flying together with one appearing to "cover" the other defensively in "wingman" type flight. In addition we find reports suggesting very high altitude photographic imaging of facilities, low level radiation emissions monitoring of atomic production plants, monitoring and sampling of fallout generated by atomic testing and even very low altitude particulate collections from both radioactive materials plants (Oak Ridge) and weapons storage sites (Killeen Base).

Other aspects of the UFO reports, including multiple objects maneuvering with each other and structured formation flights, could be viewed as matching the operational profiles of electronic and photographic missions routinely flown by the United States against Russia early in the Cold War. Yet no level of operational/mission profiles or comparisons show up in the Air Force studies and reports.

In fact there is no evidence that mission profiles/action lists for strategic reconnaissance and pre-attack familiarization flights were created and matched to UFO reports in any detailed analysis. Instead we find official Air Force intelligence studies (with both military and scientific consultant commentary) which challenge the idea of foreign UFO origins by objecting to repetitive observations (why do they keep coming back?) or the use of advanced technology aircraft (why fly your most advanced technology where you might lose it over enemy territory?) when both elements were common in the actual American foreign reconnaissance operations of the period.

The answers to such questions were discussed in the previous chapter and become obvious in the context of real world aerial intelligence collections practices. Still, we have to keep in mind that neither the technical intelligence specialists at Wright Patterson/ATIC nor their scientific consultants, or even CIA/OSI personnel were involved with covert American aerial missions. In practice such missions were highly classified and compartmentalized – and issues of security may well have kept such practices from being discussed in Air Intelligence studies. As we have mentioned, references and comparisons to several of America's most advanced rocket aircraft and even constant level photographic reconnaissance balloon developments are also missing from the same studies and reports.

Of course the other problem is that that if you are not specifically looking for such details, they are overshadowed by the more sensational aspects of the overall body of data. One of the key aspects of intentions analysis is preparing an action list that is detailed enough to catch small but important indicators. In our review the operational aspects of the UFO reports stand out because we began by profiling American reconnaissance and ferreting missions against the Soviet Union – highlighting aerial intelligence gathering practices developed for use against conventional military targets as well as in evaluating the atomic weapons development programs of first Russia and later China.

Most surprisingly, a pre-attack indicator not addressed in any specific detail in the Air Force reports of the period relates not just to intelligence collection but proactive testing of American air defenses. That includes the activities which we have referred to as "ferreting" – intentionally probing defense networks to trigger weapons system radar tracking, interception, military communications and even provocation of a military response. Those were all practices routinely carried out by both Air Force and Navy aircraft against the Soviet Bloc. It's a high risk activity and along with other American reconnaissance and ELINT/SIGINT flights resulted in actual attacks by Russian aircraft and the loss of a number of American aircraft and military personnel.

Yet while the individual Air Force reports relating to attempted interceptions of unidentified aerial objects increasingly described what pilots felt to be threatening behavior on the part of the UFOs, there is no discussion in the intelligence studies which collects and specifically evaluates patterns in those incidents. There are no trend studies focused on what appear to be changing types of interceptor engagements, changes suggesting increasingly proactive and aggressive testing of ground and air defenses. There is also no extended discussion noting trends in the specifics of the threatening maneuvers that military and even commercial pilots described.

The fact that such analysis is missing is especially notable because it is exactly at that point that comparing operational practices begins to argue against Russian involvement. Certainly it is significant that on a number of occasions the objects being observed as UFOs appear to have intentionally – and on occasion for considerable lengths of time – exposed themselves to both commercial and military aircraft. In contrast American reconnaissance flights made every attempt to avoid Soviet aircraft, at any distance.

Earlier we discussed one instance in which a SAC B-29 on a penetration/reconnaissance flight over Siberia emerged from a cloud formation to find itself in the company of a number of identical aircraft – actually a Soviet Tu-4 formation. The Russians apparently did not notice the B-29, or assumed it to be one of their own, and the American pilot did nothing to draw their attention, slipping back into the clouds and distancing himself as quickly as possible. American aircraft used in reconnaissance were specifically selected for either high speed or high altitude operations which would keep them distant from Soviet aircraft. Avoidance was planned into all missions to the greatest extent possible.

We do find a number of credible reports from pilots and aircrews that describe unidentified objects – either singly or in groups– simply passing by American aircraft at a distance, with no apparent response to being observed. However, often in dramatic contrast, we also find just the opposite. In a growing number of instances during the period of 1947-1952, UFOs not only approached passing aircraft but "engaged" with them, sometimes passively and at other times aggressively. These incidents did not involve attempted interceptions of UFOs by fighter aircraft, just the opposite, they involved approaches and obvious attention being paid to aircraft simply passing through the area in which the UFO was operating.

On December 4, 1949 the three man crew of a C-47 military transport flying over Hammond, Louisiana observed a bright silver sphere the size of a fighter approach their plane head on, then execute a turn and take a station keeping position with the aircraft. It simply held its place, bobbing up and down. The sphere then made sudden starts and stops, maneuvering in all directions. Following that it flew directly across the nose of the aircraft, departing at very high speed.

Another military transport crew, on January 24, 1950, noted a large hemispherical shaped object at a distance of five to ten miles away and a bit above their cruising altitude. The pilot began a climb towards the object and initially it moved off ahead – only to reappear after a moment, approach and hold stationary with the aircraft, oscillating or "wiggling" as it did so. After pacing the aircraft for a time the object simply moved ahead of the transport again and departed at high speed.

Some aerial encounters were even more dramatic, appearing to involve actual inspection of the aircraft. Dr. Alan Hynek discussed an incident which involved a B-36 bomber in flight over Davis-Monthan AFB near Tucson, Arizona on May 1, 1952. Two metallic discs overtook the bomber in flight, but slowed to assume positions near the bomber. One moved close enough in so as to be observed at very close range by a turret gunner.

After something like half a minute, both objects made sharp turns, resumed their original speed and flew off some miles, with one then coming to a sharp stop and remaining stationary. The entire event was observed by an Air Force intelligence officer on the ground; the officer prepared an extensive report in which several personnel on the ground corroborated the sighting. The sightings took place during an estimated three to five minutes. Following the incident the pilot requested permission to land. Although the aircraft had been in transit flight with no scheduled stop permission was granted – and the crew was debriefed at that time.[1]

Similar passive encounters and apparent close inspections were recorded by jet interceptor pilots. On October 30, 1948 near Grays Harbor southwest of Seattle, Washington, an F-82 fighter was directed by ground control intercept radar against an unknown target at an altitude of 8,000 feet. The pilot visually acquired the target, describing it as a compact formation of yellow objects which were moving to join an in-line formation of some twenty white, egg shaped objects. The formation crossed in front of the interceptor, in level flight at constant altitude. The objects then turned back to fly parallel to the jet at high speed. After a time they essentially faded from sight, while at the same time disappearing from the Air Defense radar.[2]

In contrast, we find what appear to be an equal if not greater number of incidents in which UFOs behaved anything except passively in encounters with aircraft. This appears to have developed into a trend, correlated with the rapid expansion of the nation's air defense. Certainly we find more UFO incidents involving either active avoidance or active "teasing" of interceptors as search and surveillance radars become part of the equation.[3] In an increasing number of instances the objects appeared to actively react to tracking by ground based radar or weapons radars on interceptors.

We discussed the trend towards more seemingly threatening encounters (at least from the perception of aircraft pilots and crews) and gave examples in earlier chapters. Apparent "engagements" with UFOs occurred only a handful of times up to 1950 but as interceptors were more widely deployed and radar became more frequently involved the instances of "aggressive" UFO behavior became more common. As an example, on January 22, 1950 a Navy patrol plane flying out of Kodiak Naval Air Station in Alaska detected suspicious radar targets, only to experience intense radar interference which prevented it from tracking the UFOs.

At that point watch officers on the USS Tillamook south of Kodiak observed an orange ball of fire maneuvering in their patrol area. After a time the patrol plane again picked up unknown radar tracks at five miles distance and quickly closed with the radar target. The target became visually well defined, appearing to be two orange lights, flying in formation and making barrel rolls with each other.[4] The Navy plane stayed in pursuit, only to have the object/s fly directly at it in what the pilot felt to be a threatening move. The pilot turned off his own running lights and shortly later the target flew away from the aircraft.

On July 9, 1951 near Augusta, Georgia the pilot of an F-51 fighter observed an oval disc about twice the size of his plane come out of the sun towards him, apparently flying at high speed in a head-on approach. At the last moment the UFO lowered to fly underneath the aircraft – only to pursue the fighter, position itself to the front and make a second head-on dive. That same maneuver was repeated a number of times until the UFO finally broke off and climbed out of sight. The pilot had ample occasion to obtain a very good view of the object as it approached as close as three hundred to four hundred feet.

It was definitely a physical object, round but flat on top and bottom as well as apparently spinning.

In retrospect, none of these encounters – whether passive or aggressive – between UFOs and commercial/military aircraft are what one would expect from Russian reconnaissance, especially missions being flown by craft with what surely would have been the most closely guarded technology of the Russian military. Yet there are no remarks to that effect in the Air Force intelligence studies and reports.

These types of aircraft encounters leave us with some very fundamental questions about the behavior of the UFOs. Such anomalous operational behavior – viewed from the perspective of standard reconnaissance practices – not only cast doubt on a Russian origin but raise some serious questions related to the nature of the types of reconnaissance which appears to have been in play. Why would it be that essentially all the primary targets in the nation's atomic warfare complex were being repeatedly targeted – but at the same time the UFOs were exposing themselves to casually inspect propeller driven aircraft and even balloons? Exactly why would covert Russian spy flights repeatedly approach and appear to inspect propeller driven aircraft? And why would they seem to be so interested in balloons?

A series of highly credible daylight observations suggest that UFOs found balloons interesting, not just passing directly by them but on occasion pausing or stopping to inspect the balloons. They seemed especially interested in the really big, stratospheric balloons.

In the earliest reports from 1947, it was not unusual to find observers reporting the passing of spherical and disc shaped UFOs in the vicinity of pibal weather balloons. One of the earliest series of such observations occurred in Virginia, well before the publicized wave of 1947 flying saucer reports. Dr. James E. McDonald enumerated and discussed a number of balloon incidents in a 1968 statement prepared for a House congressional subcommittee. His statement described balloon/UFO observations and provided examples beginning in 1947 and extending through 1961.[5]

The year 1947 also saw the first of what were to be ongoing launches of large, stratospheric balloons. One type consisted of very large "trains" or strings of weather balloon clusters. Individual balloons were made out of first rubber and later polyethylene plastic. The balloons themselves were not at all unique; it was the overall train of balloon clusters which was immense – over six hundred feet in length. The creation of balloon trains equipped with devices which allowed them to ascend to very high altitudes and remain aloft at a constant altitude was also a novel technique, one developed by the Japanese in their FuGo balloon weapon systems during World War II.

The second, and more spectacular balloon development immediately following World War II was the creation of clear polyethylene balloons of gigantic size, capable of carrying large instrument or photographic payloads into the stratosphere and also of taking manned observation gondolas to extreme altitudes, far above the ceilings of manned aircraft of the time. From September, 1947 until 1958 hundreds of instrumented flights as well as a number of manned ascents were made using such balloons – known as "Skyhooks". The Skyhooks were made by General Mills Inc. and operated by a combination of military and civilian launch teams. Skyhook class plastic balloons became a major business in the upper Midwest, with the hub being the General Mills facilities in Minneapolis. General Mills estimated that by 1960 there were four individual companies building the giant balloons, with sales of around seven million dollars.[6]

In and of themselves there was nothing especially secret about either the huge balloon trains or the giant polyethylene Skyhook balloons. On the other hand, the use of constant level balloon trains in a top secret Army Air Force project devoted to acoustic detection of Soviet atomic device tests was very much secret. Mogul project balloon trains were developed by New York University teams and first tested on the east coast in early spring 1947. By early summer, in June, they were being launched from the Army Air Force Base at Alamogordo, New Mexico. Polyethylene balloons rather than rubber weather balloons were incorporated into the balloon trains. Sonobouy microphone packages, derived from anti-submarine warfare, were adapted for aerial sound wave detection and radio relay.[7]

Mogul balloon train launches did produce some reports of UFOs in the White Sands area, on occasion being perceived as formations of UFOs given the multiple balloons in the train.[8] Ultimately atomic explosion acoustic detection Mogul launches were conducted from sites at Kwajalein Island, Guam and Hawaii as well as New Mexico and Alabama during actual American atomic tests in the South Pacific. Sonic detection proved viable, at ranges of up to 1,700 miles, but proved no more effective at altitude than from ground level. The Mogul project was abandoned following analysis of the detection results from the Eniwetok tests of May, 1948.[9]

Skyhook balloon scientific and manned ascents were also quite public, however Skyhook also had its classified side, with the stratospheric balloons being used in a lengthy series of global photographic reconnaissance flights taking them the length of the Soviet Union – with photographic film package recovery in the Pacific. We discussed the various classified balloon projects earlier, including numerous test flights and actual classified CIA launches which took balloons on paths over the United States in the early to mid-1950s. Several of those Skyhook flights appear to have attracted the attention of UFOs, leading to some very high quality observations. The following examples are taken from a list of personnel observations from teams working with Skyhook and constant level stratospheric balloon programs. They are sourced from Captain Ruppelt's book as well as a listing of 1500 Project *BLUE BOOK* unknowns developed by researcher Brad Sparks.[10]

In October, 1951 General Mills aeronautical engineers were airborne in a plane tracking one of their balloons when they sighted a UFO crossing its path; the object was cigar shaped and in passing leveled off over the balloon and briefly slowed. At that point it made a sharp left turn and climbed away at a steep angle, with extreme acceleration. The General Mills personnel had the object in sight for some two minutes and were convinced it was not any type of balloon or known aircraft.[11]

Another October, 1951 sighting in Minneapolis involved two observers aloft in a balloon and a ground observer team using a theodolite. The balloon crew observed two UFOs. The first was seen at high altitude, moving at speed from east to west; it then slowed and circled in an upward climb (described as a vertical "falling leaf" fashion – a motion often reported in U FO sightings) for two minutes before departing. Shortly after the first UFO departed, another passed over the area at high speed and both the airborne crew and the tracking team (advised by radio from the balloon) observed its passage. A brief theodolite view revealed it to be cigar shaped. That overall incident lasted for some five minutes.

Balloons launched from Holliman AFB over the White Sands test range and monitored from the air were also seen to be approached by UFOs. In one instance a C-47 tracker aircraft, the balloon ground launch crew and the manager of the local airport all observed two discs (flying side by side) approach a high altitude balloon, circle it and then fly rapidly away. The balloon had been quite high at the time of the encounter but still quite visible due to its size, given that the two UFOs were also quite visible the observers were led to believe that the UFOs were also quite large. When the balloon was recovered it was found to have been ripped down the side during its flight.

Perhaps the most dramatic balloon/UFO incident was one reported by a Navy Patrol aircraft off Thule, Greenland on August 29, 1952. The Navy plane was periodically monitoring a Skyhook balloon at 90,000 feet when the crew observed that the instrument pod beneath the balloon appeared to have three silver discs either attached to it – or so close as to appear to be physically attached.

The crew was using binoculars for observation and after several minutes the discs were seen to detach themselves and move into a compact V formation. They then banked away from the balloon at extremely high speed and were gone from sight in approximately three seconds.[12] In a somewhat similar incident, on February 1, 1954 the crew of a Navy aircraft monitoring a Skyhook balloon over Tuscaloosa, Alabama observed six unknown objects fly over and then around the balloon. After maintaining a stationary position by the balloon for a short time they then ascended vertically, quickly going out of sight.

The observations of UFOs approaching Skyhook balloons were certainly known to the Air Force and to *BLUE BOOK*. In his own book Ruppelt describes a visit to the General Mills offices in Minneapolis, only to be met with "disgust". The balloon teams there had seen UFOs around their launches so frequently that they simply could not understand why the Air Force was refusing to acknowledge their existence as real objects. They had no interest in making any further reports to the Air Force. Ruppelt also commented that he had personally known two Air Force C-47 balloon tracker pilots who had observed UFO's approach Skyhooks and both were absolutely convinced they had seen real craft of some sort.[13]

These sorts of UFO flight behaviors – close approach and inspection of conventional aircraft, intentional and threatening passes at jet interceptors, approach and inspection of large, high altitude balloons – all are truly anomalous in regards to any reasonable type of Soviet strategic reconnaissance. Beyond that none of the seemingly advanced technology involved in the most anomalous UFO reports ever appeared in actual Russian weapons systems and the extent of the reports of UFO activity over and around American strategic and military targets appears to be well beyond the scope of anything needed for pre-strike reconnaissance.

While reconnaissance of strategic military targets such as air bases, weapons storage sites, air defense installations, major logistics bases and command and control centers is standard practice in pre-strike planning, the repeated UFO appearances at Los Alamos, Hanford and Oak Ridge also make little sense from a Russian origins perspective. Mapping approaches to strategic targets is an operational necessity and so is estimating the types, yields and blast range of the enemy's weapons. But American strategic facilities were publicly known. Bases and security reservations were marked and clearly shown on widely available commercial maps. Beyond that, while extensive American intelligence collections were required to determine virtually every detail of Russian atomic weapons development, the world was routinely advised on exactly what types of atomic weaponry (and even delivery systems) were in the American inventory.

In summary, even a limited indications review evaluating the scenario of pre-strike Russian reconnaissance would have to be considered as negative. The indicators for reconnaissance do exist but there were also far too many aspects that simply did not support Russian involvement. Of course a reality check from our distance in time gives us an absolute and negative answer to the dual question of possible Soviet spy flights and exceptionally advanced technology Russian aircraft.

We now know that the Russians had focused on building huge numbers of conventional aircraft, primarily medium range bombers and jet interceptors. Later, following the extended SAC reconnaissance of Russia, the Soviets shifted resources to anti-aircraft rockets and built the most extensive air defense network in history. The once feared Tu-4 long range bombers were used primarily in ocean reconnaissance roles tracking the U.S. Navy. No major intercontinental Russian bombing capability – requiring large numbers of aerial tankers and refueling capability – was ever put into place. The fear of a Soviet SAC (SUSAC in popular literature of the period) turned out to be ungrounded; the Russians chose to put resources into defense against SAC, not matching it in equivalent strike capability.

Which leaves us with the obvious question, if indications of reconnaissance were indeed positive but the source was not the Russians, who were the unknown parties actively probing the American military, the nation's air defenses and its atomic warfighting capabilities? While the sightings of unknown objects over strategic military bases on the west and east coasts might be taken as an "artifact" of the flying saucer publicity during the national waves of 1947 or 1952 that provides no reasonable explanation for the months-long spikes in sightings at Los Alamos and Sandia Base in 1949, especially since any media publicity of that period related to nighttime fireballs and not the types of daylight physical objects sightings we reviewed. The Killeen base sightings surge in Texas is even less consistent, with low altitude and often stationary lights totally unlike what was being reported in the press from central New Mexico.

Similarly there is no obvious explanation for the sudden spike in reports from Hanford and especially from Oak Ridge in 1950, neither facility had reported any significant number of sightings during the initial 1947 flying saucer publicity. The timing patterns of reports from the atomic materials production facilities and weapons assembly plants simply do not parallel the waves of national UFO sightings, nor do they parallel each other. Beyond that, at a greater level of detail, those incidents at those facilities do have something in common. Each seems to display an evolving pattern in the types of sightings being reported. At each facility the early observations of unknown aerial objects describe the UFOs as being at a distance or at considerable altitude. Where interceptors were available, as at Hanford, the objects were far above the fighter's ceilings.

But over time the fly-bys and high altitude stationary object sightings evolved into observations directly over the facilities, with objects moving at lower altitudes and often at relatively high speed. At some installations there were relatively long "visits" by stationary objects at a distance. And on occasion there were lower altitude passes of multiple objects appearing to actually attract attention to themselves with violent maneuvers and apparent "dogfights".

Only after at least some of those stages are passed do we see very low altitude intrusions, sometimes virtually at ground level. Of course there are exceptions, but in general if we look at each facility over a several year period we do find a transition and trends in the operational behavior of the UFOs being observed and reported.

That suggestion of possible trends during the period of our first study leads to the question of whether even longer term patterns might be found. To examine that question, we need a new hypothesis, a new scenario and a longer term study. This leads us to a second scenario which will be a bit broader than our first – and certainly more controversial. Simply stated, through 1952 and beyond do we continue to find indications of unknown aerial objects (with a non-Russian origin) conducting ongoing military assessment, targeting and probing of American military capabilities – most specifically of American nuclear warfighting capability?

We will continue our indications review – with that expanded scenario – in the following chapter. It will be a relatively minimalist exercise but it will address several decades of data. Given that we have no record of the national intelligence community addressing the UFO problem over the longer term, certainly not with such an extended chronological study, even a limited effort should prove educational.

Chapter 17 Endnotes

1. Dr. J. Allen Hynek, *The Hynek UFO Report*, Barnes and Noble Books, 1997, 100-103

2. Sighting report from Brad Sparks, with transcriptions and reference material from Francis Ridge and Dan Wilson. NICAP material online at: http://www.nicap.org/490527hartmtn_dir.htm

3. 44 Lashup radar sites were in operation by the end of 1959. *The Emerging Shield : The Air Force and the Evolution of Continental Air Defense,* Kenneth Schaffel, 1991, p. 23

4. This particular description of two orange lights maneuvering with each other while being pursued will show up again in a following chapter, almost exactly matching the experience and observations from the pilot and co-pilot of a SAC tanker, asked to pursue a UFO which had overflown a northern tier SAC base. In that experience the dual UFOs were only visible at close range, evading the SAC aircraft, returning to it and otherwise engaging in apparent "cat and mouse" maneuvering, just as in this incident over Alaska.

5. Dr. James E. McDonald, "Meteorologists and weather observers look at the sky frequently. Why don't they see UFOs?", Statement on Unidentified Flying Objects, House Committee on Science and Astronautics, July 29, 1968 http://ufologie.patrickgross.org/books/mcdonaldhcsa68meteorologists.htm

6. Suzy Goodsell, "The Daddy of the Balloon Industry, A Taste of General Mills", August 4, 2011 http://blog.generalmills.com/2011/08/the-daddy-of-the-balloon-industry/

7. The only true secret of the Mogul project was its sound wave detection mission, in that regard the fact that sound detectors, including "sonobouys" were being carried aloft by the balloons could have raised certain questions. The sonobouys were designed for Navy anti-submarine warfare use, as floating acoustic detection devices. The bouys were designed to float on the surface of the ocean, remaining in radio communication with ships or airplanes in order to relay signals from hydrophones underneath the water. Coming across a sonobouy out in the New Mexico desert would have been unusual, to say the least.

8. Jim Eckles, *Pocketful of Rockets; Histories and Stories Behind the White Sands Missile Range*, Fiddlebike Partnership, Las Cruces, New Mexico, 2013, 438

9. Jeffery Richelson, *Spying on the Bomb*, W.W. Norton and Company, 2006, 82-84

10. "List of UFO Sightings by Mogul and Skyhook Balloon Personnel" http://roswellproof.homestead.com/balloon_ufo_sightings.html

11. Dr. James McDonald; incident originally reported in *The New York Times*, April, 12, 1952, 13

12. "Cosmic Curiosity Incident", *Naval History Magazine Reports*, August, 1952 posted by Mike Christman, September 22, 2004 http://www.ufoupdateslist.com/2004/sep/m22-022.shtml

13. Edward J. Ruppelt, *The Report on Unidentified Flying Objects*, Doubleday and Company Inc., New York, 71

Chapter 18

Parties Unknown?

In this chapter

- An extension of the reconnaissance indications study from 1946 to 1968, covering three eras in the evolution of American atomic warfare capability.

- The dramatic drop in UFO reports from atomic materials facilities.

- The "spooking" of aircraft as an indication of possible testing of the rapidly expanding continental air defense network.

- Incidents suggesting that UFOs proactively mimicked American radar transmissions including both surveillance radar emissions and elements of military aircraft identification transponder codes.

- A new trend, involving an increasing number of extended sightings from ICBM missile installations.

- A new type of UFO incident, involving low level intrusions into atomic weapons storage areas at SAC air bases and SAC underground missile wing silos.

- Indications that UFOs may have demonstrated an ability to actually interfere with military aircraft electrical and communications systems as well as with SAC ICBM missiles.

At the risk of being repetitive, it's important to register a reminder that indications intelligence is based in action lists and in the ongoing collection and comparison of observations over time. The good news is that collections of data do not go out of date, for comparison purposes they actually improve. Strategic analysis Cynthia Grabo noted that a base of knowledge involved in good indications work is "the product of years of painstaking collection".[1] Lots of observations, chronologically developed over an extended period of time are the starting point.

For this next phase of our extended study – which will continue into through the 1960s – our actions list (reconnaissance, defense probing, ferreting) stays constant. On the other hand, the nation's strategic targets definitely changed as its atomic warfighting capabilities evolved over some three decades.

Roughly speaking, and with a good deal of generalization, it's possible to lay out four major "eras" which describe that evolution. We have already dealt with the first era, the period in which the U.S. established itself not just as an atomic power but determined to cope with the huge Soviet bloc manpower advantage by committing itself to atomic warfighting and nuclear deterrence. For shorthand purposes we will refer to those years as the "Going Atomic" era.

During that period, which extended from 1946 to 1952, there were initially a very limited number of operational atomic bombs - certainly nothing like a real American atomic weapons stockpile. The strategic bombing force which would come to be called SAC had to be built, trained and proven. SAC began as a conventional strategic bombing force, it took time to turn it into an atomic warfighting machine. And there was no continental air defense. American skies were open, even the most strategic atomic plants and bases had little to no air defense. In short, it was all a work in progress and beginning in 1950 the Korea war diverted both SAC and the resources needed to build a true continental air defense. In terms of military "signature", as viewed from the outside, the most obvious aspect of what was going on in regard to America's strategic atomic capability during the period was construction, lots and lots of construction.

In examining the Going Atomic era years in the previous chapter we isolated patterns of UFO incidents from the radioactive materials manufacturing facilities - at Hanford and especially Oakridge - which appeared to be largely independent of national trends in UFO reports. Not only were the spikes in sightings and the nature of the reports anomalous but the numbers were also considerably in excess of UFO reports coming from the nation's major conventional military installations. The same can be said for the atomic weapons assembly areas and storage areas – first at Los Alamos, then Sandia Base/Manzano and Killeen Base. What we lack is sufficient report data to see if anything similar occurred as the additional Q site storage areas began to receive actual atomic weapons.

The next era, and the time frame in which we will resume our study, might best be described as "Bomb Building and Bombers". It revolved around building what can only be described as huge atomic weapons stockpiles, ranging from hydrogen fusion bombs for SAC bombers to small tactical atomic cannon shells and mines for the Army. That era, extending from 1952 through 1961 involved a dramatic increase in atomic materials production and bomb assembly. SAC also came of age during the era, evolving into a force of some 57 bomber squadrons and 60 tanker squadrons by 1961.

For both operational and deterrence purposes, SAC routinely made itself highly visible, flying very large simulated combat missions such as Power House and Road Block in 1956. Those exercises involved over one thousand bombers and tankers flying over the United States and into the Arctic. Beyond that SAC conducted a huge number of bomber and tanker flights for training and the eventual deployment of an airborne alert capability (flying some 6,000 sorties during 1959 and 1960). Beginning in 1960 SAC began a series of nuclear armed alert flights – Chrome Dome missions - to distant holding areas in both the Arctic and over the Mediterranean Sea. Those flights placed fully armed bombers at positive control points from which they could be commanded to continue on nuclear strikes into the Soviet Union.[2] During this second era, the nation's atomic visible warfighting capability lay largely in the activities and bases of the Strategic Air Command.

The Bomb Building and Bombers era was also one of massive growth in the continental air defense, including the construction of large numbers of interceptor bases, gun emplacements, anti-aircraft missile batteries, and extensive surveillance radar networks. Continental air defense reached its peak during the years of 1959-1962 when Soviet bomber attacks were still considered to be an existential threat to the United States. During 1959 alone the Air Defense Command fielded 56 interceptor squadrons. When those units were consolidated under NORAD in 1960, the total force grew to some 67 interceptor squadrons, 3 Skysweeper antiaircraft gun batteries, 2 Bomarc anti-aircraft missile batteries and 257 Nike anti-aircraft missile batteries. In addition, some 108 Air Force squadrons were available and categorized as "augmentation forces".[3] At that point the Canadian border "northern tier" and coastal surveillance radar "fences" were also in place and in the Arctic, the Distant Early Warning Line (DEW line) was operational.

With that high level picture of the nation's military activity into the 1960s as context, we can return to a chronological review of our base of UFO reports. Certain types of observations that were occurring in 1952 continued directly into 1953 and onwards – but with nothing like the spikes in numbers seen during the earlier years. The atomic materials production plants continued to produce a small number of reports, but in most instances those incidents began to involve air defense actions, attempted interceptions and some sort of evasive action by the UFOs.

On June 21, 1952 a Skywatch observer at Oak Ridge spotted a slow moving object approaching the facility. That observation was relayed to ground control intercept radar, which in turn acquired a target - only to lose tracking on it. An F-47 on combat patrol was directed towards the area and made a visual sighting. Upon closing, the fighter and the target (a light) maneuvered around each other, with the unknown making what appeared to be repeated ramming approaches towards the interceptor before leaving the area.

On March 5, 1953 at the new Savannah River atomic materials plant, an observer informed a ground radar warning unit of a silver crescent shaped object at very high altitude over the facility. Radar did pick up a plot and an F-51 was vectored towards it, only to have the plot fade. Around two hours later another radar site picked up a UFO and an F-80 was scrambled towards it. At that point the target reversed direction and went into a series of course changes. Its average speed was relatively slow, around 200 miles per hour and it was at moderate altitude, estimated at 20,000 feet. No intercept was accomplished.

On July 16, 1953, in mid-afternoon, another incident occurred at Oak Ridge, involving an interesting account of what appears to have been "hide and seek" maneuvering by the UFO. Two civilians had their attention drawn to an F-86 interceptor circling at low altitude, as low as 3,000 feet. The plane continued it's circling for ten to fifteen minutes, enough time to be observed through binoculars, only to eventually fly off towards Knoxville. As the interceptor departed, the observers watched a black, cigar shaped object emerge from a cloud in the area where the fighter had been circling. The object moved at high speed and began its own circling maneuver, continuing that for an estimated five minutes. This incident is not listed in the *BLUE BOOK* reports but researchers did find confirmation in Army documents.[4]

Two reports from Oak Ridge and one from Savannah River in 1953 - that was it as far as the atomic materials manufacturing plants were concerned. That same minimal level of activity continued into 1954, but with a dramatic radar incident over the Savannah River AEC restricted area.[5] On February 15, 1954 Dobbins AFB radar monitoring the Savannah River air space tracked a large, conventional speed target passing to the north of the facility. The target then altered course and accelerated to a speed between 700 and 1,000 miles per hour, with a flight path directly over the restricted area. Due to the airspace violation, an alert was issued. Pope AFB radar also tracked an object violating the AEC restricted area and notified Dobbins. The object made additional course changes, slowed and then accelerated to a speed over 1,000 miles an hour as it left AEC restricted air space. Once again slowing, to 600 miles per hour, it proceeded to change headings a number of times before accelerating to a speed above 1,000 miles per hour and finally fading off radar. It appears no interception was attempted – with speeds and maneuvers such as those reported it certainly would have been fruitless.

In the fall of 1954, during the period of October 1 through November 20, a number of security guards at Killeen Base in Texas reported observing oval, glowing objects passing over the facility at night. The objects traveled in level flight, frequently changed direction and exhibited what appeared to be ninety degree turns at very high speed. The file document mentions no special defensive measures being taken, much less efforts to intercept the objects being sighted. There is much less information available during this two month surge at Killeen than in previous sightings but the incident reports did make it to the *BLUE BOOK* files.[6]

Following the Killeen base incidents of fall 1954, it would be three years before sightings once again began to be reported from atomic plant facilities. While it is true that overall sightings of UFOs tailed off dramatically following 1952, there were still substantial numbers reported nationally during those years, ranging from around 600 to 800 *BLUE BOOK* reports per year.[7]

Compared to a significant, ongoing level of sightings from around the country, this absolute and abrupt drop off in reports from atomic materials facilities appears as anomalous as do their previous dramatic spikes in numbers of sightings. There is no obvious correlation between the numbers and trends in reports from nuclear facilities and national media coverage of UFOs or national waves in UFO sightings. The only constant to be noted in reports from the atomic materials facilities is the ongoing failure of their air defense to do anything beyond tracking apparent intrusions.

Another trend first noted during 1951 and 1952 – the "spooking" of aircraft – also continued, providing an indication that parties unknown might not just monitoring but actually testing the effectiveness of the evolving air defense. On October 30, 1953 a pilot and observer in a C-45 flying out of Norton AFB in California had a daylight encounter with an object which passed underneath their aircraft at moderate speed and moved directly into their path; it continued in a vertical climb until out of sight with the whole incident taking some seven minutes. The following year, on March 25 a fighter pilot flying tail end position in a three jet group experienced just the opposite type of approach in another afternoon encounter. Flying at approximately 26,000 feet he observed a ball shaped object descend on an apparent collision course with him. He took evasive action and radioed the other two pilots but while doing so he saw the object apparently come to a stop directly above him. He turned towards it but it then accelerated away and disappeared at very high speed. The pilots ahead of him missed the entire encounter.

Two months later, on May 18, 1954 a Marine fighter out of El Toro, California experienced an early afternoon encounter with a delta shaped object which approached in a head on collision course with his wingman. Before he could radio a warning it had passed between them, descending to their rear. In June, on the 23rd, 1954 an Air National Guard pilot out of Columbus, Ohio saw a round, white unknown approach his fighter from behind, flying a bit above him. The report of the incident is vague but suggests he acquired it with airborne radar and that it was tracked from the ground as it maneuvered away from efforts to engage, finally accelerating away from him.

There seems to be no obvious geographic distribution to these sorts of encounters, they literally occurred all across the continental United States beginning in 1951 and continuing in diminishing total numbers from 1953-1955. On Jan 1, 1955 a B-25 instructor and student pilot flying over New Mexico were simply paced by a disc shaped object while in flight. In July of the same year, another B-25 instructor, a student pilot, and other crew members flying out of Miami, observed an unknown object above and to their right while over Alabama. The object moved to a lower altitude and the pilot moved to pursue. The object led the B-25 downwards, itself moving almost at ground level. At that point the airplane crew observed the object leaving wind like vortex trails of dust as it moved over fields. The object left the B-25, with a maximum speed of only 300 miles per hour, behind and simply moved out and away from it. The entire incident took an estimated eleven minutes.

Nothing in those incidents was totally new but it certainly appeared that very real, physical objects were involved and that they were truly unknowns, demonstrating capabilities far in advance of the contemporary air defense and out flying the interceptors available at the time. But things were about to change. The nation experienced another general wave of UFO reports in 1957, the equivalent in total reports of 1952, and from that year on a new trend began to develop – based around an increasing number of observations from operational atomic warfare bases, most particularly sites were atomic weapons were either stored or in the process of being deployed.

From 1951 through 1955 the AEC had dramatically grown the nation's atomic materials and weapons assembly infrastructure. Construction and expansion included the addition of the new Savana River materials complex in South Carolina, the Rocky Flats works in Colorado, the Pantex assembly plant outside Amarillo, Texas and the addition of a radioactive fuel rod manufacturing facility in Ohio.[8] It was that dramatic AEC expansion of its production facilities which grew the nation's atomic inventory from 13 unassembled weapons in 1947 to 1,169 by 1953 - and would extend that to a stockpile of 22,229 by 1961.[9]

By the end of the 1950s the majority of the nation's strategic nuclear weapons (megaton class bombs and warheads) had been built. At that time the main American targets of strategic importance moved from being the radioactive materials production and bomb assembly facilities to the actual locations where the hydrogen fusion bombs/and warheads were being deployed – the locations of the delivery systems which were to carry them to war.

In 1956 SAC went to sustained alert at selected air bases and began to proceed with plans for dispersing bombers to 55 bases by the end of that year.[10] Ultimately atomic weapons storage/Q sites were expanded to include installations at Loring AFB, Maine; Ellsworth AFB, South Dakota; Fairchild AFB, Washington State; Travis AFB, California, and Westover AFB, Massachusetts. SAC gained full control over the Q Sites (which had initially been planned and developed by Sandia Laboratories) in 1962.[11] Towards the end of the 1950s, the appearance of Soviet intercontinental ballistic missiles as a new threat led to a focus on SAC bomber readiness at northern tier bases, specifically those bases with the shortest flying times to targets inside Russia.

In addition, work began on a huge construction program of building ICBM launch complexes, involving both underground missile silos and control centers. Three Atlas ICBM squadrons began to be organized in 1958, by 1959 two would be receiving missiles, and by 1960 seven squadrons were being activated. The early Atlas and Titan ICBM sites were located adjacent to existing SAC air bases: Francis E. Warren AFB in Wyoming, Lowery AFB in Colorado, Offutt AFB in Nebraska, Ellsworth AFB in Wyoming and Fairchild AFB in Washington State.

However, while missile silos were being built, weapons areas prepared and personnel trained, SAC remained very much bomber oriented. SAC's massive bomber force was on display in huge December 1956 airborne exercises. The Power House and Road Block exercises involved some 1,000 bombers and tankers flying simulated combat missions across the United States and on into the Arctic. At that point in time it might have looked very much as if SAC were preparing to go to war – to some extent that was true. SAC's guiding principles, established by General Curtis LeMay, required that the command consider itself to be in a state of virtual warfare, waiting only for the emergency action message which would send it towards its pre-defined Communist bloc targets.

In regard to our extended study, the new trends which began to emerge during the period of 1956 to 1962 evolved most specifically around SAC bomber bases, developing missile complexes and atomic weapons storage areas. There were an increasingly limited number of sightings at AEC manufacturing plants, particularly the newer ones such as Savanah River – but with nothing from Hanford or Los Alamos. In contrast, during 1957 a new type of intrusion began to occur, with the first recorded instance of what would become a series of low altitude to ground level incidents associated with atomic weapons storage areas.

On November 4, 1957 air traffic controllers in the tower at Kirtland AFB first observed a white light traveling over the runway at low altitude and called for radar verification.[12] Radar confirmed the target and the object was observed to turn across a runway and rapidly descend. The controllers were watching it through binoculars and had an excellent view, at times looking down on it. They described it as automobile sized, egg shaped and displaying a single white light. It circled and began to descend almost as if it were approaching for a landing. The object's descent was tracked on approach control radar.

Instead of landing it moved across the Air Force flight line, runways and taxiways, heading towards the control tower at a very low speed of some twenty to thirty miles per hour. Descending even lower, still at very slow speed and demonstrating extreme maneuverability, the object disappeared behind a security fence at the perimeter of a floodlit high security area – an area used for atomic weapons storage. After hovering there for some twenty to thirty seconds, it moved slowly away, and then accelerated in a steep climb at very high speed.

The tower controllers were in communication with approach radar control and radar tracked the object as it traveled east away from the base, only to circle a radio range signal station before heading north and disappearing off radar at approximately ten miles distance. Later another unknown target was picked up, hovering north of the base before disappearing. Some twenty minutes after that incident, an Air Force C-46 took off from Kirtland towards the west and radar painted an unknown object some four miles south of the runway. The object accelerated towards the runway and made a hard turn to move into formation with the C-46, maintaining proximity for fourteen miles before turning again and moving back towards the runway, where it remained stationary before fading off the radar.

The total time of visual observations had been four to five minutes; the radar tracking had occurred over some twenty minutes. The official Air Force conclusion was that the object was unidentified at the time but could conceivably have been an airplane. In *BLUE BOOK* terminology, probable airplane - statistically tallied as "identified".

In the longer perspective of our study, the Kirtland AFB incident appears to been a leading indicator in what would become an ongoing series of similar incidents which would occur during following years – incidents involving very low level, very slow and highly maneuverable UFOs moving over security fences and approaching or overflying atomic weapons storage areas. As with Kirtland AFB in 1957, future incidents would also involve a striking lack of defensive actions against the intruding objects.

Some three days after the Kirtland/Sandia Base incident in Albuquerque, another low altitude intrusion was reported, at a new AEC weapons assembly facility. On November 7, 1957 several bright, flashing objects were observed hovering over the Pantex atomic assembly plant outside Amarillo, Texas. Private security personnel reported the objects to the Highway Patrol and a Highway Patrol officer was dispatched to the plant, also observing the lights. Security guards described three objects which had been "floating" over the plant for some time. The guards felt the objects had actually landed but when attempting to approach them, the lights would be turned off and they would simply slip away. The guards were positive they were seeing actual objects, not just lights. Exactly this same type of observation would be reported at SAC air bases and missile sites in following years, with the same unsuccessful security response as at Kirtland and the Pantex plant in 1957.

The next example of such an intrusion reportedly occurred some six months later, in May, 1958 at Malstrom AFB in Montana.[13] This incident was not reported to *BLUE BOOK*, however given its nature and the national security implications involved, that would be understandable. According to information collected at a much later date from a former base security guard, an unidentified object approached the base and hovered over the SAC alert aircraft hangar, adjacent to the atomic weapons storage facility. Upon leaving, the round, metallic object departed by flying over the runway and on to the municipal airport at Great Falls, once again hovering – over a National Guard interceptor parking ramp - before finally departing. Reportedly both base and airport radar tracked the object during that part of its flight.

While that report is not documented in the *BLUE BOOK* archives, it is fully consistent with another UFO incident at Malstrom AFB which is in the records, occurring only three months later.[14] On August 4, 1958 an Air Force security guard observed a delta shaped object flying directly over the base. It was relatively small, silver in appearance and had no visible means of propulsion. The object was tracked on approach control radar as it moved over the air base, but no interceptors were scrambled. According to the report no immediate notifications or alerts had been generated at the time of the incident, lending some support to the idea that the earlier May incident might either have not been reported at all or treated strictly as a classified operational incident.

In a continuation of what we referred to earlier as a pattern of "sampling" particular types of atomic warfare facilities, no similar SAC base intrusions are on file for 1957. That point is significant in and of itself given that nationally the year 1957 generated over eleven hundred UFO reports for *BLUE BOOK*, an even greater number than in 1952. Once again this suggests that it was the appearance of real objects, physical unknowns, which were being reported from atomic warfare complex sites - not waves of incidents driven by the popular media and the wave of reports from across the United States.

The extent to which sightings from the particular atomic warfare "targets" we are focusing on in this study are disconnected from the waves of public UFO reports and media coverage of UFOs appears to confirm that security and military personnel were not just replicating incidents which were appearing in the national press. That impression is reinforced by the fact that while national UFO reporting plummeting in 1958, we find the same number of atomic complex related incidents as in 1957.

And in 1958, the focus of such reports was definitely the new Air Force ICBM installations being built and prepared for activation. On September 7 and the following day, September 8, two of SAC's newest ICBM construction areas produced extended and highly credible reports of unknown aerial objects.

The Sept 7 sightings came from Ellsworth AFB in North Dakota.[15] During the incident there were visual sightings of unidentified lights and three separate radars began tracking what initially appeared to be simply an unidentified aircraft. Further tracking indicated two objects flying extremely close to each other. At that point the targets had begun to move up and down in altitude while rapidly traveling in a circular path northwest of the base. Two interceptors were scrambled during the incident, one was vectored by radar to within three miles of the target; at that point the target disappeared from the radar and the interceptor pilot was unable to obtain a visual or to engage. The second fighter was directed into the target track three times without spotting anything, although there is a suggestion that one fighter did pick up a very low altitude radar return during the attempted intercepts.

The following day, at Offutt, Nebraska (home to another of the early ICBM installations), several SAC officers, as well as a number of airman and personnel at the base traffic control tower, observed a brilliant white, cylindrical object hovering west of the base. The cylinder was stationary and tilted in respect to the horizon. After some minutes the object became sharper in outline and a swarm of "black specks" were observed to be moving around the lower end of the cylinder, then appearing to move inside it. The cylinder then began to drop its tilt until it was stationary and level. At that time it began to decrease in apparent size until it faded out of sight in the west. During the observation the sky was totally cloudless with only minimal haze on the horizon. The entire incident involved some 25 personnel and occurred over just short of half an hour. This is incident was documented in a report which makes reference to Air Technical Intelligence but it does not appear in the *BLUE BOOK* files.

In company with what appears to be a shift in interest from radioactive materials production facilities to actual atomic weapons deployment at SAC storage areas and at ICBM sites under development, there continued to be ongoing encounters between unknowns and Air Force interceptors. The only notable change in those encounters had to do with the types of aircraft involved, not the behaviors of the UFOs being reported. The new generation of Century (F-100 series) jets were going operational, capable of supersonic speeds and carrying radar and infrared homing missiles. During 1957-1958 Century series fighters such as the F-101 and F-106 also began to carry Genie air to air rockets with atomic warheads. The Genie warheads had an explosive power of 1.5 kilotons, comparable to the bombs dropped on Japan during World War II.

On June 9. 1958 an F-102 flying out of McChord AFB, was operating at an altitude of 40,000 – 50,000 feet near Tacoma, Washington. The jet's pilot observed an unidentified cylindrical object which approached the F-102 at high speed - the pilot banked the jet to follow it. At that point the cylinder first climbed and then decelerated and turned to circle the jet three times while moving closer. The cylinder then pitched up and accelerated in a climb which quickly carried it out of sight. That encounter would become one of a number suggesting that the Century series interceptors were going to fare no better in terms of actually engaging the unknowns than their predecessors.

In addition to the new Air Defense Command interceptors and weapons which became operational towards the end of the 1950s, SAC was also conducting an extended series of operational missions. Some 6,000 bomber and tanker sorties were flown during 1958/59, testing SAC's ability to maintain a constantly airborne alert bomber force.[16] The first phase of that project, designated as Head Start, flew missions out of Loring AFB in Maine, across northern tier states and though Canada.

On March 25, 1959 a B-52 bomber operating on a Headstart II flight was flying towards the Canadian border when it made radar contact with an unknown object; the object appeared to be emitting its own radar frequencies, directed towards the bomber. The frequencies were identified and monitored by the aircraft's electronic warfare officer. The object itself was tracked on the B-52 radar for approximately an hour, closing to distances of from eight thousand to fifteen thousand yards from the aircraft.[17]

The B-52 notified air defense command and ground radar tracking was established on the target. At that point the UFO penetrated the northern air defense zone and an F-89 interceptor was scrambled. The fighter crew intercepted and made visual and fire control radar contact with the target, describing it as delta shaped. After closing to an estimated four miles radar tracked the object reversing its course, increase speed and moving away. The interceptor gave chase but the unknown easily outdistanced it and climbed away. Air defense reports refer to the incident as representing a new type of threat to the continental United States.

There may have been good reason for the Air Force to have especially threat sensitive in the spring of 1959. Only a few weeks later, on May 2, 1959 at 8:23 in the morning, five radar tracks were detected coming inbound from the Atlantic and towards Pease AFB in New Hampshire, minutes later additional tracks appeared.[18] Eventually 18 radar tracks were being monitored by three different radars including one Texas Tower radar installation in the Atlantic. An attack seemed to be in progress and all available fighter aircraft were scrambled, from Pease and other defense sector fields. SAC bombers were brought to alert, including planes at Stewart AFB, Westover AFB and Otis AFB.

Reportedly air defense artillery sites also tracked a number of unidentified objects in the area. Ultimately several of the tracks reversed course and headed outwards, back over the Atlantic, while others simply faded out as their tracks were projected inland (no mention is made of the possibility that they might have simply dropped below radar detection and then reversed course). The entire incident appeared to be a well-organized and coherent attack on SAC, however no intercepts were made and in the end the whole matter was filed as an occurrence of unexplained radar phenomena.

The early 1960s saw the next major evolution in the American military complex – the move into an era of intercontinental ballistic missiles. The Missile Era involved a shift from waging war with atomic bombers and defending against surprise Soviet long range bomber attack to a focus on warfighting with missiles, both intermediate and intercontinental range ballistic missiles. The years 1960 – 1962 were a time of transition, with nuclear warhead Atlas and Titan ICBMs (carrying hydrogen warheads in the megaton plus range) being deployed and going operational at SAC installations. The massive American ICBM construction program helped speed the transition from bombers to missiles. By the fall of 1962 there were 204 Atlas and Titan missiles deployed and operational in underground silos, beyond that American nuclear submarines were on sea patrol, with 32 operational Polaris ICBMs.

During that same period, a host of new surveillance radar systems were going into place to scan for incoming missile attacks. The first Ballistic Missile "over the horizon" surveillance radar became operational in Greenland during November 1960 (BEMEWS/Ballistic Missile Early Warning System) and the new Space Detection and Warning System (SPADATS) was placed under the control of CONAD, the continental air defense command. SPADATS included a number of search and detection tools from different sources - including the Navy's space surveillance radar fence (stretching across the continent), a computerized object cataloging system, and optical tracking of space objects via Minitrack and NASA cameras – some 200 different sources of space related data would be fed into the new system.[19]

Still, the first years of the 1960s remained a time of both missiles and bombers. As early as 1956 CIA analysis of U-2 photography had shown that fears of a huge Soviet jet bomber force were simply untrue; there was no bomber gap. President Eisenhower was advised of the information but for security reasons determined not to reveal the news to the public. Doing so would have informed the Soviets of the extent of American knowledge of Soviet military capabilities and of American intelligence collections capability.[20] As a consequence of his security decision, the hugely expensive SAGE air defense system, conceived and largely built to deal with attacking jet bomber formations, continued to completion, going fully operational in 1962.

The continental defense command continued its focus on detecting and countering Soviet bombers. In fact the years 1960 – 1962 saw the largest and most visible air defense exercises ever to occur over the North American continent. Each year, as part of Operation Skyshield, American air space was totally closed – with all commercial air traffic grounded in both the United States and Canada. During the exercises American, Canadian and British bombers flew in simulated penetration attacks through American and Canadian air space, with all the resources of NORAD and the Continental Air Defense Command devoted to detecting and intercepting them. Some 1,800 NORAD fighters flew 6,000 sorties during Skyshield II in October, 1961 and 2,900 commercial flights were canceled or delayed.[21]

It is worth noting that despite the decades of diligent research into Air Force archives, there are few reports of encounters with highly anomalous "unknowns" during the major SAC simulated bombing exercises of the 1950's, the thousands of SAC airborne alert sorties or the huge Skyshield air defense exercises. The massive air defense exercises of 1960-1961 did not trigger major new waves of UFO sightings from either the public or within the atomic warfare complex. In fact during the years of the Skyshield exercises, unidentified reports in the *BLUE BOOK* files dropped to less than six hundred annually, less than half of the reports which went into the files during national wave of sightings in 1957 or a similar wave which would occur again in 1966.

There were, however, a series of military reports in 1957 that deserve particular attention. Those incidents appear to show highly anomalous UFO capabilities and suggest that UFOs were capable of "teasing" not only air defense command interceptors, but of conducting highly directed radar spoofing – demonstrating their ability to generate signals identical to both search radars and friend or foe radar transponders. One of the most significant incidents involved extended UFO contact with an individual SAC aircraft, on July 17, 1957.

In that instance, the SAC aircraft was not a bomber, but an RB-47, a very specialized electronics intelligence platform flying with a crew of ELINT and electronic countermeasures specialists. The aircraft had been on a training flight from Kansas over the Gulf of Mexico and was returning during the early morning hours. Its initial contact with an unknown aerial object was the detection of what appeared to be a ground based search radar beam, but one whose source was apparently in motion, actually crossing the plane's flight path. From that point on the encounter involved a series of apparent radar transmissions from a maneuvering aerial object – whose movements matched those of a brilliant light that tracked the plane - and with concurrent appearances of the UFO on the aircraft's own search radar.

At times the unknown source simply tracked the plane, at other times it apparently moved ahead of it and waited for the aircraft. The entire encounter occurred over a span of approximately two hours and some 800 miles distance. The various observations and correlations are far too detailed to pursue here but they remain one of the strongest technical cases for not only a technologically unknown object but one electronically engaging a military aircraft with standardized frequencies and patterns used by the American military. Readers are referred to a detailed study by Brad Sparks, his research involves the most comprehensive technical analysis of the encounter available. His work may be found in the second edition of The UFO Encyclopedia by Jerome Clark and is also available online courtesy of the Jerome Clark, Brad Sparks and NICAP.[22]

Given the documents research referenced in Sparks' study of the RB-47 encounter, we also know that this was not a totally unique experience for SAC reconnaissance aircraft. On five separate days in June, 1955, radar operators on RB-47s flying over northern Canada detected unknown objects at ranges between two and five miles from the aircraft. Apparent radar sweeps of the SAC planes by an airborne radar beam and/or attempted radar jamming of the SAC aircraft occurred in each incident. During a June 4 encounter the unknown was visually sighted and described as a metallic cylinder. On one occasion the unknown paced the RB-47 for some nine minutes, before breaking contact and departing at high speed.

The electronics aspect of the RB-47's July 17, 1957 encounter is especially intriguing considering two other incidents, one of which occurred the day before, and the other the day afterwards. On July 16 an air defense radar station outside Las Vegas tracked an extremely high speed target (estimated at 6,200 mph) for a very short time before it became stationary. The target then departed at a similar and possibly faster speed, until it disappeared beyond radar range. During the time in which it was acquired by the search radar, it appeared to respond to an encrypted military IFF (Identification Friend or Foe) transponder signal. In short, it was sent the signal from the air defense site and in turn sent back elements of an appropriate IFF response. A similar incident had been reported two days earlier by the same night crew at the radar site; nothing like that had happened at the site before or ever happened afterwards.

The day after the RB-47 incident, another radar station in Arizona tracked a stationary target at a distance of 82 miles and an altitude of 42,000 feet. Once again the target was interrogated with an IFF query and responded with an encrypted IFF Mode 3 response. At that point the target on the radarscope also appeared to "strobe" slightly, normally a sign of jamming.

Taken by themselves each of these incidents can be questioned – although no explanation for the full RB-47 experience of July 17 has been offered in rebuttal to Spark's most recent 1997 technical reinvestigation and study of the encounter. However in combination the July electronics incidents of 1957, occurring on consecutive days, become much more suggestive. Certainly they raise the possibility that unknown aerial objects displaying aerodynamic capabilities that exceeded the performance of any known aircraft also possessed extremely advanced electronics capability and were able to mimic at least portions American radar transmissions, even transmitting elements of military IFF codes. Such a possibility could well have generated a national security inquiry but to this date we have nothing beyond the *BLUE BOOK* files on each incident

At this point it should at least be mentioned that there is a category of sightings indirectly related to our focus which we lack the space to examine in this work. There were most definitely spikes and trends in the UFO sightings associated with the development of advanced jet and rocket aircraft at the Muroc test center (later Edwards AFB), during rocket and missile testing at Holloman AFB and the White Sands Test Range, and at both the Vandenberg and Cape Canaveral missile launch facilities. Military weapons, including delivery vehicles intended to carry atomic warheads, were tested at White Sands, at Vandenberg and at Cape Canaveral. Vandenberg was even activated as an early SAC ICBM site for a time. And there are highly credible reports of unknown objects which appeared to be not only observing but actually interacting with certain tests. Those reports are documented and available in the sources we have cited, an indications study devoted to those facilities would be of considerable interest but it is beyond the scope the intentionally tight focus of this study.

Also, as we move through the 1960s and beyond, a disclaimer is needed. Increasingly the reports of most relevance come from SAC air bases and missile installations. Given that those sites routinely housed megaton class atomic weapons and the systems which were used to deliver them, it appears that in certain instances operational security concerns prevented some UFO incidents from being submitted to ATIC and entering the *BLUE BOOK* files. That is no particular surprise as we previously reviewed a number of Joint Chief's directives and Air Force regulations which restricted reporting of potentially imminent security threats. And as we pass 1970 and the end of *BLUE BOOK*, matters become even more challenging since documents related to certain CIRVIS and OPREP-3 incidents might very well be withheld, even to requests under the Freedom of Information act.

Fortunately, a number of very diligent and experienced researchers have pursued the sorts of incidents which are directly related to this study. In some instances they have actually been able to obtain official documents, in other instances technical data and at a minimum extensive oral history information - often with corroboration from multiple individuals. Researchers exploring this particular area include Barry Greenwood, Lawrence Fawcett, Robert Hastings, Robert Salas, James Klotz, Thomas Tulian, and Kevin Randle – as well as Francis Ridge and all the individuals' contributing to the Nuclear Connections Project at the National Investigations Committee on Aerial Phenomena.[23]

One of the challenges for those researchers is that there are very real limits on access to official Air Force reports and documents. Oral history work dealing with observations made years earlier also poses a known challenge in regard to well-known memory and recall issues. Such information has to be approached cautiously. As we continue this study, when referencing information outside the *BLUE BOOK* archives we will make every effort to provide sources and cite the investigator's actual research. In some instances, for the sake of space - and given that each incident is only a single data point in this study - we will only discuss summary level information, directing the reader to the full body of the source's work.[24] With that said, we can return to our study and move forward though the 1960s and beyond.

As we move further into the Missile Era, actual observations become more complex given that SAC bases were often quite large, with a variety of internally restricted areas including specially secured weapons bunkers. In the case of SAC missile squadrons, each group of missile silos were spread out to minimize damage from incoming warheads and there were separate launch control centers. A typical facility with multiple wings could involve an area of several hundred square miles. Launch personnel were and are located underground, security and maintenance teams are mobile and reporting goes through a strict local chain of command from the missile squadron back to the SAC base command.

Researchers have sometimes been forced to rely on anecdotal information from individual Air Force personnel stationed at different locations, whenever possible confirmed by security reports or similar secondary sources. Given the distances and security involved, individual observations become challenging to map to certain extended incidents – some of which occurred over several hours at multiple locations.

One of the earliest missile site incidents, from August 7, 1962 involved Titan missile sites still being prepared for activation, with missiles not yet emplaced. On that date, personnel at a Titan ICBM complex in Arizona (associated with the Davis-Monthan SAC base) observed a brilliant light descending and becoming stationary over the site. At that point the light was large enough to frighten the men, who went into the silo and notified base command. Reportedly SAC fighters were sent to investigate but as they approached the object took off and rapidly moved out of sight before the actual arrival of the aircraft. The jets loitered over the site for a bit, then returned to their base and upon their departure the UFO immediately returned. It once again descended towards the silo - only to take off vertically and disappear overhead.[25]

That report is quite similar to another from a new Atlas ICBM installation, in Oklahoma. Once again, after midnight, on May 24, 1964, a large bright light moved to a stationary position directly over a missile silo. Observed first by a security guard and later by maintenance personnel the object had first appeared hovering over the security fence on the south site of the site, The UFO remained over the silo area for some eight to ten minutes. The incident was reported to command at Altus AFB and upwards to the SAC command post.[26]

Sightings at missile sites under construction and being activated, with atomic war heads installed, continued throughout the 1960s and beyond. And as the sightings continued a new pattern emerged, new for the missile sites but in some ways reminiscent of the early years at Killian Base Site B in Texas and at Manzano Site A outside Albuquerque.

While this new - SAC focused - pattern of UFO reports was developing, another type of UFO incident seems to have been fading away. As previously noted, beginning around 1951 and increasingly though the 1950s there are numerous incidents of "spooking", the appearance of UFOs appearing to engage individual military aircraft in combat-like maneuvers. The aircraft were approached, circled, and at times engaged with head on passes and high speed maneuvering which placed the UFOs behind or above them (classic attack positions).

Such incidents increasingly occurred with interceptors which were trying to close with and identify UFOs. The UFOs were consistently able to out maneuver or outrun even the most advanced interceptors of the period. Yet by the mid-1960s we find fewer and fewer reports of that nature, a trend which continued though the end of the *BLUE BOOK* reporting period. Encounters between UFOs and with military aircraft continued to occur but they seem to have become a bit more passive and a good deal less threatening.

An example would be encounter by an Air Force KC-135 tanker aircraft in 1965. On October 14, 1965 the pilot of a tanker flying out of Sawyer AFB in Michigan reported a sharply outlined light in the west at around 7:50 in the evening. The light was seen to move over a period of several minutes, able to rapidly accelerate at will. The KC-135 was given permission to descend in altitude and investigate. At that time the light simply began to climb and accelerate away from the jet tanker; the crew reported that its speed exceeded that of any known aircraft. All in all a rather familiar type of non-threatening encounter.

Sightings of UFOs by private and commercial pilots also continued but when we pass 1970 we largely run out of military data. Fortunately NARCAP maintains a listing of aircraft encounters and is actively engaged in research and technical study of them. A scan of their listings appears to suggest that private and commercial sightings not only continued but still remain relatively common in the 21st Century.[27] The real question is whether interceptor/unknown incidents continued to occur in any numbers. The Air Force does still maintain a limited interceptor force and scrambles do still occur over certain restricted areas. Unfortunately it has become almost impossible to effectively track contemporary trends in military aircraft/UFO encounters.

Sightings by personnel at military bases continued during the 1960s, but they also decreased in number and the actual incidents became reminiscent of the earliest years of UFO reports. As an example, on July 28, 1965 an Air Force major, rated as a command pilot, and his wife observed a "manta ray" shaped object pass over Carswell AFB in Texas (a SAC bomber base) at very low altitude, under 1,000 feet. The object was quite close, the description was detailed and the craft was some 40 feet long, with pulsating white lights. The sighting was within controlled airspace, verified by other observers and confirmed by traffic control radar – which was unable to identify the object. While we have seen numerous other examples of similar UFO passes over restricted areas, the language in the Air Force report of the incident is striking, "This sighting was a positive observation, under ideal circumstances, of a definite object of an unconventional nature – possibly of foreign origin, which could be a threat to national security."[28]

Strong language – but language that might well have been increasingly applied to an entire series of incidents which began to occur around SAC's long range bomber and ICBM atomic warfighting assets. Those incidents will be our next focus, all of them could have been taken to represent immediate operational security concerns, and in total warnings intelligence analysts could well have taken them as indications of a very real and imminent threat to the nation's security.

As the 1960s progressed, individual sightings of unknown lights in the vicinity of ICBM installations – and radar confirmation of actual unknown objects – appeared to simply be a continuation of the incidents from the earliest years of Atlas, Titan and Minuteman deployments. An example would be an incident of August 11-12, 1965 at Whiteman AFB, one of the first ICBM sites built for deployment of the advanced, solid fuel Minuteman missiles. Whiteman was being built to have 15 launch control centers and 150 missile silos and on that date it produced what almost seems to be a familiar report. That August evening personnel at Base Operations and the Air Force control tower reported an ongoing series of UFOs. Fast moving lights repeatedly passed over the missile sites during a four to five hour period. One object appeared to point a spotlight at the ground; it was tracked on weather radar and height finder radar and determined to be at a height at 5,000 feet. No record of any attempt to intercept the objects was noted but the incident was reported to NORAD and ultimately found its way to ATIC.[29]

That was not the only incident involving Minuteman missiles that August. During the following two weeks unknown lights were reported in the area of and over the Minot AFB Minuteman missile complex. In the first instance, on August 16, two individuals including a Missile Maintenance Analysis Specialist, observed a football shaped light at low altitude for some twelve minutes.[30] Just over a week later, on August 24, a major sighting involving Minot security personnel, radar confirmation and the dispatch of a security strike team occurred – with radio interference report by the strike team sent to investigate reports of an object hovering at ground level.[31] This incident was investigated in considerable detail by Ray Fowler, with a follow up by Dr. Hynek; it does appear in Air Force documents – but only to a limited extent. The challenges encountered by Fowler and even Hynek in researching such an extended sighting illustrate the difficulties in obtaining information about incidents involving missile sites and SAC weapons storage areas.[32]

Beginning in 1966 we begin to find an ongoing and consistent body of similar observations, with commonalities in the observations and which seem to validate their reality – and their significance. The following year, over three weeks in March, 1967 something similar but even more concerning appears to have occurred around a series of Minuteman silos at the Malmstrom AFB complex in North Dakota. Those experiences are examined in great detail in *Faded Giant; the 1967 Missile/UFO Incidents* by Robert Salas (Salas himself worked for a time at Sylvania, for their Minuteman Program Office) and James Klotz. Other researchers including Raymond Fowler and Robert Hastings have investigated the 1966/Minot incident in great detail; the following synopsis is derived from their work and writings as well as a review and critique by Kevin Randle.[33]

The Malmstrom experience involved multiple locations, multiple witnesses, Minuteman security teams, documented military communications and reports, UFO reports from civilian witnesses in the general area (during the period of February through April, 1967) and most dramatically one confirmed incident of a full wing of Minuteman missiles going off line – along with numerous internally corroborated statements from Minot personnel that another wing of missiles had also gone offline during the same time frame.

Civilians who contacted Malmstrom Air Force Base with their own local sightings during that period were simply told that the Air Force no longer took UFO reports. As we have seen, that might be construed to be true in a fashion, reports relating to unidentified aircraft or missiles required a military response but anomalous UFOs not viewed as an air defense or imminent security issue were another matter.

What is absolutely documented in regard to the March experiences at Malmstrom is that at least one wing of missiles did go off line and was the subject of an extensive technical inquiry and report – "Report of Engineering Investigation of Echo Flight Incident, Malmstrom, Mont - 16 Mar 1967." In addition, the Air Force did investigate several reports of UFO sightings in conjunction with the outage, dealing with them officially by stating that none could be "proven". That is a far different story than was told by a number of Air Force personnel who were interviewed separately by Robert Salas and Robert Hastings. Those individuals described their personal sightings of bright lights hovering directly over missile silos, of confirmation sightings by security teams dispatched to investigate and of two incidents of missile wing outages, not the single off line experience noted in the 16 March, 1967 technical study.

All of which leads us to the possibility of one and perhaps two ICBM wing events, exposed only by the existence of a contractor technical study of one wing failure and a separate UFO incident on April 24 which forced the Air Force to respond to Highway Patrol reports and local newspaper coverage.

The April 24 incident involved a day light civilian sighting, Highway Patrol involvement and an investigation of a UFO at ground level, resulting in the dispatch of an Air Force helicopter. Newspaper articles described FAA radar tracking of a UFO and a visual confirmation from an Airman at Malmstrom – neither of which was mentioned in follow-on Air Force reports. Air Force documents do indicate that there were public relations concerns and note that no statement was to be issued other than that the possible landing of a UFO would be investigated.

The reports of unknown lights over and around the Malmstrom silo areas are consistent with incidents reported from Atlas, Titan and other Minuteman sites. However, the possibility that the presence of UFOs might be connected to complete wings of ICBMs going offline takes matters a bit further. If there was a connection it would indicate not just a passive assessment of American nuclear capability, but something beyond even the various radar/electronics contacts with SAC reconnaissance and bomber aircraft. It would have demonstrated an ability to actually interfere with the nation's most strategic military weapons systems.

Aside from that particular concern, it seems hard to deny that unknown objects were actually "probing" American ICBM missile facilities and individual missile wing silos – and doing so repeatedly over a span of several years. A very concrete example of that continuing activity comes over a year later from the Minuteman missile wings deployed around Minot AFB in North Dakota. Researchers have been able to recover extensive documentation relating to that incident, up to this point they have located and shared something on the order of 200 pages – with that date there is virtually no doubt as to multiple visual and radar observations of a UFO over the SAC facilities.

A great deal of the incident documentation has been made available by Daniel Wilson and by NICAP. It is available on the NICAP website, which also includes independent remarks and studies of the incident by Dr. Allen Hynek, Kevin Randle, Richard Haines, and Thomas Tulian. Thomas Tulian's detailed and illustrated study of the incident is particularly useful in following the multiple parties and observations involved. In addition to exploring the incident itself, Kevin Randle provides key insights into how *BLUE BOOK* responded to the incident and ultimately managed to produce an "identification".[34]

In a pattern consistent with virtually all the missile site incidents, the Minot sightings were made at night, usually after midnight, reducing the chances for any detailed visual descriptions. In this instance the observations began with a UFO sighting by a missile crew maintenance man driving near the

Minuteman complex. That individual observed a very large, bright orange/yellow light hovering in the vicinity of the missile silos. Some two hours later two other Air Force personnel independently sighted bright lights in the area. Those sightings were followed by a series of observations from maintenance personnel within the missile flight area. Maintenance team members all described a very large, bright, reddish orange light. At one point what appeared to be an actual physical object moved overhead one of the teams.

Maintenance team members continued to observe the bright UFO, which was described by some as being very large, comparable to the visual diameter of the sun - a security team was then dispatched to the area. The security team approached to within half a mile of a light and observed it to be either hovering at ground level or having actually landed. For some 45 minutes other personnel around the missile complex also observed the light, all placing it at the same location and giving similar descriptions.

Independently of events on the ground, a SAC B-52 was airborne and approaching Minot, having been engaged in earlier penetration exercises against the Minuteman complex. Upon completion of that exercise it was returning in a landing approach to the air base. Approach control advised the aircraft of a UFO being tracked on radar and the aircraft independently observed a very high speed UFO/light, which moved across its flight path to take a position an estimated mile and a half off its wing. The subsequent SAC investigation report described the air crew as stating that the UFO had "traveled approximately 2-1/2 miles in 3 sec or about 3,000 mi/hr." to position itself by the aircraft. The radar return remained off the aircraft's left wing for approximately 20 miles at which point it broke off. Radar scope photographs were taken. When the target was close to the B-52 neither of the two (radio) transmitters in the B-52 would operate properly – but when the UFO broke away the radios "returned to normal function."

Minot AFB tower was in contact with the aircraft during its approach and directed the B-52's pilot to look towards the location of the "ground light" being described by maintenance and security teams. The pilot confirmed seeing an orange light in the indicated location and was advised that ground weather radar was picking up a target at that location as well. At that point the pilot lost radio transmission and could not establish voice communication with the tower. He could hear them but not send; in response the tower requested an identification / IFF "squawk" from the aircraft, apparently to confirm its location on their radar. After a few minutes the plane's transmitter once again began to work and the pilot confirmed their earlier sighting of the UFO/light being reported by the ground personnel - as well as its position in regard to the aircraft. At that point the plane had no visual or airborne radar contact with the UFO and the personnel on the ground also had lost visual contact.

The follow up SAC investigation, directed out of 15th Air Force Headquarters, produced its own report, independently of the later *BLUE BOOK* inquiry (*BLUE BOOK* failed to even send an investigator to Minot and seems to have exhibited no particular interest in the incident). One of the most significant points made in the SAC investigation was not noted in the *BLUE BOOK* case file at all – that being the point of a series of physical security violations which had occurred along with the UFO sighting. The Air Force headquarters report stated that: "'Fourteen other people in separate locations also reported sighting a similar object. Also, at this approximate time, the security alarm for one of the sites was activated. This was an alarm for both the outer and inner ring. When guards arrived at the scene they found that the outer door was open and the combination lock on the inner door had been removed."[35]

The follow-on SAC investigation revealed the apparent physical penetration of both inner and outer ring security gates, activation of security alarms at both the outer and inner security rings, the compromise of the one door lock and the actual removal of the inner security door lock. Obviously there had been a serious physical security breach at the site and something much more serious than mysterious lights and UFO sightings was involved. Unfortunately the documents now in hand do not shed any further light on the site penetration. This leaves us with no proven connection between the physical security violations and the UFO sightings, although the hovering or landed object was described in close proximity to the area of the gate breaches. Without knowing whether or not SAC resolved the security issue in further investigations the question remains open. It does however raise the possibility of physical violation of the launch facility for a nuclear armed ICBM and should have been treated as a national security level concern.

At this point, our extended indications study has taken us from 1952 through 1968, focusing on sightings, reports and incidents which would support the tentative hypothesis/scenario that unknown parties were utilizing technologically advanced aerial devices to conduct a long term assessment of American military capabilities – and not just military capabilities in general but specifically the nation's atomic warfighting potential. In doing so we have noted changes in the types of reports, patterns in sightings and certain trends which developed (and ended) during the different eras of the nation's establishment of itself as the dominant nuclear force on the planet.

By the early 1970s the period of strategic American nuclear dominance was ending, with the Soviet Union fielding an ICBM force not only comparable size but one actually greater in number, supported by a larger atomic weapons stockpile than that possessed by the United States. And at the point in time that the total planetary atomic arsenals peaked, the UFO sightings at SAC atomic weapons storage also spiked.

Ultimately, during 1975, a series of UFO incidents - which came to be referred to as the Northern Tier wave – created what could have been viewed as a potential national security crisis. The incidents of that period were so extensive that is seems necessary to extend our hypothesis one step further. In the following chapter we will examine the possibility that the UFO activities focused on SAC installations had reached the point where they might be interpreted to represent some form of threat to the nation's atomic warfighting capability.

Chapter 18 Endnotes

1. Cynthia M. Grabo, *Anticipating Surprise; Analysis for Strategic Warning*, University Press of America, New York, 2004, 30-33

2. Ben Phillips, "Stories and memories of Col. Francis Harold Potter, USAF (1921-2009)", December 16, 2013 https://francisharoldpotter.com/2013/12/16/operation-chromedome/

3. 1959 NORAD/CONAD Historical Summary, July – December, 1959, U.S. Northern Command, December 2006 http://www.northcom.mil/Portals/28/Documents/Supporting%20 documents/(U)%201959%20NORAD%20CONAD%20History%20Jul-Dec.pdf

4. *Airspace Violation* By Black Cigar Observed Above Oak Ridge Near F-86, Nuclear Connection Project, NICAP http://www.nicap.org/ncp/ncp-oakridge530719.htm

5. Daniel Wilson, Feb. 15, 1954; Near Savannah River AEC site, South Carolina (BBU), RADCAT, NICAP chronology http://www.nicap.org/docs/540215savannah_docs.pdf

6. Daniel Wilson, Oct. 1 thru Nov. 20, 1954; Killeen Base (Gray AFB), Texas (BB), NICAP Chronology http://www.nicap.org/docs/541001killeen_docs.pdf

7. Dr. J Allen Hynek, *The Hynek UFO Report*, Barnes and Noble Books, New York, 1997, 247-248

8. Charles R. Loeber, *Building the Bombs; A History of the Nuclear Weapons Complex*, Second Edition, Sandia National Laboratories, Albuquerque, New Mexico, 2002, 84-100

9. Ibid, 83

10. George L. Butler, "Alert Operations and The Strategic Air Command, 1957-1991", Office of the Historian, Headquarters Strategic Air Command, Offutt Air Base, Nebraska, December 7, 1991 http://www.alternatewars.com/WW3/WW3_Documents/USAF/SAC_Alert/Alert_Ops_SAC_1957-1991.htm

11. Ibid

12. Dr. Allen Hynek, *The UFO Experience; A Scientific Inquiry*, The Henry Regnery Company, 1972, 76-79

13. "Object Flies Low Over Base, Tracked On Radar," NICAP subcommittee report, NICAP

14. http://www.nicap.org/580515malmstrom_dir.htm14 Brad Sparks, Delta Craft Observed & Tracked On Radar At Key Base, RADCAT Case Directory, NICAP http://www.nicap.org/580804malmstrom_dir.htm

15. "Uncorrelated Targets Vanish When A/C Approached", NICAP http://www.nicap.org/reports/580907milescity_rep.htm

16. George L. Butler, "Alert Operations and the Strategic Air Command 1957-1991", Office of the Historian, Headquarters Strategic Air Command, Offutt Air Force Base, Nebraska, December 7, 1991 http://www.alternatewars.com/WW3/WW3_Documents/USAF/SAC_Alert/Alert_Ops_SAC_1957-1991.htm

17. Brad Sparks and Daniel Wilson, "B-52 & Gnd Radar / Radar Visual / Radar Freqs From UFO" March 25, 1959, Northern Montana http://www.nicap.org/590325nmontana_dir.htm

18. Daniel Wilson, May 2, 1959; Pease AFB, New Hampshire (BBU), NICAPhttp://www.nicap.org/docs/590502pease_docs.pdf

19. Shirley Thomas, *Satellite Tracking Facilities*, Holt, Rinehart, Winston, New York, 1963, 75-79

20. Curtis Peeples, *Shadow Flights,; America's Secret Air War Against the Soviet Union,* Presideo Press, Novato, California, 2000, 150

21. "Guarding What you Value Most", North American Aerospace Defense Command, NORAD Headquarters, Peterson Air Force Base, Colorado, 2008, 9-10

22. Jerome Clark, *The UFO Encyclopedia: The Phenomenon from the Beginning,* "RB-47 Radar Visual Case", Omnigraphics, June 1998, 761-790. Article also available from NICAP http://www.nicap.org/reports/RB47_Sparks_Ency.pdf

23. Nuclear Connections Project, Francis Ridge, Coordinator, National Investigations Committee on Aerial Phenomena http://www.nicap.org/ncp/ncp-home.htm

24. In the interest of full disclosure, because of experience with other subjects, the author has certain views on how much detail can be and should be trusted from witnesses - including the amount of useful detail that can be recovered more than a few hours or a few days after any given incident. Due to that caution only the basics of the extensive oral history work done by others are used in this book, readers will find considerably more detail and other incidents in the referenced investigator's full bodies of work.

25. Robert Hastings, "UFO Over Titan Missile Silo; Oracle, Arizona; August 7, 1962", July 16, 2007, NICAP http://www.nicap.org/ncp/ncp-oracle.htm

26. Daniel Wilson, May 21, 1964; Altus AFB, Oklahoma/ Missile Site 7 (Atlas ICBM), NICAP http://www.nicap.org/docs/640521altus_docs.pdf

27. Dominique Weinstein, *Eighty Years of Pilot Sightings; A Catalog of Military, Airliner and Private Pilot Sightings from 1916 to 2000*, February 2001 http://www.narcap.org/files/narcap_revised_tr-4.pdf

28. Daniel Wilson, "RAPCON Fails To Identify Low Flying Manta Ray", July 28, 1965, NICAP http://www.nicap.org/650728carswell_dir.htm

29. Daniel Wilson, "Radar at Minuteman Site Tracks UFOs "http://www.nicap.org/650811whitemandir.htm

30. Daniel Wilson, August 16, 1966, "15 miles south of Minot, ND", UFO Report, NICAP http://www.nicap.org/minot660816dir.htm31 Francis Ridge, "Minuteman Site Jammed By UFO", NICAP

31. http://www.nicap.org/660824minot_dir.htm

32. Daniel Wilson, "Radar At Minuteman Site Tracks UFOs", NICAP http://www.nicap.org/docs/650811whiteman_docs.htm

33. Robert Salas and James Klotz, *Faded Giant; Report; the 1967 Minot Missile/UFO Incident*, Burksurge LLC, 2005; Robert Hastings, Chapter 11 "Taking Down Echo and Oscar", *UFOs and Nukes; Extraordinary Encounters at Nuclear Weapons Sites*, Anchor House, 2008 and Kevin Randle, *The Government UFO Files*, 2014, "Chapter Belt Montana and the Minuteman Missile Crisis", 203-227

34. Francis Ridge, "Minot Tracks Object, B-52 Sees & Tracks UFO", October 24, 1968, Minot AFB, North Dakota, NICAP http://www.nicap.org/681024minot_dir.htm

35. Op Cit, Kevin Randle http://www.nicap.org/reports/681024minot_randle.htm

Chapter 19

Threat?

In this chapter

- Extension of the indications study scenario to include the possibility of unknown flying objects as an actual "threat" to the Strategic Air Command's nuclear strike capability.

- The resurgence of SAC as a strategic nuclear force beginning in 1974.

- Examination of UFO intrusions during the 1970s and into the 1980s – the period of maximum global nuclear capability, involving over 45,000 American and Russian atomic weapons.

- A series of striking UFO incidents suggesting that SAC air and missile capabilities were being actively tested on their site security and defensive capabilities.

- The total military failure to engage or counter UFO penetrations of secure atomic weapons storage areas and operational ICBM sites.

- The longest and densest series of low altitude UFO observations – involving a totally new type of object and thousands of reports during 1983-1984.

It might seem that introducing the possibility of unknown flying objects as an actual "threat" is leaning a bit towards the sensational. On the other hand, it is totally consistent with the overall history of UFOs as an intelligence problem. One of the stated missions for all of the Air Force UFO projects was to determine whether or not UFOs constituted a threat to national security. That question was also fundamental to the CIA's involvement in 1952. We reviewed an internal CIA assessment from its Office of Scientific Intelligence proposing that such a threat did appear to exist, that the matter deserved immediate attention and that sightings over major U.S. defense installations were "not attributable to natural phenomena or known types of aerial vehicles."[1]

In contrast, the official Air Force position, reiterated at the time Project *BLUE BOOK* was terminated, was that no UFO reported, investigated or evaluated by the Air Force had ever indicated any actual threat to national security. In practical terms that language seems to have been a bit overstated since any unidentified aerial object submitted through CIRVIS or even OPREP-3 reporting was to be considered either an imminent threat or a matter of national security concern. Beyond that we previously noted two specific instances in which SAC field investigations of UFO incidents included language referring to national security threats.

Northern Montana / 1959 "In view of the fact that this sighting suggests a possibility of a different type of threat to the Continental United States, request this Headquarters, ATTN: ADODI, be advised of your final analysis regarding this sighting."[2]

Carswell AFB, Texas / 1965 "This sighting was a positive observation, under ideal circumstances, of a definite object of an unconventional nature – possibly of foreign origin, which could be a threat to national security.

In terms of precision it seems that the official Air Force position might have been more accurate if it had stated that there was no "proof" of any threat – a threat being by definition an intention to inflict pain, injury or damage - associated with the UFO reports it had investigated.

Given that warnings/indications analysis cannot and does not ever claim to provide absolute certainty (only cautions and suggestions) our study scenario can certainly be expanded to include "suggestions" of a possible threat to national security. The new incidents reported from SAC bomber bases and missile installations during the 1960s raised the possibility of some type of threat, especially given that UFO intrusions appeared to have specifically focused on ICBM missile silos and SAC weapons storage bunkers. This extension to our study examines UFO incidents of later years in terms of threat indications.

Once again, before we delve into the details of individual incidents - much less trends and patterns - it is necessary to establish the strategic military context for the period of time we will be addressing. That period begins in the early 1970s and extends through that decade. Three major military transitions occurred during the 1970s. The first and possibly the most significant was that the Soviet Union finally achieved atomic warfare parity with the United States. By the early 1970s the Soviets had resolved a number of earlier problems with both their ground based and submarine launched ballistic missiles and had moved to placing missiles in silos, as the U.S. had done from the beginning.

In terms of actual numbers of intermediate and intercontinental range missiles, the Soviet Union achieved missile parity circa 1970. That parity involved a massive number of strategic (megaton class) atomic weapons, between eight and ten thousand for the United States alone in the early 1970's.[3] In terms of all classes of atomic weapons (including various air to ground and air to air warheads as well as tactical nuclear devices), in 1975 the United States held 27,000 atomic weapons and the Soviet Union had some 20,000 available. From then on the United States began to reduce its total stockpile, lowering it to 23,000 weapons in 1983 – the Soviets continued to aggressively build their own inventory, by 1983 they possessed an amazing number of atomic weapons, some 35,000.

The Soviets had also built an air defense network that surpassed anything the United States had conceived, much less actually fielded. As early as 1964 American intelligence had already identified 1,892 Soviet radar sites and a staggering number of 5,985 individual defense radars. Their long distance surveillance system consisted of two rings, one of 187 stations and a secondary line with some 387 operational radars. Beyond that - with a total dedication to killing SAC during what they feared would be a preemptive American attack - they had deployed some 10,000 jet interceptors and established 1,000 anti-aircraft missile sites.[4]

SAC itself had remained a potent threat, having implemented new low level bomber attack practices, but during the late 1960s and into the early 1970s it had been redirected towards conventional bombing in South East Asia. The Chrome Dome airborne alert flights were canceled in 1968 and SAC's strategic focus was largely on deploying new generations of missiles and expanding its ICBM capabilities. Whether or not the Soviets ever considered reducing their own air defense is uncertain, however if they did, events in 1969 might have dissuaded them. In what became known as the "Madman strategy", President Richard Nixon and Henry Kissinger came up with a plan for forcing an end to the Vietnam War.[5]

The strategy involved a series of actions intended to convince the North Vietnamese and even the Russians that Nixon was willing to use atomic bombing as a weapon of necessity. The most dramatic action in that effort involved a SAC mission designated as Giant Lance. In that action Nixon ordered what amounted to a mock preemptive strike on the Soviet Union and on October 27, 1969 SAC sent eighteen B-52 bombers towards Russia. Given that the Chrome Dome missions were no longer being flown, it was a highly unusual act, even though the aircraft were ultimately held back from the most advanced "fail safe" positions. The overall Madman strategy failed in regard to Vietnam, however the sudden reappearance of a large number of SAC bombers headed towards their borders would have argued for the Russians maintaining a strong air defense.

Through the late 1960s SAC's B-52s were primarily devoted to conventional bombing missions, first in South Vietnam (and covertly in Laos and Cambodia) but increasingly in the early 1970s large scale attacks were carried out against targets in North Vietnam. Those missions were part of the ongoing effort to apply pressure in support of the peace negotiations in Paris. They also proved extremely deadly to SAC – fifteen B-52s and their crews were downed in only twelve days of Operation Linebacker II in December, 1972.

South East Asian combat commitments also led to an end of the large scale SAC strategic exercises and, in 1971, even the cancellation of the annual SAC bombing competitions. However with the end of the Vietnam conflict, the bombing competitions did resume and as in past years were a major event for SAC. In 1974 there were participants from 20 B-52 wings, 2 F-111 wings, 27 air refueling squadrons and even 4 Vulcan bombers from the Royal Air Force.[6] With its continued deployment of new missiles and a resurgence in manned bomber activity, at the end of 1974 SAC was once again the most visible element of the nation's atomic warfare force.

But in 1975, a striking series of UFO incidents created a very real concern that SAC itself might have become a target. It all began at Loring AFB, in Maine. Loring was among the northern tier SAC bases which would have been among the first to either surge an attack against the Soviet bloc – or be targeted in any preemptive Soviet strike. In 1975 Loring became the first of the northern tier SAC installation to experience what would turn out to be a wave of incidents involving UFOs maneuvering at low level over SAC atomic weapons storage areas. The incident has many similarities to the low level weapons area intrusion at Kirtland AFB which had occurred years before. But in 1975, Loring was only the first in what was to become an extended series of similar incidents, incidents which lasted into 1976.

The full story of what was to become the "northern tier wave" has been researched by a number of individuals. Barry Greenwood and Lawrence Fawcett conducted a significant amount of that research themselves and have written at length about the wave of sightings in their book Clear Intent; The Government Cover-Up of the UFO Experience.[7] The following is based on material from their work as well as documents and additional cited sources.

On October 27, 1975 the Loring AFB UFO "penetration" began in much the same fashion as many of the other incidents we have reviewed. A technician manning the base tower radar began monitoring a UFO which appeared to be circling north east of the base, at a distance of some ten miles. He tracked the object over some forty minutes until it dropped off his plot, presumably either descending below the radar beam or possibly landing. Separately a security guard patrolling the munitions storage area of the base – containing SAC special/atomic weapons – observed what he assumed to be an aircraft flying along the northern parameter of the security area.

The object then penetrated the base security perimeter, moving towards the weapons storage area at an altitude of no more than 150 feet. The security guard's alert immediately brought a quick reaction team into the area and the base command post requested fighter coverage from two separate NORAD regions. Both regions denied the support request. Assuming that the UFO might simply be a lost aircraft, routine and unsuccessful efforts including ongoing radio calls were made in an attempt at identification, with no success. The UFO continued to maneuver at low altitude over the base and after a time simply moved off to the north, tracked on radar for some ten miles before once again going off scope. The incident was reported to the National Military Command Center, to the Air Force Chief of Staff's office and to SAC headquarters. However no military action of any sort appears to have been taken at the time of the incident or in an immediate response to the intrusion.

The following evening, October 28, security guards once again observed a UFO approaching from the north, at a higher altitude, some 3,000 feet. The object was tracked on radar and appeared highly maneuverable; it was presumed to be a helicopter. The object moved over the base flight line and at that point several observers obtained a close up, well defined view – describing it as football shaped, the length of four cars and being a solid, reddish orange color. It was totally silent. Security personnel continued to respond, sweeping the base, but at that point the object apparently turned off its lights and could not be located. However radar did track an object moving away towards the north. It appears that NORAD was either not immediately informed of the incident or if so once again did not respond with fighters.

The Loring intrusions were obviously a very serious security issue for SAC and the Air Force. Parties unknown were penetrating a SAC base and apparently moving around and over an atomic weapons storage area at will. Base security forces were alerted and organized for immediate response and a security option III was recommended to several northern tier bases:[8]

"Defense against helicopter assault" – The past two evenings at one of our northern tier bases an unidentified helicopter has been observed hovering over and in the near vicinity of the weapons storage area. Attempts to identify this aircraft have so far met with negative results. In the interest of nuclear weapons security will assume Security Option III during the hours of darkness until further notice."[9]

Once again, on October 29, for the third night in a row a UFO – still presumed to be a helicopter – was sighted some 300-500 yards from the weapons storage area at Loring, AFB. Arrangements had been made for an Army National Guard helicopter to be available to track and identify the intruder.[10] The UFO was sighted in the area of the weapons storage area twice on the evening of the 29th and on both occasions the Army helicopter failed to locate it or make any sort of contact with it.[11] Other visual reports of UFOs came from within the base and beyond its perimeter. Some of those reports were confirmed by radar, including objects at a distance of ten miles; altitudes ranged from as low as 300 feet and to as high as 5,000 feet.

In the days that followed there were further reports of UFOs in the area, the investigations continued but in the end none of the intrusions at Loring were actually identified as helicopters nor were any helicopters found that could be linked to the incidents within or around the base. But almost immediately another SAC base, this time Wurthsmith AFB in Michigan, began to experience its own series of intrusions.

Beginning around 4 pm in the afternoon of either October 29 or 30 (the records appear unclear as to which date) a UFO penetrated into restricted areas at Wurtsmith. The first report on the Wurtsmith incidents is anecdotal, made well after the fact and independent of any official documentation. It comes from an individual working with a mobile approach control unit located off the base runway at the time. His report of an afternoon penetration begins with his monitoring several calls between the base tower and the mobile radar unit in regard to possible helicopters over the SAC Alert Area. The inquiries were given a "negative" as no helicopters were being observed or heard at that time.

Shortly afterwards a SAC tanker entered approach control space and began contact with the tower. At that point the tanker was asked to fly over the Alert

Area and identify a UFO in that vicinity. At that point a UFO was visible over the Alert Area, described as an aluminum colored disc about 75 feet long. The mobile radar operator stated that as the tanker aircraft approached he observed the disc go from stationary to an estimated 300 mph, departing well ahead of the approaching aircraft.[12] While anecdotal, the report is consistent with a second incident at Wurthsmith on that same date, one which is officially verifiable.

That incident involved a series of reports dealing with a nighttime penetration at Wurtsmith. It is extremely well documented. Several independent sightings, as well as the involvement of a KC-135 tanker aircraft, were reported via OPREP-3 to the National Military Command Center.[13] That night, beginning around 10 pm, several personnel at the base began to observe a low flying craft, displaying lights while flying erratically and hovering at times.[14] During the incident, approach radar appears to have tracked a number of UFOs, with multiple object plots at times, as well as individual returns.

During that same period of time, security police reported an object described as an unlighted helicopter flying directly over the back gate and into the base. It was seen moving at very low altitude directly over the weapons storage area – however reports from the security patrol in the area itself do not refer to a helicopter, stating only that they could not identify the object at all. Some personnel on the base reported helicopter noises at different times, some of the closest to the object heard no noise at all. Later approach radar picked up a target departing the base and tracked it for some thirty five miles. Once again security forces apparently were unable to engage the intruder in any fashion.

During the intrusion a KC-135 tanker returning from a refueling mission was flying a transition approach into a landing at the air base. It was redirected to pursue and identify the object and vectored towards it. The aircraft obtained a visual on a lighted UFO and pursued the object towards Lake Huron, following as it turned towards Saginaw Bay. During that pursuit the pilots were able to observe that it was not a single object but rather two objects which seemed to be signaling each other with lights.[15] A brief aircraft radar contact was also made with the targets and Wurtsmith approach control radar also had intermittent contact, further vectoring the tanker. The plane was able to move to within a mile of the objects at about 2,000 feet altitude but each time it appeared to close, the objects would speed away.

Eventually the tanker crew lost sight of the targets as they descended and appeared to move among lighted boats on the bay; the tanker pilots even felt the UFOs might have landed. But after turning back towards Wurtsmith the aircraft crew once again picked the two objects up at the rear of the aircraft, following the tanker. Upon turning the aircraft back towards the UFO, the pilot observed the light/s accelerate away at an immense speed - estimated at over 1,000 miles per hour. The tanker followed in the same direction and was advised that Wurtsmith radar was again showing a UFO, some four to five miles from them. The tanker was once again vectored towards the UFO but by that time the plane was running low on fuel and had to return to land. Upon final approach the crew again reported sighting unidentified lights, in the area of the base weapons storage facility.

Officially the Air Force continued to treat these northern tier incidents as a helicopter threat, even in the face of several contradictory close range observations. The report of the KC-135 crew, which gave chase over an extended period and failed to close with two UFOs, certainly appears to argue against them being helicopters.

With two virtually concurrent intrusions, SAC and the Air Force were faced with what can only be considered as a security crisis, with two strategic northern tier bases repeatedly penetrated by unknown aircraft which had proved impossible to engage. Craft (even if helicopters) flown by unknown parties, demonstrating the ability to enter and exit restricted air space at will - and operate directly over SAC flight lines and atomic weapons storage areas.

There are no documents available describing a broader national security dialog on the exact nature or origins of the intruders- or of any broader security threat. Individuals in higher levels of command seem to have faced two equally unacceptable options. Either they were dealing with the same types of unknown objects that had been reported over and around SAC bases for years, this time in a virtually unique wave of low level penetrations – or the Soviets were demonstrating that they had the ability to penetrate and compromise SAC at will. Helicopter borne Russian special operations (Spetsnaz) forces with tactical nuclear devices would have been a frightening alternative, especially in regard to the total failure of base security to engage or otherwise deal with the intrusions in any fashion.

And then the intrusions moved west, to the site of the previously discussed ICBM incidents of 1967, at Malmstrom AFB in North Dakota. Once again there were lights and mysterious noises and radar tracks. Once again none of incidents and observations seemed to make sense in terms of conventional aircraft, including helicopters. The incidents at Malmstrom began on November 8, 1975, after midnight, with several radar plots of a UFO at altitudes between some 9,000 to 15,000 feet. At the same time there were visual reports of unknown lights reported from Malmstrom AFB itself as well as several ICBM silo areas – there were also reports of jet noises overhead. A check with the FAA revealed no jet aircraft within a hundred miles and the radar tracks were showing UFO speeds of only 7 knots. Nothing seemed to match up.

There had been civilian reports of mysterious lights and low flying craft in the general vicinity of the base for several weeks, with many calls to the police. A number of former Air Force personnel have also described ongoing sightings over several days around launch control centers, missile launch silos and the Malmstrom base weapons storage area – however the detailed base and command level documents that should exist on the incidents, including the reporting to the National Military Command Center (similar to the documents describing the Loring and Wurthsmith incidents), have not been located.

There is no doubt something significant occurred at Malmstrom, a NORAD incident report records radar tracking, the scrambling of two F-106 interceptors, and multiple visual sightings from SAC sabotage alert teams.[16] Fortunately researchers who filed numerous Freedom of Information requests on the incidents were ultimately able to obtain the NORAD Director's log for the period in question (as well as its attachments); the attachments record additional details of the UFO incidents at Malmstrom.[17]

The incidents on the night of November 7 began with at least four ICBM missile sites reporting to their Command Post that they were observing a large reddish orange light (the same descriptions given during the Malmstrom missile incidents of 1967). The SAC command post at Malmstrom reported the incident to NORAD. Additional reports described an object actually illuminating the driveway at one Launch Command Post, other locations reported at least two objects (one overhead and one at a distance), and one object was observed to be extending some sort of black tube. As of that point in time no radar tracks were being generated for the objects being reported. The UFOs remained in view until sunrise, at which time the observers began to obtain visuals on physical objects – however at that point the objects quickly rose and disappeared out of view.

On the following evening, November 8, the sightings continued. Multiple security teams again began reporting lights and confirmed their locations. Radar picked up multiple objects at medium altitudes of approximately ten thousand feet. The plots led to estimates of from two to seven UFOs, moving at very slow speeds - some as slowly as only seven miles per hour.

Interceptors were dispatched but flight rules (mountainous terrain) required that they stay above 12,000 feet and they could not move down to the level of the UFOs to attempt an identification, even though both the UFOs and fighters were being radar tracked at the same time. The UFOs and fighters were both visually observed from several different points – but as the fighters arrived the lights would go off, only to come back on after the fighters departed. The same patterns of lights (stationary, moving and at times climbing at high speed), multiple observations, including several from commercial aircraft, and intermittent radar tracks continued all night long. It all reads very much like Washington D.C. circa 1952 – and equally futile in terms of air defense. The NORAD communications report is extensive and readers can examine it online.[18]

In regard to the other reports and communications which should have existed in regard to the Malmstrom incidents, the Air Force responded to Barry Greenwood that none were still in the files because "unidentified flying object reports are of transitory interest to the Air Force and permanent files are not maintained".[19] A similar response was given to a Congressman who also requested information on the incidents. While frustrating, such a response is not inconsistent with the regulations for routine destruction of unit files – although the continued existence of the NORAD documents suggests the possibility of recovering documents at some higher level of SAC or Air Force headquarters. Given their content, and the fact that they might well discuss much broader security and defense issues it's not hard to imagine them being classified. In fact a much higher level of headquarters concern is suggested by additional material that Greenwood was able to obtain.

At first glance the document appears relatively "tame", at least when compared to the incidents described above. It simply involves a National Military Command Center memorandum with a request to the Air Force Global Weather Center to make arrangements for ongoing analysis of temperature inversions – the request was issued in conjunction with "sightings of unusual phenomena along the northern U.S. border" and the information was to be provided to the Joint Chiefs of Staff.[20] The request itself is dated November 13, 1975.

As Greenwood and Fawcett describe it, from that point on there apparently were ongoing requests for meteorological data related to possible temperature inversions, data clearly relating to the incidents that had begun to be reported across northern tier bases. That at least suggests that the unknown helicopter scenario had to be abandoned - very possibly due to the observations at Malmstrom - and that at some higher command levels the penetrations and intrusions were receiving quite serious attention. It also suggest that there was indeed some national security level of visibility of the northern tier intrusions, up to the level of the Joint Chiefs.

In one respect, the events of late 1975 give us a positive indication in regard to our extended study scenario, not just a suggestion of unknown parties actively monitoring American atomic warfighting assets but with unidentified aerial objects actually being viewed as a potential threat. Of course the SAC Security Option III alert that was issued to ten different SAC air bases and missile installations from Maine to Washington State was not ordered using the term "UFO". Instead the threat was characterized as an unidentified helicopter and security measures were directed in terms of a defense against helicopter assault. The follow on incidents at Wurtsmith AFB and Malmstrom AFB certainly appear to have justified the alert – however the details of the intrusions at those bases strongly suggest that objects other than helicopters were involved.

By November 11, 1975, a message from Commander in Chief NORAD to all NORAD units appears to acknowledge that point; that communication refers to "suspicious objects" being sighted at Loring AFB, Wurthsmith AFB, Malmstrom AFB and the Canadian Air Force station at Falconbridge, Canada.[21] That message notes the early "characterization" of sightings as helicopters but adds the fact that Minot was "buzzed" by a noiseless object the size of a car at one to two thousand feet and that Falconbridge radar had tracked an object at altitudes of 26,000 feet up to 72,000 feet – clear indications of something other than a helicopter being involved. The message also notes failures to intercept and identify the objects by Air Guard helicopters, SAC helicopters and NORAD F-106 interceptors.

One additional incident, in January of 1976, is also documented at the level of the National Military Command Center. It involved the report of multiple UFOs in the immediate vicinity of the flight line at Cannon Air Force Base in New Mexico. The observations appear to have been made at close range; the base security police were quite specific in their description of four physical objects – twenty-five yards in diameter, with a hole in the middle, a blue light on top and a red light on the bottom. Unfortunately all we have is the NMCC memo of the initial report; it references an ongoing investigation but no further related records have been located.[22]

Cannon AFB was a Tactical Air Command (TAC) base rather than a SAC base. SAC bases and their nuclear weapons storage sites and ICBM fields appear to have been the primary focus of the 1975 UFO incidents previously described, however at that point in time Cannon AFB hosted a number of F-111 multipurpose fighter bombers. The F-111s assigned to Cannon were internally configured as conventional bombing aircraft. However F-111s were also configured and deployed with SAC for nuclear strike missions.

Over the years, nuclear capable F-111As from SAC's bomb wings at Pease AFB in New Hampshire and Plattsburg AFB in New York had been reconfigured for tactical missions and transferred to Cannon, AFB. While purely speculative, it is possible that the presence of the F-111s might have drawn some attention to Cannon AFB as a potential nuclear weapons storage site. Certainly the 1976 UFO incident is entirely consistent with the ongoing intrusions over SAC flight lines and weapons bunkers.

Unfortunately that is as far as these types of incidents can be traced with currently available information and documents. Which means that as of 1976 we reach the end of our military indications studies, simply because at that point the data itself largely ends. Public access to military UFO data had begun to diminish as early as 1954 - due to the new directives on reporting and the regulations regarding classification of sightings and observations. Those regulations were interpreted to apply not only to military personnel but to highly qualified observers such as commercial airline pilots and crew. Apart from those reporting regulations, the release of technical data and operational details has historically been constrained by security and classification restrictions.

The northern tier incidents of 1975 illustrate that even when actual UFO sightings in the area of military bases are known to the public, obtaining information at levels of SAC and NORAD is extremely challenging. Determining if a particular incident was elevated to the National Military Command Center, Air Intelligence, or even higher levels of the national security infrastructure appears to be almost impossible. Were there other incidents similar to the northern tier wave? There are rumors, leaks, suggestions - and many of the same researchers diligently continue to pursue them.

Of course there always have been and continue to be credible civilian UFO observations from outside the military complex which has been the primary focus of this work. Extending our indications exercise beyond 1976 in terms of military data remains a challenge for the future. However, there remains one body of civilian sightings so extensive, with such a degree of regional media coverage and with such a body of private research that it has to be noted before we can proceed to any final remarks. The particular body of civilian sightings and observations in question began in the spring of 1983. In terms of the quantity of ongoing, low altitude observations, it lasted far longer than any of the geographically focused military and atomic weapons complex spikes that we have previously reviewed. It appears as possibly the densest and longest lasting wave of close range UFO sightings to occur within the continental United States.

Coincidentally, or perhaps not, it occurred during what we now know was very possibly the most dangerous period of Cold War history other than that of the Cuban missile crisis. In fact many readers may be shocked to learn that in 1983 key elements of the Soviet military and political leadership were seriously considering the need for a preemptive, surgical atomic strike on the United States. They had been driven to that point by an intense fear that the West was actually preparing for its own preemptive, decapitation strike against the Soviet leadership.

The roots of that Soviet fear were grounded in the public announcement of American stealth aircraft (the F-117 Nighthawk attack bomber) and plans to deploy a new generation of nuclear intermediate range ballistic missiles in Europe. While readers may be most familiar with the F-117 from its conventional bombing missions, the new stealth aircraft was configured for B-61 nuclear weapons and capable of virtually undetectable strikes into western Russia from European bases.

In that respect, the F-117 could indeed have conducted a classic decapitation strike against both Soviet leadership and its major command and control facilities, rendering it impotent in terms of retaliation against a full scale western nuclear attack. The Russians immediately recognized the true threat of the F-117 and were deeply concerned that - when combined with new, longer range missiles in Europe - the Americans would have the ability to launch a successful preemptive strike with virtually no warning. That would have fundamentally undermined the relatively new nuclear parity between the two superpowers, as well as the long standing deterrent of Mutual Assured Destruction (MAD).

Beyond those new weapons, SAC had also reemerged as a major strategic force. And once again SAC was becoming highly visible - in 1979 it conducted its first major airborne exercise since 1956. The SAC Global Shield exercises continued each year into 1983 and involved up to 400 bomber and tanker aircraft being sent aloft in response to simulated Russian attacks.[23]

In addition to the Global Shield exercises,[24] contemporary research of recent years has surfaced information about a number of secret but highly threatening military actions made visible to the Soviets during the early Reagan Administration years.[25] Those actions involved surges of SAC aircraft across the Arctic, directly towards the Russian frontiers. Elsewhere nuclear capable fighter bombers were sent on similar missions towards Russian borders in Europe. At their peak such missions reportedly recurred several times a week. And in a related and challenging move, American Navy battle groups began operating much closer to key Soviet military bases and installations in the Soviet Far East.

These actions, combined with President Ronald Reagan's championing of a huge American military buildup and his characterization of Russia as an "evil empire" seriously worried the Soviet leadership.[26] The Russians had first become concerned over Reagan's remarks during his election campaign, that concern was only reinforced by his early speeches after taking office – they were so concerned that in 1982 they conducted a massive military exercise of their own, including the launch of a number of both defensive and offensive missiles. They also initiated an extremely secret and elaborate human intelligence collections effort designated as RYaN. Its goal was to monitor America's NATO allies – especially the British – for activities that would suggest a preemptive attack from the West was imminent. In essence RYaN was a very covert program of short term indications intelligence.

It took several decades for this full story to emerge, including the fact that the point of gravest risk occurred during a huge NATO exercise in 1983, which the Soviets perceived as a cover for an actual attack. The story of this highly dangerous period late in the Cold War is far too extensive to cover here, however it clearly was a point in time when major military activities were occurring within both blocs. A single element of the 1983 NATO Autumn Forge exercise involved 170 separate Air Force transport aircraft missions to Europe; an associated exercise named Able/Archer sent B-52 bombers to Europe to participate in simulated bombing missions.[27]

In that context (and based on the history covered in this work), with major SAC airborne exercises resuming in 1979 and continuing into 1983, with a major Soviet military exercise in 1982 and with the huge Autumn Forge and Able/Archer exercises of 1983 – involving major aerial movement of transports and SAC bombers – we might well expect to find a series of military related UFO incidents. Given the 1975 intrusions it might even be expected to be more intense, and more dramatic.

And what we actually find is – nothing. At least nothing in regard to military observations, operational reports, security alerts or a surge in civilian reports around SAC air bases or missile complexes. Of course it may well be that incidents of that nature occurred and researchers have just not yet been able to develop that military story. What is visible in terms of a surge in UFO activity is something quite different. Beginning in October, 1983, dozens, then hundreds and ultimately thousands of people did begin to sight something they could not identify, aerial objects of a totally new sort. What they saw were very large, very "structured" and very low altitude unidentified flying objects. Objects which the Air Force was apparently not "seeing", or at least not acknowledging.

The new UFOs were being reported from north of New York City, up the Hudson River to the Indian Point Nuclear Complex on the west bank of the river and east into western Connecticut – from Brook Haven down to Bridgeport. Private citizens, police, Highway Patrol officers, security officers and a host of other people across the Hudson River Valley began to encounter huge, triangular/boomerang shaped objects, consistently described as being larger than a football field. Some encounters were during the day or at twilight, the vast majority were in early evening after nightfall. In some instances the objects carried a variety of lights, including groupings not unlike aircraft running lights, in other observations they were totally unlit.

For months reports of similar sightings appeared in area newspapers, but the huge black triangles never went national – nothing at all similar to the UFO waves of 1952, 1957, 1960 or 1966. In terms of sheer number of sightings, it was comparable to the huge national wave of 1947, but compressed into a relatively small, densely populated suburban area just north of New York City. It was a literal tidal wave of UFO reports, involving as many as 5,000 sightings over five years, with the majority made during 1983 and 1984.[28]

The Hudson River Valley sightings were explored in depth and remain a matter of study by a number of researchers; they are the subject of a book by Dr. J. Allen Hynek, Philip J. Imbrogno and Bob Pratt, *Night Siege; The Hudson River Valley UFO Sightings*.[29] Imbrogno remains active in investigating the huge black triangles, which continued to be reported in some numbers well into the 21st Century. In themselves the objects represented the greatest change in UFO physical structure since the discs, ovals and cylinders which were first profiled by the Air Force in 1947 and remained consistent in the military and pilot reports through several decades. While triangular or delta shaped UFOs had been intermittently reported beginning in the earliest years, they were relatively few and generally of small dimensions, the largest estimated to be bomber aircraft size.

The objects repeatedly seen and described in great detail in the Hudson Valley River sightings represented an entirely new form. Most often these UFOs were observed at very low altitudes – 1,000 feet or lower – and the objects being reported were described as huge in size, 200 to 300 feet. The closest observations describe solid physical objects, constructed more on the order of a bridge, with crisscross struts, tubular bracing and essentially an open, "pipe like" structure. Numbers of different colored lights were reported, mounted throughout an essentially open framework construction. As one witness described it, they appeared to be like "something built with an erector set". An erector set with a great number of lights, lights that not only changed color but strobed and at times assume various patterns.[30]

The only constant in regard to the lighted objects was that observers noted the lights did not move in relation to each other – their physical relationship stayed the same, supporting the impression that they were attached to or within a solid structure. While UFOs of earlier decades were often lighted - surprisingly "observable" even during appearances over and within restricted security areas - the Black Triangles were even more prominent. In one sense they seem to specifically designed to attract maximum attention – huge in size, constructed differently than any conventional aircraft, moving at low altitudes and often displaying not only bright lights but changing patterns of different colored lights.[31]

Given those characteristics and their tendency to appear over well populated areas, including over major highways, it is little wonder that these new UFOs drew so much attention and produced such a large number of sightings. It's almost as if they were designed and operated for that specific purpose - while retaining an aura of mystery due to their largely twilight and nighttime appearances. In successive years, and into the 21st Century, sightings and discussions of large black triangles largely replaced the traditional saucers and discs as a theme in civilian UFO sightings.

Over the years sightings of large black triangular objects, suspected of being secret Air Force developments, spread far beyond the Hudson Valley, although in far smaller numbers – hundreds rather than thousands.[32] On occasion they drew national attention, but only for a limited time. One striking sighting example, from Illinois on January 2, 2000, involved multiple witnesses, watching a huge black triangular object moving slowly above them at only a few hundred feet in height. It passed along a well-defined flight path, carrying it over three different Illinois towns where it was seen by numerous police officers – before it ultimately turned and moved away at high speed just as the sun was rising. The flight of the object was reported by so many people, and confirmed by so many law enforcement officers that the incident received coverage in newspapers as far distant as the Los Angeles Times.[33]

Certainly the appearance of a new physical profile for UFOs is interesting. Yet while the shape may have changed, certain elements of black triangle observations remain quite familiar and could have applied to many of the military observations we have reviewed. What seems more relevant to our particular intelligence "problem" is that the Hudson Valley River sightings and continuing reports of large black triangular craft made no impression at all on major news outlets or national, mainstream media.

In 1947, a relative handful of initial UFO sightings triggered trigger national media coverage. Several hundred sightings over some three months sustained that attention, creating what the Air Force perceived as a major crisis in public confidence. The summer time flying discs/saucers of 1947 were a national news event and led to ongoing media attention even in the face of constantly dismissive and reassuring Air Force statements.

In contrast, hundreds of civilian sightings coming out of a densely populated area just north of New York City produced nothing comparable in 1983/84. And as far as is known they produced no Air Force response of any type - much less a proactive investigation. Civilian attempts to approach the Air Force were met with the standard Air Force response that it simply no longer takes UFO reports; the same response was given by the FAA. If actual aircraft are involved it's another matter. Unidentified or unresponsive aircraft are a military concern, as they always have been and will continue to be – but the subject of truly anomalous "unknowns" is simply no longer part of the Air Force mission. That position effectively resolved what had become an increasingly uncomfortable public relations problem and neither the Air Force nor any other government agency appears to be eager to entangle itself with that problem again.

As to the larger and more fundamental intelligence challenge of the true "unknowns", that is a problem which appears to have been simply deferred - perhaps referred would be more accurate - rather than resolved. That will be the subject for our final chapter, which will address certain practical realities of the national intelligence community. It will also explore the various scenarios in our indications studies and offer some final observations on what the studies suggest.

Chapter 19 Endnotes

1. CIA memorandum, Dr. H Marshall, Chadwell to CIA Director Walter B. Smith, December 2, 1952; *THE CUFONSM 1952 CIA UFO-RELATED DOCUMENT SAMPLER*, Part 1 of 2 Parts, Corrections provided by researcher Brad Sparks added 23-Mar-2004 by J. Klotz, http://www.cufon.org/cufon/cia-52-1.htm

2. Brad Sparks and Daniel Wilson, "B-52 & Gnd Radar / Radar Visual / Radar Freqs From UFO March 25, 1959", Northern Montana http://www.nicap.org/590325nmontana_dir.htm

3. Gerald E. Miller, *Stockpile; the story behind 10,000 strategic nuclear weapons*, Naval Institute Press, Annapolis, Maryland, 8-10

4. Larry Hancock, *Surprise Attack*, Counterpoint Press, Oakland, California, 2015, 246

5. William Burr and Jeffry Kimbell, "Nixon's Nuclear Ploy: The Vietnam Negotiations and the Joint Chiefs of Staff Readiness Test", October 1969, The National Security Archive, December 23, 2002http://nsarchive.gwu.edu/NSAEBB/NSAEBB81/

6. Norman Polmar, *Strategic Air Command; People, Aircraft and Missiles*, The Nautical and Aviation Publishing Company of America, Annapolis, Maryland, 1979, 134

7. Barry Greenwood and Lawrence Fawcett, *Clear Intent; The Government Coverup of the UFO Experience*, Prentice Hall Inc, Englewood Cliffs, New Jersey, 1984, 1-56

8. Ibid, 21

9. Security Option III related to practices related to "defense against helicopter assault", the closest protocol matching the intrusions initially reported at Loring AFB

10. AFB Penetration, *Memorandum for the Record*, The National Military Command Center, October 29,1975 http://www.nicap.org/reports/751027loring_1-6.htm

11. AFB Penetration, "Memorandum for the Record", The National Military Command Center, October 29, 1975 http://www.nicap.org/docs/NMCC_assort1.pdf

12. Mark A.K. Singh, "Shiny Disc Hovers Over Restricted Area, Oct. 29 (or 30th), 1975 Wurtsmith AFB, Michigan" http://www.nicap.org/751029wurtsmith_dir.htm

13. Donald M. Davis, "Memorandum for the Record," National Military Command Center, 31 October, 1975 http://www.nicap.org/wurtsmith18-21.htm

14. Francis Ridge, "UFO Chased By KC-135 Tanker, October 30, 1975, Wurtsmith AFB, Michigan"http://www.nicap.org/docs/751030wurtsmith_docs.pdf

15. This report is similar to a number of observations noted in earlier years - UFOs tracked as individual radar returns but upon close approach by aircraft, visually observed to be two discrete objects/lights, flying in extremely close proximity and flawlessly maneuvering with each other even during extended pursuits.

16. NORAD Command Directors Log, entry for November 8, 1975, Headquarters Aerospace Defense Command http://www.nicap.org/foia_002.htm

17. NORAD Command Directors Log (1975), 24thNORAD Senior Directors Log (Malmstrom AFB, Montana), Francis Ridge, NICAP http://www.nicap.org/docs/norad95-101.pdf

18. Ibid.

19. Barry Greenwood and Lawrence Fawcett, Clear Intent; The Government Coverup of the UFO Experience, 55

20. Ibid, 10-11

21. Ibid, 50-51

22. Paul Dean, *UFO's Documenting the Evidence*, "OPREP-3, A Classified US Military Reporting Channel for UFO Incidents", Part 7, November 7, 2016 http://ufos-documenting-the-evidence.blogspot.com.au/2016/11/oprep-3-classified-us-military.html

23. "400 SAC Planes Take Part In Response to Mock Attack", *The New York Times*, February 9, 1981http://www.nytimes.com/1981/02/09/us/around-the-nation-400-sac-planes-take-part-in-response-to-mock-attack.html

24. STRATEGIC AIR COMMAND - THE GLOBAL SHIELD - 1980 USAF DOCUMENTARY - Ella73TV; Ella73TV - A curated collection of old films, newsreels & archive footage spanning the 20th century. #Military https://www.youtube.com/watch?v=dFQQB-Dn5CQ

25. Benjamin B. Fischer, *A Cold War Conundrum: The 1983 Soviet War Scare*, Center for the Study of Intelligence, Central Intelligence Agency, March 19, 2007 https://www.cia.gov/library/center-for-the-study-of-intelligence/csi-publications/books-and-monographs/a-cold-war-conundrum/source.htm

26. Ronald Reagan, "Evil Empire" speech to National Order of Evangelicals, March 8. 1983, Orlando, Florida, Miller Center, University of Virginia http://millercenter.org/president/speeches/speech-3409

27. Nate Jones and Lauren Harper, *The 1983 War Scare: "The Last Paroxysm of the Cold War Part III*, The National Security Archive, May 22, 2013 http://nsarchive.gwu.edu/NSAEBB/NSAEBB428/

28. Dr. J. Allen Hynek with Philip Imbrogno and Bob Pratt, *Night Siege; the Hudson Valley UFO Sightings*, Ballantine Books, New York, 1987

29. Op Cit

30. Ibid, 11, 12, 21, 59, 91

31. Readers familiar with the B-2 Spirit, a very large delta winged bomber, may immediately think of it in regard to the Hudson River Valley sightings. For reference, the B-2 was under highly secret development up to November, 1988 when it was shown (only from the front) in a strictly restricted presentation area. Its first public flight did not occur until July, 1989, on a trip from the Northrup plant in Palmdale, California to Edwards AFB. The first operational B-2 was only delivered for military service in 1993. While a large aircraft, with a wingspan of 172 feet and a length of 69 feet, the aircraft is designed for high subsonic speed and is not capable of the type of low altitude "loitering" flight described in the majority of the Black Triangle reports. "B-2 Spirit" US Air Force Fact Sheet, December 16, 2016 http://www.af.mil/AboutUs/FactSheets/Display/tabid/224/Article/104482/b-2-spirit.aspx

32. John B. Alexander, *UFO's; Myths, Conspiracies, Realities*, St. Martin's Press, New York, 2011, 251

33. Ibid, 249-250

Chapter 20

Observations

There is simply no doubt that unidentified flying objects have been taken seriously by military intelligence. Beginning during World War II, first field intelligence groups, then headquarters groups and eventually scientific advisors all wrestled with reports of mysterious nighttime lights, generally referred to as "foo fighters" in Europe or as rumored derivatives of the "baca bomb" manned suicide rockets deployed by Japan towards the end of the war in the Pacific. Allied intelligence used all the standard methods of conventional intelligence including extensive observer debriefings, interrogation of prisoners, and solicitation of information from defectors and refugees. In a few instances scientific advisors even flew with air crews on missions, hoping to make observations for themselves.

In the end they failed to connect the lights with any specific new German or Japanese weapon, no actual attacks on Allied aircraft were documented and extensive technical collections work in the final months of the war failed to identify any specific weapons developments which would have provided a military explanation for the mystery nighttime lights. Given no proven threat and no positive identification of unconventional technology which could be directly connected to the observations, the matter was dropped.

That war time experience established the paradigm for the military intelligence work with UFOs which we have followed during successive decades. During both combat and peacetime, military intelligence actively involved itself with unidentified aerial object reports which might signify imminent or even potential threats. In 1946 both British and American intelligence, including the new Central Intelligence Group, covertly investigated the Flyer X / Ghost Rocket reports from Scandinavia.

Certain observations, as well as limited technical intelligence (in the form of radar tracking) led both the Americans and British to take the matter seriously, associating certain incidents with the Russians and with missile launches from Peenemunde, the former German rocket development site on the Baltic Sea, as well as other possible locations. Those indications were sufficient to send a Central Intelligence Group assessment to President Truman, advising him of probable Soviet involvement and the possible motive of intimidation in the form of a new type of psychological warfare. That assessment supported an ongoing but covert series of technical collections - involving both radar monitoring and aerial photographic missions - for two more years, long after the civilian wave of sightings had ebbed.

In 1947, a wave of UFO reports over both the continental United States and certain overseas American military bases produced a similar but more in depth response. Initially the Army Air Force conducted a low key, conventional intelligence effort – developing a target profile, formalizing official collections guidelines and applying the standard practices of field and technical intelligence. There was also a frantic search for relevant information on advanced German aeronautical developments – revisiting the war time Lusty collections, interviewing German scientists and scouring Europe for information on the Horton brother's flying wing aircraft designs.

Despite early hopes for a quick solution to the UFO problem, human collections work quickly put to rest the initial assumptions relating to Soviet adaptation of advanced German technology. In addition, technical intelligence collection was frustrated by the lack of physical samples as well as the inability to gather even the most basic information from radar path tracking or altitude measurements. Surveillance radar assets for tracking UFOs were simply not available within the continental United States. Neither were interceptors, virtually no military aircraft camera photos were obtained during the early Air Force investigations. More importantly, no clear threat emerged. There was no firm connection to the Soviets, there were no attacks and no indications of anything more than possible reconnaissance or probing of air defenses – the same sorts of measures the U.S. was already conducing to a limited extent, and preparing to dramatically escalate.

No identification, no proven threat – but a public relations headache, just like the foo fighters during the recent war. By 1947 Russia was being viewed as an existential threat to America; it had become an article of faith that Russia intended to engage the Western bloc and that it would do so militarily as soon as it was in a position to do so. In that context, even the possibility of a Russian UFO connection demanded that Air Force intelligence continue to monitor UFO reports. Public and press interest continued unabated and UFOs became a perennial challenge for Air Force PR personnel at base level and at the Pentagon – and an issue that senior staff officers were unable to ignore.

Events in Eastern Europe, the Korean War and the unexpected early appearance of Soviet atomic weapons only served to reinforce Americans concerns over continental air defense. During the early 1950s increasing numbers of unidentified radar tracks and interceptor patrol encounters with UFOs served to maintain concerns over the possibility of Soviet reconnaissance or pre-strike probing.

By early 1952 the air defense network had significantly improved but even the newest and most capable interceptors were still unable to engage and resolve a significant number of UFO incidents, even with improved radar and ground controller support. Air Intelligence took the issue quite seriously, under General Samford there was an increased interest in resolving the issue of truly anomalous sightings and a serious move towards a program of expanded scientific investigation. Driven by the high profile Washington D.C. UFO incidents of that summer, and with President Truman's personal interest, for several months in the second half of 1952 the CIA became directly involved with the intelligence problem of UFOs.

By December, the CIA's Office of Scientific Investigation had reached the opinion that there was a very real and fundamental national security problem associated with at least a core of the UFO incidents. OSI pressed the CIA Director to elevate the issue to the National Security Council, making it an issue for the broader intelligence community and a subject of extended scientific investigation. As previously discussed, inter-service and inter-agency politics appear to have surfaced at that point, aborting any such effort. In the end the UFO problem was left to the Air Force, as a matter of UFO identification related to air defense.

The very real issues with the Air Force "incident by incident" approach and its failure to address the fundamental UFO intelligence problem faded away in the wake of the CIA's own scientific study panel report. That study took place in January 1953 - with only three days of meetings on the subject – including the preparation and formalization of a final report. By 1954 new regulations, new directives and new headquarters attitudes within the Air Force ensured that the Air Force intelligence work would continue to be "incident oriented", a matter of identification, classification and filing.

The reality is that military intelligence and for that matter the intelligence community in general focuses on active threats and potential threats from known adversaries. National security is the mantra and intelligence tasking is built around that focus. If UFOs didn't come from the Communist bloc and represent new technologies which must be countered (or possibly exploited), if they were not provably hostile, then they were not tasked as a topic of national security and addressed by the analysts of the broader national intelligence community.

Without an identifiable source, without being proven to be an existing or potential threat, anomalous aerial object reports fell outside the primary intelligence mission and simply constituted a diversion of resources. Only the need for public reassurance was seen to justify a minimal UFO desk/public relations effort - which became the ultimate role of *BLUE BOOK*.

In the larger view, if the core "unknowns" - even the most anomalous UFO incidents – could not be confirmed as an actual threat, then as a class of observations they were simply a "phenomenon", a matter for the scientific and academic community. The scientific community was free to explore whichever aspects of the phenomena it felt to be of interest and value - and sets its own priorities. Intelligence groups always have fewer resources than required for their own missions, UFOs as a class of observations were best deferred to the academics who could use their own resources – and budgets – if they considered it worthy of study. And from a career standpoint, any radical conclusions they might reach would only be affecting their career paths. A slightly simplistic assessment, but a pragmatic one, seemingly consistent with the history which we explored in this work.

Both conventional military intelligence and technical intelligence proved ineffective in regard to the challenge of the most unconventional core of UFO reports – leaving them simply classified as "unknown". An immense quantity of detailed witness interviews and investigations eventually ended up in the *BLUE BOOK* archives, but in each instance there was deemed to be insufficient data for the Air Force - or its scientific advisors and consultants - to conclusively accept that any individual observation was not a misidentification, or natural phenomena not yet fully understood. At its most positive, the official attitude was that if sufficient resources could be made available perhaps enough technical data could have been collected to move past that point, identifying all of them.

Over the years, and privately, a number of individuals became convinced that there very real physical objects involved, intelligently controlled and possessing vastly superior technology. But there was just never enough proof for the scientists – and for whatever reason a number of items of hard data ranging from artifacts to instrumented observations and data never received a broad or comprehensive scientific review.

Beyond the official position statements on UFOs, what it all really comes down to is rather simple. If you choose to accept that within the total number of observations there are a set of credible witnesses, that witness have been able to accurately describe very real and unconventional aerial objects later positively identified, that credible observations by experienced radar operators (including radar screen shots) exist, that interceptor gun camera photographs confirm real and maneuvering objects (even if they are a bit blurred or hazy) then the "unknowns" remain an open issue and a challenge. Edward Ruppelt captured the basic quandary of the situation by relating an exchange which occurred during a Pentagon level briefing on UFOs.

A colonel chose to speak out during the meeting, questioning a particular incident involving a military aircraft encounter observed by multiple air and ground witnesses. The colonel's question was simple but fundamental – why did *BLUE BOOK* always pick an explanation, however improbable, that explained away UFO sightings - "why not believe that most people know what they saw?"[1]

Ruppelt's response was to turn to scientific method, answering that if you cannot prove what it is, then you have to leave it as unidentified and unexplained. The exchange also captured the point that under Ruppelt *BLUE BOOK* had continued to approach the UFO challenge according to the standards of scientific proof. Unfortunately, as we discussed in some detail earlier, even scientists such as Dr. Hynek ultimately pondered whether UFOs were a problem that was addressable with scientific methodology.

Yet as we have pointed out, there was and is another approach and another tool available, an approach now routinely used in both strategic intelligence and business intelligence. While it doesn't provide proofs, it does evaluate scenarios, delivering insights and either validating or rejecting them. It will not identify the unknowns; it will not tell you where they come from nor will it prove they exist.

However it has successfully been used to reveal trends, identify patterns, characterize anomalies and with a long enough baseline, it can at least offer suggestions on possible intentions. It has repeatedly proven to be extremely effective in all those things – so effective it had become an accepted practice not only in national military and geopolitical intelligence but has been widely adopted in business, from strategic planning to marketing and even in investment management.

We do not absolutely know that some degree of indications intelligence work was not conduced against the UFO problem. Such studies could have occurred inside the Air Intelligence staff groups; building activity lists and monitoring indicators is a well-accepted military practice. It could have been assigned within the Intelligence Advisory Council or performed by the

National Indications staff. But that tasking would have had to come down from the National Security Council and other than the period when UFOs were suspected of being Soviet devices it seems unlikely that such an assignment would have been a priority for the relatively small indications staff.

Given the apparent lack of records we are unlikely to resolve that question but conceptually such work would have had a limited time frame, specifically tied to possible UFO/Soviet associations. What seems especially hard to imagine is that any long term, chronological indications analysis of UFOs as a potential military threat would have followed the official positions taken by the Air Force during 1953/54.

Indications analysis requires continual examination of developments, of activities which could suggest changes, trends, anomalies – anything suggestive of a step towards new actions, in the case of warnings intelligence, a step towards hostilities. Above all it requires continuity and the building of a reliable base of observations, consistent observations from the same types of sources. In that regard, at its most fundamental level it requires that any analysis be preceded by "separating the wheat from the chaff" in building the study base.

With that caution, it's time to return to our own admittedly minimalist studies which addressed some 22 years of Air Force archival reports, focused strictly on the military aspect of unknown aerial objects – objects observed to be capable of speeds, maneuvers and activities beyond those of not only conventional aircraft but of manned aircraft in general.

The scenarios which we examined included : (a) military reconnaissance and ferreting by the Russians, expanded to (b) assessment by unknown parties of American atomic warfighting capabilities, c) testing the defenses assigned to the atomic warfare complex, and finally (d) indications of an actual threat specifically targeting that same complex. That degree of focus obviously leaves out a tremendous amount of data that occupies most discussion and theorizing about the general subject of UFOs. Of course that is by intention, since this sort of analysis requires a tight focus and our focus is the national security challenge of UFOs. As a side benefit, a tight focus on strategic "targets" diminishes the possibility of spending too much time with observations and incidents which could potentially represent deception or diversion.

The possibility of deception is always a concern (in both military and business data collection), and often impossible to verify during the period of the study. As a precaution, time spent on incidents that divert attention (sometimes referred to as "bait") from the actual focus involved in the study scenario needs to be minimized.[2] Examples of possible diversions could include the Green Fireball wave over a wide area of central New Mexico in 1948, the southwestern wave of 1957 (in which incidents involving apparent UFO interference with civilian vehicle engines drew extensive media attention)[3] and a variety of other incidents involving apparently random civilian encounters, isolated "landings", and even certain "contact" experiences not mentioned in this work. It is impossible to know, speculation is largely fruitless – the solution is simply to focus on the specific types of incidents related to the indications/actions list defined in the study scenario.

The final consideration in establishing the baseline for any scenario study is to "weed" the mass of potential data. To do that we focused on observations from military personnel, commercial pilots, and to a much lesser extent security and law enforcement officers. We also focused on incidents involving multiple observers, whenever possible including observations supported by instruments or technical resources such as radar tracking. As a check, we primarily selected incidents corroborated by official reports and documents.

In some instances, in an effort to be as critical as possible, we chose to leave out considerable witness detail not verified by the documents. There is a risk in that since it becomes clear that some official documents relating to UFOs have been either "sanitized" for security purposes or simply worded to be consistent with the official Air Force position. Examples of that include daylight, physical object sightings in New Mexico and Texas which were discussed only under the broad category of "green fireballs" and objects reported during the Northern Tier incidents which were officially described as "helicopters" - in the face of eyewitness observations which clearly described objects with physical appearances and performance characteristics which were obviously not helicopters.

Readers choosing to dig more deeply into the sources we cited are advised to apply one very important witness evaluation criteria, highlighted by Peter Ainsworth in his writings on eyewitnesses and perception. He describes perception as a highly subjective matter, witnesses are not video cameras.[4] Expectations have a great impact on perception, as do personal experiences. People see what they expect to see and make identifications in terms of the known, not the unknown.

This suggests that UFO witnesses whose immediate perception is that what they are seeing is an aircraft, a helicopter or a meteor but who are forced to change that initial identification by subsequent details in the observation make especially credible witnesses. That is of particular importance in regard to reports from military and commercial pilots with extensive flying histories and for scientists and technicians who have spent great lengths of time in astronomical observations or tracking missile and balloon launches. If those people originally perceive an object as being conventional and familiar, and are then forced to change their minds based on actual details of the observation, they are most likely worthy of particular consideration.

Which brings us back to the observations detailed within our indications studies. We established our baseline in terms of reports from strategic military facilities during 1947 - 1952. The baseline incidents included a series of sightings over high security atomic materials production facilities (Hanford), over Albuquerque (emerging as the home for the nation's newest atomic weapons assembly facility and what would become Manzano Base, the first atomic weapons storage complex). There were also observations from major air logistics and air defense bases on the West Coast as well as northern frontier air fields in Alaska and Newfoundland.

Those sightings included a considerable number of daytime events, with observations of well-defined physical objects. Several of the sightings involved multiple objects, at times in apparent formation flight. Others involved rapidly moving objects, in high speed passes by or over strategic installations. Significantly, in some incidents the object's maneuvers were what would be expected in low altitude reconnaissance of potentially hostile targets, ranging from dashes and zigzag maneuvering to the appearance of one object flying in what appeared to the observers as defensive cover for the other.

Such incidents corroborate the remarks in an Air Intelligence report issued late in 1947, suggesting that that certain UFO sightings indicated the possibility of foreign photo reconnaissance or ferreting of defensive capabilities.[5] Without saying so specifically, the remarks certainly implied Soviet involvement.

That initial 1947 suggestion of a pattern of reasonably broad military reconnaissance and ferreting did not continue or further develop during the following year. During 1948 the only sign of an ongoing strategic target focus was the report of a UFO appearing over Albuquerque, with the object staying stationary for an extended period – some ten minutes. If aerial reconnaissance was continuing it did not appear to broaden to other major military facilities and at best was highly selective.

It should be noted that Albuquerque appears to have remained a special area of UFO interest for several years. That constant is itself an indication since Albuquerque was where the atomic warfare capability of the nation was coming together, where the bombs were being built and stored, with Kirtland Air Force Base serving as the bomb pick up and distribution point for the Strategic Air Command. SAC bombers had to fly into Kirtland, load bombs and fly out on missions. If there was a central nexus to the early day atomic warfare complex, it was in Albuquerque. When and if UFO sightings in Albuquerque significantly decreased or ceased, a serious change in focus would be suggested – and that would not happen for a full decade.

Any analyst would have been hard pressed to make a solid case for UFO related military warnings at the end of 1948. And it would be the better part of a year before signs of a new trend began to develop – a trend which was not in the direction of a broader military reconnaissance effort. Throughout 1949, as in 1948, there was simply no overall pattern in observations that supported that scenario. The daytime group and formation flights reported in 1947 did not continue. The low altitude, high speed passes over strategic air bases were not in evidence. Daylight observations from atomic materials production plants continued, but only in regard to single objects and single observations at Hanford and Oak Ridge.

In contrast, we find the first incidents of two newly developing trends, both appearing in sightings and reports at atomic warfare facilities. The first trend involved detection and evasion. An airspace surveillance radar detected a UFO over the Hanford reservation restricted area and an interceptor was scrambled. After obtaining an aerial radar contact, the pilot was unable to engage the UFO, which faded from his screen during the attempted pursuit.

That sort of incident would become a constant during following years, appearing to change only as air defenses improved. Initially attempts at interception based on visual sightings were generally met with simple evasive responses - in the earliest incidents the UFO would simply move to altitudes where interceptors could not follow. With the advent of radar directed interceptions and more capable interceptors, the target either exited the area at high speed in advance of the fighter's arrival or disappeared from radar while the aircraft were being directed to the target. The disappearing targets were generally officially explained as equipment problems or false radar returns related to atmospheric conditions such as temperature inversions. Interceptor pilots were often of the opinion that the unidentified targets might have simply outmaneuvered them, quickly dropping to low altitudes, out of radar detection - or accelerating away too quickly to be tracked.

In later years, UFO evasion became more involved. When UFOs were tracked and closed upon they actively avoided the interceptors with aerial maneuvers, turning rates and acceleration (G forces) far outside the capabilities of manned aircraft. In an increasing number of incidents they appeared to "tease" interceptors or even threaten them, making head on passes or moving to positons above or behind the fighters. The one constant over time was the suggestion that the UFOs could detect radar scans and move either below or beyond effective radar tracking at will.

The second trend in UFO appearances would only become clear during 1950; it was more substantive in nature, and more warnings related. It began with a series of medium altitude, low altitude and even near ground level intrusions at the Killeen base in Texas. Killeen base/Site B being one of the new secure storage areas that were a critical part of the AEC/SAC plans for distributing atomic weapons in support of the Strategic Air Command.

The significance of the Killeen base intrusions is magnified not only by their frequency and intensity, but by the total lack of any active defense against the unidentified objects – which at times remained visible for periods long enough for triangulated instrument readings to allow firm estimates of both their altitude and size. In terms of indications, the events at Killeen base can be interpreted to suggest actual testing of military defenses – and the willingness of any defense to use force against intruders.

Three months of very high visibility sightings at Killeen/Site B (the majority involving nighttime observations of very obvious, brightly lit objects) suggests something beyond basic reconnaissance. As with their appearances over the weapons facilities in Albuquerque, the UFOs in Texas made no effort to be covert, repeatedly exposing themselves to possible anti-aircraft fire or fighter engagement. Killeen base was adjacent to an Army artillery training area and some UFO sightings actually occurred over firing ranges. Yet we have no evidence that any military action was taken to actually engage the UFOs. If a foreign power had been involved, they would certainly have determined the limitations of the American defense of its strategic atomic assets.

The outlines of the new, more intrusive patterns in UFO behavior began to solidify the following year, with reports from Los Alamos and Sandia Base / Kirtland; particularly notable were the UFO appearances over the ordinance storage area at Kirtland. However the multiple observer reports from Albuquerque began to raise an interesting point – the reports discuss viewer impressions that the objects doing flyovers wanted attention, they almost appeared to be performing exhibitions. There were even impressions that the objects themselves were maneuvering with each other - "dogfighting" - as they passed.

That level of visibility, a daylight repeat of the nighttime light shows at Killeen base, is a counter indicator, suggesting more complex intentions than simple reconnaissance. For reference, we noted something roughly similar in SAC formation flights over major Soviet cities, especially in the Far East. Those flights went beyond pure reconnaissance and target mapping. They were more in the way of military "statements" (force projection), intended to send a message from SAC – and General LeMay. We can reach you, we are watching, you can't stop us and it would be best not to threaten us. Admittedly this is pure speculation in regard to the UFO observations noted above, however it is consistent in terms of military intentions and motives.

In support of that interpretation, 1950s UFO incidents continued to develop the trend of fruitless efforts by interceptors to engage with and identify UFOs. That was illustrated in a dramatic incident from Selfridge AFB, a northern tier air defense base. We discussed that incident in detail, including the repeated and apparent back and forth "teasing" or "spooking" of the interceptor by the UFO. Clearly that is a subjective observer impression but those involved in the interception clearly viewed the UFOs maneuvers as either a threat or a message; the pilots in such encounters leaned towards regarding them as threatening.

The same sort of UFO behavior was repeated in a number of other incidents, including an extended series of abortive intercepts over and around the restricted security area at Oak Ridge, Tennessee. Oak Ridge had radar coverage available and interceptors were on call – yet over several months of visual and radar alerts, no interceptor scrambles were successful in terms of close range contact, much less identification. If the northern tier encounter with the Selfridge interceptors had been a message, the repetitive "teasing"/"spooking" over the security area at Oak Ridge was an even firmer statement.

By the end of 1951, a significant body of observations had indeed accumulated, suggesting that certain specific areas within the atomic warfare complex were being repetitively visited - and beyond that very possibly tested in terms of potential defenses. It was a clear picture, as well defined as the physical and maneuvering profiles of the unknown aerial objects had been in the fall of 1947. In December, 1951 Captain Ruppelt briefed the new Director of Air Force Intelligence, Major General John Samford.

As part of that discussion Ruppelt highlighted the point that UFO sightings appeared to be focused on the areas housing the nation's most strategic assets, including both atomic weapons production facilities and weapons storage sites. That pattern was evident, however other aspects of the earliest sightings were no longer being reported. As an example, the earliest years' daylight reports of multiple UFOs, of groups and even formations performing overflights and maneuvers over conventional military facilities and air bases had become much less frequent.

While certain patterns of UFO activity were becoming increasingly clear at the end of 1951, during the following year, a virtual explosion in both quantity and breadth of observations obscured those developing patterns, adding little more than ambiguity. Interestingly, the overwhelming of intelligence collections with large amounts of information – conflicting information if possible - is a very well established technique in the practice of deception. In her review of "the problem of deception" Cynthia Grabo notes that "flooding" collections channels with masses of conflicting reports can obscure key indications – as well as overwhelm intelligence analysts.[6]

"...a mass of material compounds immeasurably the problem of analyst fatigue....and may tend to generate a series of 'cry wolf' alarms which reduce the credibility of the authentic warning when it is received".

Going into 1952 Air Force memoranda still speculated on possible Soviet involvement. Advanced Soviet technology was discussed as in the early months of 1952, including the possibility of a secret Soviet delivery system being tested in advance of their building sufficient atomic weapons for a surprise, nuclear attack. But as the early months passed, in terms of UFO reports it began to look as if it was 1947 again. At first it was a continuation of sightings from Kirtland AFB, Sandia base and the Manzano bomb storage facility. In addition to quick fly overs, UFOs were observed stationary for extended periods of time, to the east of the Albuquerque facilities, and then to the west – doing nothing more than simply holding their positions. Once again it appears no interceptors were scrambled or approached them during those extended observations. Other sightings followed at Hanford, over the new Savannah River nuclear plant and over both Los Alamos and Killeen base.

Strategic and military target related sightings were widespread in 1952, including observations in the vicinity of the huge Navy logistics base at Hampton Roads adjacent to Norfolk, Virginia and in a wave of sightings across the metropolitan/population corridor in the Northeast – always considered a primary strategic target in any surprise Soviet attack. Sightings also began coming from a number of air defense installations and interceptor bases, ranging from forward defense sites on the polar routes to major bases around the perimeter of the nation. SAC air bases across the northern tier states also appeared to be the target of probing – northern tier incidents included Rapid City AFB (later Ellsworth) for the first time since 1947, Great Falls AFB in Montana, as well radar tracking which brought interceptors flying out of air defense bases in Michigan and Ohio.

An analyst searching for indications of Soviet pre-strike reconnaissance would certainly have found them in 1952, and in far larger quantity than 1947. Yet the sheer numbers and breadth of the sightings across military and strategic installations actually argued against Soviet involvement. There were simply too many sightings over too many different facilities, with the UFOs demonstrating the capability to avoid or evade any effort to engage them.

At the end of the year the CIA's Assistant Director of the Office of Scientific Intelligence described the speeds and altitudes of UFOs being reported over major U.S. defense installation as something beyond what could be attributed to either known aerial vehicles or natural phenomena. Based on Air Force memoranda and Ruppelt's own remarks it appears that senior Air Force intelligence officers had begun to lean towards a similar assessment, enough so to propose an investment in a very serious new technical collections effort. Of course now, with the advantage of decades of hindsight - including a considerable body of military history which came out of Russia during the years of post-Soviet Union information exchange - we know for a certainty that neither the technology nor the "unknowns" were coming out of Russia.

Which leaves us with no explanation at all for the highly anomalous reports which perplexed both senior Air Force officers and the CIA. With a rejection of Russian involvement we also lack any obvious explanation for the earlier spikes in reports from Hanford and especially from Oak Ridge in 1950. Neither facility had reported any significant number of UFO sightings during the initial 1947 flying saucer publicity – in fact the same could be said of all the strategic atomic warfighting facilities, with the possible exception of the Albuquerque area.

In terms of indications from our baseline years study, we are simply left with data suggesting that over some five years each atomic materials production plant, each weapons assembly area and at least some of the initial atomic bomb storage facilities appear to have been observed, repeatedly visited and in the case of select facilities, more intensely "ferreted" in a test of their defenses. If that had not been the Soviets, who was doing the probing? And for that matter why would the Russians have spent so much time and effort at Oak Ridge or Killeen Base – they could find out all about the American atomic bombs just by reading American newspapers; even the basics of how to build a fission bomb had been put into the public domain.

Moving on to a broader look at the UFO sightings in the years following 1952, we found a significant change in the pattern of incidents, and emerging indications of a new focus. During the next two years there were a few, but only a few, UFO sightings at atomic materials production plants. The newer facilities including Savannah River, and the Pantex plant outside Amarillo Texas did produce a few incident reports but that was it. Oak Ridge recorded a handful of sightings during 1953 and 1954 and Killeen base reported another two months of overflights of oval, glowing objects.

And then it was over, for the better part of two years the atomic materials production and weapons assembly facilities experienced no significant UFO activity (at least none visible in the available records) – making the earlier months' long spikes at those sites even more anomalous. Indications of pre-strike or imminent hostile action associated with UFO activity largely faded away. It appeared that if the nation was going to be attacked – as was still anticipated - it would be by conventional Russian jet bombers carrying atomic weapons, not by some totally new and unconventional type of "bomb carrier" which had been an Air Force concern as late as 1952

It would be 1957 before a new pattern of indications began to emerge from the atomic warfare complex, not so much a change in any operational sense, but rather a change in focus. First the indicators reflected a new focus on "bombers and bombs", then that focus expanded to include "missiles and warheads". The new pattern emerged from the types of strategic facilities generating UFO reports as well as in the density and nature of the reports.

In terms of the nation's total nuclear warfighting capability, the years from 1955 to 1962 represented an almost unbelievable growth in atomic weapons – ranging from warheads for ground to air missiles, air to air missiles, atomic shells for Army artillery guns and warheads for short range tactical missiles, even atomic land mines. The Navy also deployed a number of atomic weapons including depth charges and torpedoes. Atomic weapons were quite literally everywhere, including in rings of Nike anti-aircraft batteries surrounding major American cities.

Despite the huge number of atomic weapons and their broad distribution, the nation's truly strategic striking power resided first in the numbers of megaton class, hydrogen fusion bombs carried by SAC long range bombers and later in the hydrogen warheads mounted on the intercontinental ballistic missiles that began to be emplaced during the early 1960s. A search of the *BLUE BOOK* archives does reveal a handful of UFO reports from NIKE anti-aircraft missile sites, but nothing comparable to the UFO incidents which became focused on SAC. It was the SAC bomber bases – especially those "front line" bases in the northern tier – and their associated ICBM silo fields that began to generate the sorts of spikes in UFO reports that were comparable to those seen earlier at Los Alamos, Sandia Base, Killeen Base, or Oak Ridge.

It would be SAC and its strategic weapons that would receive first UFO flyovers, then "loitering" incidents and finally near ground level intrusions. But the clusters of incidents at SAC facilities did not begin during the huge national wave of UFO reports in 1957, it came later and independently. We found the surges in sightings at the nuclear production and assembly sites to be out of sync with the general UFO waves of both 1947 and 1952. In the same fashion the focus on SAC appears to have begun after 1957. There are anecdotal suggestions of a series of incidents at SAC northern tier bases in 1958, with one low level weapons storage flyover. But 1959 produced a sensational and threatening SAC incident which is definitely documented.

The appearance of inbound UFOs apparently targeting Pease AFB, recorded and tracked on multiple radars, created a major air defense alert. It had all the appearances of an actual attack, clearly something far more than covert probing. It's tempting to speculate that if that type of activity had continued, intelligence attention to "unknowns" as a strategic threat might have resurfaced. Yet given our earlier review of the Northern Tier incidents of 1975, it's hard to imagine that happening given anything short of documented physical attacks.

Following the Pease incident in 1959, the UFO probing reports definitely shift to a focus on SAC and its ICBM squadrons. That appears to be a clear trend in sightings and more intrusive incidents. Once the majority of the strategic weapons stockpile had been built and deployed (first to AEC Q sites and later to special weapons storage areas at SAC air bases and onto emplaced missiles), the most anomalous UFO reports move from the atomic materials production plants and weapons assembly centers to the actual locations of weapons deployment.

The shift in geography is clear, however certain patterns in the operational aspects of the UFO activity remain familiar and consistent. At Atlas, Titan and Minuteman sites it almost became a routine. First mysterious nighttime lights passing around the construction sites, or at altitude over them – with radar tracking of unidentified objects. Then lower altitude approaches, descents into the actual restricted areas of the silos or launch control centers and visual confirmations of actual objects.

But it was all far from covert. It was a repetition of Killeen base or of Oak Ridge. No purely military operation would be so obvious. Attention catching bright lights were the rule - up to the points at which ground security personnel approached or an aircraft appeared. Then the lights went off and the UFOs apparently moved away or just stayed dark until the aircraft left. Only then would the lights return, at least for a time.

From a military standpoint that type of activity is anomalous irrespective of the technology involved. The UFOs appeared to intentionally make themselves visible, to telegraph their intentions, to probe as far as the actual locations of the bombs or warheads – and then depart, sometimes in a highly visible fashion, other times very stealthily. Subjectively such behavior has more the look and feel of "messaging" than any serious military activity - which would be far more covert.

Those types of incidents were reported from 1958 through 1965 – in New Mexico, Missouri, Nebraska, the Dakotas and Oklahoma. They moved from state to state as missile site construction proceeded, continuing until the sites became operational. From an indications standpoint it would be difficult to conceive of such incidents as simple reconnaissance. After all, SAC air bases and the new missile complexes were huge, highly visible facilities, they were marked on road maps and on FAA flight charts, all clearly designated as restricted areas.

The types of missiles in each complex were written about extensively, the general specifications showed up in plastic model hobby kits for children – all built to actual blueprint specifications according to the claims on the packages. Exactly what the UFOs might be doing during their appearances around SAC sites is unclear but certainly it appears more similar to the "antics" at Killeen base or Oak Ridge than the apparent incoming attack targeting against Pease AFB. Whatever the "unknowns" are, in regard to the new focus on SAC there are indications of a change in geography, but a repetition of "practices", including apparent stages in their activities.

In a broad sense, through 1970, a case can be made that there is a strong suggestion that unknown parties did actively observe the development of the American atomic warfare complex. In addition there is indication of selective sampling in that process – each facility did not produce an equal number of reports but over time each type – radioactive materials production, weapons assembly and weapons storage – had one or more sites which were intensely visited. At least one of each type of facility reported a particularly notable surge in UFO reports, ultimately extending down to apparent ground level intrusion.

Beginning in 1947 and extending though the end of the 1950s this pattern appears to suggest not only observation by truly anomalous and unconventional aerial objects but of apparent intelligent analysis. It appears that after a general survey, each type of atomic warfare site was intensely "sampled" at only one location. The number and types of reports from Oak Ridge are significantly different from those at Hanford. The number, type and duration of incidents at Sandia Base are quite different from those at Los Alamos. Site A (Manzano) and Site B (Killeen) certainly stand out from the other early Q sites in terms of number and types of reports. And if such "sampling" did in fact occur, it implies that the different types of facilities were profiled and differentiated.

While not often mentioned, there is also a suggestion that certain UFO sightings might be related to an active effort by "unknowns" to sample radiation clouds from atomic testing, especially during the early series of atomic tests in Nevada. The United States itself devoted an immense effort to particulate sampling of Soviet weapons development tests and continued that effort in the early years of Chinese atomic testing.[7]

Conventional aircraft including F-84Gs, B-29s and B-47s were all used at various times, especially in the earliest years of testing. Later highly specialized, very high altitude aircraft (including variants of the U-2, the RB-57Ds and the WB-57F) were adapted to collect particulate matter from atomic tests around the world, including American weapons testing. B-57B aircraft were adapted to carry a sampling rocket to 50,000 feet and launch it upwards from that altitude; the rockets enabled sampling the air from the very first minutes of the nuclear explosion - at the extreme altitudes at the top of the mushroom cloud, an area of extreme radiation.[8]

Sampling was considered vital in order to fully evaluate and chemically profile the radioactive materials involved; it also proved key in determining the composition and type of Soviet and Chinese atomic weapons. Collection and laboratory analysis allowed the differentiation between radioactive materials produced by atomic reactors, atomic test explosions or the detonation of specific types of atomic weapons.[9]

Particulate sampling remains a key tool of atomic intelligence, even in the 21st Century – currently being carried out to assess North Korean weapons development.[10] Even satellite surveillance of atomic testing is unable to provide the level of analysis obtained by the chemical testing of radiation cloud particulate matter.

The United States faced that challenge in its monitoring of Chinese atomic developments. A series of satellite intelligence collection systems – beginning with the early SAMOS and Corona satellites and extending to the advanced Gambit and Keyhole "birds" were able to image Chinese atomic facilities - but an extensive series of offshore aerial materials collections was also conducted. In 1963 alone the aerial sampling fleet involved some 67 aircraft, operated by the Air Weather Service and by SAC.[11]

Yet given the public information available to the Soviets and the wealth of information gained from their World War II spying on the Manhattan Project, there is no obvious reason for them to have carried out any high risk of aerial intrusions and sampling at the Oak Ridge and Hanford facilities during the late 1940s and 1950s. In the same vein, Soviet aerial observation and covert particulate sample collections directed towards domestic American atomic tests was simply unnecessary. If a concrete case could be made for true "unknowns" engaging in sampling and collections at production sites and from weapons tests it would be extremely suggestive. Further exploration of trends and patterns in credible unidentified object sightings related to American atomic development stands out as an important area for further research.

The shift of UFO incidents from production and assembly facilities to weapons deployment locations could also be taken as an indication that the most destructive (hydrogen fusion; megaton class) weapons were identified and actually tracked in their movements. In that regard, once again a sampling effort seems to have been conducted, not every SAC base or missile site received the same treatment, but samples of each did – SAC bomber bases, Atlas, Titan and Minutemen missile sites. Some level of selectivity certainly seems indicated and the concentrations and quantity of incidents certainly show no correlation to national waves of UFO reports.

In terms of our final scenario question – threat or no threat - incidents such as the inbound tracks targeting Pease AFB in 1958 and the northern tier intrusions of 1975 ended with no overtly hostile action and during the decades since 1947 (or even 1944) no known hostile action has been documented. In that regard, the final assessment of our studies would seem to be – no threat; probable messaging; possible warning.

In conclusion, we can offer the following as a general summary of the studies. We do have indications that unknown parties, possessing unconventional technology, monitored the development of the nation's strategic atomic military capability. Over time that included its design and production facilities, its stockpiles and the deployments of its most strategic and powerful weapons. That observation and monitoring could hardly be considered covert – it was more on the order of SAC's missions over Russia. Again, in purely subjective terms, we are here, we see what you have, you can't stop us.

In contrast to SAC's missions over Russia, the UFO activities which appear to have targeted the American atomic complex were actually far more intrusive, either by design or simply due to the fact that even over four decades nothing could be done to offer any meaningful opposition to them. The harsh reality, in terms of the data available, is that at no time over some four decades was the nation's defense able to effectively engage the most unconventional UFOs.[12] Which in very pragmatic terms may explain why a large proportion of the attempted intercepts resulted in UFO reports either being filed by the Air Force as simply "unknowns" - or otherwise listed as "probable aircraft, balloon, astronomical object".

A military intelligence analyst might well assess that certain highly unconventional aerial objects did exist, that they were intelligently controlled, and possessed the "capability" of presenting a threat to national security. Basically all the actions that they would need to take to prepare for preemptive military action did occur, repeatedly, over several decades. Which leaves two choices: (a) despite having the capability they present no actual threat or (b) there is an active threat but the time frame involved is beyond our understanding.

This would be an appropriate place to stop – in terms of the basic UFO intelligence problem it would be as far as it could be taken even by the admittedly subjective practice of indications study. But after hours, and off the record, one other observation might be added; one that requires not only going outside the box but looking back from the outside towards it.

Consider the fact that this particular class of unconventional objects showed up either during an immense, global war or immediately afterwards. From an external perspective, the general observation that could be made both then and in later years is that warfare is a constant - either open warfare, or constant preparation for warfare. It would also be obvious that immense resources are routinely devoted to both defense and offense.

Through decades of monitoring America's strategic military capability, it would be increasingly obvious that major efforts were being made in air defense. There are anecdotal reports of anti-aircraft artillery being given firing orders against UFOs, of individual fighter aircraft opening fire on them with machine guns or even air to air rockets. Yet even if true those appear to be isolated incidents, not part of any broader, coordinated military action against the unknowns. And when objects hovered over nuclear weapons dumps or flew directly over quick reaction security forces we have no record of effort to actually fire at them, from either ground or air forces.

No matter how clearly frustrated the defenders were, no matter how close the UFOs came to security personnel – at Killeen, at Oak Ridge, at SAC weapons bunkers or missile silos – nobody actually fired weapons. With all the encounters, the tension, the fear of the unknown; with all those air to air and antiaircraft missiles that were in place (many with nuclear warheads) – there appear to have been no consistent, repeated efforts to actually damage or destroy UFOs. Security teams at the Northern Tier sites was armed and able to fire. But they didn't. UFOs were simply not routinely fired on during their most intrusive facility penetrations, either in anger, or frustration.

And in later years, when gigantic, brilliantly lighted craft maneuvered just north of New York city for months and years - at extremely low altitude where hundreds and thousands of people could see and report them, the military didn't even came to look, much less threaten them. There were no interceptors, no helicopters, nothing. From outside does it appear that there is a huge disconnect in human behavior? Is it possible that fundamentally we remain as much of an intelligence challenge to the "unknown parties" as they remain to us?

Chapter 20 Endnotes

1. Edward J. Ruppelt, *The Report on Unidentified Flying Objects*, Doubleday and Company Inc., New York, 1956,148-149

2. Cynthia M. Grabo, *Anticipating Surprise; Analysis for Strategic Warning*, University Press of America, Lanham, Maryland, 2004, Chapter 7 "The Problem of Deception", 120

3. The Southwestern wave of 1957 primarily involved civilian incidents and reports; readers unfamiliar with it are referred to the following: Antonio F. Rullan, "The Southwestern UFO Wave of 1957", National Investigations Committee on Aerial Phenomena http://www.nicap.org/reports/SW_UFO-wave-of-1957.htm

4. Peter B. Ainsworth, *Psychology, Law and Eyewitness Testimony*, John Wiley and Sons, New York, 1998, 7-20

5. "Analysis of Flying Saucer Reports", Memorandum for the Record, To Director of Intelligence,Director of Research and Development, December 18, 1947

6. Cyntia M. Grabo, *Anticipating Surprise; Analysis for Strategic Warning*, University Press of America, Lanham, Maryland, 2004, 128

7. "History of Air Force Atomic Cloud Sampling", Armed Forces Special Weapons Center, January, 1963 http://nsarchive.gwu.edu/nukevault/ebb249/doc07.pdf

8. Robert C. Mikesh, *Martin B-57 Canberra; The Complete Record*, Schiffer Military History, Atglen, Pennslyavania, 1995, 162-164

9. Jeffery T. Richelson, *Spying on the Bomb*, W.W. Norton Company, New York, 2006

10. Brad Lendon, "US to fly 'radiation sniffer' jet off Korean Peninsula", CNN Politics, September 9, 2016 http://www.cnn.com/2016/09/08/politics/us-air-force-radiation-sniffer-jet/index.html

11. Jeffery T. Richelson, *Spying on the Bomb*, 187

12. American reconnaissance flights over Russia were engaged and fired upon by interceptors and missile batteries, with losses of aircraft and crews. Although American air defense protocol did allow firing on unidentified aircraft which refused to communicate or respond to interceptors, there are no known record of any air or ground missile launches against UFOs. There are credible anecdotal stories that in the early years, fighters may have fired machine gun or cannon at evading targets, with no apparent effect.

CPSIA information can be obtained
at www.ICGtesting.com
Printed in the USA
LVHW041800010920
664770LV00010B/916